A PLUME BOOK

EVERYTHING YOU NEED TO KNOW
ABOUT LATINO HISTORY

HIMILCE NOVAS had a distinguished career in journalism in New York City and is the author of seven acclaimed books, both fiction and nonfiction. She is an expert in Latino history, culture, and literature and has taught English and Latino literature as visiting author at Wellesley College, the University of California, Santa Barbara, Clark College, Tulane University, and other colleges and universities. She lectures across the country on a variety of artistic and academic subjects, and on human rights, and is a frequent guest on radio programs. She is at work on new fiction and lives in Arizona and California. Visit her Web site, http://supernovas.org.

ALSO BY HIMILCE NOVAS

*Everything You Need to Know About
Asian-American History*
(with Lan Cao and Rosemary Silva)

Princess Papaya, a novel about *Santería* and a Jewish
Cuban American family. Arte Público Press,
University of Houston, December 2004.

Mangos, Bananas and Coconuts: A Cuban Love Story.
University of Houston, Arte Público Press, 1996;
Riverhead Books/Putnam, 1997. Excerpts of this
novel have been reprinted in many prestigious
publications, including *The Prentice Hall Anthology of
Latino Literature*.

Latin American Cooking Across the U.S.A. (Knopf Cooks
American) coauthored with Rosemary Silva
(Knopf, 1997).

*The Hispanic 100: A Ranking of the Latino Men and
Women Who Have Most Influenced American Thought
and Culture*. Citadel Press, 1995.

*Remembering Selena: A Tribute in Pictures and
Words/Recordando a Selena: Un tributo en palabras y
fotos*, an illustrated, four-color, bilingual biography of
the queen of Tejano music. St. Martin's Press, 1995.

Among others. Author's Web site:
http://www.supernovas.org

HIMILCE NOVAS

EVERYTHING
YOU NEED TO
KNOW ABOUT
LATINO
HISTORY

2008 Edition

Ⓟ

A PLUME BOOK

PLUME
Published by Penguin Group
Penguin Group (USA) Inc., 375 Hudson Street, New York, New York 10014, U.S.A. •
Penguin Group (Canada), 90 Eglinton Avenue East, Suite 700, Toronto, Ontario, Canada
M4P 2Y3 (a division of Pearson Penguin Canada Inc.) • Penguin Books Ltd., 80 Strand,
London WC2R 0RL, England • Penguin Ireland, 25 St. Stephen's Green, Dublin 2,
Ireland (a division of Penguin Books Ltd.) • Penguin Group (Australia), 250 Camberwell
Road, Camberwell, Victoria 3124, Australia (a division of Pearson Australia Group Pty.
Ltd.) • Penguin Books India Pvt. Ltd., 11 Community Centre, Panchsheel Park, New
Delhi – 110 017, India • Penguin Group (NZ), 67 Apollo Drive, Rosedale, North Shore
0632, New Zealand (a division of Pearson New Zealand Ltd.) • Penguin Books (South
Africa) (Pty.) Ltd., 24 Sturdee Avenue, Rosebank, Johannesburg 2196, South Africa

Penguin Books Ltd., Registered Offices: 80 Strand, London WC2R 0RL, England

First published by Plume, a member of Penguin Group (USA) Inc.

First printing, October 1994
First printing (revised edition), October 1998
First printing (second revised edition), June 2003
First printing (third revised edition), December 2007
10 9 8 7 6 5 4 3 2

LIBRARY OF CONGRESS CATALOGING-IN-PUBLICATION DATA
Novas, Himilce.
  Everything you need to know about Latino history / Himilce Novas. — 2008 ed.
    p. cm.
  Includes bibliographical references and index.
  ISBN 978-0-452-28889-8
  1. Hispanic Americans—History. I. Title.
  E184.S75N69 2008
  973'.0468—dc22   2007032941

Printed in the United States of America

*For my mother and father, and for Rosemary Silva,
my brilliant, steadfast* compañera,
*whose help and scholarship made this work possible,
and the journey joyous.*

Contents

Contents

Introduction

Latinos, also known as Hispanics, comprise the largest minority group in the United States, a distinction they have enjoyed since 2003, and are also the nation's fastest-growing ethnic minority. According to the Pew Hispanic Center tabulations of the U.S. Census Bureau's 2005 American Community Survey, Latinos numbered 41,926,302 in the year 2005. This figure represents a dramatic increase in numbers since 2000, when the U.S. Census Bureau counted 35,305,818 Latinos, and is nearly double the 1990 U.S. Census tally of 22,354,059 Latinos.

Latinos have also been measured in terms of their economic clout. In 2006, Latino consumers enjoyed a buying power of $798 billion, according to the Selig Center for Economic Growth at the University of Georgia. The Selig Center estimates that Latino buying power will reach $863.1 billion in 2007. To meet the demand for goods and services, the number of Latino-owned businesses in the United States has risen exponentially in the last decade. In 1997, the U.S. Census Bureau counted 1.2 million Latino-owned businesses, and in 2006 the Small Business Administration tallied about two million such businesses. Mainstream businesses, realizing that Latinos represent a gold mine at the cash register, have directed many more advertising dollars toward this ethnic group than ever before. As Latinos have grown in visibility economically, corporate America has awakened to the realization that this minority group has much to contribute in the boardroom as well. The number of Latinos in the top echelons of major American corporations—from the late Roberto C. Goizueta, CEO of the Coca-Cola Company, to the family-owned and family-operated Bacardi International Limited—is mounting.

Latinos have achieved prominence in every arena, from the arts, science, technology, and politics to law, finance, journalism, and sports. In the post–*I Love Lucy* decades (after long years when Desi Arnaz and maybe Charo and Xavier Cugat were among the truly recognizable "Latins" around), Latinos have become household names: Antonia Novello, U.S. surgeon general during the Bush (senior) administration; Henry Cisneros, former mayor of San Antonio and Department of Housing and Urban Development secretary under President Clinton; the late congressman Henry B. González, who represented Texas in the U.S. House of Representatives for thirty-seven years; Joan Baez, Linda Ronstadt, Gloria Estefan, Jon Secada, Mariah Carey, Selena, Christina Aguilera, and Shakira, music superstars; Pancho Segura, Rosie Casals, and Mary Joe Fernández, top professional tennis players; Anthony Quinn, José Ferrer, Rita Hayworth, Rita Moreno, and Chita Rivera, legends of the stage and screen; and many, many others.

Still, in spite of enormous demographic and social changes in recent years, mainstream society's greater recognition of Latinos, and the extraordinary number of Latinos who have contributed immensely to this nation throughout history, most Americans know relatively little about their Latino neighbors, about their culture, their rich history, their diversity, and their dreams for the future.

The history of Latinos goes back as far as American history itself. In fact, you could say that without Latinos, there would be no United States of America as we know it today. Christopher Columbus's voyages to the New World, under Isabella I and Ferdinand II's flag, excited the imagination of the Spanish crown and the Spanish people, who were in the throes of empire building. Spanish explorer Hernando de Soto, who discovered the

Mississippi River in 1541, dreamed of finding hidden caves of gold in Florida. Francisco Vásquez de Coronado, who explored the American West in the early 1540s, thought he had found there a brave new world destined for Spanish conquest.

Then, after the formation of the thirteen English colonies, peoples with Spanish blood from Mexico, Puerto Rico, Cuba, the Dominican Republic, Colombia, and other Spanish colonies in Latin America began venturing north to seek their destiny or, as is the case for the ancestors of scores of Mexican Americans and much later for Puerto Ricans, suddenly found themselves a part of the United States due to shifting borders and American imperialism. As a result of the Spanish-American War; the Cuban Revolution and the Cuban Missile Crisis; a bloody dictatorship and authoritarian leaders in the Dominican Republic; the civil wars in Nicaragua, Guatemala, and El Salvador; military dictatorships, war, and crimes against humanity in Colombia and Chile; and hundreds of other political, economic, and social upheavals from Tijuana to the Argentine pampas, people from Spanish-speaking Latin America have settled in the United States by the millions and become Latinos. In the process, they have changed the face of the nation.

In spite of my own Latino roots, the Spanish education I received at home, and my very early years spent in Cuba, I began this project, over a decade ago, cherishing some of the same misinformation and stereotypes subscribed to by many with no real knowledge of Latinos. After all, I experienced the American school system at a time when the "Anglo" perspective on history was the only valid one, when the word "bilingual" was used mainly when referring to an especially gifted secretary, and when Puerto Rican fare was called "Spanish food."

I had virtually no exposure to Latino history in high school, and for my introduction to Latino culture, I depended almost exclusively on mainstream American writers' observations of Latinos, rather than Latinos' commentary on themselves. For instance, my reading assignments in New York City public schools included Stephen Crane's "A Man and Some Others," which offers a rather simplistic portrait of Latinos; John Steinbeck's *Tortilla Flat*, which, while attempting to honor Mexican Americans, paints a picture of them as lazy drunkards; and the works of Ernest Hemingway, Katherine Anne Porter, Jack Kerouac, and countless others who wrote passionately about Latinos but often missed the key thread of their existence and presented naive, stereotyped images of them.

Regrettably, the works of Latino writers of that era, such as Piri Thomas's *Down These Mean Streets*, José Antonio Villarreal's *Pocho*, and Tomás Rivera's *And the Earth Did Not Devour Him*, among many others, were nowhere to be found in school libraries. A good number have surfaced only in recent decades and sit only on the shelves of libraries in urban areas with large Latino communities.

I have learned much in the process of unearthing my own roots, which has amounted to a lifelong pursuit. In some cases, I have been as astounded by what I have uncovered as Columbus must have been when he first tasted chiles.

In answering some basic questions about Latino history, this book is more an act of *abrir la puerta* (opening the door) to a rich and enduring culture than an effort to cover a vast and complex history in one fell swoop—an impossible feat. I have tried to present historical facts and events fairly, from the perspective of those whose history they represent.

How to Read This Book

This edition of *Everything You Need to Know About Latino History* is organized just like the first three: in a question-and-answer format that allows the reader to zero in on those topics of Latino history and culture that are of most interest to her or him. Of course, the book may also be read from cover to cover so that all the fascinating pieces of Latino life fall into place.

The term "Latino" embraces a multitude of peoples who came to the United States from the different corners of Spanish-speaking Latin America, each with its own history and culture, or whose ancestors did. As in the previous editions, I have divided the chapters according to the various Latino subgroups. I have devoted entire chapters to the largest of these subgroups, in descending order of population, namely, Mexican Americans, Puerto Ricans, and Cuban Americans. In this edition, as in the last two, Dominican Americans, whose numbers are growing rapidly, are afforded their own chapter.

As in the last two editions, I have expanded the commentary on Americans of Central American descent and have grouped their histories together in one chapter, "The Newest Immigrants," since their collective experiences in America are strikingly similar. Salvadoran, Guatemalan, and Nicaraguan Americans, whose communities are the largest, are the focus of this chapter, but Honduran, Panamanian, and Costa Rican Americans are touched upon as well. Also covered in this chapter are Americans of South American descent (with the exception of those with roots in Brazil, a country conquered by Portugal, not Spain), who, although they are relatively few in number by comparison, wield a disproportionate amount of clout and are exerting an undeniable influence on American life. This chapter zooms in on Colombian, Ecuadoran, Peruvian, Argentinean, and Chilean Americans but also briefly considers Venezuelan, Bolivian, Uruguayan, and Paraguayan Americans.

This edition of *Everything You Need to Know about Latino History*, like the previous three, contains four chapters that present background and cultural information on Latinos as a group, all of which has been updated. I have incorporated some new information in the boxes filled with facts about Latinos and in the list of Internet addresses relevant to Latino history and culture.

As in the first three editions, I have sought not to merely compile dates and details, but to air out American history just a bit and provide fresh perspectives on one of the richest and most invigorating cultures of all time. In examining Latinos' place in the American landscape, I have shattered a few myths and taken a poke at some stereotypes so that the truth may be known about a marvelous people who have made valuable contributions to this nation and who continue to shape American life.

EVERYTHING
YOU NEED TO
KNOW ABOUT
LATINO
HISTORY

UNO

Latino: Sí y No

What's in a name?

When it comes to the term "Hispanic," there is a great deal to say. "Hispanic" is derived from *España*, the Spanish name for Spain, the country that led the conquest (as in the conquistadores) of the New World. But Hispanics are more than just the descendants of New World Spanish conquistadores and settlers. As it turned out, in the Americas, the Spanish encountered many different native peoples, known generally as Amerindians, and they engaged in a fair share of intermarriage and interbreeding with those they conquered. Add to that all the peoples whom the Spanish eventually brought from Africa to the Americas as slaves (and with whom they also mixed), and you get the whole enchilada known as Spanish-speaking Latin Americans, the "relatives" of Hispanics.

Over the centuries, many peoples from Spanish-speaking Latin America have either made their way to the United States to forge a brand-new life or found themselves citizens due to shifting U.S. borders and American imperialistic pursuits. For the sake of clarity, Spanish-speaking Latin America is comprised of

Cuba, Puerto Rico (which is a U.S. commonwealth, not a sovereign nation), the Dominican Republic, Mexico, Nicaragua, Costa Rica, Guatemala, El Salvador, Honduras, Panama, Venezuela, Colombia, Ecuador, Peru, Bolivia, Chile, Argentina, Uruguay, and Paraguay. All U.S. citizens and residents of the United States who originated from these nations or from the Commonwealth of Puerto Rico, or whose ancestors did, are known as Hispanics. The U.S. Census Bureau also includes Spanish Americans—Americans whose forbears came directly from Spain—among Hispanics, but many scholars limit the definition to those of Spanish-speaking Latin American origin.

While European Americans in the United States have been categorized by their country of origin (for instance, those with roots in Ireland are called Irish Americans), in the mainstream culture, Hispanics, with roots in the eighteen sovereign nations and one U.S. commonwealth (Puerto Rico) listed above—each with its own distinct culture, history, indigenous language(s), religions, culinary traditions, and individual philosophies—are classified by their own or their ancestors' mother tongue, Spanish, in the name of "simplicity." The term "Hispanic" is so entrenched in American culture that some give no regard to Hispanic individuals' country of origin or to that of their forbears, as if "Hispanic" referred to a person from Hispania. (Incidentally, *Hispania* is a Phoenician word meaning "the land of the rabbits." The Romans used it to refer to a region they conquered, one that encompassed Spain. Some scholars believe that the word "Hispanic" is related to Hispania.)

In Spanish-speaking Latin America, people, of course, do not call one another Hispanic. Each Latin American country is a marvelous melting pot of diverse peoples, many of whom speak ancient indigenous languages in addition to Spanish, and thus "Hispanic" is not an appropriate appellation. National identity takes precedence. Thus, Mexicans call themselves *mexicanos*; Puerto Ricans, *puertorriqueños*; Cubans, *cubanos*; and so forth. For the recent immigrant from Spanish-speaking Latin America, the realization that he or she is no longer viewed by popular American culture as Nicaraguan, Mexican, Cuban, or Colombian, but rather as part of a collective called Hispanics, is often startling. The majority of Hispanics, new immigrants and fourth- or fifth-generation Americans alike, identify primarily with the subgroup to which they belong, be it Mexican or Cuban, while a small percentage refer to themselves first and foremost as Hispanic or as American.

No matter how they view themselves individually, Hispanics as a whole have benefited greatly from the rise of a pan-ethnic consciousness or solidarity among the subgroups. As a large united front, Hispanics have been able to fight ethnic and racial discrimination, which at times has run rampant in American society, and have acquired the political clout necessary to effect positive social change.

Why has there been a panic over "Hispanic"?

Many Americans with roots in Spanish-speaking Latin America prefer the pan-ethnic terms "Latino" or "Latina" (the feminine form) over "Hispanic." Some have made the case that "Hispanic" is a U.S. government census term that was forced upon them, or that it encapsulates the Spanish colonization of Latin America without reflecting the African and Indian heritage of many of those who fall under its umbrella. Others find it archaic, or even downright offensive, likening it to the terms once used to describe African Americans.

Mexican American novelist **Sandra Cisneros**, author of such books as *The House on Mango Street* (1984), *Woman Hollering Creek and Other Stories* (1991), and *Caramelo* (2002) is so adamantly against the term "Hispanic" that she refuses to allow her work to appear in anthologies that mention the word. To Cisneros, "Hispanic," an English word, connotes colonization and a desire to be embraced by the non-Latino majority. " 'Hispanic' is English for a person of Latino origin who wants to be accepted by the white status quo," she told an interviewer in an article that appeared in the January 7, 1993 issue of the *New York Times*.

Some remain unperturbed when it comes to the Hispanic-Latino debate. While he holds with those who favor "Latino," Puerto Rican–Colombian American actor, comedian, writer, and producer **John Leguizamo**, who first earned accolades in the early 1990s for his one-man shows *Mambo Mouth* and *Spic-O-Rama*, has said that he does not consider "Hispanic" offensive. "I don't consider it a negative term. Now 'wetback, greasy spic'— *that's* derogatory," he told an interviewer in an article published in the *New York Times* on November 15, 1992.

However, "Latino" has not been popular across the board,

either. **Enrique Fernández,** former editor of *Más,* a Spanish-language entertainment magazine, and currently a music critic at the *Miami Herald,* said in the aforementioned November 15, 1992 *New York Times* article that "Latino" does not suffice, because, taken back to its roots, it signifies "an even older empire. That's the one that took over Spain." Others fall neither in the "Hispanic" nor the "Latino" camp, arguing that both lead to assimilation "beyond recognition," a state of no ethnicity or heritage at all. They prefer to be known as European Americans are known—by their or their forbears' country of origin—that is, as Mexican American, Cuban American, Dominican American, and so forth, or as plain old American.

Are Brazilian Americans Latinos?

No. Brazilian Americans have roots in Brazil, a South American country that was conquered by the Portuguese, not the Spanish. On April 22, 1500, Portuguese navigator **Pedro Álvares Cabral** landed at what is present-day Pôrto Seguro, Brazil, and claimed the region for Portugal, in keeping with the Treaty of Tordesillas, which Spain and Portugal ratified in 1494, and which, to separate the two nations' areas of settlement and trade, divided all the world beyond Europe between them along a north–south meridian set 370 leagues west of the Cape Verde Islands. (The Spanish took the lands to the west of the meridian; and the Portuguese, the lands to the east.) Portugal would rule Brazil for about the next three hundred years. Historians have speculated that Spanish explorers may have sighted, and even visited, the coast of Brazil before the Portuguese put up stakes.

Brazilian Americans are of Portuguese, not Spanish, ancestry and, therefore, do not qualify as Latinos. Nonetheless, many Brazilian Americans consider themselves part of a larger pan–Latin American diaspora and have forged close ties with the Latino community.

Just how many Latinos are there, and where do they live?

According to the Pew Hispanic Center tabulations of the U.S. Census Bureau's 2005 American Community Survey, the total Latino population (not including the residents of Puerto Rico) stood at 41,926,302 in 2005. This figure represents a significant rise in numbers since 2000, when, according to Census 2000 figures, Latinos numbered 35,305,818 and constituted 12.5 percent of the American population. What is even more remarkable is that in 2005 nearly twice as many Latinos were tallied than in 1990, when the U.S. Census Bureau counted 22,354,059 Latinos. The Latino population has grown at such a fast rate that in 2003 it was announced that, based on population estimates from July 1, 2001, and their comparison to Census 2000 figures, Latinos, with 37 million strong in 2003, had edged past African Americans, who numbered 36.2 million in that year, becoming the largest minority group in the United States, a phenomenon that demographers had long anticipated. The data also show that in this period the Latino population expanded by 4.7 percent, the African American population by just 1.5 percent, and the white population by a scant 0.3 percent.

It is estimated that the Latino population boom will continue for at least another generation, owing to robust Latin American immigration to the United States and to the Latino predilection for larger families (2.5 children on average as compared to 1.8 children for non-Latino Caucasians). Experts anticipate that in the not-too-distant future, the Latino population growth will level off, owing to two developments: favorable economic conditions for a greater proportion of Latinos will translate into lower fertility rates, and an increased rate of Latino intermarriage with other ethnic and racial groups will result in offspring that self-identify as another racial or ethnic group, or as a racial or ethnic admixture. The Latino population boom will have profound ramifications for American society. Ever since the New World colonies that became the United States adopted African slavery on a large scale in the 1660s, a central issue in American society has been black-white race relations and the racial divide. As they constitute an ever-larger percentage of the American population, and as they disperse across the country in response to job growth, Latinos, a rainbow of races and nationalities, will alter this dynamic completely, to the point that it will disappear. Black and white America will completely give way to multiracial America.

Not only did the Latino population mushroom in the years 1990–2005, its composition also changed. Mexicans retained their status as the largest Latino subgroup by a long shot, and Puerto Ricans and Cubans remained in second and third place in terms of numbers. However, these three subgroups did not exhibit the fastest growth of all Latinos, as in the past. That distinction went to Latinos with roots in the Dominican Republic and in Central and South America.

According to Census 2000 data and the Pew Hispanic Center tabulations of the Census Bureau's 2005 American Community Survey, in recent times, Latinos have been settling not only in all the traditional states with established Latino populations, including California, Texas, Florida, Illinois, Arizona, and New Jersey (states that combined were home to three in four Latinos in 2000), but in all corners of the United States—and in some cases in significant numbers. In fact, in virtually every growing county in the United States for which Census 2000 data exist, the Latino population growth outpaced the overall population growth in the 1990s. And in that decade the Latino population growth was greater than the overall population growth in *every* county in a total of eleven states. Some counties witnessed an astronomical rise in the number of Latino residents in the 1990s. For example, rural Clarke County in Iowa saw its Latino population expand by 1,842 percent. Between 2000 and 2005, the Latino population grew in every state except West Virginia and Vermont, and in most states the increase was substantial. For instance, in twenty-three states, the Latino population rose more than 30 percent during this five-year span, and it more than doubled in four states, Tennessee, South Carolina, Arkansas, and North Dakota.

In what way is Census 2000 problematic when it comes to counting Latinos?

Census 2000 data suggest that the Central American, South American, and Dominican populations in the United States are far smaller than experts estimate and the facts indicate. Some attribute this discrepancy to a reluctance by Dominicans and Central and South Americans to divulge their identity, a reluctance that stems from an increasing desire on the part of Latinos to see beyond these subgroups and embrace a pan-Latino identity, one that transcends Latin America's borders. Many others argue, perhaps more realistically, that the U.S. Census Bureau undercounted Dominicans and Central and South Americans in the United States by providing on the Census 2000 form specific boxes to mark for those with Mexican, Puerto Rican, and Cuban roots, but only a generic "other Hispanic" box for all other Latinos. The problem arose when "other Hispanics" had to give details about their ancestry. Unlike on the 1990 census form, they were not afforded sample answers to guide them (such as "Argentinean" or "Nicaraguan"), and a large number—over six million—chose general terms, such as "Hispanic," without providing greater detail. Based on the U.S. Census Current Population Survey for 1998 and 2000, the Lewis Mumford Center for Comparative Urban and Regional Research at the University of Albany calculated that the actual size of the Central American, South American, and Dominican populations in the United States in 2000 was much larger than Census 2000 data suggest.

One consequence of the Census 2000 undercount is that Latinos with no identified national origin theoretically constitute the second-largest group of Latinos after Americans of Mexican descent. A more serious consequence is that undercounted may metamorphose into underrepresented, underserved, and underappreciated—as is often the case.

Why is it so difficult to count all Latinos?

Contrary to popular belief, most Latinos are U.S. citizens. A small minority are legal resident aliens with green cards, and an unknown number are undocumented—mostly workers who slip across the U.S.-Mexico border illegally, to earn a measly sum in the fields and factories of America, which they send back home to keep their families afloat.

Based on its analysis of the March 2005 Current Population Survey, a monthly survey conducted jointly by the U.S. Census Bureau and the Bureau of Labor Statistics, as well as other data, the Pew Hispanic Center estimated that in March 2006, 11.5 to 12 million unauthorized immigrants lived in the United States. In 1990 the U.S. Immigration and Naturalization Service (now U.S. Citizenship and Immigration Services), in a draft report to the House immigration committee, estimated that 3.5 million unauthorized immigrants resided in the United States. Thus, in the years 1990–2006 the unauthorized immigrant population in the United States more than tripled in size. Neither the Census Bureau nor INS/USCIS provides a breakdown of the illegal immigrant population by ethnicity, but the general consensus is that Mexicans comprise nearly half of the undocumented population in the United States. Since the actual number of undocumented immigrants from Spanish-speaking Latin America who live in the United States is unknown, it is impossible to achieve an accurate count of Latinos.

LATINOS BY THE NUMBERS

1. In the year spanning July 1, 2004, through July 1, 2005, approximately one of every two individuals added to the U.S. population was Latino. (2006 U.S. Census Bureau report)

2. By July 1, 2050, the Latino population of the United States is projected by census experts to reach 102.6 million and to constitute 24 percent of the country's total population. (2004 U.S. Census Bureau report)

3. In 2005, for every 100 Latinas, there were 107 Latinos. By contrast, in the general population, there were just 97 males for every 100 females. (2006 U.S. Census Bureau report)

4. By 2050, nearly a quarter of all women in the United States will be Latina. (The HispanTelligence® research report *Hispanic Women in Profile 2005*, released in mid-2005 by Hispanic Business Inc.)

5. Latinos' median age in 2005 was 27.2 years, as compared to 36.2 for the overall population. (2006 U.S. Census Bureau report)

6. According to July 1, 2004, population estimates, 49 percent of all Latinos resided in California (12.4 million) and Texas (7.8 million). (2005 U.S. Census Bureau report)

6. In 2003, 57 percent of Latinos twenty-five years or older had at least a high school education and 11 percent had earned a bachelor's degree or higher. (2004 U.S. Census Bureau report)

7. At the end of September 2001, 109,487 Latinos were in the enlisted ranks of the U.S. armed services. (Pew Hispanic Center's 2003 "Hispanics in the Military" fact sheet)

8. In 2005 the median income of Latino households was $35,967. (2006 U.S. Census Bureau report)

9. In 2006 the homeownership rate among Latinos was 49.4 percent, as compared to over 75 percent for Caucasian Americans. (Hispanic PR Wire)

10. The Latino consumer market enjoyed an estimated buying power of $480 billion in 2006. (Selig Center for Economic Growth at the University of Georgia)

11. Latino-owned businesses in the United States numbered 1.6 million in 2002 and generated $222 billion in revenues, an increase of 19 percent since 1997. Women owned a little more than a third of all Latino-owned businesses in 2002, up from 28 percent in 1997. (2006 U.S. Census Bureau report)

12. Over sixteen million Latinos went online in 2006. Of these, 77 percent had access to broadband service. (*2006 U.S. Diversity Markets Report*, released by Synovate's Diversity Group)

Mexican Americans: As many as the stars in the night sky?

According to the Pew Hispanic Center tabulations of the Census Bureau's 2005 American Community Survey, 26,784,268 Mexican Americans and Mexican nationals resided in the United States in 2005, and 10,993,851 were foreign born. Census 2000 counted 20,640,711 people of Mexican origin in the United States in 2000, up from 13,393,208 in 1990, an increase of 54 percent. At 26,784,268 strong, the Mexican community constituted 63.9 percent of the nation's Latinos in 2005.

According to the U.S. Census Bureau, the five states with the largest Mexican American population in 2000 were California (8,455,926), Texas (5,071,963), Illinois (1,144,390), Arizona (1,065,578), and Colorado (450,760). As in 1990, California and Texas ranked as the two top states for Mexican Americans and Mexican-born residents in 2000, and more people of Mexican descent called Los Angeles home than any other city in the world except Mexico City. Census 2000 also indicates that in the way of all Latinos, Mexican Americans and Mexican-born residents have flocked to places in the United States where they have not traditionally settled. For instance, North Carolina saw its Mexican population rise 655 percent in the 1990s as Mexican Americans and Mexican-born residents moved there to take advantage of jobs in the manufacturing and meatpacking industries.

The 2000 census figures do not take into account the population known as Hispanos, the descendants of residents of the region of Mexico annexed by the United States after the Mexican War (1846–48), under the Treaty of Guadalupe Hidalgo. Hispanos include both the direct descendants of the Spanish conquistadores and mestizos, or those of mixed Spanish and Amerindian blood. Hispanos, some of whose ancestors were here before the Pilgrims sighted Plymouth Rock, live mostly in New Mexico. Many have been assimilated into the non-Latino population of the United States. Due to the Hispano assimilation, it is virtually impossible to ascertain precisely how many Latinos of Mexican origin make their home in the United States. This matter is further complicated by the scores of undocumented Mexican workers in the United States, who are trying to piece together a living in the underground economy while avoiding U.S. immigration authorities.

Mexican Americans' educational attainment has lagged behind: According to the U.S. Census Bureau's 2004 Current Population Survey, 51.9 percent of Mexican Americans twenty-five years or older had a high school diploma or better, as compared with 58.4 percent of all Latinos, 90.4 percent of non-Latino whites, and 80.9 percent of non-Latino blacks. However, to get an accurate picture of Mexican American educational attainment, it is imperative to distinguish between the native born and the foreign born, since such a large percentage of the Mexican American community is foreign born. The data indicate that immigration and intergenerational assimilation into the American mainstream are decisive factors in Mexican Americans' educational deficit: second- and third-generation Mexican Americans perform significantly better than the first generation. In 2004, 71.3 percent of second-generation and 75.3 percent of third-generation (or more) Mexican Americans had graduated from high school or better, as compared to 36.6 percent of first-generation Mexican Americans. The foreign-born Mexican American educational deficit translates into a wage gap. Data from the Pew Hispanic Center tabulations of the Census Bureau's 2005 American Community Survey show that 56.7 percent of foreign-born Mexican households earned under $20,000 in 2005. Education affords native-born Mexican Americans about the same economic payoff as all other native-born Americans, and so, over time, more and more Mexican Americans will enter the economic mainstream.

Puerto Ricans: Why aren't they considered immigrants?

Because they aren't—not on the island of Puerto Rico and not on the isle of Manhattan, either. Puerto Ricans are American citizens by birth, thanks to Spain's defeat in the Spanish-American War and its subsequent cession of Puerto Rico to the United States in 1898, the extension of U.S. citizenship to Puerto Ricans in 1917, and the island's status as a U.S. commonwealth since 1952—an issue that has been hotly debated for over half a century by those who favor the status quo, U.S. statehood, or independence for Puerto Rico. Thus, Puerto Ricans' movement between Puerto Rico and the U.S. mainland is categorized as the internal migration of Americans and does not constitute immigration. Historically, Puerto Ricans have migrated to the U.S. mainland both in response to unemployment and overpopulation in Puerto Rico, and in search of job opportunities, better pay, and a higher quality of life.

Mainland Puerto Ricans comprise the second-largest Latino group but trail far behind Mexican Americans in number. According to the Pew Hispanic Center tabulations of the Census Bureau's 2005 American Community Survey, Puerto Ricans numbered 3,794,776 on the U.S. mainland in 2005, almost as many as lived on the island. (Some say that there are actually more mainland Puerto Ricans than island Puerto Ricans because not all islanders are Puerto Ricans.) Census 2000 counted 3,406,178 mainland Puerto Ricans, an increase of about 28 percent from the 1990 census figure of 2,651,815, and it tallied 3,808,610 island Puerto Ricans. With 3,794,776 Puerto Rican mainlanders counted, the stateside Puerto Rican community comprised 9.1 percent of the nation's Latinos in 2005. Thus, compared to Mexican Americans, mainland Puerto Ricans comprise a much smaller piece of the Latino pie, and their numbers are increasing at a slower pace.

The states with the largest number of Puerto Ricans in 2000 were New York (1,050,293), Florida (482,027), New Jersey (366,788), Pennsylvania (228,557), Massachusetts (199,207), and

Connecticut (194,443). From the early days of Puerto Rican settlement in the continental United States until 1990, New York City was the number one destination for islanders, and the number of Puerto Ricans in the city rose with each passing year, reaching 896,763 in 1990. However, during the 1990s, the Puerto Rican population of New York City fell by 12 percent, to 789,172. Experts have cited a declining birth rate; the increased popularity of other states, especially Florida, among migrants; Puerto Ricans' movement to the suburbs; and retired Puerto Rican New Yorkers' return migration to the island of Puerto Rico as reasons for the decline in numbers. Despite this decline, New York City remains the very heart of Puerto Rican mainland life.

Of mainland Puerto Ricans ages twenty to fifty-nine, 60.7 percent were employed in 2000. A smaller percentage of Puerto Rican women on the U.S. mainland participated in the labor force that year. Even though one-half of Puerto Rican mainlanders held professional, managerial, technical, and administrative support jobs in 2000, only 30 percent of those working full time throughout the entire year earned over $35,000 in 2000. Puerto Ricans' high unemployment rate and lower earnings, as compared to the national average, are related to their low overall educational attainment: in 2000, only 64.3 percent of mainlanders had earned a high school diploma.

Cuban Americans : What makes them different?

According to the Pew Hispanic Center tabulations of the Census Bureau's 2005 American Community Survey, Cuban Americans and Cuban-born residents in the United States numbered 1,462,593 in 2005. Census 2000 tallied 1,241,685 people of Cuban descent in 2000, which represents an increase of 18 percent from 1990, when 1,053,197 were counted. In 2000 the overwhelming majority of them—833,120, to be exact—lived in Florida, particularly Miami, which Cuban Americans, with their love of enterprise and distinct Latin rhythms, succeeded in transforming from a backwater into a chic, cosmopolitan metropolis and a center for international business. After Florida, the states with the largest Cuban population in 2000 were New Jersey (77,337), California (72,286), New York (62,590), and Texas (25,705). The figures for New Jersey and New York represent a decline in numbers since 1990.

Communist dictator **Fidel Castro**'s seizure of power in Cuba in January 1959 unleashed a mass exodus of Cubans from the island. In the 1960s and 1970s, Cuban refugees fled their home for America each of the numerous times Castro opened the floodgates on emigration. Some Cubans did not wait for Castro to swing open the door and tried to escape undetected on makeshift rafts and small boats—as they do to this day. In 1966 the U.S. Congress passed the Cuban Adjustment Act, which gives—to this very day—all Cubans seeking asylum in the United States the special status of political refugees. As refugees, Cuban immigrants confront none of the restrictions governing U.S. immigration, such as presenting proof of persecution in the home country.

In 1980 a group of Cubans known as the Marielitos (because they departed Cuba from the port of Mariel) reached the United States as part of a seven-week airborne and seaborne exodus from Cuba. Their journey to America and subsequent resettlement were aided by the U.S. government. In 1994 many thousands of Cubans arrived on America's shores during the rafter refugee crisis. Seeking to prevent a replay of this mass arrival of Cubans on American soil, **President Clinton** signed migration accords with Cuba in 1994 that afford the United States the discretion to return to Cuba all Cubans picked up at sea—but not those who manage, literally, to reach dry land in the United States—in exchange for permitting twenty thousand Cubans to immigrate to the United States annually through a legal visa-lottery system established in Cuba. The accords have had the effect of curbing the exodus from Cuba considerably.

Cuban Americans have long identified with European refugees who came to our shores fleeing Nazism, communism, and other totalitarian regimes, and like those refugees of old, they have actively pursued the American dream. As a result, the first wave of Cubans, the refugees who came to America by the hundreds of thousands in the 1960s and 1970s, and their children are now largely middle class. Their assimilation into the American mainstream has been more rapid than that of most other Latinos, whose primary reason for immigrating has not been political but economic, and whose communities include fewer Caucasians than the Cuban community and therefore face more discrimination.

Of all Latinos, Cuban Americans enjoy the most formal education (although some Americans of South American descent are close behind), and thus a higher income, which has helped them progress in American society. In 2004, according to the Pew

Hispanic Center's analysis of the Census Bureau's 2004 American Community Survey, 25 percent of Cubans twenty-five years or older had a college degree, and Cuban American households enjoyed a median income of approximately $38,000, as compared to $36,000 for other Latinos and $48,000 for non-Latino whites. And 68 percent of Cuban Americans owned their own home in 2004, as compared to 47 percent of all other Latinos and 74 percent of non-Latino whites. Foreign-born Cuban Americans who arrived in the United States before 1980 have been particularly successful: their rate of home ownership was 72 percent in 2004.

Since Castro's revolution forced Cubans to flee the island, generations of Cuban Americans have forged lives for themselves in the United States. Some of those who had a Cuban life before an American one still profess the desire and determination to return someday to their homeland. However, those who were raised mostly or entirely in the United States, such as singer and songwriter **Gloria Estefan**, say they hope merely to visit a democratic, prosperous Cuba one day.

Dominican Americans: What has brought them to the United States since 1961?

According to the Pew Hispanic Center tabulations of the Census Bureau's 2005 American Community Survey, there were 1,135,756 Dominican Americans and Dominican-born residents in the United States in 2005, up from the 764,945 counted in Census 2000. It should be noted, however, that the Lewis Mumford Center for Comparative Urban and Regional Research at the University of Albany determined, based on the U.S. Census Bureau's Current Population surveys for 1998 and 2000, that the actual number of Dominican Americans and Dominican-born residents in the United States in 2000 was 1,121,257, and that the Dominican population in America grew by 106 percent in the 1990s.

According to Census 2000 figures, the five states with the highest number of Dominican Americans and Dominican-born residents in 2000 were New York (455,061), New Jersey (102,630), Florida (70,968), Massachusetts (49,913), and Rhode Island (17,894). New York City is home to more Dominicans than any other place in America. Dominicans have been the city's largest immigrant group since 1970, and the city boasts the largest Dominican population outside of Santo Domingo. According to Census 2000, 332,977 Dominicans called New York City home in 2000, down from the 407,473 counted in 1990. (However, Mumford Center statistics reveal that New York City's Dominican community actually grew to 652,347 strong in the 1990s.) The Dominican community in New York City is centered in Manhattan's Washington Heights, Inwood, and Hamilton Heights and in Corona in Queens. Dominicans are fond of calling Washington Heights Quisqueya Heights (after the native name for the island of Hispaniola, two-thirds of which constitutes the Dominican Republic and one-third of which is Haiti).

Stratospheric real estate prices and rents in New York City have unleashed a secondary Dominican migration in recent times: a growing number of Dominican New Yorkers have uprooted themselves and settled outside the city, in places like Yonkers; Union City, New Jersey; the Poconos; and as far afield as Reading, Pennsylvania, where a house can be snapped up for what amounts to a down payment in Manhattan. Census 2000 tallied just 1,696 Dominicans in Reading, but by mid-decade, that figure had risen to 5,912, according to the Census Bureau's 2005 American Community Survey.

From 1930 until 1961, the Dominican Republic experienced one of the most ruthless dictatorships in world history, that of **Rafael Trujillo**, who answered dissent with genocidal massacres, torture, and terror, inflicted by his secret police. Due to Trujillo's severe restrictions on travel abroad, few managed to escape his brutal rule, which ended only when the dictator was assassinated in Santo Domingo in 1961. Trujillo's death unleashed the first substantial wave of Dominican immigration to the United States. It also created a power vacuum, and in 1963 a civil war erupted in the Dominican Republic, which sent the U.S. Marines rushing to the Caribbean nation and Dominicans fleeing to America's shores with even greater urgency. Even though the Dominican Republic endured a series of bumbling authoritarian leaders in the decade after the civil war, living conditions improved, thanks to an economic boom. By 1978, however, the boom times were over. The country found itself mired in hyperinflation, a collapsing infrastructure, mass unemployment, and widespread poverty, which unleashed uncertainty, then social panic. In the 1980s and the first half of the 1990s, the number of Dominicans immigrating to the United States skyrocketed.

The possibility for a brighter future finally materialized in 1996, when the Dominican Republic's first democratically elected leader, **Leonel Fernández**, took office. The Dominican economy experienced sustained growth in the late 1990s, but without a comprehensive poverty reduction strategy to aid them, many people did not enjoy its fruits, and having lost all hope for a prosperous future and a stable life, a significant number left their nation during Fernández's presidency. In 2000, **Hipólito Mejía** was elected president, but his attempts to stamp out banking fraud and government corruption failed, and a deteriorating economy cost him reelection in 2004, when voters pinned their hopes once again on Leonel Fernández, who pledged fiscal austerity and a crackdown on corruption to pull the country out of its economic crisis. Since his reelection, the Dominican economy has grown, and signs of progress are everywhere, but corruption, inflation, and unemployment remain nagging problems.

The Dominican emigration trend since 1961 explains why 545,262 of the 764,945 people of Dominican descent counted in 2000 were foreign born. With so many foreign-born Dominicans struggling to gain a footing in a new country, the level of educational attainment in the Dominican community as a whole has historically been low. In 2000 only about 51 percent of Dominican Americans twenty-five years or older had graduated from high school or more, as compared to 80 percent of the general population. But, as with Mexican Americans, this statistic is misleading. If native-born and foreign-born Dominicans are analyzed separately, the intergenerational educational divide becomes apparent, with the native born far outpacing the foreign born. In 2000, nearly 60 percent of native-born Dominican Americans twenty-five years or older had attended college, and 21.9 percent had received a bachelor's degree or higher, nearly the percentage in the overall population (24.4 percent). The foreign-born Dominican educational deficit has long translated into rampant unemployment, poverty, and a wage gap, distorting the socioeconomic profile of the Dominican American community as a whole. In 1999, the mean per-capita household income for all Dominican Americans was $11,065, half the national average that year, and in 2000 about 64 percent of Dominican men and 53.1 percent of Dominican women participated in the labor force, figures that are substantially lower than those for the overall U.S. workforce. With their much higher levels of educational attainment, native-born Dominican Americans have done substantially better in terms of employment and income, proof positive that time and educational progress are the keys to the American dream for Dominican Americans.

Americans of Central and South American descent: Why are they the new Latinos?

Approximately 78 percent of all Americans and foreign-born residents of Central American descent had roots in El Salvador, Guatemala, and Nicaragua in 2000, when the U.S. Census Bureau counted 655,165 Salvadorans, 372,487 Guatemalans, 217,569 Hondurans, 177,684 Nicaraguans, 91,723 Panamanians, and 68,588 Costa Ricans. In the years 2000–2005, the Central American community in the United States grew enormously: according to the Pew Hispanic Center tabulations of the Census Bureau's 2005 American Community Survey, in 2005 the United States was home to 1,240,031 Salvadorans, 780,191 Guatemalans, 466,843 Hondurans, 275,126 Nicaraguans, 141,286 Panamanians, and 111,978 Costa Ricans. The majority of Americans and foreign-born residents with roots in Central America reside in California, though a significant number also live in New York and Florida. Los Angeles has the largest Guatemalan and Salvadoran communities outside of Central America. These are poor communities; however, the people are extremely hardworking, and they have great aspirations to acculturate, learn English, and provide their children with the educational tools needed for socioeconomic advancement.

About 75 percent of Americans and foreign-born residents of *Spanish-speaking* South American descent had roots in Colombia, Ecuador, and Peru in 2000. Census 2000 reported 470,684 Colombians, 260,559 Ecuadorans, 233,926 Peruvians, 100,864 Argentineans, 91,507 Venezuelans, 68,849 Chileans, 42,068 Bolivians, 18,804 Uruguayans, and 8,769 Paraguayans residing in the United States in 2000. The South American community in the United States also expanded significantly between 2000 and 2005. The Pew Hispanic Center tabulations of the Census Bureau's 2005 American Community Survey indicate that in 2005, there were 723,596 Colombians, 432,068 Ecuadorans, 415,352 Peruvians, 189,303 Argentineans, 162,762 Venezuelans, 105,141 Chileans, 68,649 Bolivians, and 51,646 Uruguayans. (No figure for Paraguayans was provided.) As a group, Americans and foreign-born residents with roots in Spanish-speaking South American countries are well educated and middle class, and have enjoyed about the same level of success as Cuban Americans.

Since Central American immigrants began arriving in the United States in significant numbers only in the final decades of the twentieth century, and a large percentage of Spanish-speaking South American immigrants came to the United States after 1980, together they could be called the new Latinos.

DOS

Roots

If Columbus was Italian, why do Latinos celebrate Columbus Day?

Columbus Day is known among Latinos as *El Día de la Raza*, meaning "the Day of the Races," or the day celebrating the union in the Americas of two racial groups: the Spanish and the Amerindians. Among Mexican Americans in contemporary society, *la raza* means "the people," that is, the Chicanos, and is an expression of solidarity. Columbus Day is an official holiday throughout Latin America, Spain, and Latino America, and Latinos celebrate it with much fanfare.

Given the Spaniards' brutal repression of the native peoples of the Americas, it may seem puzzling that Latinos celebrate the day on which the Spanish and the Amerindians came together. But Latinos represent both cultures: collectively, they are the direct descendants of the native peoples of the Americas and of the Spanish who conquered and then settled the Americas. They pay homage to their Spanish ancestry on Columbus Day, with spectacles and floats that proudly reenact the bravery and daring of the

Spanish explorers who sailed perilous and uncharted seas and who were, after all, the first to "discover" and conquer the New World.

Although **Christopher Columbus**, called **Cristóbal Colón** in Spanish, originally hailed from Genoa, Italy, hardly anyone in Spain considers him anything other than Spanish. Columbus's voyage was commissioned by **King Ferdinand** and **Queen Isabella** of Spain, the explorer sailed under the Spanish flag, and he commanded a crew that was mainly Spanish.

Did Columbus really discover America?

Christopher Columbus, of course, is credited with discovering America, and without him, there might not be an America at all, certainly not as it exists today. But the America that Columbus discovered was not the landmass we know today as the United States, but rather the Caribbean islands and other regions of Latin America, parts of which constitute the ancestral lands of Latinos.

Since a land already populated with advanced ancient civilizations cannot really be *discovered*, Columbus could more accurately be said to have discovered a water route from Europe and North Africa to the Americas. It was all an accident, as we know, since the mariner believed his course would take him to the Indies, then taken to mean all of South and East Asia and later called the East Indies, and even died thinking he *had* found a water route there.

It is also certain that Columbus was not the first European to cross the Atlantic. The Vikings reached the New World around AD 1000, and evidence suggests that both the English and the Portuguese may have landed in Newfoundland and Labrador during the fourteenth century.

What was Columbus really in search of?

In the fifteenth century, a time of intense imperialistic and hegemonic ambitions in Europe, several European nations, Spain included, sought to accrue wealth and power through new trade routes and trade partners; the establishment of colonies; and the acquisition of valuable goods, including gold, the coinage of the European economy at the time. With the fall of Constantinople, the capital of the Byzantine Empire, to the Muslims in 1453, Europeans lost access to a fine land route to Asia, a source of silk, spices, and other prized goods. Other land routes from Europe to Asia were quite treacherous to traverse, and the Portuguese took to sailing all the way around Africa to reach Asia, a roundabout route. Miscalculating the earth's circumference, **Columbus** mistakenly concluded that there was an uninterrupted, direct nautical route from Europe to Asia, which, he misreckoned, stretched for approximately 3,700 kilometers and lay in a westerly direction. Seeking a competitive edge in imperialist Europe, **Ferdinand II** and **Isabella I** of Spain lent Columbus the financial backing required to set in motion his plan of finding a sea route to Asia.

Two things motivated Columbus to cast himself headlong into perilous voyages and, quite possibly, into the abyss: The first was the possibility of unearthing large quantities of gold, gold, and more gold, which would facilitate the Spanish crown's efforts to transform Spain into a global superpower, and which, in fact, he did. The second was to meet the Great Khan of the Mongol Empire, a wish inspired by Columbus's hero, the Venetian explorer **Marco Polo**, who had written extensively in 1298 and 1299 about one Great Khan, **Kublai Khan**, in *The Travels of Marco Polo*, his account of his journey through the Middle East and Central Asia. Columbus's fascination with the Great Khan is apparent in his *Lettera rarissima* of July 7, 1503, addressed to Ferdinand and Isabella. In it he quotes Marco Polo as having said that "the emperor of Cathay some time since sent for wise men to teach him one religion of Christ." (Cathay is the name Marco Polo gave to northern China.) Columbus clearly envisioned himself the wise man who could teach the religion of Christ to the "heathen" Chinese emperor.

But Columbus's grand aspirations did not end there. He believed he could procure enough gold in Asia, and enough clout with the Spanish crown, to enable him to organize a crusade to liberate Jerusalem from the Arabs and transform it into a Christian city. Just before he set sail that day in 1492, Columbus asked for Isabella I's promise that should he find a westward route to Asia, she would fulfill his aspiration to free Jerusalem. The queen agreed but later changed her mind, feeling that she had enough on her plate—namely, a whole New World—with which to contend.

What did Columbus first lay eyes on when he reached America?

All in all, **Christopher Columbus** made four voyages to the New World. In his first foray into the Americas, he set sail on August 3, 1492, from Palos, Spain, with three small ships, the *Santa Maria*, the *Pinta*, and the *Niña*. On October 12, 1492, he made landfall on an island in the Bahamas and immediately took possession of it for Spain, christening it San Salvador (nowadays it is also called Watling or Watlings Island). This was the first of thousands of names the Spanish gave the New World—from Amarillo and El Paso, Texas, to San Diego and Palo Alto, California—in an effort to claim the land for all time.

On October 28, 1492, Columbus reached the northeast coast of Cuba, and delegations from his ship went ashore to seek the court of the Great Khan and demand gold. A few weeks later, on December 5, Columbus's expedition made landfall on the island of Hispaniola (present-day Haiti and the Dominican Republic). When, on Christmas Eve, the *Santa Maria* was shipwrecked off the northern coast of Hispaniola, Columbus sent thirty-nine of his men ashore to remain on the island, in a settlement he christened La Navidad, while he sailed back to Spain on the *Niña* to inform the queen of his remarkable discoveries. Columbus was well received in Spain, and in keeping with his contract with the Spanish crown, he was given the title Admiral of the Ocean Sea (the "Ocean Sea" was the Atlantic Ocean) and made governor general of all new lands he came upon.

On September 24, 1493, Columbus set sail again for the New World from Cádiz, Spain, with a fleet of seventeen ships carrying 1,500 colonists. His voyage took him through the Lesser Antilles and the Greater Antilles, and he reached Puerto Rico on November 19, 1493. He continued on to Hispaniola, where he discovered that the La Navidad settlers had been slaughtered for looting the native settlements and raping the women. This event marked the beginning of a tumultuous relationship between the Spanish and the native peoples scattered across the Caribbean, Mexico, Central America, South America, and North America.

On his third voyage to the New World, Columbus departed Sanlúcar, Spain, on May 30, 1498, and reached the island of Trinidad before exploring South America and then returning to Hispaniola. On Hispaniola, he found that he had incurred the ire of many Spanish settlers, who, with little to show for their efforts, felt he had misled them about the bounty of the New World. Upon returning to Spain, some of the settlers aired their grievances about Columbus before the Spanish court, and in 1500 the Spanish monarchs recalled Columbus to Spain. The explorer convinced them that he had matters under control in the New World, and on May 11, 1502, he set sail on his fourth voyage to the New World.

He made his way to Martinique, Hispaniola, and Jamaica before exploring the coasts of Honduras, Nicaragua, Costa Rica, and Panama. In a storm off Cuba, his ships beached in Jamaica on June 25, 1503. About a year passed before he was rescued, and he finally returned to Spain on November 7, 1504. Having been relieved of his duties as governor of the Indies, Columbus failed to secure the 10 percent of all the profits that Spain made in the lands he discovered, which had been promised him. Still, when he died on May 20, 1506, he had accumulated a small fortune from the gold he and his men had uncovered on Hispaniola.

What was Columbus's most amazing feat?

In the end, **Christopher Columbus** proved to be a mediocre, tyrannical administrator, and his handling of the Spanish settlements in the New World was judged inept. Present-day historians attribute Columbus's greatness to his "discovery" and colonization of a brave new world—which, with exploration, yielded abundant gold and silver, forever altering the history of civilization—and to his ability, despite major errors in his navigational computations, to find his way back and forth between Europe and the New World again and again.

Who were the native peoples Columbus encountered in the Americas?

The native peoples who greeted **Christopher Columbus** and his alien-looking crews when they made landfall on islands in the Caribbean Sea, which are known collectively as the West Indies, were the Amerindian group called the Arawak. The Arawakan subgroups that Columbus encountered were the Siboney, who inhabited the Antillean islands (the islands of the West Indies, with the exception of the Bahamas), and the Taino, indigenous inhabitants of both the Antilles and the Bahamas. It is not known how many Taino and Siboney populated the West Indies at the time of Columbus's arrival, but judging from the records of **Friar Bartolomé de las Casas**, a Spanish missionary who was the first ordained Roman Catholic priest in the New World and who chronicled the atrocities that the Spanish conquistadores and colonists committed against the indigenous peoples of the Americas, an estimated thirty to fifty thousand Taino called the Caribbean home in 1492. The Taino and the Siboney enjoyed highly developed social and economic systems based on farming and fishing. They were peaceful, disciplined peoples who carried out elaborate harvest ceremonies and held naturalistic beliefs in bush spirits that foretold the coming of messiahs.

Just a short time before the Spanish conquistadores reached the Caribbean, the Caribs—fierce inhabitants of the Lesser Antilles; that is, the Antillean islands of the southeast (namely, the Leeward Islands, the Windward Islands, and the Leeward Antilles)—had driven the Arawak off the Lesser Antilles. The Spanish subdued the Caribs, forcing them, along with the Taino and Siboney, to convert to Catholicism and to adopt Spanish ways. Hundreds perished from overwork at the hands of the Spanish and from the diseases the Europeans brought with them, for which the native peoples had no immunological defenses.

The Taino, Siboney, and Caribs are the ancestors of many of the peoples of the islands of the Caribbean Sea. However, since these native peoples either succumbed to disease, overwork, or acts of barbarism at the hands of the Spanish or were forced to adopt Spanish values, their culture and traditions faded and are not readily apparent in the Caribbean today. The gentle Siboney and Taino spirit must still live on in the peoples of Latin America with Arawak genes, as well as in Latinos who walk the streets of New York, Miami, Los Angeles, and places in between.

Who else lived in the Americas before Columbus got there?

Aside from the Arawak, three highly advanced indigenous cultures were thriving in the Americas at the time of the Spanish conquest. These were the Aztecs of central Mexico; the Maya, who still inhabit their ancestral lands in Yucatán and much of Guatemala; and the Incas, whose empire took shape in the Andean highlands of Peru and ultimately encompassed a large swath of western South America.

In addition, the Spanish had a great deal of interaction with the Seminole Indians of Florida and the Pueblos (Spanish for "town") of the southwestern United States, descendants of the prehistoric Anasazi peoples, including the Hopi of northeastern Arizona and the Zuni of western New Mexico and the Rio Grande pueblos.

THE MESOAMERICAN AND ANDEAN PEOPLES: THE MAYA, THE AZTECS, THE INCAS

The two main cultures that dominated Mexico and Central America before the Spanish *conquista* were those of the Maya and the Aztecs. Their civilizations are known as Mesoamerican, or Middle American. The Olmecs, who prospered from about 1200 BC to 400 BC—though scholars have diverging opinions about the Olmec timeline—along the southwestern gulf coast of Mexico, in the modern-day states of Tabasco and Veracruz, are widely viewed as Mesoamerica's first major civilization and as the fountainhead for all subsequent Mesoamerican civilizations. (Though in a minority, some Mesoamerican archeologists have contested the theory that the Olmecs were the "mother" culture, arguing that they were in reality a "sister" culture interacting with neighboring societies.) The Olmecs' highly evolved, innovative culture would exert an influence throughout the region for many centuries to come. Echoes of the Olmec political system, religion, art, rubber-ball games, and the Olmec rulers' ceremonial dress are clearly evident in burgeoning Mesoamerican civilizations, including the Maya.

The main culture that dominated South America before the Spanish *conquista* was that of the Incas, an Andean people whose empire began around AD 1100 as a small enclave in the Cuzco Valley in the highlands of Peru and then underwent a major expansion around 1438. By the time the Spanish conquistadores first stepped foot in the Inca territories of Peru in 1532, the Inca empire, then at its pinnacle, spread from South America's Pacific coast over the Andes mountains to the Amazon rain forest, and from what is present-day Colombia approximately 2,500 miles southward to what now constitutes central Chile.

Why is it said that the Maya were conquered but never defeated?

Between 1500 BC and AD 1000, the Maya, descendants of the Olmecs, flourished in southern Mexico, especially in the modern-day states of Chiapas, Tabasco, Campeche, Yucatán, and Quintana Roo, as well as in northern Central America, that is, in the modern-day states of Belize, Guatemala, Honduras, and El Salvador. At its peak, the vast Mayan empire, which was comprised of numerous city-states, was home to approximately two million inhabitants, with about one hundred thousand alone living in Tikal, the largest population center.

While the Maya were not the first Mesoamerican civilization to develop a writing system, findings published in *National Geographic* in 2006 suggest that their system may date back as far as 400 BC, which would make it nearly as old as the oldest Mesoamerican writing system uncovered thus far, that of the Zapotecs. The Maya inscribed their texts on stone monuments, palace walls, stone slabs, pottery, and tree bark (in a book format known as a codex). Approximately ten thousand Mayan texts have been found, but the Maya produced many more. At the onset of the Spanish conquest, Spanish priests burned all the bark codices they uncovered; only four codices have survived to the present day, and all that is left of one of them is a few pages. Most of the Mayan inscriptions in existence chronicle the Mayan dynasties and wars, but some that have been found actually tell of women's lives.

The Maya were the most advanced of all the pre-Columbian civilizations in the Americas in the areas of architecture, sculpture, painting, mathematics, and astronomy. They also employed very sophisticated and diverse agricultural methods. They are recognized in particular for their monumental architecture, which is on a par with Greek and Roman architecture. The Maya constructed great pyramids, religious and governmental buildings, royal palaces, and ball courts (for ritual ball games) at the center of their cities. Around this ritual core stood smaller temples and individual shrines, and, beyond that, the modest abodes of commoners. While the Maya lacked many advanced tools, such as pulleys, metal tools, and perhaps the wheel, they still managed, through the use of man power, to construct large-scale edifices of stone. The Maya's skill in mathematics was extraordinary; they formulated the first system of numeration by position that includes the concept of zero. Although earlier Mesoamerican civilizations, including the Olmecs, utilized calendars, with their mathematical erudition, the Maya were able to create the most sophisticated calendric system, and one readily accessible to scholars.

In the eighth century AD, the Mayan civilization began to decline. Theories abound as to what precipitated this: scholars have cited foreign invasion, peasant revolts, climate change, natural disasters, disease, famine, and the dissolution of trade routes as possible explanations. By the time the Spanish first entered the Mayan territories in 1519, most of the Mayan city-states were in decay. Still, it took the Spanish until 1697, over 175 years, to gain control over all of them, in part because there was no single Mayan capital to subdue. While they were overpowered, the Maya managed to salvage their culture in large measure. The Mayan civilization was so resilient that between 1554 and 1558, decades after the Spanish first set foot on Mayan territory, an anonymous indigenous person or persons from Quiché, a Mayan kingdom in the highlands of Guatemala, penned the *Popol Vuh*—an epic of Mayan creation and a history of the Quiché kingdom—which is the most important surviving work in Mayan literature in the Latin alphabet. (The text was written in the Quiché language using Spanish orthography.) That Mayan culture survived intact on the shores of the Apasion-Usumacinta river system in Central America, in the highland plains encircled by volcanoes, and in the lowland forests of that region is a testimony to the resilience of the Maya. Nowadays many there speak a version of their ancestral language and worship the same gods as the Maya of old. It is said that the Maya's roots went so deep and their bond to their mother earth was so strong that although they were seemingly conquered, in the end they were never truly defeated.

What are the Halls of Montezuma, anyway?

At the time that the Spanish conquistadores arrived in the New World, the Aztecs of central Mexico had the most advanced civilization in the Americas. When the first Spanish explorer, **Hernán Cortés**, set foot in Aztec territory in 1519, **Montezuma II**, also known as **Moctezuma II**, was ruling over the Aztec empire, the heart of which was the Valley of Mexico and the Aztec capital, Tenochtitlán (present-day Mexico City). And Montezuma had halls, all right.

Tenochtitlán, founded in 1325, was a raised city built on an islet in the middle of Texcoco Lake. Three wide causeways led to colossal palaces and elaborate pyramids and temples. During his reign, from 1502 to 1520, Montezuma II dwelled in a lavishly decorated palace, surrounded by obsequious nobles and thousands of slaves who catered to his every whim. The place was neat as a pin and ran as efficiently as a Swiss watch, since order and harmony were divine requirements, and every effort was made to keep the emperor happy. Montezuma II came from royal lineage (he was believed to be directly descended from the gods), and as such, his subjects owed him endless homage. On the other side of town, though, life was quite different for the drones. *Chinampas*, farms situated on the shallow lake beds, surrounded the city, and the farmers lived in wattle-and-daub huts, gazing on the "halls" of Montezuma from afar with wonder and reverence.

The firsthand accounts of Montezuma II were written by Spanish conquistadores bent on his demise, including Hernán Cortés, and by a Franciscan missionary to the Aztecs, **Bernardino de Sahagún** (1499–1590), who gathered information from native peoples disenchanted with the Aztec ruler. They are filled with bias, depicting him as a weak-minded ruler who was more interested in Aztec religion and prophecy—and the good life—than in preserving his great empire and saving his subjects from certain domination. It can probably be said without a doubt, though, that Montezuma II was unprepared for Cortés and the Spanish conquest. At first, so the story goes, the Aztec ruler was uncertain whether the Spanish were gods or men. But after consulting soothsayers and uncovering omens, he concluded that the conquistadores were, categorically, white gods, and that his reign was up.

Rather than battle the Spaniards, who had formed a strategic partnership with the inhabitants of Tlaxcala, a city-state of central Mexico that the Aztecs had failed to conquer, Montezuma II tried everything else to entice them to leave—from gifts to sorcery. When none of his stratagems worked, and he could neither buy the Spanish off nor make them magically disappear, Montezuma II invited Cortés to enter Tenochtitlán. They met for the first time on November 8, 1519, and before long, Cortés's forces took Montezuma II prisoner. Violence erupted between the Spanish forces and the Aztecs in June 1520. According to Cortés's account, Montezuma II was mortally wounded by a stone cast by one of his own people, presumably in reprisal for his purblindness and folly. In July 1520 the Spanish fled from Tenochtitlán, and the Aztecs managed to keep them at bay for a while, but eventually the Spaniards prevailed, thanks to their weaponry and a smallpox epidemic that ravaged Tenochtitlán. The entire Aztec empire fell under Spanish domination in 1521.

As for his halls, the Spaniards, who were horrified by the Aztec religious rites involving human sacrifice, ruthlessly destroyed Montezuma II's temples. The Spanish missionaries who converted the Aztecs to Catholicism completed the desecration of their temples by burning the records and smashing the idols.

Why were they called the heart-eating Aztecs?

In the Aztec religion there were hundreds of gods, who ruled over certain days and even over certain hours of the day. The Aztec gods personified the forces of nature, and numerous Aztec religious ceremonies were aimed at appeasing the gods by performing rites that often involved human sacrifice. For instance, at the dedication in 1487 of the Great Pyramid of Tenochtitlán, with its shrines to the deities Huitzilopochtli (god of sun and war) and Tlaloc (god of rain and fertility), the Aztecs sacrificed eighty-four thousand captives as an offering to the gods. The captives were led up the steps of the high pyramid, where priests slit open their bodies and tore out their hearts, considered the most precious organ to offer the gods. During some religious ceremonies, the Aztecs engaged in ritual cannibalism, an act they believed would imbue them with their victims' virtues.

Besides the halls, what else did the Aztecs have to brag about?

The Aztecs could be said to have been brilliant imitators rather than privileged originators. They absorbed much from the cultures of earlier, more advanced Mesoamerican peoples, including the Toltecs, Zapotecs, and Maya. For instance, they learned the fundamentals of architecture and engineering from the Toltecs, and then built magnificent temples, as well as the remarkable city of Tenochtitlán. The Aztecs also imported Mixtec crafts and even brought in Mixtec craftsmen, whose work they replicated. The Aztecs developed an advanced agricultural system. Their chief crops, which they bartered using cacao beans as change, included pears, tomatoes, corn, beans, chiles, squash, and cotton—all of which they cultivated with a high degree of uniformity harvest after harvest.

How did Mexico get its name?

The Aztecs, who spoke Nahuatl, which is related to the languages of the Pima and Shoshone tribes of the western United States, referred to themselves as the Mexica people. "Mexica" might have derived from the Nahuatl word for the sun; from Mexitli, the name of a great Aztec leader and war god; from the word *mexitli*, the Nahuatl name of a weed that grows in Lake Texcoco; or from the word *mexicatl*, which translates as the "weed people," a reference to the Aztec practice of eating the weeds of Lake Texcoco to ward off starvation. The whole of Mexico is named after the Mexica people, the Aztecs.

Are there any Aztecs left?

Though the Aztec population plummeted from fifteen million at the onset of the Spanish conquest to under two million by 1581, neither Spanish explorer **Francisco Fernández de Córdoba**, who "discovered" the Yucatán in 1517; nor **Juan de Grijalba**, who, beginning in 1518, furthered Fernández de Córdoba's explorations (and was the first to hear about **Montezuma II**'s Aztec empire); nor Spanish conquistador **Diego de Velázquez**, who authorized Grijalba's expedition in 1518; nor **Hernán Cortés**, who actually dethroned **Montezuma II** and brought about the collapse of the Aztec empire in 1521; nor the Spanish settlers who followed them were able to completely destroy the Aztecs. Incalculable numbers of native peoples and mestizos dwelling in Mexico today, as well as countless Mexican Americans, are the descendants of the proud Aztec people. Aside from their obvious genetic legacy, the Aztecs left a wealth of wisdom, artistry, and folklore, which lives on in the hearts and minds of their heirs.

SOME PLACES WHERE YOU
CAN RELIVE LATINO HISTORY

1. **The De Soto National Memorial**, Bradenton, Florida

This twenty-five-acre national park commemorates the arrival and legacy of Spanish explorer Hernando de Soto's expedition in Florida in 1539. The park features Camp Uzita, a reproduction of the sixteenth-century Indian village that De Soto and his men used as a base camp during their explorations. At the camp, park rangers and volunteers dressed as Spanish soldiers of the period show young visitors the fine points of the military crossbow and Spanish harquebus, provide them the opportunity to try on Spanish armor, and demonstrate colonial cooking and blacksmithing.

2. **Castillo de San Marcos National Monument**, St. Augustine, Florida

In this twenty-acre national park stands the original *castillo*, or "fort," that the Spanish erected at the entrance to St. Augustine's harbor between 1672 and 1695 to protect what was then Spain's northernmost outpost in the Americas from invasion and to guard the shipping lane from St. Augustine to Spain. The Castillo de San Marcos is the oldest masonry fort and the oldest extant seventeenth-century fort in North America.

3. **Cabrillo National Monument**, San Diego, California

This park, which lies at the tip of the Point Loma Peninsula, west of San Diego, and was established in 1913, commemorates the voyage of discovery of Spanish explorer Juan Rodríguez Cabrillo, the first European to set foot on what is now the West Coast of the United States. On June 27, 1542, Cabrillo and his crew set sail from Navidad, Mexico, and on September 28, 1542, they sailed into San Diego Bay and claimed all of the surrounding territory for the Spanish crown. Sometime later during the expedition, Cabrillo died, but his crew pushed forward, possibly sailing as far north as present-day Oregon before winter storms forced them to turn back.

4. **The California Missions**, coastal California

The twenty-one Franciscan missions that dot *El Camino Real* (the King's Highway), which runs parallel to the California coast, from San Diego up to Sonoma, were founded between 1769 and 1823 by Spanish Franciscan friars. They established the mission system to bring Catholicism to the native peoples of California and to settle the land. Father Junípero Serra founded the first of the missions, in San Diego, in 1769. In 1988 Pope John Paul II beatified Father Serra at the Vatican, granting him the title "blessed," which signifies that the Catholic Church has attributed at least one miracle to him.

5. **Columbia State Historic Park**, Columbia, California

Situated three miles north of Sonora, Columbia is one of myriad settlements that sprang up during the heady days of the California gold rush, which began in 1848. From the 1850s to the 1870s, mines in the town's vicinity yielded over $500 million in gold (at today's value), but by 1860 all of the most accessible gold had been mined, and Columbia's population plummeted from ten thousand to five hundred citizens. While many of the gold rush settlements fell victim to abandonment, fire, vandalism, and the elements, Columbia remained in fair condition. In 1945 the California state legislature turned this gold rush town into a historic park, and nowadays visitors can explore its original schoolhouse and its historic saloons, hotels, restaurants, and shops, and even pan for gold, tour an active gold mine, and ride a one-hundred-year-old stagecoach.

6. **The Alamo**, San Antonio, Texas

Originally call *Misión San Antonio de Valero*, the Alamo is considered the shrine or cradle of Texas liberty and is the state's biggest attraction. The Spanish began construction on the mission in 1724, and until 1793, when it was secularized, it was home to missionaries and their native converts, who farmed the land. The chapel and barracks are all that remain of the original mission and fort, where a small band of American soldiers, fighting for Texas's independence from Mexico during the Texas Revolution (1835–36), battled General Antonio López de Santa Anna's Mexican army of thousands for thirteen days before being defeated on March 6, 1836. Nowadays visitors can tour what remains of the mission and view exhibits about the Texas Revolution and Texas history at the Alamo's 4.2-acre complex, which has been managed by the Daughters of the Republic of Texas since 1905.

7. The Mexican Museum, San Francisco, California

The Mexican Museum, which opened its doors in San Francisco's Mission District in 1975 and will soon relocate to the city's Yerba Buena Arts District, houses a permanent collection of more than twelve thousand objects. Among them are preconquest artifacts (that is, those that predate the Spanish conquest of Mexico and the Americas); examples of colonial art from Mexico; art by Mexican artists, including Diego Rivera; Chicano art dating from the 1960s to the present; and works by other Latino artists.

8. El Museo del Barrio, New York, New York

Founded in 1969 in New York City's East Harlem as an educational institution devoted to Puerto Rican art, El Museo del Barrio, which has called the Heckscher Building on Fifth Avenue home since 1977, nowadays boasts a rich permanent collection of Caribbean and Latin American art, as well as some works by Latinos. The collection is comprised of pre-Columbian Caribbean artifacts; traditional art objects from Puerto Rico, Mexico, Chile, and Peru; a Puerto Rican print collection; over five hundred paintings by leading Latin American artists; sculptures and installations by such artists as Pepón Osorio; and photography and film/video collections, replete with footage of life in El Barrio as early as the 1970s. In addition to expanding its collection, the museum also stages exhibitions, such as the highly touted Frida Kahlo exhibition in 2002.

What was so great about the Incas, and what did they do with all that gold?

After founding the capital of Panama in 1519, Spanish conquistador **Pascual de Andagoya** headed southward to Colombia, where he learned of a gold-laden territory, called Birú (Peru). Andagoya attempted to reach this distant territory but failed. His health in decline, he returned to Panama and relayed the news of the existence of Birú and its riches. Andagoya's account of Birú, and reports of **Hernán Cortés**'s gold finds in Mexico, captured the imagination of Spanish conquistador **Francisco Pizarro**, who after two unsuccessful expeditions to the south of Colombia, finally reached the Inca territories of Peru in 1532, saw for himself the region's productive goldfields, and immediately succumbed to gold fever. But, to the Spaniard's amazement, the citizens of the mammoth Inca empire—which had begun as a small entity in the Cuzco Valley of highland Peru around AD 1100 and, at its zenith, stretched from the Pacific coast of South America across the Andes to the Amazon rain forest, and from present-day Colombia some 2,500 miles southward to present-day central Chile—did not consider gold, or even silver, a commodity. Unlike the Europeans, for whom gold served a monetary purpose, the Incas relied on a system of barter.

The worship of the sun was at the core of the Incan religion. The Inca emperors were regarded as divine beings directly descended from the sun god. Since gold symbolized the sun, the precious metal was used exclusively by the Inca emperors and the elite for decorative and ritual purposes. They sported gold brooches, buckles, and headdresses, and even had knives, plates, and entire walls made from gold. While gold was not coinage for the Incas, they held it in as high esteem as the Spanish.

The Incas are known for much more than their appreciation of gold. Theirs was an advanced and wealthy society; Cuzco, the center of the Inca empire, earned the reputation as the richest city in the Americas. When it comes to the arts, few cultures on earth have approximated the accomplishments of the Inca. They were skilled at handweaving, created exquisite jewelry, and were also extraordinary architects. Among the most superb examples of Incan architecture are the ruins of the granite ceremonial buildings and houses that comprise the remote Incan city of Machu Picchu. Built on a high mountain ridge above the Urubamba Valley in Peru beginning around 1440, the city was not discovered by the Spanish and thus remained intact—unlike Cuzco, the Incan capital, which the conquistadores almost completely destroyed.

The Incas were also adept farmers, developing innovative methods for irrigating thousands of miles of valleys, and they built an intricate system of roads throughout their immense territory, which aided in the distribution and trade of foodstuffs and goods and enabled Inca emperors to keep tabs on their subjects. In addition, the Incas created a highly organized and effective system of governing, which kept their vast empire prosperous no matter what the sun or rain gods did in any particular season. For instance, if crops failed in one locality, government records would indicate where the harvest had been more abundant, and the shortage would be made good by drawing on public warehouses in those districts.

Are potatoes a gift from the Incas?

Archeological discoveries indicate that the potato was cultivated in Peru more than seven thousand years ago, and DNA tests on potatoes have pinpointed a narrow region of origin, southern Peru, and not a wider area stretching from Peru to northern Argentina, as was thought until very recently. The Incas grew the starchy tuber, even employing freeze-drying techniques to render potatoes light enough for the Incan armies to carry them in adequate quantities. The Incas also cultivated quinoa (a highly nutritious, grainlike annual herb of the goosefoot family that is grown for its seeds), corn, tomatoes, peppers, sweet potatoes, cassava (known to most Latinos as yuca, not to be confused with yucca, a tropical New World plant with white flowers), and other vegetables and fruits. Impressed by the potato's hardiness, versatility, and flavor, Spanish explorers took the tuber back to Spain around 1570. From there, the potato spread throughout Europe, and, later, English settlers introduced it to North America.

Why were the Incas really not Incas at all?

Originally, the name Inca referred strictly to the first Inca royal family and its forty thousand descendants who governed the empire. However, the Spanish used the term to refer to all the inhabitants of the vast Inca empire. These inhabitants spoke an assortment of different languages, but Quechua and Aymara were the major languages of the empire. Quechua is still the lingua franca of many of the indigenous peoples of Peru, Ecuador, Bolivia, Argentina, northern Chile, and southern Colombia. Nowadays it can be heard on American streets, among Latinos with roots in these countries and regions, who pepper their Spanish with words from the ancient tongue.

How did the Incas get so big?

The Incas were big, as in powerful, but they were short in stature by contemporary American standards: An Incan man stood an average of four feet tall. For that matter, most of the Spanish conquistadores were pretty short, too. (Check out the Spanish armor at the Metropolitan Museum of Art in New York City.)

The Incas were also big in terms of the dimensions of their empire, the largest in the pre-Columbian Americas. The beginnings of the Inca empire are shrouded in mystery because Incan mythology and history were closely intertwined. The Spanish recorded Incan history just as it was conveyed to them, but the Incas may have relayed more fiction than fact. **Manco Capac** is believed to be the founding ruler of the Inca empire, although he may have been mythological. The Inca empire remained small until **Pachacuti Inca Yupanqui** was made emperor around 1438 and set about absorbing, by conquest and assimilation, surrounding cultures, swallowing up over a hundred nations in the space of thirty years. Thus, by the time **Francisco Pizarro** stepped foot on Inca territory in 1532, the Incas had amassed a vast empire. To this day, it remains the largest native state to have ever existed in the Western Hemisphere.

How did the Incas lose their empire?

When **Francisco Pizarro** entered Inca territory in 1532 and established San Miguel de Piura, the first Spanish settlement in Peru, that very same year, the legendary **Atahuallpa** was the Inca emperor. Unlike **Montezuma II**, the Aztec ruler whom **Hernán Cortés** easily subdued, Atahuallpa was someone to be reckoned with. He was not about to hand over his treasures and sacrifice his subjects to the greedy conquistadores without a valiant struggle. When Atahuallpa refused to welcome Pizarro, the conquistador unleashed his forces on the Inca army in the battle of Cajamarca on November 16, 1532. The Spanish won the battle, and in the end, they captured Atahuallpa and then executed him on August 29, 1533, to show the Incas that their fierce emperor was, in fact, a man of flesh and blood who had not feet of gold, but of clay.

Atahuallpa's treacherous half brother, **Manco Inca Yupanqui**, collaborated with the Spanish in Atahuallpa's capture. The Spanish then installed Manco as a puppet ruler, but they mistreated him, and, finally, in 1536 he fled Cuzco for Vitcos, a city on the edge of the jungle, where he built a fortress from which to begin reconquering his land. The Spanish proved too mighty, and, ultimately, Manco Inca Yupanqui was forced to negotiate a surrender in exchange for his life. Other Incan nobles continued the courageous resistance against the Spanish. They won an impressive number of skirmishes and left a trail of decapitated Spaniards along the Andean mountainsides, but they lost the war when the last Incan leader, **Túpac Amaru**, was captured and executed in 1572.

Under Spanish domination, the Incan regional capitals were immediately transformed into Spanish towns bearing Spanish names, and most of the Incas were forced into slavery—principally as gold miners and laborers, who filled the Spanish galleons and the king's coffers to the brim. As with most of the indigenous populations that the Europeans conquered, the Incas and their culture could not be entirely erased. Quechua, a main language of the Inca empire, as well as Incan religious beliefs, artistic and culinary traditions, and even philosophy, are still kept alive by the descendants of the Incas.

Why is there a Cadillac named Eldorado?

El Dorado is Spanish for "the gilded one." Soon after they first arrived in South America, the Spanish conquistadores learned of a South American Chibcha Indian legend that told of a land swimming in gold somewhere between Bogotá, Colombia, and Lima, Peru. The legend probably stems from a ritual that the Chibcha performed in the highlands of Colombia, which involved anointing a new chief with resinous gums and decorating him with gold dust as an offering to the earth gods, while the people tossed gold bars and emeralds into the water. This ritual of the Man of Gold, or *El Dorado*, had died out long before the Spanish set foot in the region, but tales of a city of gold, also called El Dorado, buried somewhere in the land persisted.

The Spanish took these tales very seriously and organized expeditions in search of El Dorado from around 1569 until 1617. One of the most important expeditions was led by **Gonzalo Jiménez de Quesada**, who, during his first foray in the New World in the 1530s, had conquered the Chibcha of the great central plain of Colombia, had founded the city of Bogotá, and had amassed a vast quantity of emeralds and gold. In 1569 Jiménez de Quesada set off in search of El Dorado but came up empty-handed. A few decades later, the English adventurer, scholar, and courtier **Sir Walter Raleigh** got into the act. In 1595 Raleigh led an expedition of four ships in search of the fabled city of gold, sailing up the Orinoco River into what is now known as Guiana (a region in South America that includes present-day Guyana, Suriname, and French Guiana). He came upon several gold mines but little else. In 1617 a resolute Raleigh launched a second search for El Dorado, which took him once more to Guiana. Stricken with fever, he was unable to lead his party up the Orinoco and sent his lieutenant in his place. His men found no gold, then burned a Spanish settlement, and Raleigh's son Walter lost his life in the ensuing skirmish.

Although El Dorado was never found, the impassioned search for it resulted in the exploration and conquest of much of northern South America. El Dorado, the mythical land of the Man of Gold, has come to connote a golden dream, which is probably why General Motors chose Eldorado as the name for one of its convertibles when it debuted in 1953. An upmarket vehicle, the 1953 Eldorado came, naturally, with eye-catching custom coachwork, luxury accessories (most everything standard), and a hefty $7,750 base price tag. (The average cost of an automobile in 1953 was $1,850.) Not surprisingly, one of the color choices for the 1953 Cadillac Eldorado was Aztec red.

THE "SPANISH" in "HISPANIC"

Latinos have Spanish roots, but where do the Spanish people come from?

Obviously, the Spanish people come from Spain, a country in southwestern Europe that occupies about five-sixths of the Iberian Peninsula (the last sixth encompasses Portugal, the British possession of Gibraltar, and the microstate of Andorra). The Canary Islands, off the northwest coast of Africa; the Balearic Islands, in the western Mediterranean; Melilla and Ceuta, city enclaves perched on the Moroccan coast; and three island groups near the Moroccan coast also fly the Spanish flag. In all, Spain comprises an area about the size of Arizona and Utah combined.

The Spanish enjoy one of the oldest and most diverse cultural and ethnic heritages in Europe and, thus, can be said to come from many different places. To be exact, they are descended from the Carthaginians, Celts, Romans, Vandals, Visigoths, and Moors. Also, a large number of Jews settled in Spain, particularly in the south, as the result, not of an invasion, but rather a migration, and contributed vastly to Spanish society. The inhabitants of each of the seventeen autonomous regions of Spain—Castile and León, Andalusia, Galicia, Catalonia, the Basque Country, Asturias, Cantabria, Rioja, Aragon, Valencia, Murcia, Extremadura, Castile-La Mancha, Madrid, Navarra, the Canary Islands, and the Balearic Islands—have their own distinct customs, dialects, and character, and regional devotion runs deeper than national pride.

For instance, the Castilians—who live in Spain's heartland and whom most foreigners consider "real" Spaniards, because Castilian Spanish, *castellano*, is the official state and literary language of Spain—are known for their austerity, deep sense of pride, and fortitude. On the other hand, the Andalusians, on Spain's light-drenched southern coast, who, in addition to *castellano*, speak the Andalusian dialect, are known for their gaiety and love of horses and dance. The Galicians (*gallegos*), whose roots are Celtic, or Gaelic, like the Irish, speak *gallego*, a language closely related to Portuguese (some linguists contend that Galician and Portuguese are dialects of the same language). They live in the lush, rainy northwest corner of Spain, and are regarded as a hardworking, frugal, and somewhat melancholy folk, just like the Irish. In contradistinction, Catalonians, who speak Catalan, a language related to Provençal, a dialect of Occitan spoken in southern France, and reside in the northeastern corner of Spain (the Parliament of Catalonia defined Catalonia as a nation in 2005) are generally considered brisk, industrious, and artistic people. (Three of the twentieth century's greatest artists hailed from Catalonia: **Pablo Picasso**, **Salvador Dalí**, and **Joan Miró**.)

Then there are the Basque people, who speak Basque (or Euskera), which is a language isolate, meaning it is not derived from a single ancestral tongue common to any other language and is, therefore, the sole language within its language family. Ethnic nationalism runs deep in the Basque Country, and the Basques have long sought to sever ties with the rest of Spain. From 1968 until it renounced violence and declared a "permanent cease-fire" on March 22, 2006, *Euskadi Ta Askatasuna* (ETA, Basque Homeland and Liberty), a militant Basque separatist group founded in 1959, sought to establish an independent Basque state by terrorizing Spanish society, assassinating and killing with bombs over eight hundred people, among them

Spanish government officials, Spanish security forces, military personnel, and civilians. ETA's actions have also come at a high monetary cost: from 1994 to 2003, the Spanish government spent almost $11 billion on ETA-related police and intelligence operations, the provision of bodyguards to thousands of potential victims, and compensation to victims. Over the decades, an overwhelming majority of Basques have condemned ETA's violence. Now most are hoping that the "permanent cease-fire" translates into lasting peace.

Are Latinos the descendants of people from all over Spain?

Spaniards from all corners of Spain conquered and later settled the New World. Thus the character of each region of the country was added to the prodigious melting pot—or, more accurately, distinctive stew—of the Americas and, eventually, Latino America. It should be noted that Extremadura—one of Spain's most unspoiled regions, whose harsh, rugged landscape generated a tough, robust people—was home to a great number of conquistadores, including **Hernán Cortés**, **Francisco Pizarro**, **Hernando de Soto**, **Vasco Núñez de Balboa**, **Pedro de Alvarado**, and **Pedro de Valdivia**. For this reason, Extremadura earned the title Cradle of the Conquistadores.

What is the Spanish "lisp," and where did it really come from?

The Castilians, as well as Spaniards from other regions of Spain, pronounce the letters c and z like the interdental fricative "th" when they precede the vowels i and e, and thus they are said to "lisp." For instance, they pronounce "San Francisco" as "San FranTHisco." The interdental fricative "th" in Spanish, contrary to popular opinion in the United States, cannot be traced to a Spanish king who lisped. Rather, it is an example of the Greek influence on Latin and, later, on its first cousin Spanish.

The "th" sound, like some wine, did not travel well and was completely dropped by Spanish speakers in Latin America, where c and z are pronounced like s before the vowels i and e, just as they are in Andalusia and other areas of Spain. This does not mean that Spanish-speaking Latin Americans do not speak Castilian Spanish. They do indeed, and, not only that, it is the official language of all the Spanish-speaking Latin American countries. Thus there is no such thing as, say, the Cuban or Puerto Rican language. However, Cubans and Puerto Ricans (and each Latino subgroup) speak Spanish with their own unique accent and pepper their speech with words that the indigenous peoples of the Americas, and African slaves and their descendants, lent to New World Spanish over the centuries.

Why do Latinos have two last names?

In Spain, newborns are given both their father's last name and their mother's maiden name. Thus if the surname of María's father is Pérez and her mother's maiden name is López, María's full name will be María Pérez López. When María becomes a mother, she will pass on her father's name to her child. Thus if María's husband has the surname González, the baby will have González Pérez as a surname. And so the patriarchal line prevails. The Spanish and Latin Americans still adhere to this dual-surname tradition, but most Latinos drop their mother's name.

Why do Spaniards say olé?

Olé is a Spanish word adapted from "Allah," the Arabic name for God. So when Spaniards cry *"¡Olé!"* at a bullfight, they are saying "Praise Allah!"—even if they really mean *"Viva,"* which is Spanish for "Long live!" or "Live!" or, in some circles, "Man alive!" No single word encapsulates as much Spanish history as that three-letter word *olé*—seven centuries of history involving the Moors, to be precise.

Another Spanish word derived from "Allah" is *ojalá*, which means "hopefully." At its root is the Arabic word *Inshallah*, meaning "if God be willing," which Arabic speakers sometimes employ when describing future plans.

Who were the Moors, and how did they manage to dominate Spain?

From AD 415 to AD 711, the Visigoths, an East Germanic tribe, ruled Spain. In the seventh century, Arab armies swept across northern Africa and conquered the Berbers, engendering a new mixed race of Muslims known as the Moors. In AD 711 the Moors crossed the Strait of Gibraltar into Spain and overthrew the Visigoths at the battle of Guadalete. By 714, Muslim armies controlled all of Spain except for the mountainous regions in the north, where the Visigoths found refuge. Thus began seven centuries of Muslim domination in Spain, evidence of which can be found to this day in Spanish, Latin American, and Latino culture, music, literature, art, architecture, and philosophy. For instance, Latinos consider lucky the numerical combination 7-11, the year that the Moors made their way to Spain. It was certainly lucky for the Moors—since seven hundred years, by anyone's calculations, is a very long winning streak.

The Moors left their stamp on all of Spain except the northern regions that were controlled by Christian kingdoms. With their ingenious methods of irrigation, the Moors transformed the arid coastland and southern hills of Spain into lush, palatial gardens. They rebuilt the old Roman cities in the Arabic style, with mosques and elegant courtyards complete with fountains. Ceramic tiles, fine silk, beautifully crafted leather goods, and metalwork became the trademarks of Moorish Spain.

The Moors also exhibited great intellectual prowess. They transformed the city of Córdoba, in Andalusia, into a glorious caliphate, which emerged as a center of learning. Scientists, mathematicians, philosophers, and writers flourished there and in other regions of Moorish Spain.

Why did the Jews settle in Europe, and how did they fare in Moorish Spain?

After the destruction of Jerusalem by the Roman army in AD 70, many uprooted Jews settled in North Africa or in Mediterranean cities. Later they made their way to other parts of Europe, especially Spain. Spanish Jews and their descendants are known as Sephardim. Their customs, rituals, and pronunciation of Hebrew differ somewhat from those of Ashkenazic Jews, who settled in eastern European countries. In the more than one thousand years that the Jews have inhabited Spain, they have experienced periods both of relative acceptance and of intense persecution and pressure to convert to Christianity.

The Christian Visigoths, who ruled Spain from AD 586 to AD 711, were the first to vigorously impose virulently anti-Jewish policies, with the result of nearly decimating the Jewish population. When the Moors conquered Spain in AD 711, they granted Jews a high degree of religious and intellectual freedom. So began what is known as the Golden Age of Spain, during which Spanish Jews produced a large body of scholarship and creative work. Jewish literary tradition, music, and philosophy became deeply embedded in Iberian culture. Among the prominent Jewish scholars and philosophers of eleventh- and twelfth-century Spain were **Judah ha-Levi**, **Solomon ibn Gabirol**, and **Moses Maimonides**. With the freedom the Moors gave them, the Jews also excelled as financiers and tradespeople.

Around the mid-twelfth century, the Almohads, a fanatical Muslim sect from North Africa, founded around 1120 by **Abu 'abd Allah Muhammad Ibn Tumart**, swept across North Africa and into Moorish Spain. The Almohads persecuted Spain's Muslims, whom they believed practiced an impure form of Islam, and non-Muslims alike. Jews faced certain death if they did not either convert to Islam or escape Spain; many fled to northern Spain, where Christian rulers were organizing efforts to reconquer the Iberian Peninsula, as well as to the south of France. The Christians in northern Spain forged alliances with the Jews, which lasted a while, until a new era of Christian fervor. In 1212 the Almohads were finally suppressed, and the Jews in Moorish Spain once again enjoyed religious freedom.

Who were the Marranos?

Eventually, Christian fanaticism took hold of northern Spain to the same extent that Almohad zeal had gripped the south. For three months in 1391, Spanish Christians massacred over fifty thousand Jews, striking every Jewish community in Spain, with the exception of Zaragoza. In Valencia, not a single Jew survived the slaughter. The Spanish Christians forced those Jews they spared, or who managed to escape, to convert to Christianity and be baptized. The converted Jews, or *conversos*, were called Marranos, Spanish for "swine," by the old Christians—a term that has lived on. Many Marranos achieved high positions at court and in the church, but countless others were suspected of practicing Judaism in secret and were persecuted and killed. Some were the victims of autos-da-fé—the burning of heretics at the stake. As a result of these pre–Spanish Inquisition policies in Spain, Spanish Jews came to value highly the mystical doctrines of the kabbalah.

What role did Queen Isabella and King Ferdinand play in the Christian reconquest of Spain?

A decisive one. The reconquest, or *reconquista*, of Spain, which commenced in about AD 1000, was a five-hundred-year campaign by Spain's remaining Christians, who inhabited the northern territories of the Iberian Peninsula, to push the Moors out of Spain and reestablish Christian rule there. The reconquest was not a continuous process but occurred in fits and starts. By the time **Isabella I** acceded—with a little bit of dynastic fortune and an ounce of luck—to the throne of Castile, a kingdom in central and northern Spain, in 1474, the Christian armies had long reconquered all of Moorish Spain except for the Kingdom of Granada, on the southern Mediterranean coast.

When Isabella's husband, **Ferdinand II**, became the rightful heir to the throne of Aragon, in northeastern Spain, in 1479, the two most influential kingdoms of Spain outside the Moorish Empire, that is, the Kingdom of Castile and the Kingdom of Aragon, were joined in a union of crowns. And, as luck would have it, both the queen and the king, who together were known as the Catholic Kings, were savvy leaders single-heartedly committed to the joint rule of Castile and Aragon, which had the effect of pulling together, and conferring legitimacy on, a new Christian Spanish state, and of strengthening the Christian armies. Isabella I and Ferdinand II launched a massive assault on the Moors of the Kingdom of Granada, who fell in defeat. The final blow to Moorish rule came with the Catholic Kings' conquest of the Moors' last refuge, the city of Granada, in January 1492.

What was the fate of the Jews in Spain after the reconquest?

In 1478, while the reconquest of Spain was still under way, **Isabella**, with the permission of **Pope Sixtus IV**, created an Inquisition in the Kingdom of Castile as a means of achieving religious unity in what was a multireligious society comprised of Catholics, Jews, and Muslims, and thereby consolidating power. The Spanish Inquisition involved the creation of ecclesiastical tribunals for the discovery and punishment of Christian heretics, and in the Kingdom of Castile, it was presided over by two Dominican monks, **Miguel de Morillo** and **Juan de San Martin**. Tribunals were set up in Seville and Córdoba, and *conversos*, both Marranos (converts from Judaism) and Moriscos (converts from Islam), suspected of religious infidelity were put on trial. Infidels were locked up, dispossessed of their land and belongings, subjected to torture, and burned at the stake or otherwise executed. On October 17, 1483, the pope established the Inquisition throughout all the kingdoms of the Spanish monarchy, and **Tomás de Torquemada** was made the grand inquisitor of Aragon, Valencia, and Catalonia. During the first dozen years of the Spanish Inquisition, which was not officially abolished until 1834, thousands of *conversos*, the majority Marranos, were executed.

Under the Spanish Inquisition, practicing Jews were not subjected to persecution, but they constantly aroused suspicion as they were viewed as a source of temptation to Marranos, who might at any time renew their ties to Judaism. Once the last Moorish rulers fled to North Africa, and Spain was newly unified, Isabella I and **Ferdinand II** dealt with this threat to Catholic unity by issuing the Alhambra Decree, an edict of expulsion aimed at the professing Jews in Spain, the largest Jewish population in Europe at that time. Under the edict, which was issued in the spring of 1492, all professing Jews were ordered to convert to Christianity or, if they refused, to leave their homeland of over a millennium or face certain death. With the issuance of the edict, approximately half of the two hundred thousand Jews in Spain in 1492 fled the country.

Many of the professing Jews who converted to Catholicism under the edict, the "New Christians," managed to lead peaceful, prosperous lives in Spain, rising to positions of power in all spheres of Spanish life, but especially in politics and finance. A few took an active role in the conquest of the New World. For instance, Dominican friar **Diego Durán**, who was born in Spain in 1537 and was the son of a converted Jew, made the journey at the age of five or six to Mexico. There he joined the Dominican order in 1556 and devoted all of his energies to converting Amerindians to Christianity. Around 1581, Durán wrote *Historia de las Indias de la Nueva España e islas de la tierra firme* (*History of the Indies of New Spain and Islands of the Terra Firma*), in which he eloquently describes the glories of the Mesoamerican civilizations. It is an astounding historical text and one of the few surviving accounts of the Aztec people.

What else happened in 1492?

The year 1492 was a triumphant one for Spain. It saw the fall of Granada, marking the final defeat of the Moorish empire on Spanish soil and the reunification of Spain. It was also the year of **Christopher Columbus**'s first voyage to the Americas and the beginning of febrile Spanish expansionism in the New World. In myriad ways, the Inquisition that gripped Spain at the end of the fifteenth century carried over to the New World: the Spanish conquistadores, missionaries, and settlers subjugated the peoples of the Americas, destroyed their religious iconography, and ultimately forced them to convert to Catholicism. Nonconverts were considered subhuman and were treated as such.

THE AFRICAN PEOPLE

Why do more Latinos than Anglos have African roots?

From the very start, the Spanish conquistadores and settlers in the Americas appropriated the indigenous peoples as a labor force. However, the indigenous populations proved unsuitable for forced labor: Unaccustomed to the rigors of agrarian work and the sheer brutality meted out to them, and highly susceptible to European diseases, they were swiftly depleted. In desperate need of laborers to work in agriculture and mining, the Spanish in the Caribbean resorted to importing slaves from Africa, a practice begun by the Portuguese, who, facing a labor shortage in Brazil, transported the first shipload of African slaves to the Americas in 1502. It should be noted that the European slave trade in Africa started about a half century before, in 1441, when the Portuguese, lacking in agricultural laborers, took twelve Africans they captured in Cabo Branco (modern-day Mauritania) back to Portugal.

In the sixteenth century, the Spanish and the Portuguese were not the only Europeans to engage in, and reap the monetary gains of, transatlantic African slave trading: the English, Dutch, and French also brought large numbers of African slaves to their New World colonies. In fact, the Atlantic traffic in African people by Europeans became such big business that the great shipping companies across Europe bid against each other for shipments. Only the best "specimens" were brought across the ocean, and even then, hundreds of thousands did not survive the Middle Passage, which they spent shackled in extremely close quarters below deck, with barely enough water, food, and air to sustain them.

Given the propensity to work the African slaves to death and then simply replace them, especially in the Caribbean, it is estimated that from the sixteenth to the nineteenth century, between nine and fifteen million Africans were transported to the New World. About 40 percent of these enslaved Africans were taken to the Caribbean, and another 40 percent to Brazil, with the rest transported to the United States and to territories outside of the Caribbean that were controlled by Spain. Most of the African slaves brought to Spain's Caribbean colonies came from eastern Nigeria, the Gold Coast, and the Congo basin. Despite the odds, they managed to preserve some of their religious and cultural traditions, and over time their gods, art, music, and food preparation techniques entered Caribbean mainstream cultures. In present-day Puerto Rico, the Dominican Republic, and Cuba, it is difficult to unthread the African cultural strands from the larger culture. Even African terminology, such as *kimbombo*, Yoruban for "okra," made its way into colonial Spanish in the Caribbean and now enlivens the speech of Americans with roots in the region.

The lucrative transatlantic African slave trade endured for over three centuries. In 1807 Britain finally abolished the slave trade on its own territory for moral, humanitarian, and economic reasons—as well as in response to growing African resistance to enslavement—and in 1833 the British parliament abolished the institution of slavery itself, allowing for a six-year "apprentice" transition and compensation to slave owners. Before the end of the century, Spain, France, Portugal, Denmark, the Netherlands, the United States, Brazil, and other nations would put an end to slavery in their territories, with Brazil the last holdout, eradicating slavery only in 1888.

As to the reason for a greater *mestizaje*, or racial, ethnic, and cultural synthesis, in the former Spanish colonies as compared to the English colonies, there are three prevailing interpretations. The first is that the ratio of Africans and native peoples to Caucasians was higher in the Spanish than in the English colonial world, and therefore miscegenation was inevitable. According to the second interpretation, which is related to the first, the Spanish conquistadores and settlers first journeyed alone to the New World, leaving their families behind in Europe, while the English, Dutch, Germans, and other settlers of the Americas tended to bring their families with them and had, therefore, less of a desire to stray. The third premise is that the Spaniards found the African and native peoples generally pleasing in their physiques and personalities and had rather casual attitudes toward interracial and interethnic unions and hybridity. The English, whose society was dominated by class hierarchy, which was tied to heredity (noble blood lines), and for whom upward mobility was rarely an option, asserted and preserved their social status through class segregation and distancing. Naturally, they rejected the notion of racial and ethnic integration, wherein lay certain social demotion. Of course, this is not to say that once in the New World, the pride and prejudice of the upper classes behind them, the English did not from time to time overcome the cultural proscription against intermingling with Africans and Native Americans, as a cursory glance across North America reveals.

TRES

Mexican Americans

The history of Mexico and that of the United States are so inextricably linked that these nations have been compared to Siamese twins who, before enduring a radical and painful separation, shared the same heart. Mexican Americans are not an ethnic minority who merely *crossed* U.S.-Mexico borders and then, by slow assimilation, became incorporated into the great American mosaic. They have ancestral roots in part of the territory within the boundaries of what *now* constitutes the United States, that is, the areas that formerly belonged to Mexico. As the saying goes among Tejanos, Texans of Mexican origin, "We never crossed a border. The border crossed us."

Who are the Chicanos?

The word "Chicano" is derived from *mexicano*, meaning "Mexican," and was originally a pejorative term used by both Anglos and Mexican Americans to refer to Mexican-born unskilled workers in America, particularly recent immigrants. But since prejudice seldom makes fine distinctions, all Mexican Americans, no matter how many centuries their families have lived in the territory that is now the United States, are liable to be labeled Chicanos.

When Mexican American civil rights leader **César Chávez** organized a labor revolt in the 1960s, Mexican Americans began to forge a positive ethnic identity and to fight for social justice. In the process, they claimed racial slurs such as "Chicano" as their own in order to rid them of their negative connotations. Many Mexican Americans began calling themselves Chicanos to assert their ethnic pride and show their solidarity with *la raza*—the people.

Who are the Anglos?

To Mexican Americans, as well as to other Latinos, the term "Anglo" does not refer strictly to Americans of Anglo-Saxon descent but encompasses all European Americans. Thus Italian Americans and Hungarian Americans qualify as Anglos even if they do not have a drop of Anglo-Saxon blood coursing through their veins.

Who are the gringos?

"Gringo" was originally the Mexican word for a foreigner of English or Anglo-American descent. Some Mexican Americans use the terms "gringo" and "Anglo" interchangeably, but "gringo" seems to be slowly falling into disuse in America. Theories abound as to how it entered the Mexican parlance. A common assumption among historians is that it evolved from a phrase Mexicans ofttimes uttered during the Mexican War to American soldiers, who were clad in green uniforms: "Green, go home," or "Green, go away."

THE CONQUISTADORES IN MEXICO

When did the Spanish begin their conquest of Mexico?

In February 1519, approximately two years after the Spanish conquistadores began their exploration of Mexico, Spanish explorer **Hernán Cortés**'s expedition of eleven vessels, which carried 508 men as well as horses and artillery, dropped anchor off the coast of the Yucatán, near what is present-day Veracruz. By 1521,

Cortés and his men had conquered the Aztecs, who were at the time the mightiest and most advanced civilization in Mexico and all of the Americas. For all intents and purposes, Mexico was in the hands of the Spanish.

The swiftness of the Spanish takeover of the Aztec lands of Mexico can be attributed in part to the belief of Aztec emperor **Montezuma II** that the Spaniards were gods, and that their conquest had been divinely preordained to punish the Aztecs for having subdued and enslaved the Toltecs and other indigenous peoples. But the conquistadores owed their success to several advantages they had over the Aztecs. For one, the brave Aztec warriors had in their arsenal only wooden clubs and spears and were thus no match for a Spanish army equipped with cannons, harquebuses, and horses. The Spanish also unwittingly utilized biological warfare: they had brought with them smallpox and other diseases, to which the native peoples succumbed by the thousands. Finally, the Spanish enlisted Montezuma II's longtime enemies, among them the Tlaxcaltecs, as powerful allies against the Aztecs.

IMPORTANT DATES IN MEXICAN AMERICAN HISTORY

1521	Spanish conquistadores defeat the Aztecs of Mexico.
1810	Father Miguel Hidalgo y Costilla unleashes the Mexican movement for independence from Spain with his *Grito de Dolores* (Cry of Dolores).
1821	Mexico wins its independence from Spain.
1848	The Treaty of Guadalupe Hidalgo is signed.
1910	The Mexican Revolution, a long, bloody civil war, commences.
1924	The U.S. Border Patrol is created.
1943	Discrimination against Mexican Americans turns brutal during the Zoot Suit Riots in Los Angeles.
1962	César Chávez launches the National Farm Workers Association.

Did Mexico become Spanish right away?

In principle, yes, but in practice, no. While **Hernán Cortés** swiftly conquered the Aztecs, razing their prize city, Tenochtitlán (Mexico City was later built at the site), the rest of Mexico fell gradually under Spanish dominion. The Maya in the south, for instance, were difficult to subdue, and the Spanish left them undisturbed for quite a while. Similarly, the Chichimec people of the north continued in their traditional ways almost uninterrupted by the Spanish.

How did the Spanish rule in Mexico?

With two goals in mind: to Christianize the "heathens" of the New World and to fill Spain's coffers with gold and more gold.

The Spanish conquistadores and early colonists, aided by armies of missionaries, imposed Catholicism on the native peoples from the very start. In fact, Catholic friars accompanied **Hernán Cortés**'s 1519 expedition to Mexico. The Spanish confiscated the native peoples' gold, often telling them that Spaniards suffered from a strange disease only gold could cure. They also put the native peoples to work mining for gold and, later, silver.

Cortés gave the early Spanish colonists *encomiendas*, grants that afforded them ownership and control over native land and goods in perpetuity. As a means of establishing a labor pool, the *encomenderos* were each given as many as twenty thousand native peoples to cultivate the land and perform other tasks. The native peoples received no compensation for their work; thus, the institution of the *encomienda* essentially constituted the codification of slavery in Mexico. The *encomenderos* committed a range of abuses and atrocities against their native workers, forcing them to labor with little rest, robbing them of their possessions, beating them badly, and even killing them. Many clergy members, such as **Friar Bartolomé de las Casas**, who was called the "defender of the Indians," objected vehemently to the *encomiendas*. From time to time, the native peoples revolted against Spanish control, but with little lasting success.

One of the native peoples' most successful campaigns against Spanish domination occurred in 1680. **Popé**, a distinguished Pueblo medicine man in New Mexico who practiced his own religion and called for an end to Spanish rule, led the Pueblo Indians in a revolt against their oppressors. Hundreds of Spanish colonists and missionaries in northern New Mexico were killed in what is known as the Popé Rebellion. Once his people were free of Spanish domination, Popé set about to restore the old Pueblo way of life, even rinsing clean the Pueblos who had been baptized. In 1692, soon after Popé died, the Spanish again subdued the Pueblos.

As for the *encomienda* system, it proved so profitable that although the Spanish instituted reforms to lessen the native peoples' suffering, they did not dismantle the system entirely until 1786.

What role did women play in the conquest, and was there such a thing as a conquistadora?

While Englishwomen accompanied Englishmen to the Eastern seaboard in the early days of the colonization of the present-day United States, Spanish women remained behind in Europe, leaving the exploration and settlement of the New World to Spanish men. This was a fundamental reason why the Spanish mixed with the native peoples of the Americas, giving rise to the mestizos, or peoples of mixed race, in Mexico and throughout Latin America.

Both the Spanish and the native peoples of the Americas had patriarchal systems, and women, by and large, were treated as chattel. The following account, written on October 28, 1495, by **Michele de Cuneo**, a Ligurian nobleman who sailed with **Columbus** on his second expedition, is a fine example of how the Spanish treated the women of the Americas from the very outset. It is also testimony of the universality of both sexism and racism:

> While I was in the boat, I captured a very beautiful Carib woman whom the aforesaid Lord Admiral gave to me, and with whom, having brought her into my cabin, and she being naked as is their custom, I conceived the desire to take my pleasure. I wanted to put my desire to execution, but she was unwilling for me to do so, and treated me with her nails in such wise that I would have preferred never to have begun. But seeing this, I took a rope-end and thrashed her well, following which she produced such screaming and wailing as would cause you not to believe your ears. Finally, we reached an agreement such that, I can tell you, she seemed to have been raised in a veritable school of harlots.

Not only is the nameless native woman taken hostage and raped, but once subdued, she is called a whore. She was not only the object of a double rape—sexual and racial—but once overpowered, she, like the native peoples as a whole, is accused of liking and accepting European "civilization" with the alacrity of a harlot.

Decades later, when Spanish women began making the journey to the Americas, they were held accountable for the enslavement, forced conversions, and brutalization of the native peoples by their husbands, brothers, and fathers, even though they played no active role. This is not to say, of course, that Spanish women did not share the belief in the white man's superiority to the native peoples, or that they did not disdain native religions and consider primitive the sophisticated indigenous cultures of the Americas. They did, of course, in the same way that most Englishwomen did, but they did not actively participate in the decimation of the native peoples.

Who was La Malinche, how did she help the Spanish conquer Mexico, and is she a villain or a hero?

La Malinche, known as Malintzin to the Aztecs and baptized Doña Marina by the Spanish, played a vital role in **Hernán Cortés's** conquest of the Aztecs. A Nahuatal from Mexico's gulf coast, La Malinche was sold or given as a slave to the Maya after her father's death and her mother's remarriage. In 1519 the Maya gave her to the Spanish conquistadores as a gift. The minute he set eyes on her, Hernán Cortés was enchanted with La Malinche and offered her to **Alonzo Hernández Puertocarrero**, the most highborn conquistador on his expedition. When Puertocarrero set off for Spain, Cortés took La Malinche as his own mistress.

La Malinche remained dutifully at Cortés's side during the conquistador's conquest of the Aztecs and their capital city, Tenochtitlán, where most Aztec wealth was amassed. She was able to communicate with the conquistadores and to serve as their interpreter in dealings with the Aztecs, because she spoke her native Nahuatl, the language of the Aztecs, as well as Yucatek Maya, the Mayan language of the Yucatán Peninsula, a language that one of Cortés's men, the Spanish priest **Gerónimo de Aguilar**, had learned while held captive by the Maya. Until she picked up

Spanish, La Malinche served as a Nahuatl–Yucatek Maya interpreter and Aguilar as a Yucatek Maya–Spanish interpreter. As a language interpreter for Cortés, La Malinche enabled the conquistador to forge strategic alliances with the enemies of the Aztecs and to participate in the historic meeting with **Montezuma II**, on November 8, 1519. In his firsthand account of the Spanish conquest of Mexico, *Historia verdadera de la conquista de la Nueva España (A True History of the Conquest of New Spain)*, **Bernal Díaz del Castillo**, a Spanish conquistador and *rodelero*, or swordsman, who joined Cortés's 1519 expedition to Mexico and participated in the military campaign against the Aztecs, testifies to the essentialness of La Malinche's linguistic skills in Cortés's imperialist undertakings in Mexico: "Without the help of Doña Marina we would not have understood the language of New Spain and Mexico." Cortés himself acknowledged her invaluable contributions to his military successes, writing in a letter, preserved in Spanish archives, that "After God we owe this conquest to Doña Marina."

Some historians have opined that Cortés would not have succeeded in his conquest of the Aztec empire without La Malinche for reasons beyond her linguistic facility, hypothesizing that La Malinche might actually have persuaded Montezuma II that he stood no chance against the Spanish invaders and his reign was over, and that she made no effort to sabotage the Spanish conquistadores' efforts to subdue the Aztecs. According to this historical view, La Malinche was motivated both by her strict allegiance and fidelity to Cortés and by the grudge she bore against the Aztecs for having sold her into slavery.

Whatever her actual role in the Spanish conquest, over the centuries the critical consensus among Mexicans and Mexican Americans has been that La Malinche was a betrayer of her people and a linchpin in the brutal colonial subjugation of Mexico. The word *malinchista* means "deserter" and "coward," among other things, and *malinchismo*, "the act of deserting one's country or race by inviting in outside influences." It is important to point out, however, that an opposite interpretation of La Malinche has long been bandied about. According to this intepretation, she was both a victim of Spanish imperialism and a hero—because she might have saved thousands of indigenous peoples from imminent death during the Spanish conquest of Mexico, and therefore an entire Mesoamerican civilization, owing to the enormous clout she wielded with the conquistadores and her uncanny ability to conduct diplomacy.

In Mexico and Mexican America, myths about La Malinche endure to this day. According to one, she drowned the son she bore Hernán Cortés in 1522, **Don Martín Cortés** (who has been called one of the first mestizos), when the conquistador insisted on taking the child back to Spain with him and leaving her behind. According to some myths, La Malinche still weeps over the tragic loss of her child. For this reason, she is the central figure in some versions of the Mexican and Mexican American folktale about La Llorona, "the Weeping Woman," who is the inconsolable ghost of a young woman who committed infanticide (usually drowning her children) after her husband abandoned her.

NORTHERN EXPOSURE, OR HOW NEW MEXICO CAME TO BE KNOWN AS NUEVO MÉXICO, AND CALIFORNIANS AS CALIFORNIOS

When did the Spanish explore areas north of the present-day Mexico-U.S. border?

After informing Congress on May 25, 1961, that it was "time for this nation to take a clearly leading role in space achievement, which in many ways may hold the key to our future on earth" and to put a man on the moon, **President John F. Kennedy** made the following remark in an address on the nation's space effort delivered at Rice University on September 12, 1962: "We choose to go to the moon in this decade and do the other things, not because they are easy, but because they are hard." The Spanish, too, pushed northward from present-day Mexico not because it was easy, but because it was hard—and because the North American continent was a huge tract of real estate devoid of borders and potentially rich in gold, silver, and other valuable commodities that were ripe for the picking. But it was a race against time, since Spain's Old World rivals, especially England, France, Portugal, and Russia, were also bent on colonizing North America. All in all, it took the Spanish from around 1527 to 1781—the year a Spanish expedition out of St. Louis, Missouri, reached Niles, Michigan, and captured Fort St. Joseph—to complete their exploration of, and to claim for Spain, territory north of what is present-day Mexico. During all or part of that time, the Spanish controlled all or a portion of present-day New Mexico, Texas, California, Arizona, Colorado, Utah, Florida, Alabama, Mississippi, Oklahoma, Louisiana, Arkansas, Missouri, Kansas, Iowa, Nebraska, Minnesota, North Dakota, South Dakota, Wyoming, Montana, Idaho, and Michigan.

Spanish exploration of the vast territory north of the present-day U.S.-Mexico border was the result of great planning, as well as mishaps and a bit of luck. In June 1527, Spanish conquistador **Pánfilo de Narváez** set sail from Sanlúcar, Spain, for Florida, which the Spanish had first set foot on in 1513, when **Juan Ponce de León** made landfall on the peninsula's east coast. After enduring desertions and storms, Narváez finally made landfall on the Florida coast, near Tampa Bay, in April 1528. After sending his ships on to Mexico, he headed inland in search of gold and other treasures with a party of around three hundred men. Plagued by starvation and unrelenting attacks from the native peoples, Narváez's expedition returned to the coast, constructed five makeshift vessels, and set sail for Mexico in September 1528. The journey ended in utter disaster when three of the vessels sank and the other two were shipwrecked on an island off the Texas coast, conceivably Galveston or Mustang Island. **Álvar Núñez Cabeza de Vaca**, the treasurer of the expedition, was one of the few who managed to survive the ordeal. He was taken captive by the natives but managed to escape, only to wander, with three other survivors, for eight years across what constitutes present-day Texas, New Mexico, and Arizona, as well as northern Mexico, before finally meeting up with fellow conquistadores in Culiacán, Mexico. Cabeza de Vaca brought them news that would change the course of history in the region that would become the American Southwest.

Cabeza de Vaca's encounters with the native peoples during his eight-year journey sparked in him a remarkable spiritual awakening, which afforded him an entirely new outlook on life and so-called different people. But his awakening was of no interest to the Spanish. What did cause a great stir among his gold-hungry compatriots were the reports Cabeza de Vaca sent to the king of Spain in which he revealed that during his travails in the New World, he had learned of the fabulous Seven Cities of Gold, otherwise known as Cíbola, situated somewhere beyond the region he had traversed. Cabeza de Vaca's reports prompted **Fray**

Marcos de Niza, in 1539; **Francisco Vásquez de Coronado**, in 1540; and **Hernando de Soto**, in 1541 to launch in earnest their own explorations of what is the present-day American Southwest. None of them found Cíbola or the fabled gold, but they did encounter a land populated by the Pueblo Indians. But then, rich silver mines were discovered in Michoacán, Zacatecas, San Luis Potosí, and Guanajato, and the Spanish left the idea of conquering the Southwest on the back burner for the next fifty years.

What was Cabeza de Vaca's spiritual awakening all about?

Shipwrecked, the mighty conquistador **Álvar Núñez Cabeza de Vaca** was taken captive by the Pueblo Indians inhabiting regions of what is present-day Mexico and Texas. The Pueblos believed the white man possessed divine powers, and they ordered him to heal the sick in exchange for food and his life. At first, the conquistador argued that he was a soldier and could not perform such supernatural feats, but the Pueblos refused to back down. Faced with certain death, Cabeza de Vaca fell on his knees and prayed sincerely and earnestly for the recovery of the sick. Amazingly, the sick were healed. The Pueblos then escorted the Spaniard from village to village to perform his "miracles." In the process, Cabeza de Vaca was transformed from a bloody soldier into a mystic and an admirer of the Pueblo people.

Cabeza de Vaca wrote to the king of Spain that in his encounters with the Pueblos, he had learned to practice primitive Christianity and its lost element of healing—something that the strict priestly and hierarchical Catholic Church of his day deemed heretical. In fact, *iluminados*, or mystics, were burned at the stake by the Spanish Inquisition, along with the Moors and the Jews of Spain, for having unauthorized religious experiences. Even more startling, perhaps, than his ability to heal and his bold confessions to the king was Cabeza de Vaca's newfound pacifism, as evidenced by this line in his writings: "If we reach Spain, I shall petition His Majesty to return me to this land, with a troop of soldiers. And I shall teach the world how to conquer by gentleness, not by slaughter."

What was the Northwest Passage, and what role did Sir Francis Drake play in the Spanish conquista of the Southwest?

The Northwest Passage, a water route connecting the Atlantic and Pacific oceans through the northern extremities of North America, eluded European navigators for centuries. It was the carrot in front of the donkey for European explorers seeking an easily traversed route to India and China, one bypassing altogether the European colonial empires of the New World and their blocked trade routes. While the search for the Northwest Passage commenced at the end of the fifteenth century, it was not discovered until the mid-nineteenth century, when **Sir Robert McClure** traversed it by ship and sled (after his ship became trapped in ice) in the years 1850–54. It took about a half century more before an expedition party actually traversed the Northwest Passage by ship only, a feat accomplished in 1906 by Norwegian navigator **Roald Amundsen**, who completed the voyage in three years in a herring boat.

The Northwest Passage has since been judged impractical as a commercial shipping route: The northern waters remain icebound for most of the year, and sections of the waterway are quite shallow. Canada has long claimed that the passage sits in Canadian internal waters, but the United States and other nations contend that it is an international waterway. Thus far, these conflicting claims have garnered little attention, but with the likelihood of global warming freeing the Northwest Passage for longer periods during the year, making it a viable major shipping route, challenges to Canadian claims of sovereignty over the Arctic archipelago are sure to surface.

In the late 1570s, the famed English privateer **Sir Francis Drake** sailed through the Strait of Magellan, up the west coast of South and North America, across the Pacific, and around the world. The Spanish were certain that Drake had at long last found the Northwest Passage, which in those days was believed to lie just north of Mexico. Seeking to protect this area from a possible English incursion, and still hoping to locate the Seven Cities of Gold, especially since the Spanish crown's coffers needed refilling after the Spanish Armada's defeat at the hands of the English, Spain at last settled the American Southwest. In 1595 **Philip II** authorized the northward expedition to the upper Rio Grande Valley by Spanish explorer **Juan de Oñate**, who set off in 1598 with several hundred colonizers. Oñate did not find the Seven Cities of Gold, but he did found the province of Nuevo México in 1598, which encompassed most of what is now New Mexico and bits of present-day Texas, Arizona, Colorado, and Utah, in addition to establishing the permanent settlement of San Gabriel de los Españoles (nowadays the town Chamita). It was nine years before the English would establish Jamestown, their first permanent settlement in the Americas. About a decade later, in 1609, the Spanish established Santa Fe de San Francisco, the first permanent settlement near the Rio Grande, and in 1610 they founded the town of Santa Fe on the settlement's site. Santa Fe holds the distinction of being the oldest capital city and the second-oldest surviving city (after St. Augustine, Florida, which was founded in 1565) founded by Europeans on territory that constitutes the present-day United States.

THE SPANISH SETTLEMENT OF TEXAS AND CALIFORNIA

Parlez-vous *Texan? No way!*

The English were not the only Europeans who posed a threat to Spain's territorial claims in North America and its efforts to expand them. By the end of the seventeenth century, France, whose colonizing efforts in North America had begun in 1534, with French navigator **Jacques Cartier**'s exploration of the Saint Lawrence River, had laid claim to a large portion of North America, an area that became known as New France. This territorial claim hinged on alliances forged with various native tribes rather than settlement and economic development. In 1682 French explorer **René-Robert Cavelier**, **Sieur de La Salle**, who had realized the Mississippi River's potential as a major inland trade route, pushed southward and reached the mouth of the Mississippi by canoe. He claimed the entire Mississippi drainage basin for France, naming it Louisiana after the French monarch **Louis XIV**. By that act, the vast but largely underpopulated territory of New France stretched east to west from Newfoundland all the way to Lake Superior and north to south from the Hudson Bay to the Gulf of Mexico.

In 1684 La Salle set sail once again for North America, with the intent to first fortify the mouth of the Mississippi River, setting up a French colony there. En route, he lost one of his ships to pirates in the West Indies. Then, by a terrible miscalculation, his remaining ships made landfall at Matagorda Bay in Texas instead of at the mouth of the Mississippi, which lay five hundred miles east. To make matters worse, one of the ships sank in Matagorda Bay and another ran aground. After establishing the settlement of Fort Saint Louis in 1685 near what is present-day Victoria, Texas, La Salle conducted several fruitless journeys on foot in search of the Mississippi before realizing his error. With no end in sight, his men, who had long grown impatient and fearful, mutinied and murdered La Salle in 1687 near present-day Navasota, Texas.

France's southward expansion in North America, its foothold on the Mississippi drainage basin (which Spanish conquistador **Pánfilo de Narváez** had discovered back in 1528), and its establishment of Fort Saint Louis on what Spain considered its territory were cause for alarm to the Spanish. To protect their investment in Texas, the Spanish destroyed Fort Saint Louis (or what was left of it, since the Karankawas, a group of Native American tribes of the Texas gulf coast, had already killed most of its French settlers), and they established Mission Santísimo Nombre de María on the Neches River in Texas in 1690. The following year Texas was declared a Spanish province, and before long, six missions and a presidio, or fortress, were erected in the province. By 1718 San Antonio de Béxar, now known simply as San Antonio, was settled.

In the end, the French were no match for the colonizing forces of Britain. When they went head-to-head against the British in the French and Indian Wars (1689–1763), the French and their Native American allies lost ground, owing to the British colonies' larger populations and greater productivity. With the signing of the Treaty of Paris on February 10, 1763, ending the last of the French and Indian Wars, known simply as the French and Indian War (1754–63), France handed over all of its North American possessions east of the Mississippi River (except for two small islands off of Newfoundland) to Britain. Spain ceded Florida to the British and as compensation acquired the portion of the vast French colonial territory of Louisiana that lay west of the Mississippi (some 530,000,000 acres), as well as New Orleans, from France. In 1800 France and Spain secretly negotiated the

Treaty of San Ildefonso, which retroceded Spain's portion of the territory of Louisiana to the French. Questioning the feasibility of hanging on to so much land, in 1803 France sold the territory to the Americans for a song—about $27 million, to be exact—a transaction called the Louisiana Purchase.

Who were the Californios?

In the 1760s, the Spanish crown received word that the Russians were coming—not to Spain, but to North America, descending southward from Alaska and toward the Pacific Northwest—and that the British, who occupied the East Coast of North America and had acquired all of Canada with their victory over the French in the French and Indian War (1754–63), had suddenly acquired a great yen for West Coast real estate. With a lot of land on the line, the Spanish scrambled to settle Alta California, now known simply as California.

Spanish explorer **Gaspar de Portolá** commanded the second expedition to Alta California, setting out from Baja California in 1769. Portolá's job was to extend Spanish dominion north to the Monterey Peninsula, which Spanish explorer and merchant **Sebastián Vizcaíno** had discovered in 1602. Portolá established a small colony at San Diego Bay in 1769 and the mission and presidio of San Carlos on Monterey Bay in 1770. Accompanying Portolá to San Diego Bay was Spanish Franciscan missionary **Junípero Serra**, who remained behind to erect a mission at San Diego, while the rest of the party headed north. It was the first in a chain of twenty-one Franciscan missions that Father Serra and other missionaries would establish by 1823 along the California coast, from San Diego all the way up to Sonoma.

The Franciscan missionaries in California sought to convert the native peoples, whom they also put to work in the fields and in raising cattle. The early Spanish-Mexican colonists who followed the missionaries into California were mostly Caucasians of Spanish descent and mestizos, and were called Californios. Like the missionaries, the Californios took advantage of the state's abundant sunshine, gentle climate, and fertile soil, pursuing farming and cattle ranching.

MEXICO VS. SPAIN

In 1776 thirteen of Britain's colonies in mainland North America declared themselves independent of the Kingdom of Great Britain. This declaration of independence eventuated in the American Revolution, which began as a colonial struggle between the thirteen colonies and Britain, then escalated in 1778 into an international war—waged between France, Spain, and the Netherlands on one side and Britain on the other.

Hoping to deal the British crown a blow, France, Spain, and the Netherlands had all provided the American revolutionaries with financial backing from the very start of the war. The Spanish governor of Louisiana, **Bernardo de Gálvez**, who assumed the governorship on January 1, 1777, sold munitions to the American rebels and permitted them to traverse Spanish Louisiana and use the port at New Orleans. However, once the United States defeated the British and gained its independence in 1783, Spain refused to recognize U.S. sovereignty. To the Spanish crown, American independence was synonymous with anticolonialism, a sentiment it sought to squelch in the Spanish colonies. But Spain's refusal to recognize U.S. independence would do little to stem the tide of rising anti-Spanish sentiment in its colonies, Mexico included: Trouble had already long been brewing for the Spanish empire.

Where did Spain go wrong?
(Don't blame it all on the Spanish Armada!)

Latinos, Latin Americans, and Spaniards tend to view the typical English and American explanation for the disintegration of Spain's global empire—namely, **Queen Elizabeth I**'s defeat of the Spanish Armada in 1588—as another example of jingoism. It seems that **Philip II**, king of Spain from 1556 to 1598, was a zealous Catholic who viewed the English Protestant Reformation with aversion. He also considered Queen Elizabeth I, a Protestant, both a heretic and a military threat. Concerned that she might stir up trouble in his colonies, Philip II launched a preemptive strike, ordering his fleet, the Spanish Armada, or "Armed Navy," to sail up the English Channel and invade England. Elizabeth I reacted swiftly, turning her "sea dogs" loose on the Spanish Armada's 130 ships. The Spanish fought valiantly but were no match against the sea dogs.

Although England's defeat of the Spanish Armada inflicted great psychological damage and cost a good deal, it did not by any means break the rich Spanish bank or undermine Spain's ability to defend and control its colonies. It was actually another naval defeat, the defeat of an allied French and Spanish fleet by England's Royal Navy in the Battle of Trafalgar, over two centuries later, on October 21, 1805, that undercut Spain's ability to retain and defend its empire. Ultimately, however, it was political and social unrest—the chorus of voices calling for independence—within the Spanish colonial empire that caused it to unravel. In the first three decades of the nineteenth century, Spain was divested of all of its colonies in the Americas with the exception of Cuba and Puerto Rico.

What was the Grito de Dolores?

As the nineteenth century dawned, Mexico was getting really antsy. From the beginning of Spanish colonization and domination in the region, the peoples of Mexico had suffered social and economic injustice and had rebelled on numerous occasions. For instance, in 1541 the Zacatecas Indians led a major uprising to protest the Spaniards' brutal treatment of the native peoples of Michoacán, Jalisco, Nayarit, and Sinaloa. The battle was fierce, and the Spanish, though they emerged the victors, lost hundreds of soldiers. The final skirmish, fought in the Mixton hills, near the city of Guadalajara, ended in the slaughter or enslavement of most of the native rebels. However, this act of suppression only fueled the flames of discontent and strengthened the native peoples' resolve to rid themselves of their Spanish oppressors.

Mexico's criollos—individuals of pure Spanish blood who were born in the Spanish colonies, as opposed to in Spain—were even more fervent in their resolve to end Spanish domination than the native peoples. From the Spaniards' perspective, birthplace meant everything, and thus, even though the criollos were Caucasians of strictly Spanish lineage, they were also New World progeny, which rendered questionable their allegiance to the Spanish crown. Consequently, the Spaniards born in Spain, known as *peninsulares*, treated them as second-class citizens: The criollos were deemed superior to the mestizos (those of mixed Spanish and native blood) and the native peoples, but inferior to the *peninsulares*. At the hands of the *peninsulares*, the criollos endured rampant discrimination, as well as "taxation without representation." And criollos were seldom afforded the choice parcels of land or the best jobs; these were reserved for the *peninsulares*, who also had the final say in local government affairs.

By the time the nineteenth century dawned, the criollos had had enough of the Spanish colonial caste system and Spain. On September 16, 1810, **Father Miguel Hidalgo y Costilla**, the criollo parish priest of the small Mexican village of Dolores, uttered the famous *Grito de Dolores* (Cry of Dolores), a clarion call to action that ignited Mexico's revolution for independence from Spain. "Long live the Virgin of Guadalupe!" he shouted to the assembled crowd. "Down with the Spaniards!" Incidently, *Grito de Dolores* is a double entendre in Spanish: It means both the "Cry of Dolores" and the "Cry of Pain," the pain that Spanish colonial rule inflicted on the people of Mexico.

The native peoples and mestizos, who had for centuries been subjugated and marginalized, also answered the call for social change in Mexico. Led by Father Hidalgo, fifty thousand natives and mestizos banded together as an army and marched toward Mexico City. Along the way, they pillaged the haciendas of wealthy *peninsulares*. Father Hidalgo's powerful army defeated Spanish forces at Monte de los Cruces on October 30, 1810. His army could have won a final victory and seized control of Mexico City, but for some reason, the priest turned his troops away from the capital. His army reorganized at Guadalajara, only to be overpowered by Spanish forces and defeated at Calderón Bridge on January 17, 1811. As for Father Hidalgo, he headed north to seek refuge in the United States but was captured en route. He was defrocked by the Spanish Inquisition and then executed.

A close friend of Father Hidalgo, **Father José María Morelos y Pavón**, a mulatto, took up the baton and waged guerilla warfare against the Spanish, capturing Orizaba, also known as Citlaltépetl, and Oaxaca in 1812 and Acapulco in 1813. While his forces battled on, Morelos called a congress and, with other leaders, declared Mexican independence in November 1813. But it would not be so easy. In 1815 Morelos was captured, defrocked by the Spanish Inquisition, and shot. Mexico's war of independence waged on. Finally, in 1821, when Mexican rebels entered Mexico City, Spain recognized Mexican sovereignty, and the first Mexican Empire was created. In 1824 Mexico was proclaimed a federal republic with an elected president. Before the end of the decade, Spain attempted to reconquer Mexico by force, but the Mexican army, under the leadership of **Antonio López de Santa Anna**, defeated the Spaniards. In 1832 Santa Anna seized the reins of power. He would emerge as a major player in the Texas secessionist movement of 1836, in the Mexican War (1846–48), and in the Gadsden Purchase in 1853, when he sold southern Arizona to the United States for $10 million.

THE ANGLO CONNECTION

What did the Anglos' westward expansion mean for Mexicans?

The westward movement, or expansion, across North America by English-speaking people commenced not long after the thirteen British colonies on the continent's eastern seaboard won their independence from Britain. With the exhortation "Go west, young man" ringing in their ears, the Anglo colonists settled the territory up to the banks of the Mississippi River between 1776 and 1800. Then, when **Napoléon Bonaparte** clinched the sale of the French colonial territory of Louisiana—a vast tract of land extending from the Gulf of Mexico to British North America, and from the Mississippi River to the Rockies—to **Thomas Jefferson** in 1803, the American republic instantly doubled in size. The young nation was well on its way to consummating a mission in the making, a mission that would later be called Manifest Destiny, an expansion westward—to spread democracy and freedom—which would culminate in the occupation by Anglo-Saxon Americans of a territory stretching from the Atlantic Ocean to the Pacific.

A good deal of that territory between the Atlantic and Pacific belonged to Mexico, and thus it was not long before the Anglos came in contact with the Mexicans. Around 1790 Kentucky mountain men began trespassing on Spanish-Mexican land in New Mexico to trap beavers, which were coveted for their fur. They trapped without licenses, and they traveled where they pleased. Sometimes their loot was confiscated, but, no matter, they kept coming back for more. These frontier beaver trappers were grubby, bearded, and uncouth; they cussed and spat and picked fights willy-nilly. Often the native peoples and mestizos of New Mexico would hold perfumed cloths to their noses if they had to stand next to the Anglo trappers. And so, the relationship between the fledgling United States and Mexico got off to a rough start.

What exactly was Manifest Destiny?

In an editorial he wrote in support of the annexation of Texas that ran in the July–August 1845 edition of the *United States Magazine and Democratic Review*, a political and literary journal that was published monthly in Washington beginning in 1837, **John O'Sullivan**, the magazine's cofounder and editor, put into words what the citizens of the nascent American republic had been feeling from the start and coined the phrase "Manifest Destiny." In his editorial, O'Sullivan maintained that "our manifest destiny [is] to overspread the continent allotted by Providence for the free development of our yearly multiplying millions." In a nutshell, Manifest Destiny was an Anglo-American version of the national supremacy theory and justified the aspirations of the United States to extend its borders from sea to shining sea. The phrase took, and so did the sentiment. Politicians of all persuasions made mention of Manifest Destiny in articles and speeches everywhere, and they felt as full of imperialist zeal and purpose as the Spanish conquistadores had.

In the first half of the nineteenth century, the American republic would work especially hard at manifesting its destiny. Acquiring Mexican territory seemed like a logical step in American expansion, although the more extreme exponents of Manifest Destiny spoke of pushing America's borders as far north as the arctic circle and as far south as Tierra del Fuego. Several Mexican observers have remarked that viewed from a different perspective, Manifest Destiny could have been called "Mexican Fate," since the nation that suffered the most from this doctrine was Mexico.

What was the Santa Fe Trail?

On the heels of the Anglo trappers in New Mexico came the Anglo merchants, who wanted to capitalize on the region's new, untapped market. These traveling salesmen needed a way to enter New Mexico without being spotted by Spanish-Mexican authorities, who viewed them as interlopers. By approaching New Mexico from the north rather than the east, the merchants were able to sneak into Spanish-Mexican territory undetected, with wagons laden with goods—from snake oil to women's underwear.

In 1821 trader **William Becknell** spread the news among the Anglos that Mexico was free from Spanish rule, the Mexicans had eased restrictions on commerce with foreign countries, and the town of Santa Fe invited trade with the Americans. In 1822 Becknell led the first group of traders from Independence, Missouri, to Santa Fe, a 780-mile trek over rugged terrain along a route that became known as the Santa Fe Trail. That same year, caravans began making the forty- to sixty-day trip to Santa Fe along the Santa Fe Trail on a regular basis. The Santa Fe Trail fell out of use in 1880, when the newly built Santa Fe Railroad reached its terminus in Santa Fe. In 1987 the Santa Fe Trail was designated a national historic trail.

How did the Santa Fe traders foster Anglo expansionism?

Soon after **William Becknell** led that first group of Anglo traders along the Santa Fe Trail in 1822, it became a highway of opportunity. Business boomed for the Anglos who transported their wares into New Mexico. They had hit pay dirt in a territory sorely in need of essential goods, which the Mexican government could not supply. The first official American traders transported only $5,000 in goods to Santa Fe, but by 1855, $5 million worth of merchandise had been carried to the town.

Merchandise was not all the Americans took to New Mexico. They also introduced a distinctive weltanschauung. Unlike the beaver trappers, these Anglos dressed smartly and were generally well mannered, and the New Mexicans welcomed them with open arms. However, the Americans also harbored ethnic prejudice, which would soon surface and create a painful rift between the two countries. The Americans considered themselves superior to the Mexicans of New Mexico, who they viewed as lazy and uncivilized—the same opinion the Spanish conquistadores had had of the indigenous peoples of the Americas three centuries earlier.

As more Anglos poured into New Mexico, and in some cases married and stayed for good, the Mexican government began to worry about the long-term effects of this foreign influence in a region so removed from Mexico City. In an attempt to turn back the clock, Mexican president **Antonio López de Santa Anna** outlawed trade between Anglos and New Mexicans. But the people of New Mexico had grown accustomed to their new way of life. They protested loudly, and Santa Anna was forced to rescind the law in 1844. The residents of New Mexico were beginning to feel separate from their government to the south. By then, however, the Anglo economic domination of New Mexico was a done deal. There was no going back.

HOW TEXAS WAS WON—OR LOST

Who was Stephen F. Austin, and why is he called the father of Texas?

Stephen F. Austin was an American frontiersman with a special interest in Texas. His father, **Moses Austin**, had obtained a colonization grant from Spanish authorities in 1821 to settle Americans in Texas. As he lay dying, Moses Austin requested that his son Stephen be permitted to carry out his settlement plan. Stephen Austin had the grant confirmed—on the grounds that he and his fellow American colonists would obey Mexican law, become Mexican citizens, convert to Catholicism, and bar slavery on their lands—and he chose an area between the Brazos and Colorado rivers as the site for his settlement. In December 1821, Austin led three hundred Anglo-American families to the site and established the first legal settlement of Anglo-American colonists in Texas. He allotted 117 acres to each family willing to farm the land and 4,428 acres to those who wanted to raise livestock. The frontiersman took almost one hundred thousand acres for himself as a bonus for organizing the territory.

Mexico's newly independent government found Austin's settlement satisfactory and offered land grants to other Americans. Within a decade, the number of Americans living in Texas as Mexican citizens had risen to about fifty thousand, outnumbering the Mexican settlers. The Anglo Texans formed their own insular society and did not always abide by Mexican law. For instance, many, including Austin, brought in hundreds of African slaves to labor in the fields. Others refused to convert to Catholicism. Alarmed at the Anglo Texans' behavior, Mexico imposed stricter controls on the settlements. Tensions mounted, and in 1830 Mexican general **Manuel de Meir y Terán** led his soldiers into Texas territory, with the intent of expelling Stephen Austin and the Anglo Texans from Mexican land and preventing the influx of other Anglos. His efforts failed, and the seeds of animosity between the Anglo Texans and the Mexican government were sown.

By 1832 Texas was in a state of chaos. Its citizens—Anglo Texans and Mexican Texans alike—were convinced that the only way to ease tensions with the Mexican government was to establish a separate state within the Mexican federation. While Anglo and Mexican Texans had begun to view themselves as distinct from other Mexicans, they did not advocate secession. Yet when they applied for statehood at an 1833 Mexican convention, **President Santa Anna** misinterpreted their petition as a request for independence. Even after the confusion was cleared up, Santa Anna was still fuming; he refused to grant the Texans any of their requests and jailed Stephen Austin for eighteen months. Upon his release, Austin demanded in a speech that Texas be permitted to secede from Mexico. It was the bugle call that heralded the beginning of Texas independence.

Why should we remember the Alamo?

Driven by independence fever, **William B. Travis**, one of **Stephen Austin**'s men, stormed the Mexican customs garrison at Anáhuac during the fateful summer of 1835. Skirmishes with Mexican forces quickly metamorphosed into a decisive military crusade for independence. The Texas Revolution erupted in early October 1835, with the battle of Gonzales, which was triggered by Mexican efforts to retrieve a cannon given in 1831 to the American settlers at Gonzales, who were the target of attacks by Tonkawa Indians. The Americans refused to surrender the cannon, and a minor battle ensued. On December 5, 1835, Texan armies, with both Anglo Texans and Mexican Texans in the ranks, raided a military supply depot at the Alamo mission, and San Antonio, the leading city in Texas, fell to the Texan rebels. Just a few months later, on March 2, 1836, Texas declared its independence at a convention at Washington-on-the-Brazos.

In retaliation, **President Santa Anna** organized an army numbering in the thousands and prepared to lead his forces in attacking Texas. The Texan rebels, guessing that Santa Anna would strike through the city of Matamoros, withdrew most of their men from the Alamo garrison and stationed them in Matamoros. On March 6, 1836, Santa Anna led his impressive army right into El Alamo territory, slaying 182 Texans barricaded behind the mission walls. The besieged Texan forces, under the command of William Travis, defended the fort valiantly for five days. Among the Texan heroes killed at the Alamo garrison were frontiersmen

Davy Crockett and **James Bowie**. According to Mexican American legend, though, Crockett was nothing more than a mercenary soldier, who the Mexicans captured and executed.

Santa Anna won a great victory with his preemptive strike, but he was unaware that an enraged Texan army, led by **Samuel Houston** and armed to the teeth, was in hot pursuit of his men. Houston's army caught up with Santa Anna's soldiers at the San Jacinto River and Buffalo Bayou, shouting, "Remember the Alamo!" When the smoke cleared on April 21, 1836, six hundred of Santa Anna's men, but only six Texans, lay dead on the battlefield. The Texas Revolution was over, with the Texans the victors. As for the fate of Santa Anna, the Texans captured him, forced him to recognize the independence of Texas, and imprisoned him for six months. He managed to return to power in 1841 but was driven into exile in 1844. A tenacious Santa Anna again became president of Mexico in 1846 (such resurrections were not uncommon in early Mexican politics), but the Mexican government forced him out of office and into exile for humiliating his country when, as commander of the troops during the Mexican War, he met with defeat at Buena Vista, Cerro Gordo, and Puebla, and lost Mexico City. He returned from exile and in 1853 was once again restored to office.

As for Texas, with the enactment of the Texas Declaration of Independence on March 2, 1836, it became an independent republic under the Burnet flag (the Lone Star flag was adopted in 1839) and its interim president, **David G. Burnet**. (Burnet served until October 22, 1836, when newly elected president and war hero Sam Houston took office.) Though quite vulnerable to attack by Mexican forces, the Republic of Texas was on its own for nearly a decade, until 1845, when the United States finally admitted it as the twenty-eighth state in the Union.

Why do Mexican Americans cringe when they hear "Remember the Alamo"?

When **Santa Anna**'s forces stormed the Alamo and killed 182 Texans, Anglo hatred against Mexico and anything Mexican exploded with a vengeance, and the seeds of ethnic prejudice and intolerance that lay beneath the surface sprouted like prickly cactus across the Texas landscape. Suddenly, the Anglo Texans turned on the Mexican Texans, whose families had lived within the borders of Texas for untold generations, denouncing them as defenders of Santa Anna. The truth was that most Mexican Texans had sided with **Sam Houston**, and a great number had fought and died for Texan independence. The vast majority had pinned their hopes on the Anglos, who they believed understood the needs of the immense, proud, and complicated land they called *Tejas*. And yet, they became the enemy within. Before long, the phrase "Remember the Alamo!" was uttered as a warning to Mexican Texans that they better watch out.

What role did African Americans play in Texas history?

After the Texas Declaration of Independence was signed on March 2, 1836, the United States, as well as Great Britain, France, and the Netherlands, recognized the Republic of Texas as a sovereign nation. But even at the outset, it was difficult for the young republic to survive on its own. For one, Mexico kept remembering the Alamo, too, and continually organized raids on Texan cities and towns, particularly Goliad, San Antonio, and Nacogdoches, which had a large Anglo population. In addition, the Apache and other Native American peoples had declared war on the Anglos, and their attacks claimed lives and valuable property. The cost of maintaining the Texas Rangers to protect Texans from Mexican and Native American raids, as well as low credit overseas and problems with the land system, drained Texas's coffers. The solution to the republic's woes seemed clear to most Anglo Texans: join the United States. In September 1836, Texans voted for annexation.

But there was a hitch. At that crucial moment in American history, the issue of slavery weighed heavily in the balance. The states were evenly divided on the issue of slavery's abolition, and since most Anglo Texans hailed from Southern states and owned slaves themselves, Texas would tip the scale in favor of the slave states and the preservation of slavery. Texans waged the battle for annexation for ten long years, thanks to the abolitionists, who were determined to keep Texas out of the republic. Finally, on December 29, 1845, the U.S. Congress admitted Texas as the twenty-eighth state in the Union, with slavery permitted according to its state constitution. In 1861 Texas would secede from the Union, but it was readmitted in March 1870, after ratifying the Thirteenth, Fourteenth, and Fifteenth Amendments to the U.S.

Constitution, which abolished slavery and involuntary servitude, extended equal protection of the laws to former slaves and all people of color, and granted them (men only) the right to vote.

THE MEXICAN WAR

Just why did the American republic fight against Mexico?

In 1845 the Mexican government broke off diplomatic relations with the United States on the grounds that the annexation of Texas was an act of aggression aimed at Mexico. The Mexicans not only mourned the loss of their Mexican state, they worried that the imperialistic Americans had other tricks up their sleeve—namely, the acquisition of more of Mexico's territory. Their worries were perfectly justified as **President James Polk**, who steered a nation in the throes of Manifest Destiny, had publicly proclaimed that the United States had every intention of acquiring California.

When, in 1845, President Polk sent diplomat **John Slidell** to Mexico, with an offer to buy California and New Mexico, part of which Texas claimed, for $25 million, an outraged Mexican government refused to negotiate. Reacting with the full zeal of Manifest Destiny, President Polk ordered U.S. general **Zachary Taylor**, who was stationed in Texas at the time with a volunteer army as a show of force against Mexico, to advance to the Rio Grande.

How did the phrase "a Mexican standoff" come to be?

General Zachary Taylor reached the mouth of the Rio Grande in March 1846. Instead of attacking the American invaders, the Mexican army decided to wait and see what General Taylor's men were up to. Both armies hunkered down on opposite sides of the river, measuring each other's military might, shouting insults back and forth, even joking. It was a war of nerves, with each side goading the other to make the first move, which finally happened when the armies clashed on April 25. It was from this military checkmate, or waiting game, that the phrase "a Mexican standoff" was coined.

If all Zachary Taylor had was a small volunteer army, how did the United States win the war?

At first, the Mexicans, under the command of **General Pedro de Ampudia**, were confident of a swift victory: Their army was three times larger and far better trained than the paltry U.S. volunteer army, with adventurers, vagabonds, and escaped criminals in its ranks. But once the United States officially declared war on May 13, 1846, Congress authorized the formation of an army of fifty thousand soldiers and appropriated $10 million for the war effort. There was no contest. The fact that Mexico was torn by civil strife at the time and that some of its states refused to band together as a united front did not help matters for the Mexicans. On August 24, 1847—scarcely a year and a half after the Mexican standoff—Mexico accepted an armistice. As for **Zachary Taylor**, his decisive victories against the Mexicans made him a popular hero and earned him the nomination for U.S. president on the Whig ticket. He won the election and in 1849 became the twelfth president of the United States.

What is the Treaty of Guadalupe Hidalgo?

The Treaty of Guadalupe Hidalgo, signed on February 2, 1848, is the formal agreement between the United States and Mexico that ended the Mexican War. By the terms of the treaty, Mexico handed over California, Utah, Nevada, and parts of Colorado, Wyoming, New Mexico, and Arizona—approximately 525,000 square miles of territory—to the United States. With the acquisition of this land, the map of the United States was almost complete.

By a single stroke of the pen, a large group of Mexican citizens, right in their very own homes, found themselves smack in the middle of another country, whose laws, political and social institutions, and fundamentally WASP (white Anglo-Saxon Protestant) traditions were alien to them. A critical aspect of the Treaty of Guadalupe Hidalgo concerned the fate of these Mexicans who now resided in ceded American territory. They were given a year to decide whether they wanted to retain Mexican citizenship or become U.S. citizens. Nearly eight thousand Mexicans living in the new American territory opted for U.S. citizenship, while about two thousand, in order to preserve their Mexican citizenship, relocated south of the Rio Grande, which formed part of the new northern boundary between the two countries.

How did the Anglos treat the new American citizens?

Article IX of the Treaty of Guadalupe Hidalgo specifically provided that Mexicans living in the new U.S. territories would have the right to retain their property. In utter disregard for Mexican tradition and the Treaty of Guadalupe Hidalgo, the Anglos, who settled in droves in the newly acquired territories, ousted Mexican grantees from the most desirable properties (those near water) and then claimed that they had the right to homestead vacant lands. The Mexican system of property laws, with its lack of surveys, dependence on verbal agreements instead of legally binding documents, and adherence to communal tradition, hindered the Mexicans in their attempts to retain ownership of their real estate. Unable to produce written proof of ownership deemed adequate by Anglo-American law, many lost their land and their homes.

What was the Gadsden Purchase, and why did Mexicans say they needed it like a hole in the head?

In 1853 the U.S. government sent **James Gadsden** to Mexico to settle minor territorial disputes between the two nations. During his varied career, Gadsden had served under **General Andrew Jackson** in the U.S. Army during the War of 1812 and as president of the South Carolina Railroad Company from 1840 to 1850. Gadsden was a proponent of plans being bandied about to build a transcontinental railroad along the southern tier of the United States. His mission in Mexico resulted in the Gadsden Purchase, the acquisition by the United States in December 1853 of a strip of northern Mexican territory, what is now southern Arizona and extreme southern New Mexico, for the sum of $10 million. Gadsden understood that this territory constituted the most practical southern route for a railroad west to the Pacific. As fate would have it, the territory was inhabited by Mexicans who, in the aftermath of the Mexican War, had moved there from parts north so that they could retain their Mexican citizenship.

The terms of the Gadsden Purchase covered a number of other issues, such as the right of Americans to cross the Isthmus of Tehuantepec, and the reestablishment of commerce between the United States and Mexico. According to the terms of the Gadsden Purchase, the United States agreed to pay Mexico $5 million in claims for damages resulting from protests by native peoples over the loss of their ancestral lands to the U.S. government, in return for the deletion of Article XI of the Treaty of Guadalupe Hidalgo, which made the United States liable for raids on Mexico perpetrated by native peoples.

Mexico had no choice but to accept the terms of the Gadsden Purchase; rejecting them would have meant another costly war and another defeat. So, much as it was touted as the treaty that finally ended the U.S.-Mexico conflict, most Mexicans believed they needed the Gadsden Purchase like a hole in the head. On a positive note, the Gadsden Purchase reaffirmed the civil rights of Mexican Americans and guaranteed their land titles—a covenant that, not surprisingly, was not entirely heeded.

CALIFORNIA DREAMING

What was the Bear Flag Revolt, and how did the Californios feel about joining the United States?

In 1827 explorer, fur trader, and trapper **Jedediah Strong Smith**, traveling from the Great Salt Lake across the Colorado River and the Mohave Desert, made the first American journey overland to Alta California (the Spanish province of California was split into Alta California and Baja California in 1804), but Anglos did not settle in Alta California in significant numbers until 1841. The very first Anglo settlers in the region adopted the culture of the California Mexicans, or Californios, as the criollos and mestizos in the Mexican territory of Alta California were known. Many even married into Californio families, who lived mostly on large ranchos, and became Mexican citizens. But, before long, a different breed of Anglos began arriving in California via the Oregon Trail. These newcomers, who settled mainly in northern Alta California, brought their families, refused Mexican citizenship, and inhabited remote areas, far from Mexican supervision. Inspired by Manifest Destiny, they carried within them a spark of rebellion, which would rock Alta California just about a month after the United States' official declaration of war against Mexico in the Mexican War.

This rebellion in California, known as the Bear Flag Revolt, was instigated by American explorer and soldier **John Charles Frémont**, who spread rumors that the Mexican authorities were planning to oust Anglo settlers from California. In response to this perceived threat, a group of Anglo settlers in northern Alta California—who were generally disgruntled by the way the Mexican authorities handled affairs in California and wished to be backed by the mint and might of the U.S. government—strode into the town of Sonoma on June 14, 1846; hoisted a flag sporting a grizzly bear and a star, for them an emblem of a new, independent republic, the Bear Flag Republic; and captured the Mexican *comandante* of northern Alta California, **Mariano Guadalupe Vallejo**. The Bear Flag Republic, with **William B. Ide** as its president, endured for three and a half weeks, until news of the U.S. declaration of war against Mexico reached California.

The bearer of that news was **Commodore John D. Sloat**, whose U.S. naval ships wrested control of the port of Monterey from the Mexican Coast Guard on July 7, 1846. Relinquishing the notion of the Bear Flag Republic altogether, Ide, other Bear Flaggers, and the northern Californios, who were by then feeling separate from Mexico, joined forces with the United States, flying the Stars and Stripes. However, the Californios in southern Alta California, where far fewer Anglos had settled, resisted U.S. imperialism. The southern Californios would have acquiesced to the American takeover had the U.S. government selected someone other than U.S. Marine captain **Archibald H. Gillespie** to take command of California. Gillespie imposed a draconian form of martial law, enraging the southern Californios, who, in turn, took up arms against the American invaders. The southern Californios and military forces from other parts of Mexico fought the good fight, even retaking U.S.-occupied Los Angeles and forcing Gillespie to flee on September 30, 1846, in what is known as the Siege of Los Angeles, but U.S. general **Stephen W. Kearny** and his army, together with **Commodore Robert F. Stockton** and his naval forces, eventually got the best of them.

Peace was negotiated with the southern Californios under the Treaty of Cahuenga, which was signed in 1847 in an adobe house in what is now North Hollywood, and when the Treaty of Guadalupe Hidalgo was approved on February 2, 1848, a united Alta California was officially handed over to the Americans. California did not have to wait as many years as Texas had to join the Union, thanks largely to the discovery of gold and the California gold rush. On September 9, 1850, it was admitted to the Union as a nonslavery state. Many wealthy Californio ranchers participated in laying the necessary groundwork for California's admission to the Union and in fulfilling the tasks related to statehood. Among the delegates who helped draft the California State Constitution were such influential Californios as **Pablo de la Guerra**, **Mariano Vallejo**, and **José Antonio Carrillo**, who had fought against the Americans just years before. While Southern Californians harbored much proslavery sentiment, the state, nonetheless, remained in the Union during the Civil War (1861–65) and was little affected by the devastating conflict.

What was the California gold rush, and how did Mexico miss out on it by a couple of days?

As fate would have it, just as the United States and Mexico were negotiating the Treaty of Guadalupe Hidalgo in early 1848, gold—what seemed like a veritable Seven Cities of Gold, which had eluded the Spanish conquistadores and colonizers in their forays into the Southwest—turned up unexpectedly and in large quantity not very far from the Southwest. It was a discovery that unleashed one of the great gold rushes of the nineteenth century and changed forever the course of American history.

On January 24, 1848, an American contractor named **James W. Marshall**, who was building a sawmill for **Captain John Sutter** at present-day Coloma, on the south fork of the American River, in the Sacramento Valley of California, noticed some shiny yellow rocks while overseeing the digging of the millrace. Upon closer examination, Marshall realized that he had found not just a few gold nuggets, but the mother lode. Four days later, he broke the news of his discovery to Sutter, who wanted to keep the whole thing a secret. Sutter knew that the fate of a nation was at stake, that if the news of gold got out, Mexico would probably never agree to surrender its territory, especially Alta California, to the Americans. After all, had not an entire hemisphere been conquered and colonized for gold and more gold? But Sutter's most immediate concern was that his workers, struck by gold fever, would abandon Sutter's Fort, the trading and agricultural outpost near the junction of the American and Sacramento rivers that he had established for new arrivals to Alta California, and that left alone, he would not be able to defend Sutter's Fort from the onslaught of gold-hungry fortune seekers.

In the months after the Treaty of Guadalupe Hidalgo was signed on February 2, 1848, word of gold in California spread slowly and then like wildfire across America. Newspapers, including the *New York Herald*, ran feverish headlines detailing the find, and soon after **President James Polk** corroborated the report of gold in an address before Congress on December 5, 1848, prospectors from all over the world descended upon California to claim their fortune. Virtually overnight California's population exploded, and San Francisco, which was still a small settlement up until the time of the California gold rush, was transformed into a boomtown. And what of John Sutter? His worst fears were realized. Abandoning their posts, his workers made a beeline for the goldfields, allowing gold-seeking strangers to overrun his land, trample and steal his crops, butcher his livestock, and pilfer his tools. Bankrupt, Sutter spent his remaining days seeking compensation for his losses from the state and the federal government. On June 16, 1880, the U.S. Congress adjourned before passing a bill that would have granted $50,000 to John Sutter as compensation. Two days later, Sutter, still empty-handed, passed away.

What role did Latinos play in the success of California mining?

Gold-hungry Anglos, Californios, and Native Americans from around California were the first to descend upon the goldfields. Then came prospectors from Oregon, people from Hawaii, Mexican Americans and Anglos from the Southwest, Mexicans (many of whom hailed from the mining districts near Sonora), Peruvians, and Chileans. The first Peruvian and Chilean prospectors reached California by sailing up the Pacific coast of South and North America, a perilous journey. It seems fitting that descendants of the Incas, whose culture both revered gold and had been destroyed for it, would be among the forty-niners; that is, the first California prospectors. As 1849 dawned, miners from across the United States and the world—particularly Australians, New Zealanders, French, Chinese, Filipinos, and Basques—began arriving in California in droves, risking en route life and limb against attacking Native American tribes, the elements, disease, and seemingly impassable mountains and plains.

The Anglo prospectors soon outnumbered the Mexican American, Mexican, Chilean, and Peruvian miners. With no experience panning for gold, the Anglos turned for help to the Latin Americans and Mexican Americans, who taught them how to extract the placer gold from the rivers and streams with a flat-bottomed pan with sloping sides; to use an *arrastra*, a mill that pulverized rock and made it possible to extract gold from quartz; and to refine the gold with mercury, a process the Spaniards had devised to refine silver in northern Mexico three centuries earlier.

Having mastered gold mining at the feet of Latin Americans and Mexican Americans, the Anglos then decided that since California was a U.S.-occupied territory—and after September 9, 1850, a U.S. state—the gold belonged to them. Amid a barrage of racist attacks from the Anglos, the Mexican American and Latin American miners, as well as the Chinese and others, took to working away from the Anglos, in the southern part of the mother lode. Before long, however, the Anglos began invading the southern mines. Seeking to drive foreigners out of the mines, the nascent state of California passed a law taxing all non-Americans heavily. The Latin American miners protested, and revolts broke out all over the mines. In ensuing years, Mexican Americans and Latin Americans faced constant threats of bodily harm and even death, and some were murdered over gold. Under such an assault, a good number simply forfeited their right to the gold and fled. It would not be the first nor last time that Mexican Americans and Mexican nationals would confront bald-faced discrimination in the United States—without legal recourse.

Allá en el rancho grande: *What happened to the Mexican American rancheros during the gold rush and after?*

An old Mexican folk song that lives on among Latinos begins: *"Allá en el rancho grande, allá donde vivía . . ."* ("Back there on the big ranch, the place where I used to live . . ."). It's a song that romanticizes life on the rancho, or ranch, a landscape filled with handsome rancheros (ranchers) and vaqueros (cowboys), beautiful señoritas, big sombreros, and wide-open spaces.

During the California gold rush, hordes of Southern Californians rushed north to try their luck at a pot of gold, and quite a number of towns in Southern California turned into virtual ghost towns. However, the ranchos of central and southern California flourished. An exploding California population meant that a large number of people needed to be fed, and beef was the entrée of choice for most of the new and often nouveau riche citizens. A good number of the California ranchers were Californios whose families had long inhabited the Spanish-style *haciendas* of the ranches and who were accustomed to running their enormous estates like small fiefdoms. They hired vaqueros, who wore *chaparreras* (a word Anglos shortened to "chaps") and roped cattle with *la riata* (which the Anglos called a lariat). While not all gold-seekers profited richly from the California gold rush, it was good to the rancheros and vaqueros—at least until the tide turned. First, cattle ranchers in the Plains states undercut the Californians' prices, causing demand for California beef to dwindle in just a few years. In 1861 winter floods ravaged Southern California, devastating the cattle herds. The floods were followed by two years of drought, which also had a disastrous effect on the cattle.

As if these catastrophes were not enough, the Californio rancheros confronted anti-Mexican laws that were put in place in California in the decade after the Mexican War. Whereas the Treaty of Guadalupe Hidalgo had rendered legitimate the land titles of Mexicans living in Mexican territories that the United States absorbed under the treaty, the Federal Land Grant Act of 1851—drafted with California very much in mind—stipulated that all Spanish and Mexican land grants had to be presented for verification within two years and that those that were not would automatically be rendered null and void. However, most land grants had not been recorded on paper, in keeping with Spanish and Mexican traditional protocol, and families had divided and subdivided their lands over the centuries for inheritance purposes.

With no papers to show, many of those who had managed to keep their ranches after the Treaty of Guadalupe Hidalgo was signed now had to turn them over. Adding insult to injury, the California Supreme Court upheld an English law of riparian water rights (i.e., individuals, not communities, owned water rights), which meant that many a ranchero was forced to sell cheap or give up his property because neighbors could dam up his water and parch his land as they pleased. Very few rancheros were able to survive, and Anglo speculators bought up their properties for a song. As a result, scores of thriving Californio landowners became a homeless, bankrupt underclass overnight, forced to seek menial jobs across the vast American frontier.

DESPERADOS AND THE
MEXICAN REVOLUTION OF 1910

What is a desperado, anyway?

The word "desperado" is derived from the Spanish *desesperado*, meaning "desperate one," and is defined as a desperate, dangerous criminal. In the frontier years of the second half of the nineteenth century, desperados, both Mexican and Anglo, roamed the American Southwest.

One Mexican desperado who went down in history is **Joaquín Murieta**, although his existence has never been confirmed. The story goes that Murieta, who hailed from Sonora, Mexico, was a peaceful California gold miner until Anglos took away his gold-mine claim and murdered his brother in about 1850. In a desperate attempt to avenge the injustices done him, other Mexicans, and Mexican Americans, Murieta robbed, ransacked, and killed anybody who got in his way. He was compared to Robin Hood, but his random acts of lawlessness only served to deepen the bitter animosity Anglos felt toward Mexicans. When it was suspected that Murieta was responsible for raiding Calaveras County, California, and for setting the devastating fire that consumed the mining town of Stockton in 1850, California put a price on his head: $1,000, dead or alive. Some California rangers reported later that they had killed Joaquín Murieta, but his identity was never verified.

Another desperado destined for infamy in American annals was Mexican folk hero **Juan Nepomuceno Cortina**, nicknamed Cheno Cortina and the Red Robber of the Rio Grande, whom Mexican Americans have likened to **Daniel Boone** and other intrepid frontiersmen. Born into a wealthy family of cattle ranchers in Mexico in 1824, Cortina fought the Americans in the Mexican War and then settled on ranch lands that were part of an enormous land grant his mother had inherited near Brownsville, Texas. Cortina could not swallow the injustices the Anglos perpetrated against Mexicans in the United States after the war.

When a sheriff unfairly arrested a vaquero (cowboy) on Cortina's ranch in 1859, the desperado apparently grew so enraged that he shot the sheriff in the shoulder on July 13, 1859, which marks the start of the First Cortina War (1859). Two and a half months later, on September 28, Cortina, with several dozen men, stormed into Brownsville, took the town hostage, freed all the Mexican prisoners at the local jail who he felt had been imprisoned unfairly, murdered four Anglos who had killed Mexicans but were never punished, and attempted to hoist the Mexican flag at Fort Brown before finally agreeing to leave town on September 30. In May 1861, Cortina invaded Zapata County (in southern Texas), in what came to be called the Second Cortina War, and was defeated by Confederate colonel **Santos Benavides**, one of the highest-ranking Mexican Americans in the Confederate Army during the American Civil War. Over time, Cortina became more and more a scofflaw and an "avenging angel." He was held accountable for inciting dozens of riots, including the angry riots that broke out in El Paso in 1877 after Anglo profiteers tried to take the salt mines away from the Mexicans and Mexican Americans. This incident, known as the Salt War, cost many lives and caused thousands of dollars in damage.

Acts of destruction on the part of Mexican and Mexican American desperados who felt persecuted and disenfranchised after the Mexican War gave rise to armies of American vigilantes in California and the American Southwest, and to the feared Texas Rangers, an organization that was founded unofficially in 1823 by **Stephen F. Austin**. The Texas Rangers became a quasi-military unit for the Republic of Texas (1836–45) and then the state of Texas, and in 1935 were made an official state law-enforcement agency. The Texas Rangers earned notoriety for the "law and order" violence they perpetrated against innocent Mexicans and Mexican American citizens, creating an atmosphere of antipathy and suspicion toward Mexicans, which, some say, still lingers in the Lone Star State.

Was Pancho Villa a desperado?

Mexican revolutionary **Francisco "Pancho" Villa**, whose real name was Doroteo Arango Arámbula, was a hero of the Mexican Revolution of 1910, in which Mexicans fought to depose ruthless Mexican dictator **Porfirio Díaz** (who had held power since 1884) and institute a pluralistic democracy that would return the land to the peasants, and food and hope to the people. Like **Juan Nepomuceno Cortina** and **Joaquín Murieta** to the north, Pancho Villa became disgusted with the establishment and decided to take the law into his own hands. As a young man, he took to the hills and launched a career as both a guerilla fighter for democracy and a bandit who terrorized northern Mexico, robbing banks and trains and ransacking mining towns.

When the United States recognized as president of Mexico **Venustiano Carranza**—one of several Mexican leaders who had literally battled each other for the post during the Mexican Revolution—after Carranza assumed the executive powers in August 1914, Villa became enraged over what he perceived as U.S. intervention in his country's internal affairs. In retaliation, he killed sixteen American engineers on board a train that had entered Mexico from the United States, and in early 1916, he attacked Columbus, New Mexico, slaughtering seventeen Americans. In a matter of days, U.S. general **John J. Pershing** and his large army were given the order to capture Pancho Villa and bring him to the United States to stand trial. The guerilla fighter, who knew the difficult Mexican terrain like the back of his hand, slipped into hiding, and Pershing's army came up empty-handed. Pancho Villa became a hero overnight.

What was the Mexican Revolution all about, and how did the United States get involved?

The Mexican Revolution of 1910 was a lengthy, bloody, and catastrophic civil war that altered Mexico forever. Precipitated by both class and racial struggle, it was in many ways similar to the Bolshevik Revolution in Russia, which followed seven years later. By 1910 the rich of Mexico had grown richer (and so had foreign investors), and the native peoples and mestizos, who were at the bottom of the pecking order, had gotten poorer. Finally, they said *basta ya* (enough is enough) and revolted.

It was a complicated revolution, with numerous factions vying for power—some more liberal and inclusive, and others more radical, virulent, and unforgiving. Much of the protest was waged against the Catholic Church. Native peoples and mestizos stormed Catholic churches and toppled religious statues, just as the early Spanish missionaries, seeking to convert the peoples of Mexico to Catholicism centuries before, had smashed images of Aztec and Maya gods. Interestingly, when the Mexicans demolished statues of Roman Catholic saints, they often uncovered figurines of Mexican gods encrusted in the plaster, proof that rather than a complete conversion to Catholicism, a kind of cultural and religious syncretism, a mixing of Spanish and native traditions, had gone on from the very beginning.

The Mexican Revolution erupted in November 1910, when Mexican liberal leader **Francisco Madero** organized a revolt against Mexican dictator **Porfirio Díaz**. A year later Díaz resigned and Madero became president, but in 1913 Madero was overthrown by one of his generals, **Victoriano Huerta**, and then murdered. Huerta proved to be just another dictator, and the Mexican people, led by **Emiliano Zapata**, a native peasant who had backed Madero, and **Pancho Villa**, revolted. They destroyed railroads and most of the nation's crops and livestock, unleashing a food shortage of crisis proportions, which led to mass starvation, uncontrollable disease epidemics, and death. All hell broke loose south of the border.

In response, U.S. president **Woodrow Wilson** ordered an arms blockade against Mexico in 1913. It was the eve of World War I, and the United States feared that Germany might take advantage of the chaos in Mexico and meddle in the hemisphere. U.S. involvement in Mexico escalated in April 1914, when the Mexicans arrested a battalion of U.S. sailors who had made landfall in Tampico, Mexico, to pick up supplies. **Henry T. Mayo**, then commander of the U.S. Atlantic fleet, demanded an apology and a salute to the American flag from the Huerta government, and when the Mexican dictator refused to comply, President Wilson dispatched a squadron of U.S. naval ships to Veracruz, and the United States prepared to invade Mexico and declare war.

At the eleventh hour, Argentina, Chile, and Brazil interceded, and war between Mexico and the United States was averted. Huerta resigned, **Venustiano Carranza** was named president of Mexico, and the United States saw no reason for further overt hostility against the Mexican people. Civil war erupted again in Mexico in 1914, but Carranza got the country under control by 1915, although his foes Pancho Villa and Emiliano Zapata continued their raids on both sides of the border until the Mexican Revolution ended in 1917.

How did the Mexican people fare during the Mexican Revolution?

Terribly. Over a million Mexicans perished, and an untold number suffered political persecution and violence and lost their homes, their possessions, their financial well-being, and their hope.

The misery caused by the Mexican Revolution unleashed the

first significant wave of Mexican *immigration* (not absorption due to shifting borders) to the United States. Between 1910 and 1930, nearly 10 percent of Mexico's citizens fled their homeland in search of a brighter future. Most of the refugees (about seven hundred thousand) chose to forge a new life in the United States. By the hundreds of thousands, they walked endless miles to the promised land of the American Southwest and California. They waded across the shallow Rio Grande, belongings and babies on their backs, seeking refuge from the devastation. Many were upper-middle and middle class; many were poor, uneducated peasants. The Mexicans who fled the Mexican Revolution and joined the American workforce exerted a positive influence on their adopted nation's economy. They also enriched America's cultural heritage and nurtured future generations of leaders in all walks of life, leaders who would not only reshape Mexican American communities, but the nation as a whole.

What did the Mexican Revolution have to do with Henry B. González's long and distinguished career as a U.S. congressman?

Henry B. González's parents were among the scores of middle-class Mexicans who were forced to flee their homeland during and after the Mexican Revolution. They settled in San Antonio, Texas, where the future democratic congressman and highly respected leader of the Mexican American community was born on May 3, 1916. Several decades later, on November 4, 1961, Henry B., as he was affectionately called, was elected to represent Texas in the U.S. House of Representatives. There he would earn the distinction of chairing the powerful Committee on Banking, Finance, and Urban Affairs for three terms. Henry B. González served on Capitol Hill until January 3, 1999. Less than a year later, on November 28, 2000, he passed away in San Antonio, the place where his vision of a better America for the downtrodden had been conceived.

A TIME OF TROUBLES:
MEXICAN AMERICA, 1920-50

When did the United States begin
policing the border with Mexico?

In 1924 U.S. immigration laws were put in place that established quotas for people entering the country from various parts of the world. Northern Europeans were favored; Southern Europeans could gain entry in limited numbers. Almost all Asians were excluded. However, no quotas were established for immigrants from the Western Hemisphere, thus enabling Mexico, due to its proximity, to become the United States' largest supplier of cheap labor.

Ever since Mexico gained its independence from Spain in 1821, going *al norte*, "north," to the United States, had been a logical step for Mexicans seeking to improve their lot, and they had entered the United States with no questions asked. Countless Mexican farmhands, shepherds, cowboys, and miners, in search of better and more highly paid work, had crossed the border unimpeded. So, too, had political refugees fleeing the many upheavals during Mexico's formative years as a sovereign nation, especially after the Mexican Revolution of 1910. While in 1924 the United States did not impose immigration quotas on Mexicans seeking to enter the U.S. territory, that year it did make showing proof of identity and other documentation a mandatory requirement to gain legal entry. Many Mexicans entered the United States legally, but others viewed the paperwork as an impediment and began dodging the border patrol. Before long, the term "illegal immigrant" entered the American vocabulary.

Why do Mexican Americans say that the
United States was built on their backs?

The Mexicans who fled the Mexican Revolution for the United States were accustomed to meager wages and appalling living conditions, and they were grateful just to have a job, even one with low pay. Mexican agricultural workers were willing to plant, tend, and harvest crops from sunup to sundown without a break, which enabled commercial farms throughout the American Southwest and California to flourish. By the 1920s, Mexicans and

Mexican Americans had emerged as the single most important source of agricultural labor in California (and they remain so to this day), replacing the Chinese and the Japanese, who had worked the fields at the turn of the century. The early 1920s saw the expansion of the Southern Pacific Railroad, and Mexicans and Mexican Americans also went to work on the tracks. A 1929 government report indicates that as many as 70–90 percent of all workers on the southwestern railroads were of Mexican origin. The Baltimore and Ohio Railroad also heavily recruited Mexicans and Mexican Americans.

Manufacturing and other industries also benefited from the influx of cheap labor from Mexico. In the 1920s, Mexicans and Mexican Americans found employment in steel factories, meat-packing plants, utility companies, trucking, the construction industry, and dozens of other industries in the Midwest. They also worked in agriculture in the Midwest, such as in Michigan's sugar-beet fields. Due to this influx of Mexican workers into the region, Chicago's Mexican and Mexican American populations swelled from four thousand to twenty thousand between 1920 and 1930. People of Mexican origin met with much discrimination in their new home in the Midwest, especially from other ethnic groups, such as Italian Americans and Polish Americans, who, by the 1920s, considered themselves true Americans and the Mexicans foreigners. As they contributed to the nation's prosperity, Mexican American families endured physical and economic hardship as well. They often dwelled in substandard housing on the wrong side of the tracks, that is, in overcrowded Mexican ghettos, known as barrios and *colonias*.

What's a barrio, and what's a colonia?

A barrio is a Latino neighborhood in a city or town. Many Mexican American barrios bear the name of the region of Mexico from whence the first inhabitants came. Since they were first established, barrios, like other immigrant ghettos, have afforded their dwellers a semblance of the old country. Many Mexican Americans eventually left the barrios and acculturated to mainstream American society, a phenomenon that holds true for all Latinos. In recent years, new generations of Latinos have chosen to return to the barrios where their parents or grandparents once lived, to reclaim part of their heritage.

Colonias, Spanish for "colonies," refer both to Mexican

neighborhoods in towns and to Mexican communities in unincorporated rural areas all along the U.S.-Mexico border. (Texas alone has over 1,500 *colonias*.) Since they dot the border, *colonias* have served over time as rest stops for Mexican newcomers to the United States who are in search of work. The *colonias* are homes away from home, places where new immigrants explore potential employment opportunities or simply pause for a warm meal and a friendly chat on their way to "somewhere." Most of the more permanent residents of *colonias* are impoverished Mexican Americans, not illegal immigrants, as is the widespread opinion. In fact, *colonias* are among the poorest neighborhoods and communities in the nation. Many have bad roads; primitive sanitary, water, and sewer systems; unsafe, substandard dwellings, sometimes abutting much grander abodes built with drug money; and a high rate of preventable diseases, such as diabetes, which go with the socioeconomic territory.

Chicano, go home? Why were Mexicans and Mexican Americans repatriated during the 1930s?

As the 1920s came to a close, the Great Depression, a dramatic worldwide economic decline precipitated, in an immediate sense, by the Wall Street crash of 1929, was looming over the United States. During the Depression era (1929–41), the U.S. unemployment rate rose higher than 20 percent, with the number of unemployed Americans skyrocketing to over thirteen million. Wages plummeted from an average of thirty-five cents an hour to fifteen cents an hour. Stockbrokers and financiers were rumored to be leaping out of windows in New York City, and college graduates were selling apples in the streets.

Mexican nationals and Mexican Americans, like most Americans, found themselves out of work all across the land. Work at the nation's railroads, automobile manufacturing plants, meatpacking plants, and steel mills, which had employed so many Mexicans and Mexican Americans, came to a screeching halt. In New Mexico, cattle ranchers laid off Mexican American ranch hands indefinitely, and many New Mexican Hispanos forfeited their property because they could not afford to pay the taxes or the assessments for the Middle Rio Grande Conservancy project.

Consequently, thousands of Mexican Americans and Mexican nationals joined other Americans in roaming the country in search of whatever work they could get. Anglo migrants from the

Dust Bowl and other regions headed west, where they competed for the jobs that Mexicans and Mexican Americans had traditionally filled. For instance, by 1937 over half the cotton pickers in Arizona came from out of state. The Mexican Americans, who were at the bottom of the opportunity ladder, had nowhere to turn. In Texas alone, the number of jobless Mexican Americans hit four hundred thousand during the Great Depression.

Recognizing that the Great Depression was having an especially deleterious effect on Mexican Americans, **President Franklin D. Roosevelt**'s New Deal administration established a number of agencies and projects aimed at ameliorating their situation. The Federal Emergency Relief Administration, an outcome of the Federal Emergency Relief Act of 1933, one of President Roosevelt's first New Deal acts, provided financial assistance to Mexican American workers. And the Works Progress Administration, the largest New Deal agency, which was created in May 1935, put Mexican Americans to work as carpenters, masons, and unskilled laborers in the construction of bridges, libraries, and other municipal structures. In the midst of great anguish, this was a moment of pride for Mexican Americans, who were publicly recognized for their long tradition as master builders—a tradition harking back to the glory days of the Maya and Aztecs.

In spite of Franklin Roosevelt's and **Eleanor Roosevelt**'s efforts on behalf of Mexican Americans during the 1930s, a repatriation movement, which demanded that Mexicans and Mexican Americans be sent to Mexico, gathered enormous support during the Depression days. Many Anglos considered both Mexicans and Mexican Americans to be foreigners or itinerant laborers, who, in their view, had no right to take the few existing jobs from "real" Americans at a time of such extreme economic duress. In complete disregard for Mexican Americans' civil rights, local government agencies began rounding up anyone who looked Mexican and sending them "home." Frequently, they targeted undocumented immigrants, but they also sent first-generation Mexican Americans to Mexico, as well as Mexican Americans whose families had lived in the United States for centuries. Many Americans of Mexican descent could not bear the idea of being deported and fled to Mexico before they could be loaded onto the Southern Pacific or other railroads and dumped over the U.S.-Mexico border, in towns along the Tijuana and Brownsville lines.

All told, during the 1930s approximately half a million people of Mexican descent, illegal immigrants included, were deported from the United States. About 132,000 of the deportees were from Texas, which had the nation's largest Mexican American community. California was second in the number of deportees, followed by Indiana, Illinois, and Michigan. Mexican Americans in New Mexico suffered the least: only 10 percent of repatriates came from that state. This phenomenon can be attributed to the fact that New Mexico was less industrialized than other states and, thus, less affected by the Depression, and that Mexican Americans in New Mexico were more integrated into the mainstream Anglo society.

Faced with such a high number of deportees, a distraught Mexican president, **Lázaro Cárdenas**, set up resettlement camps in the Mexican states of Guerrero, Michoacán, Oaxaca, and Chiapas, as well as a small colony in Matamoros, in the state of Tamaulipas. In the end, however, the Mexican economy could not absorb this influx, and few deportees became fully integrated into Mexican society. This situation served only to increase the outrage and disillusionment of Mexican American deportees, who felt that the United States, their own country, had brutally betrayed them.

During World War II, when the United States faced a shortage of workers, U.S. authorities ceased in their efforts to divest the country of Mexicans, and Mexican Americans who had been transported over the border found their way back to their old towns in America. Mexican Americans' experience of abandonment by their country, and Mexican nationals' bitter experience of being sent "home" when they were no longer needed and sent for again when cheap labor was in demand, intensified both groups' mistrust of Anglos, a mistrust many Mexican American families had harbored for generation after generation.

The great injustice done Mexican Americans and Mexican nationals in the 1930s—which has been compared to the forced relocation of Japanese Americans and Japanese nationals to internment camps in the United States, such as Tule Lake, in California, during World War II—also led numerous American politicians to take a fresh look at the Mexican and Mexican American "question" and to seek ways to improve working and living conditions in the United States for minorities. The sad repatriation experience also stirred the desire in many Mexican nationals and Mexican Americans to empower themselves and their communities. Some entered the mainstream political arena. Others launched publications and radio programs with a political bent.

What was the Bracero Program?

The Bracero Program—in effect from August 1942 until December 1947 and then from December 1948 to December 1964—brought millions of Mexican nationals to the United States as temporary workers. The U.S. government initiated the first Bracero Program in 1942 in response to the labor shortage that developed when America's men and women went off to fight in World War II or to labor in arms factories for the war effort. During the first Bracero Program, about a quarter of a million braceros were hired to work seasonally in agriculture in the United States, as the crops required. A contract usually lasted one year. Some braceros found themselves returning year after year to work in the same region and even for the same employer.

The second phase of the Bracero Program was much more ambitious in terms of numbers. From 1948 until the beginning of the Vietnam War, more than 4.5 million Mexican nationals came to toil in the United States, most migrating seasonally to plant and harvest crops. Braceros accounted for 25 percent of all farmworkers in the United States while the second Bracero Program was in effect, and their work greatly benefited the states of Texas, California, Arizona, New Mexico, Colorado, Arkansas, and Michigan. Thousands also drove trucks that delivered crops and manufactured goods to American marketplaces or worked on the Southern Pacific Railroad, despite opposition by U.S. labor.

Before the Bracero Program, Mexican nationals toiling in the United States had tolerated deplorable conditions and little pay—and sometimes none at all, in the way of indentured servants. When ironing out the details of the Bracero Program, the Mexican government stipulated that the United States had to ensure that the itinerant Mexican workers would earn no less than the minimum wage, that their health and well-being would be protected, that labor practices would be fair, and that the workers would have the right to take legal action against American employers refusing to comply with the above stipulations. The labor shortage during World War II, coupled by the hue and cry over the illegal deportation of Mexican Americans during the Great

Depression, prompted the U.S. government to agree to abide by mutual treaties that ensured the Mexican workers' basic rights.

Even with the laws on the books, many prejudiced American employers treated the braceros abominably. Mexican workers complained of bad food (their provisions often consisted exclusively of such things as tripe, chitterlings, pig's feet, chicken necks, and leftovers from earlier meals); excessive wage deductions, which left them with very little money to support themselves or send to their families back in Mexico; harassment and physical mistreatment; miserable housing, which often amounted to nothing more than enlarged chicken coops; rampant bigotry; and exposure to deadly pesticides. Conditions for Mexican workers, braceros or not, were so wretched in Texas that the Mexican government at one point barred its citizens from working in that state.

Why did Texas pass a law declaring that all Mexicans were white?

In response to the Mexican government's vehement protests about the subhuman treatment of some Mexican nationals and Mexican Americans in Texas, the Texas legislature passed the Caucasian Race Resolution in 1944, which declared that all people of Mexican descent were Caucasian and endorsed equal rights in public places of business and leisure for all Caucasians. In a strictly segregated society, this seemed like the only way that the Texas legislature could grant Mexican nationals and Mexican Americans some rights. But the Mexican government considered Texas's efforts insufficient, and the state was forced to comply with the guarantees stipulated in the Bracero Program before Mexico again allowed its citizens to work north of the border.

The U.S. government was also put on the hot seat from time to time about the maltreatment of braceros. For example, in the early 1960s, various human rights organizations, including the National Catholic Welfare Council, Americans for Democratic Action, the National Council of the Churches of Christ in the USA, the National Farmers Union, and the AFL-CIO, alerted the U.S. Congress about the unfair wages being paid braceros. The U.S. government was forced to take action to right the wrong and discourage further injustice. **Secretary of Labor Arthur Goldberg**, a prominent labor lawyer who was later appointed a Supreme Court justice, established a minimum wage law that stipulated that braceros were to receive at least a dollar an hour in pay.

What was the El Paso Incident?

In 1948 Texas was at the center of further controversy over working conditions for Mexican nationals. That autumn, as the cotton harvest in Texas drew nigh, the Mexican government demanded that Mexican cotton pickers crossing the border into Texas receive a minimum wage of $3.00 per hundred pounds of cotton harvested. Texas farmers refused to pay more than $2.50 to Mexicans, although they were paying the going rate of $3.00 to all other workers. The Mexican government stood firm and forbade its nationals from going north, guarding the U.S.-Mexico border with armed tanks. In October, worried Texas farmers informed the U.S. Immigration Service that their crops would rot on the ground if Mexican workers did not start coming across the border fast.

La migra (the U.S. immigration authorities) responded by simply opening the El Paso border with Mexico to Mexican workers. In spite of the Mexican Army's blockade of the border, Mexicans crossed into the United States by the thousands, braving their own government's bullets. Upon stepping foot on American soil, they were loaded onto trucks by agents representing the Texas growers and delivered to the cotton fields, with the full approval of the U.S. immigration service.

The Mexican government protested so vociferously that the Mexican workers were ordered to leave the Texas cotton fields and the United States extended an official apology to Mexico— but not until all the Texas cotton was harvested.

Mojados: *Illegal or undocumented?*

In the decades when the Bracero Program was in effect, *mojados*, or wetbacks, streamed into the United States illegally, undocumented, unsupervised, and unprotected by U.S. laws. The *mojados*, which literally means "the wet ones," earned this name because they often swam across the Rio Grande, which forms part of the U.S.-Mexico border, to American soil in pursuit of work. (Incidentally, those who nowadays enter the United States illegally along the western stretch of the U.S.-Mexico border, especially in California, which is lined with high wire fences, are referred to as *alambristas*, the word *alambre* being Spanish for "wire.")

When the first phase of the Bracero Program came to an end in December 1947, *mojado* smuggling increased sharply because American agribusiness depended on Mexican labor for the planting, harvesting, and distribution of crops. While it is impossible to determine the exact number of *mojados* who crossed into the United States from Mexico after the first phase of the Bracero Program ended, the fact that between 1947 and 1955 alone over 4.3 million undocumented workers were apprehended on U.S. soil and returned to Mexico gives some indication of the magnitude of the *mojado* migration.

Many of the undocumented Mexican workers who eluded *la migra* in the 1940s and 1950s and toiled in the United States later returned to Mexico by choice, but countless others stayed and became part of the growing Mexican American community. The arrival of *mojados* in the American Southwest stimulated a migration northward of Mexican Americans with roots in that region. The Mexican Americans headed to industrial cities in the Northeast and Midwest, where they would not have to compete with Mexican newcomers for the low-paying jobs of the frontier states. During the 1960s, Mexican Americans moved to the Midwest and Northeast in record numbers. In fact, for every *mojado* that entered the United States, one Mexican American moved north.

In the United States, the *mojados* suffered prejudice, exploitation, and abuse because of their undocumented, or "illegal," status. "Undocumented" is the preferred term for these individuals since "illegal" suggests criminality, which, if the situation is seen in its proper light, does not apply to these impoverished workers who crossed the U.S.-Mexico border in search of honest work for honest pay, a practice that the U.S. government had sanctioned from time to time, and were the backbone of agriculture and other industries in the American Southwest and elsewhere in the nation.

What was Operation Wetback?

Another instance of grave social injustice perpetrated against Mexican citizens. By the late 1940s and early 1950s, the number of *mojados* in the United States had grown exponentially. While the U.S. Border Patrol had apprehended 91,000 *mojados* in 1946, it caught 865,000 in 1953. The public hue and outcry in America over the stream of undocumented Mexicans entering the country grew louder, and in response, the U.S. government launched Operation Wetback in June 1954, a campaign aimed at apprehending and expelling from the United States undocumented immigrants—Mexicans were the main target—in an effort to dissuade others from crossing into the United States illegally and to compel U.S. employers to hire Mexican laborers under the Bracero Program. During Operation Wetback, which targeted undocumented workers in the states of California, Arizona, and Texas, some eighty thousand Mexican nationals were rounded up or left the United States voluntarily, propelled by the terrifying military-style sweeps conducted by the United States Immigration and Naturalization Service (INS).

What brought an end to the Bracero Program?

In November 1946, with World War II over, the U.S. government informed Mexico that it wished to terminate the Bracero Program. However, most farm bosses in the United States had come to rely on the braceros, and they lobbied to keep the program alive. In 1947 the U.S. House of Representatives introduced a law that kept the Bracero Program in place for seventeen more years. In 1956, a year when 445,000 Mexican braceros were processed, the postwar Bracero Program reached its peak.

Increased mechanization in agriculture, coupled with U.S. organized labor's growing opposition to the hiring of Mexican nationals, led to the final dissolution of the Bracero Program in 1964. Even after the program was officially terminated, braceros continued to work on American farms for several more years: Braceros and their employers simply negotiated labor contracts without government intervention.

In 2001, nearly forty years after the Bracero Program ended, Mexican president **Vicente Fox** expressed interest in recovering the millions of dollars that had been deducted from the paychecks of braceros in the World War II era, in keeping with an agreement between the United States and Mexico, but never disbursed. Ten percent of the braceros' weekly salaries had been deducted and then forwarded to Mexican banks—to be paid to the braceros upon their return to Mexico—as a way for them to save and as an incentive to head home. The Mexican government never did pay the braceros what was due them, and the where-abouts of those millions is anybody's guess.

What was the Sleepy Lagoon case?

An incident that occurred in 1942 is just one of the myriad en-counters with ethnic intolerance that Mexicans and Mexican Americans have withstood in the United States over the centuries. On August 2, 1942, a twenty-one-year-old Mexican American named **José Díaz**—who in 1923 had fled Durango, Mexico, and the devastation of the Mexican Revolution, with his family—was found beaten and unconscious near the Sleepy Lagoon reservoir in southeast Los Angeles. He later died, never regaining con-sciousness. The blame for Díaz's murder was placed squarely on Mexican American youths, and newspapers, among them the Hearst-owned *Los Angeles Examiner*, ran a series of sensationalist articles on the dangers that Mexican American gangs posed to so-ciety. The public grew hysterical, and to calm fears, the LAPD rounded up over six hundred Mexican American youths who it alleged were somehow connected to the Sleepy Lagoon case. Twenty-two of the Mexican American youths were indicted for murder.

Their three-month trial, one of the largest mass trials in American history, made a mockery of justice. First of all, the youths were denied haircuts and a change of clothes so that they would appear more menacing, and they were made to sit in a "prisoners' box," apart from their lawyers. Secondly, not a single witness provided valid evidence that placed any of the defendants at the crime scene at the time José Díaz was assaulted. Thirdly, the youths were vilified in the courtroom; one expert from the sheriff's department even testified that "this Mexican element feels a desire to kill or at least draw blood." Finally, the press also expressed hostility toward the defendants, referring to them as "Sleepy Lagooners," then simply as "goons."

Despite the serious flaws in the prosecution's case, only five of the twenty-two youths were acquitted. The other seventeen were convicted on charges ranging from first-degree murder to assault with a deadly weapon. Nearly two years later, an appellate court overturned all the convictions against the youths, arguing that the first ruling had been marred by ethnic prejudice. Still, twelve of the youths had spent almost two precious years of life in prison for a crime the court found they did not commit.

What were the Zoot Suit Riots?

The Sleepy Lagoon case fanned the flames of ethnic and racial hatred in Los Angeles and led to another racially motivated incident that left a wake of devastation in the Mexican American community. During the 1940s, Mexican American teenagers commonly dressed in long jackets and high-waisted, baggy pants and sported extremely long watch chains. They called themselves pachucos. The pachucos' outfits resembled the zoot suits worn by young men in Harlem. To Anglos, zoot suits were clothes that only hoodlums wore. Newspapers and magazines in Los Angeles ran stories about the sharp rise in the city's crime rate and openly laid the blame on the pachucos, whom they dubbed "zoot suiters." Hatred toward people of Mexican descent boiled over in Los Angeles when, on June 3, 1943, eleven sailors and soldiers on shore leave allegedly got into a brawl with a group of Mexican Americans, pachucos supposedly, in one of the city's barrios. Although the Mexican Americans had not instigated the brawl, anti-Mexican coverage of the incident in LA newspapers fueled the fear and fury of Anglos in Los Angeles and of the sailors' comrades aboard ship.

The next day, two hundred sailors and other servicemen hired a fleet of taxis, circled the Mexican American barrios of Los Angeles, and beat to a pulp Mexican-looking young men who crossed their path. They mistook several African Americans and Filipino Americans for Mexican Americans or beat them up just because they were not Caucasian. In the days that followed, the violence only escalated, and by June 7 thousands of civilians had joined in the riots. The Mexican Americans of Los Angeles fought back, but they were often outnumbered and outmaneuvered, and the police prone to look the other way and even arrested victimized Mexican American youths. On June 7, military authorities declared downtown Los Angeles off-limits to military personnel, but by then the riots had become widespread. Soon other parts of the country got caught up in the bloody campaign of violence against Mexican Americans. The Zoot Suit Riots sparked similar attacks in Beaumont, Texas; Chicago; San Diego; Detroit; Evansville, Indiana; Philadelphia; and New York City.

A citizens' committee appointed by California governor **Earl Warren** (later a Supreme Court justice) and headed by **Bishop Joseph McGucken** of Los Angeles determined that racial prejudice had sparked the riots and that the police and press had further fanned the flames of racial discord and violence. In spite of this, the Los Angeles City Council actually debated a proposal that would make it illegal to wear zoot suits. Shortly after the Zoot Suit Riots ended, the Los Angeles Commission on Human Rights was established to study the "race question" and prescribe measures to prevent future outbreaks of hate crimes in the city.

The Zoot Suit Riots are memorialized in a highly acclaimed play entitled *Zoot Suit*, by **Luis Valdez**, the son of Mexican migrant workers and the creator of the Teatro Campesino, a theatrical group originally comprised of members of the United Farm Workers, a union that was headed by Mexican American **César Estrada Chávez**. *Zoot Suit*, which premiered on Broadway in 1979, was made into a motion picture by the same name in 1981. Incidentally, Luis Valdez also wrote and directed the 1987 film *La Bamba*, a chronicle of the life of **Ritchie Valens**, the Mexican American rock-and-roll star who died tragically in 1959, just as his career was taking off, in the same plane crash that took the lives of **Buddy Holly** and **Jiles Perry (J. P.) Richardson**, a tragedy that will forever be known as "the day the music died."

The Sleepy Lagoon case and the Zoot Suit Riots triggered the first stirring of a Mexican American civil rights movement. This movement would gather full steam in the 1960s and 1970s under the leadership of César Chávez, known to millions simply as César.

CROSSING THE BORDER: MEXICAN MIGRATION AND IMMIGRATION, 1965 to present

How have Mexicans entered the United States since the Bracero Program ended?

The Bracero Program ended in December 1964, having afforded millions of Mexicans with dismal job prospects in Mexico the opportunity to secure legal temporary employment in the United States. Since then millions of Mexicans have come to the United States to live permanently or to work temporarily. They have entered the country as legal immigrants with green cards; as border commuters with green cards, living in Mexico but working legally on the U.S. side of the border; as border commuters with border crossing cards, who are permitted to enter but forbidden to work in the United States, and so work illegally; as guest workers, who are mostly agricultural laborers holding seasonal jobs on farms, for which they are granted temporary agricultural work visas; and as undocumented immigrants, who cross the U.S.-Mexico border illegally and work illegally in the United States.

The phenomenon of America's undocumented Mexican population is rather easy to explain. Ever since the Bracero Program ended in December 1964, small-scale U.S. guest-worker programs, employing just a tiny fraction of Mexican transnational job seekers, have been the norm. The absence in 1964 of an organized, large-scale guest-worker program to replace the behemoth Bracero Program, coupled with new restrictions on immigration adopted in 1965—which imposed numerical limitations, making it difficult for Mexican unskilled and semiskilled workers to procure U.S. labor certification—unleashed a tremendous wave of undocumented Mexican immigration, which continues unabated to this day. (A key provision of the 1965 immigration policy, related to family reunification, exempted Mexicans with close relatives in the United States from the law's numerical limitations, making it easier for them to enter the United States.) Since the end of the Bracero Program, millions of Mexicans desperate for a paycheck have had no other alternative but to cross into the United States as undocumented immigrants and find work on their own. It should be noted that over the decades a sizable proportion of undocumented immigrants have not been settlers, but sojourners, making trips across the border to take temporary or seasonal jobs in the United States and then returning to Mexico. While the crossing into the United States is a potential death trap, the return trip to Mexico has always been a breeze for the undocumented, who drive, fly, and walk across the border, virtually without impediment.

By 1980 the INS was apprehending some one million undocumented Mexicans annually. In an effort to stem the flow of undocumented Mexicans over the border, the U.S. government enacted the Immigration Reform and Control Act of 1986, which provided amnesty to undocumented immigrants continuously present in the United States since 1982 but also subjected U.S. employers to penalties if they hired undocumented immigrants. Low-cost Mexican labor was so critical to the success of their businesses that American employers en masse simply ignored the Immigration Reform and Control Act and continued hiring undocumented workers. With jobs aplenty north of the border, in the years 1991–94, approximately 450,000 undocumented immigrants, mostly Mexicans, entered the United States annually, and from 2000 to 2004, that number topped 600,000. The demand for low-cost Mexican labor shows no signs of diminishing, which keeps undocumented Mexicans coming to the United States. In 2006 the Consejo Nacional de Población, a Mexican government agency, estimated that approximately 400,000 undocumented Mexicans would enter the United States every year until 2015, after which the flow would taper off, sinking to about 325,000 by 2050.

Around the year 2000, after decades of logjam on the issue of guest-worker programs, American labor unions, lawmakers, and growers associations came out in favor of increasing the number of guest workers in the United States, who that year numbered about forty thousand. Echoing this sentiment, in 2001 Mexican president **Vicente Fox** and **President George W. Bush** opened negotiations on immigration policy, with President Fox calling for an overhaul of the U.S. guest-worker program so that more Mexicans would be permitted to work legally in the United States, and for blanket legal residency status for some of the three million Mexican workers without papers in the United States. The September 11, 2001, terrorist attacks, and the Bush administration's consequent focus on beefing up border security, derailed the talks. Finally, in 2004 President Bush issued a sweeping plan to reform U.S. immigration laws, which included a guest-worker program that would give illegal immigrants living in the United States on January 7, 2004, temporary work permits for a period of three years, but no path to permanent residency. Bush's plan faced resistance on Capitol Hill, with members of his own party in favor of securing America's porous borders and stemming the flow of illegal immigrants, rather than legalizing illegal immigrants already in the United States. In 2007 the Senate, at odds over whether to provide undocumented immigrants with an avenue to citizenship, failed to pass a broad immigration bill.

How have undocumented Mexican immigrants made it over the border?

In the 1960s, 1970s, and 1980s, some undocumented Mexican immigrants commonly crossed the border without guides, an extremely dangerous undertaking, then roamed the Southwest and California until finding work. Others were led or transported across the border after paying a large sum to smugglers, known as coyotes, who profited in the millions in this human traffic. These practices continued in the 1990s and are still prevalent today, but a policy of stricter law enforcement in urban areas along the U.S.-Mexico border, first implemented in 1994 under Operation Gatekeeper, forced border crossers farther and farther off the beaten path and into remote desert areas of eastern California and Arizona to avoid detection, making the crossing all the more perilous. In the years 1993 to 1996, almost 1,200 persons, by official counts, lost their lives in border crossing attempts due to exposure to heat and cold, dehydration, snakebites, injury, and murder.

Increased vigilance at the U.S.-Mexico border after the September 11, 2001, terrorist attacks has made the journey over the U.S.-Mexico border even costlier and riskier, and the death toll remains high, with August the deadliest month of the year. Ironically, some of the dead, usually those with no identification on their bodies, make it to the United States, to a pauper's grave. The hardening of the border has also caused a drop in return migration, with sojourners electing to remain on the U.S. side of the border, rather than returning home and later risking life and limb trying to reenter the United States. In the years 1979–84, the average probability of return was 47 percent, but in the years 1997–2003, it was just 27 percent.

Over the decades, a small number of Mexicans have actually been smuggled into the United States against their will, an atrocious situation that has been likened to the African slave trade. For instance, in 1997 U.S. federal authorities uncovered a smuggling ring that had brought more than fifty deaf and speech-impaired Mexicans into the United States over the course of four years. The ring's bosses lured the Mexicans into servitude with promises of good-paying jobs and a nice lifestyle in the United States. Instead, the enslaved Mexicans were forced to peddle trinkets in airports and on the streets of Los Angeles, New York City, Chicago, Boston, Philadelphia, Washington, and Baltimore. Beatings, electroshock, and threats of violence were used to subdue them.

Who are the border commuters?

Mexican border commuters, or "dailies," are Mexican citizens who live in Mexico and work in the United States, crossing the border with a green card or a border crossing card. Border commuters holding a green card are permitted to work in the United States as long as they maintain continuous employment. Theoretically, they are supposed to reside within the United States, but the INS has looked the other way. In contradistinction, border commuters with a border crossing card, and not a coveted green card, are barred from working in the United States, from remaining in the country for over seventy-two hours, and from traveling more than twenty-five miles from the border. Over the decades, many commuters with border crossing cards have ignored the restrictions and secured employment in the United States. Until rather recently, a common practice among these commuters, once in the United States, was to mail their border crossing cards to Mexico so that if INS authorities apprehended them, their cards would not be confiscated. Commuters sent back to Mexico simply retrieved their border crossing cards and headed north again. Nowadays it's not so easy to execute such a swift return if they are caught.

Some with border crossing cards have managed to remain in the United States by buying round-trip airline tickets to a destination far from the border as soon as they enter the country. Once in Chicago, Detroit, or some other place, they join friends or relatives, who may have found them a job. In the old days, when security at U.S. airports was lax, they would sell their return airline tickets, which provided enough money until the first paycheck. The new arrivals would then lose themselves in the crowd and join the vast underground American economy—but, of course, without legal recourse, and always under the threat of discovery and deportation.

How much money do Mexican immigrants send to Mexico?

The vast majority of legal Mexican immigrants, guest workers, and undocumented immigrants at work in the United States send a portion of their paycheck back home on a regular basis, as financial support for relatives in Mexico. The monies wired home are known as *remesas*, or remittances, and for some Mexican families they are the primary source of income. The Migration Policy Institute estimated that remittances from the United States to Mexico totaled between $6 billion and $8 billion in 2001. By 2005 they had more than doubled, topping $16 billion. The Mexican economy depends heavily on *remesas*; in 2007 they constituted Mexico's second largest source of revenue, after petroleum.

IDENTITY, ACTIVISM, AND *VIVA LA RAZA*

How have Mexican Americans served their country?

Mexican Americans and other Latinos have fought valiantly for their country, and they continue to defend America and the cause of freedom. More than three hundred thousand Latinos, mostly Americans of Mexican ancestry, served proudly in the American armed forces during World War II, and hundreds of thousands more fought in the Korean War, the Vietnam War, the Gulf War, and in the U.S. invasion of Afghanistan. In those conflicts, thousands upon thousands died defending their country, as detailed congressional records, names carved on the Vietnam Veteran's Memorial, and the countless photographs in Latino homes of lost loved ones wearing the uniform attest. At a ceremony honoring Latino war veterans that was held at Santa Ana College on Veterans Day 2001, California governor **Gray Davis** reminded Americans that "Latinos fought bravely for freedom; Latinos died for freedom; Latinos did more than their part to secure victory. Theirs are stories of bravery and sacrifice, and they are stories of America." Mexican Americans and other Latinos continue the brave fight on missions in Afghanistan and in the Iraq War.

World War II, which set the standard for Latino participation in U.S. military campaigns, was also a catalyst for Mexican American self-awareness and self-empowerment. For many Mexican Americans, enlistment meant leaving the crowded barrios for the very first time. Once in the military, they shed their second-class citizenship for the first time as well: In the military, they were treated with far more dignity by whites, alongside whom they trained and fought, than they had been as civilians. Service in World War II also provided Mexican Americans with the opportunity to learn new skills—some drove a vehicle for the very first time—skills that they could not have developed in rural America or in the barrios, and with the chance to further their education. After the war, many took advantage of the GI Bill and enrolled in college. Finally, during and after World War II, a good number of Mexican Americans left the towns of the Southwest and went to work in urban centers that were predominantly white or multiethnic, affording them fresh opportunities and perspectives.

The Mexican Americans who joined mainstream society after the war met with new forms of discrimination. They were discriminated against when it came to employment, since they were competing with Anglos for better blue-collar and white-collar jobs, as well as to housing, jury selection, law enforcement, and public accommodations.

How did Mexican American activism get its start?

Before World War I, Mexican American watchdog groups existed at the local level. One such group was the *Alianza Hispano-Americana*, which was founded in Tucson, Arizona, in 1894, as a Mexican American fraternal benefit society. It offered life insurance at modest rates in an era when citizens could not look to the federal government, labor unions, or commercial life insurance to pay benefits to a family when it lost its chief provider. Chapters of the *Alianza Hispano-Americana* spread across the Southwest, stretching to Texas by 1916. By the mid-1960s, the organization had essentially fulfilled its mission of protecting Mexican American families when no other safety nets existed and had halted most of its operations.

In the aftermath of World War I, several larger Mexican American organizations formed, with the League of United Latin American Citizens (LULAC) at the forefront. LULAC was organized in 1929, a time when Mexican Americans faced virulent discrimination and prejudice, and when their civil and human rights were routinely denied. The organization sought to right the wrongs and to empower Mexican Americans by providing them with legal aid, by fighting for their right to vote wherever it was denied, and by participating in other activities to ensure their equal rights. Over time LULAC came to represent not only Mexican Americans, but all Latinos. Today it remains committed to the betterment of life for Latinos, addressing such important issues as discrimination, poverty, immigration, educational inequality, and the Latino student drop-out rate. In the over seventy years it has existed, LULAC has branched out to every state in the Union, as well as to Puerto Rico, and now boasts over six hundred councils across the nation.

In response to a lack of educational opportunities for Mexican Americans, excessive abuse by the police, discrimination in government services, widespread prejudice, and, ultimately, the Zoot Suit Riots, **Antonio Rios**, **Edward R. Roybal**, and **Fred Ross Sr.** formed the Community Service Organization (CSO) in 1947, with financial backing from **Saul Alinsky**, the pioneering Chicago community organizer. The CSO's cofounders recognized that reversing the tide of anti–Mexican American prejudice and discrimination required a unified Latino voting bloc, as well as Latino political representation. Toward these aims, they organized voter registration drives and get-out-the-vote drives in Latino communities throughout California and, together with other Mexican American organizations, groomed Mexican Americans for public office. In its heyday in the 1960s, the CSO was one of the most influential organizations in the state of California.

One Mexican American politician with CSO backing was CSO cofounder Edward R. Roybal, who had run unsuccessfully for a seat on the Los Angeles City Council in 1947. With the support of the CSO, Roybal won election to the Los Angeles City Council in 1949. Realizing what political organization could do for Mexican Americans, in 1960 **Eduardo Quevedo** and **Bert Corona** founded the Mexican American Political Association (MAPA) in Fresno, California, which in its long history has been devoted to getting Mexican Americans elected to political office. Corona, a union organizer and political activist, dedicated much of his life to improving conditions for Mexican American workers. Other groups, such as the American GI Forum, which was organized by a Mexican American veteran, fought discrimination in the workplace and in public arenas.

On the heels of **John F. Kennedy**'s election to the U.S. presidency in 1960 (in which he garnered 85 percent of the Mexican American vote), leaders from MAPA, LULAC, the CSO, and Cuban American and Puerto Rican groups met in Phoenix, Arizona, with spokespersons from the Viva Kennedy Club, a Latino organization that had campaigned for Kennedy. This historic meeting led to the creation of the Political Association of Spanish-Speaking Organizations (PASSO), headed by **Albert Peña**, commissioner of Bexar County, Texas. PASSO was committed to the advancement of Mexican Americans through the enactment of social and economic measures. At the outset, PASSO concentrated much of its effort in Texas, where in 1963 it managed to defeat the entrenched Anglo machinery by having an all–Mexican American city council elected that year in the South Texas town of Crystal City. This was accomplished by organizing the town's large number of Mexican Americans—who were mostly farm laborers or cannery laborers at Del Monte Foods, the town's largest employer—into a powerful political bloc. Crystal City's all–Mexican American city council was a stunning first for Mexican Americans and a harbinger of things to come.

In 1968 the Mexican American Legal Defense and Educational Fund (MALDEF) was founded in San Antonio, Texas, to defend the civil rights of Latinos and to empower them through community education. MALDEF has evolved over the years into the nation's preeminent nonprofit Latino litigation, advocacy, and educational outreach organization. For about four decades, it has been at the vanguard of civil rights litigation, winning landmark cases that have secured Latinos equal access to employment, the political process, and education. In addition, MALDEF has offered Latinos leadership development programs, in which they are given the tools and know-how to serve on policy-making boards and commissions at the local, state, and national levels. Lastly, the organization has empowered generations of Latino parents by instructing them on how to secure a quality education for their children.

Who was César Chávez?

César Estrada Chávez was a Mexican American migrant worker who rose from the agricultural valley of Yuma, Arizona, to organize America's first successful farmworkers' union. **Robert F. Kennedy** once described the agrarian labor leader as "one of the heroic figures of our time."

Born on March 31, 1927, César Chávez spent his early years on his family's small farm near Yuma, Arizona. During the Great Depression, his parents lost their land, and the family moved to California to labor in the fields as migrant workers. César joined his parents, harvesting carrots, cotton, and grapes under the burning sun wherever they could find work. The family pulled up stakes so often that young César attended over thirty elementary schools, many segregated, and then dropped out in the seventh grade to harvest crops full time.

After serving in the U.S. Navy during World War II, Chávez settled in Delano, California, where he met **Helen Fabela**, whom he married in 1948. It was here that he resolved to help his people out of the miserable working conditions they had accepted for generations. In 1952 Chávez joined the Community Service Organization (CSO), which was formed in 1947 by **Antonio Rios**, **Edward R. Roybal**, and **Fred Ross Sr.**, and was devoted to building a unified Latino voting bloc and fostering Latino political representation as a strategy to ending prejudice and discrimination aimed at Mexican Americans. Chávez's job was to register Mexican Americans in San Jose, California, to vote, and to serve as their advocate before welfare boards, immigration authorities, and the police. In 1958 Mexican American **Dolores Huerta** became his principal assistant.

By the early 1960s, César Chávez had turned his full attention to the plight of exploited Mexican American farmworkers, who worked for extremely low wages, enjoyed no seniority rights or fringe benefits, and had no power to confront their bosses' abuses or unfair labor contracts. In 1962 Chávez left the CSO to form a union, the Farm Workers Association (FWA), which was the forerunner of the National Farm Workers Association (NFWA). By 1965 he had recruited 1,700 families and had persuaded two large California growers to raise the wages of migrant workers. A year later the NFWA merged with the Agricultural Workers Organizing Committee (AWOC), an organization of primarily Filipino farmworkers that was led by **Larry Itliong** in Delano, to form the United Farm Workers Organizing Committee (UFWOC).

The UFWOC went to work immediately picketing table-grape growers in Delano who paid unfair wages. This marked the beginning of *La Huelga* (The Strike), a strike against grape growers in California's San Joaquin, Imperial, and Coachella valleys, which lasted five years and raised America's consciousness about the horrendous conditions and slave wages Mexican and Mexican American farmworkers had endured in the United States for many decades. To gain support for his cause, which he called *La Causa*, César Chávez staged hunger strikes, peaceful marches, and sing-ins, in the spirit of the Indian political and spiritual leader **Mahatma Gandhi**. He also had himself and UFWOC members arrested in order to garner attention.

Although he was a rather meek and self-effacing person, whose gifts lay not so much in public speaking as in leading, César Chávez was able to rouse the multitudes with his deeply felt convictions. He also captured the imagination of fair-minded people all across the nation: Seventeen million Americans, from the Oregon coast to the rivers and dales of Pennsylvania, supported his boycott and refused to buy California table grapes for five straight years. Priests, nuns, rabbis, Protestant ministers, unionists, writers, artists, college students, schoolchildren, and influential politicians, including **Hubert Humphrey** and **Robert F. Kennedy**, lent their support, demanding long-overdue justice for Mexican and Mexican American farmworkers.

In 1970, after losing millions of dollars to *La Huelga*, the California grape growers capitulated, agreeing to grant rights to workers and to raise their minimum wage. It was the first of many successful boycotts that César Chávez was to lead on behalf of grape pickers, lettuce pickers, and all the other disenfranchised groups so dear to his heart. Chávez believed in fairness, equality, and opportunity for all people; he fought for civil rights for African Americans, women, and, in later years, for gays and lesbians. In 1975 the California legislature passed the first collective bargaining act for farmworkers in the continental United States, due in large measure to César Chávez's efforts. La Causa had its share of setbacks after that first victory in 1970, and membership in the UFW, as the UFWOC was renamed in 1972, waned, but Mexican Americans never lost faith in César Chávez, their beloved leader, whom they likened to Moses, bringing them across the desert into a land of possibilities, with greater justice for all.

César Chávez's untimely death on April 23, 1993, at the age of sixty-six, elicited eulogies and expressions of bereavement from national and international leaders and an obituary on the front page of the *New York Times*. Since his death, dozens of schools, libraries, streets, parks, and other public spaces across the nation have been renamed in his honor. In 1994, at a White House ceremony, **President Bill Clinton** posthumously awarded César Chávez the Medal of Freedom, the nation's highest civilian honor. A decade later, in 2004, the United States Postal Service honored this crusader for social change with a postage stamp. Eight states (Arizona, California, Colorado, Michigan, New Mexico, Texas, Utah, and Wisconsin) have declared March 31 an official holiday in honor of César Chávez.

What is the Chicano movement?

The Chicano movement emerged in the 1960s from the unrest fomented by the Vietnam War and the African American civil rights movement led by **Martin Luther King Jr.** By forming one of the first unions to fight for the rights of Mexican Americans, **César Chávez** did much to propel the Chicano movement, and in many ways he has remained the symbolic leader of *la raza*. But several other early Mexican American civil rights advocates and groups also contributed to the formation of the Chicano movement.

In the 1960s, Chicano student organizations, such as the United Mexican American Students (UMAS) and *Movimiento Estudiantil Chicano de Aztlán* (MEChA), became actively involved in educating Mexican Americans about the injustices they had suffered as a people and in urging them to fight for their rights as American citizens, creating an awareness of "Mexicanism" and Latino heritage. The student organizations held demonstrations, demanding that their language, culture, and contributions be recognized in all educational institutions, from elementary schools to universities. The famous civil rights organization the Brown Berets—a self-defense group supporting Chicano community action and patterned after the Black Berets—was formed in 1967 by **David Sanchez** and spawned dozens of chapters throughout the Southwest. The Brown Berets' platform, while committed to nonviolence, vigorously emphasized the inclusion of Mexican American contributions in all school curricula, as well as a permanent place for Mexican American writers and artists in cultural and civic institutions.

One of the legends of the early Chicano movement is **Reies López Tijerina**, an activist born in Texas, whose family land had been seized by Anglos. Convinced that the social problems that Mexican Americans faced were connected to the loss of their ancestral lands, Tijerina organized a separatist movement called the *Alianza Federal de Mercedes* (Federal Alliance of Land Grants) in 1963. The organization, which grew to around twenty thousand members, demanded that millions of acres in New Mexico, Colorado, Utah, California, and Texas be returned to the descendants of their original Mexican owners and proposed that part of the "reclaimed" land be converted to a utopian Mexican American separatist community.

Tijerina and *Alianza* members made their demands known

in myriad ways. In July 1966, Tijerina led a three-day, sixty-two-mile march from Albuquerque, New Mexico, to Santa Fe, where he presented New Mexico governor **Jack Campbell** with a petition requesting the passage of legislation that would allow for an investigation of Mexican land grants. Tijerina announced that he represented six thousand Mexican Americans who were direct heirs to lands that had been seized unlawfully from their forbears. In 1966 Tijerina and *Alianza* members briefly took over part of the Carson National Forest, in northern New Mexico. Then, in June 1967, he and twenty of his followers stormed the courthouse in the little town of Tierra Amarilla, near Chama, New Mexico, to make a citizen's arrest of the Tierra Amarilla district attorney, who had tried to block a mass meeting of *Alianza* members. In the hunt for the district attorney, a sheriff and a jailer were shot, two police officers were beaten, and a reporter was detained.

Tijerina fled the scene, and a massive search for him and his cohorts ensued. Police caught up with the activist two weeks later in Albuquerque. He was arrested and tried on two counts of assault to commit murder, kidnapping, possession of a deadly weapon, and destruction of state property, but in 1968 Albuquerque jurors found Tijerina innocent of all charges. Later he was convicted on federal charges related to another incident and spent several years behind bars in El Paso. In 1970 Tijerina resigned as leader of the *Alianza*. While his efforts to secure Mexican Americans their ancestral acreage were unsuccessful, Tijerina's speeches and demonstrations served to focus attention on Mexican American grievances and the fight for equal rights. Tijerina recounts his efforts to reclaim Mexican Americans' ancestral land and his time spent in jail in his autobiography, *They Called Me "King Tiger": My Struggle for the Land and Our Rights*, originally self-published and then published by Arte Público Press in 2000.

Another Mexican American activist with a separatist vision is **Rodolfo "Corky" Gonzáles**, who in Denver in 1966 founded *La Cruzada para la Justicia* (the Crusade for Justice), an organization seeking to address social ills in Mexican American communities. Among his goals was to persuade the United Nations to hold a plebiscite in the American Southwest to determine independence for *la raza* and the creation of a separate Mexican American state. Toward that aim, Gonzáles created *El Plan Espiritual de Aztlán*, the Spiritual Plan of Aztlán. (Aztlán is the name Mexican Americans have given to their ancestral lands in the American Southwest. It is a mythical homeland where the Aztecs, a nomadic tribe, are said to have dwelled before journeying southward in 1325 and founding Tenochtitlán, the capital of the Aztec empire, on the site of present-day Mexico City.) The Spiritual Plan of Aztlán, which was voted on in 1969 by two thousand representatives from one hundred Chicano organizations, called for a revival of Mexican American values and the creation of a political party based on self-determination. While a separate Mexican American state was never created under the plan, it served to reinforce Mexican American identity and self-respect, and to inspire Mexican American youth.

Corky Gonzáles is also well known for the 1967 epic poem he penned, *"Yo soy Joaquín"* ("I Am Joaquín," a reference to **Joaquín Murieta**). In the poem, Gonzáles explores Mexican Americans' plight and admonishes Chicano youth to aim high and seize their rightful place in American society. *"Yo soy Joaquín"* is read in many Latino history and literature courses in the United States today and continues to inspire millions of young Mexican Americans and other Latino youths.

Named one of the "100 Outstanding Latino Texans of the Twentieth Century" by *Latino Monthly* in 2000, **José Ángel Gutiérrez**, another Chicano leader, was a founding member of the Mexican American Youth Organization (MAYO), which formed in San Antonio in 1967, and of the political party *La Raza Unida* (Mexican Americans United), which was organized in 1970, with the aim of ending discrimination against Chicanos by helping them gain access to mainstream politics and financial institutions. At the time, Gutiérrez also advocated bilingual and bicultural education, which he viewed as a means of preserving Mexican American identity.

César Chávez, Reies López Tijerina, Corky Gonzáles, José Ángel Gutiérrez, and other leaders of the Chicano movement were instrumental in righting many of the wrongs that the Mexican American community had withstood for centuries. Through their efforts, Mexican and Mexican American workers won the right to fair pay and humane treatment; public infrastructure, such as sewage and water systems and utilities, was introduced in impoverished Mexican American communities; poor Mexican American children gained access to vital health care and better education, and doors to higher education institutions were opened to Mexican Americans (and eventually Chicano studies programs were put in place); and works by Mexicans and Mexican Americans made their way into libraries. These leaders were also instrumental in the election of hundreds of Mexican Americans to political office, school boards, and civic organizations, who continue to effect positive change.

How many Mexican Americans are there?

Constituting 63.9 percent of the nation's Latinos in 2005, Mexican Americans are far and away the largest Latino subgroup. A total of 26,784,268 Mexican Americans and Mexican nationals—10,993,851 of them foreign born—lived in the United States in 2005 according to the Pew Hispanic Center tabulations of the U.S. Census Bureau's 2005 American Community Survey. This figure represents a substantial increase in numbers from five years earlier, when Census 2000 tallied 20,640,711 people of Mexican origin in the United States, and it is double the number counted a decade earlier, in 1990, when the U.S. Census Bureau tallied 13,393,208 Mexican Americans and Mexican nationals residing in the United States.

Census 2000 data indicate that the five states with the largest Mexican population in 2000 were California (8,455,926), Texas (5,071,963), Illinois (1,144,390), Arizona (1,065,578), and Colorado (450,760).

MEXICAN AMERICAN WOMEN: REVOLUTIONARIES, THINKERS, HEALERS, AND MOTHERS

What exactly is machismo?

The word "machismo" has the same root as *macho*, which is Spanish for "male gender." But, of course, machismo is much more than that: it connotes strength, bravery, power, and importance, ideal qualities in a patriarchal culture. The term "macho man," coined by the late-1970s disco band Village People in their 1978 hit song "Macho Man," refers to a tough hombre (another word Americans borrowed from Spanish, meaning, of course, "man") who struts his stuff and gets no guff.

With machismo in place, it is no wonder that historical accounts of Mexican Americans and of all Latinos, until recent times, give short shrift to women's contributions. In this respect,

Mexican American history is no different from Anglo history as it has been traditionally chronicled: men are almost always the protagonists.

Is there such a thing as macha?

There is one aspect of machismo that has eluded Anglos but that is essential to the Mexican American—and, to a lesser extent, Latino—outlook on the world. This is that a woman can also be very macho (*muy macha*). In fact, mariachis on both sides of the border sing dozens of popular songs about *macha* women. This does not mean that these women are masculine or imitate men. Rather, they are brave, strong, and resolute, and they probably drink tequila straight and eat jalapeño chiles whole—all macho virtues, but not necessarily limited to the male gender. Thus, Mexicans and Mexican Americans might refer to a gutsy woman as *muy macha* without challenging her womanliness in the least. If anything, being *muy macha* adds to it. After all, if a society holds certain qualities in high esteem, doesn't it figure these qualities enhance all individuals who possess them?

Still, institutionalized machismo, together with ethnic discrimination, has relegated Mexican American women and other Latinas to secondary status. Only in recent decades have Mexican American women strived to claim the respect that they deserve. In her book entitled *To Split a Human: Mitos, Machos y la Mujer Chicana* (1985), feminist scholar **Carmen Tafolla** delineates the nature of Mexican American women's struggle: "the Chicana may . . . find herself curiously placed on a borderland between two forces. In one camp, her struggle against sexism is trivialized. In the other, her struggle against racism is ignored."

What's a curandera?

A *curandera* is a Mexican or Mexican American woman who practices the ancient art of spiritual or herbal "folk" healing that is rooted in the Americas. (Male folk healers are called *curanderos*.) Many *curanderas* combine their faith in the Virgin of Guadalupe and a reverence for the ancient Maya and Aztec gods with knowledge of herbology. Across America, thousands of cases have been documented of *curanderas* healing children and adults of every illness known to humanity—from whooping cough to cancer. *Curanderas* are so highly esteemed among Mexican Americans that some medical doctors, acknowledging at the very least the spiritual and emotional healing that *curanderas* promote, have them on staff at medical clinics and also consult them in psychiatric cases. Some *curanderas* have gained enormous recognition and give packed lectures and workshops on the art of *curanderismo*.

What's a partera?

A *partera* is a midwife—and much more. In economically deprived Mexican American communities, where increasingly children are born into households headed by single women, *parteras* not only deliver babies at home, they serve as *curanderas*, help keep families running while mothers recover, and even babysit. Some rural and urban Mexican Americans, especially in the Southwest, prefer to give birth at home, not only for financial reasons, but for the comfort derived from having someone they know well and trust in charge of the birth.

Who are the notable women in Mexican and Chicano history?

Even when their voices were silenced, the influence of Mexican and Mexican American women was felt profoundly throughout history.

Chicano feminists include in their pantheon of heroines **Francisca de Hozas**, who accompanied Spanish conquistador **Francisco Vásquez de Coronado** during his exploratory expedition (1540–1542) of what is now the American Southwest, and **Gertrudis Bocanegra**, who took part in the revolt against Spanish colonial rule that was sparked by the *Grito de Dolores* in 1810, and was later taken prisoner and executed by Spanish loyalists. During Mexico's struggle for independence, **Manuela Medina**, nicknamed *La Capitana*, led an entire company of rebels and won several crucial battles, while **Doña Josefa Ortiz de Dominguez**, called *La Corregidora* (the Chief), fought valiantly, distinguishing herself with her flawless marksmanship.

During the frontier days, hundreds of Mexican and Mexican American women struggled bravely for their rights and sometimes paid with their lives. In 1863 **Doña Chepita Rodríguez**, who had fled to Texas with her father after **General Santa Anna** rose to power in Mexico in 1835, fought off the advances of two Anglos who stormed into her cabin. She was accused of murdering one of the Anglos when his body was found a little while later. She has gone down in history as one of only three women hanged by the criminal justice system in Texas. In California, **Josefa Segovia** was lynched for stabbing a drunken Anglo miner who tore down the door of her cabin on July 4, 1851, and called her a whore when she asked him to pay for the damage.

Chicano feminists also include in their pantheon of heroines *Las Adelitas* (the Little Adeles), who were the women warriors of the Mexican Revolution (1910–17), and those women who stayed behind the front lines, cleaning equipment, preparing meals, nursing the wounded, and burying the dead. (The original **Adela** was **Pancho Villa**'s lover, and she often rode with him astride his horse, blasting away at the hacendados, or ranch owners, with a shotgun.) *Las Adelitas* became a symbol of feminist empowerment for the Chicano movement after the 1970s.

In 1938 **Emma Tenayuca**, a natural-born leader at a time when women and Mexicans in America had no voice, organized the first successful strike of Mexican women pecan shellers in San Antonio, Texas, and lit the flame of possibility that would later burn in **César Chávez**'s heart. During the mass deportation from the United States of Mexican nationals and Mexican Americans in the 1930s, **Josefina Sierro** organized an underground railroad in the tradition of **Harriet Tubman**, bringing back home to the United States hundreds of American citizens of Mexican descent who had been deported to Mexico. She also single-handedly negotiated with **Vice President Henry Wallace** to make Los Angeles out of bounds to military personnel during the Zoot Suit Riots—an act that helped bring an end to the violence being perpetrated against the city's Mexican American youth. (One aspect of the Zoot Suit Riots that is often overlooked is that the attacks were not only racially motivated, but also sexually charged. The sailors and Anglo civilians who hunted down Mexican Americans to beat up also raped dozens of Mexican American women.)

Among the leaders of the Chicano labor movement of the 1960s and 1970s were **Marcela Lucero-Trujillo**, an activist in **Corky Gonzáles**'s Crusade for Justice; **Virginia Musquiz**, who was instrumental in organizing *La Raza Unida* party; and **Dolores Huerta**, who worked side by side with **César Chávez** in organizing Mexican American farmworkers into the United Farm Workers Organizing Committee (UFWOC). Huerta played a critical role in the union's success in *La Huelga*, the strike against grape growers in California. In 1988 she was brutally attacked by police officers in front of a hotel in San Francisco where **President George Bush** (senior) was attending a campaign dinner party. She was conducting a peaceful demonstration in response to the president's remarks that he would not support the UFWOC boycott of table grapes.

CULTURAL HERITAGE: A MOVABLE FIESTA

Who are some of the great contemporary Mexican American writers?

In the Southwest, where hundreds of ethnic jokes aimed at Mexican Americans make the rounds, there is one that goes: "Why is there no Mexican literature?" Answer: "Because spray paint hasn't been on the market for very long!" This double-edged joke insinuates that Mexican American mural artists paint nothing but graffiti and that Mexican Americans have created no body of literature, and thus no culture. This, of course, could not be further from the truth. In fact Mexican Americans and other Latinos have for decades been among the most dynamic writers on the contemporary American literary scene.

There are far too many Mexican American fiction and non-fiction writers to list, but here are the most prominent, with just a few of their works cited. Among women writers (in alphabetical order) are **Ana Castillo**, *The Mixquiahuala Letters* (1986), *Loverboys: Stories* (1996), and *I Ask the Impossible: Poems* (2001); **Denise Chávez**, *The Last of the Menu Girls* (1986), *Face of an Angel* (1993), and *Loving Pedro Infante* (2001); **Sandra Cisneros**, *The House on Mango Street* (1984), *My Wicked Wicked Ways* (1987), *Woman Hollering Creek and Other Stories* (1991), and *Caramelo* (2002); **Roberta Fernández**, *Intaglio: A Novel in Six Stories* (1990); **Montserrat Fontes**, *First Confession* (1991) and *Dreams of the Centaur* (1996); **Maria Hinojosa**, *Raising Raul: Adventures Raising Myself and My Son* (1999); **Patricia Preciado Martín**, *Images and Conversations: Mexican Americans Recall a Southwestern Past* (1983), *El Milagro and Other Stories* (1996), and *Amor Eterno: Eleven Lessons in Love* (2000); **Demetria Martínez**, *Mother Tongue* (1994), *The Devil's Workshop* (2002), and *Confessions of a Berlitz-Tape Chicana* (2005); **Pat Mora**, *House of Houses* (1997); **Cherríe Moraga**, *This Bridge Called My Back: Writings by Radical Women of Color* (1981; coedited with **Gloria Anzaldúa**) and *Loving in the War Years* (1983); **Estela Portillo**

Trambley, *Rain of Scorpions and Other Stories* (1975), *Trini* (1986), and *Sor Juana and Other Plays* (1983); **Alma Luz Villanueva,** *Blood Root* (1977); and **Helena María Viramontes,** *The Moths and Other Stories* (1985), *Under the Feet of Jesus* (1995), and *Their Dogs Came with Them* (2007).

Among the men (in alphabetical order) are **Oscar Zeta Acosta,** *The Autobiography of a Brown Buffalo* (1972) and *The Revolt of the Cockroach People* (1989); **Rodolfo "Rudy" Acuña,** *Occupied America: A History of Chicanos* (1981) and *Anything but Mexican: Chicanos in Contemporary Los Angeles* (1995); **Rudolfo Anaya,** *Bless Me, Ultima* (1972), *Tortuga* (1979), *Shaman Winter* (1999), and *Elegy on the Death of César Chávez* (2002); **Jimmy Santiago Baca,** *Winter Poems Along the Rio Grande* (2004) and *The Importance of a Piece of Paper: Stories* (2004); **Rodolfo "Corky" Gonzáles,** *I Am Joaquín / Yo soy Joaquín* (1964) and *Message to Aztlán: Selected Writings* (2001); **Rolando Hinojosa,** *Estampas del valle y otras obras / Sketches of the Valley and Other Works* (1973), *The Useless Servants* (1993), and *We Happy Few* (2006); **John Rechy,** *City of Night* (1963), *Numbers* (1967), *Marilyn's Daughter* (1988), *The Miraculous Day of Amalia Gomez* (1991), *Our Lady of Babylon* (1996), *The Life and Adventures of Lyle Clemens* (2003), and *Beneath the Skin: The Collected Essays of John Rechy* (2004); **Tomás Rivera,** *. . . y no se lo tragó la tierra / And the Earth Did Not Devour Him* (1971) and *The Harvest: Short Stories* (1989); **Luis J. Rodriguez,** *The Concrete River* (1991) and *Always Running: La Vida Loca: Gang Days in L.A.* (1993); **Richard Rodriguez,** *Hunger of Memory: The Education of Richard Rodriguez* (1981), *Days of Obligation: An Argument with My Mexican Father* (1992), and *Brown: The Last Discovery of America* (2003); **Gary Soto,** *The Tale of Sunlight* (1978), *Black Hair* (1985), *Living Up the Street* (1985), and *The Effects of Knut Hamsun on a Fresno Boy: Recollections and Short Essays* (2000); **Sergio Troncoso,** *The Last Tortilla & Other Stories* (1999) and *The Nature of Truth* (2003); **José Antonio Villarreal,** *Pocho* (1970); and **Victor Villaseñor,** *Macho!* (1971), *Rain of Gold* (1991), *Thirteen Senses: A Memoir* (2001), *Burro Genius: A Memoir* (2004), and *Crazy Loco Love: A Memoir* (2006).

Is Chicano mural painting a recent phenomenon?

Chicano mural painting has its roots in ancient Mexico and the early Olmec tradition of adorning walls with paintings. The Mexican mural tradition underwent a renaissance in the 1920s, with internationally acclaimed Mexican artists, including **José**

Clemente Orozco, **David Alfaro Siqueiros**, and **Diego Rivera**, known together as the Big Three, leading the way. While the Works Progress Administration, the largest New Deal agency, was in effect from 1935 to 1943, the U.S. government commissioned these Mexican mural masters to create public murals in America that promoted the New Deal agenda, the core of which was social and economic reform and relief to benefit the poor and the working class, who were hit hardest by the Great Depression.

Through their work in the United States, Orozco, Siqueiros, and Rivera laid the foundation for the emergence of the Chicano mural tradition in the 1960s and 1970s as an expression of the Chicano movement. In these decades, hundreds of young Mexican Americans took to the streets of cities in California, the Southwest, and the Midwest to celebrate their cultural heritage and to transform, with large murals, the bleak urban landscape of the barrios and working-class neighborhoods.

One of the founders of the mural movement in Los Angeles is nationally renowned Mexican American muralist, activist, and academician **Judy Baca**, who in 1974 launched the city's first mural program, which created over four hundred public murals during its ten years in operation. Judy Baca's most celebrated work is *The Great Wall of Los Angeles*, a half-mile-long mural—the world's longest—adorning the San Fernando Valley's Tujunga Wash, a section of the drainage system in Los Angeles, and chronicling the history of California's ethnic peoples from their origins to the 1950s. It took the efforts of forty artists and nearly 450 young people, from different ethnic backgrounds, over seven summers, from 1976 to 1984, to complete the project. The work was sponsored by the Social and Public Art Resource Center (SPARC) in Venice, California, a nonprofit, multiethnic arts center that Baca cofounded in 1976. SPARC creates, preserves, and documents community-based public artworks, which, the organization asserts, are an avenue for addressing social issues. It encourages youth involvement and community participation in art making and also offers educational programs. In 1988 Judy Baca developed another city mural program, the Great Walls Unlimited: Neighborhood Pride program, at the request of LA mayor **Tom Bradley**. The program enlisted more than a thousand at-risk youths, who created over eighty murals in nearly every ethnic neighborhood in the city.

Other Mexican American muralists painting politically motivated work in Los Angeles and in other California cities in the

1970s were members of the group called Los Four: **Frank Romero, Carlos Almarez, Gilbert Sánchez Luján,** and **Beto de la Rocha**. In the same decade, an artist by the name of **Gronk**, and others, under the guidance of **Charles Felix**, contributed to the most extensive mural project in East Los Angeles, the murals at Estrada Courts, a low-income housing project in Boyle Heights. The murals, with their larger-than-life images of Aztec gods, Our Lady of Guadalupe, members of the United Farm Workers, and others, serve to remind Chicanos of their origins, trials, and triumphs.

Chicano Park in Logan Heights (Barrio Logan), a largely Mexican American and Mexican immigrant community in southeast San Diego, where Mexicans first began settling in the 1890s, contains some of the finest muralist art in the tradition of the Mexican mural movement of the 1920s and 1930s. It all started in the late 1960s, when some Logan Heights residents were evicted from their dwellings and businesses were closed to make way for the San Diego–Coronado Bridge, which opened in 1969. As compensation for these losses, the community earned the right, not without a fight, to build a park and a Chicano cultural center in the area under the bridge. What had been a jungle of ugly concrete pillars metamorphosed into a park adorned with murals depicting decisive moments and key figures in Mexican American history. Murals at the freeway entrances portray **César Chávez** addressing Mexican Americans and the struggles of Mexican workers and peasants from the past, such as **Zapata**'s guerillas. The documentary film *Chicano Park* (1989) offers a fascinating look at some of the artists, musicians, and activists who contributed to the transformation of Barrio Logan and who expressed in their art and activism the cultural and social aspirations of a people whose voices were just then beginning to be heard.

How many holidays do Mexican Americans celebrate?

There are far too many to count, because most hamlets, towns, and cities with a sizable Mexican American population have their own distinct holidays, some of which involve celebrating patron saints (*santos*). An important Mexican holiday that binds all Mexican Americans, though all do not partake in it, is *El Día de los Muertos* (the Day of the Dead), which represents an amalgam of pre-Columbian and Roman Catholic beliefs. *El Día de los Muertos* falls on November 1 and 2, coinciding with All Saints' Day and All Souls' Day. During the festivities, Mexican Americans do not mourn deceased family members and friends, who are believed to pay a visit to the earthly realm on this holiday, but rather honor their lives and interact joyously with their souls, in the belief that but a fragile boundary separates the living and the dead.

In keeping with Mexican tradition, Mexican Americans commonly set up *ofrendas*, or miniature altars, in their homes and at festivals, which they bedeck with candles, incense, favorite foods and objects of the deceased, flowers (especially yellow marigolds, the traditional flower of the dead), loaves called Bread of the Dead (customarily in the shape of skulls and crossbones), and colorfully decorated miniature candy skulls. Also in keeping with tradition, celebrants flock to the cemetery to tidy the graves of loved ones and hold a picnic for the dead souls, who are said to regain their appetite on this holiday, consuming, it is believed, the smell of the food and drink.

Another important holiday that Mexican Americans celebrate en bloc is the Feast of Our Lady of Guadalupe, the patron saint of Mexico and the Americas, who is honored on December 12. The holiday memorializes the appearance of the Blessed Virgin Mary (Our Lady of Guadalupe) to a converted native named **Juan Diego** in Mexico in 1521. Our Lady of Guadalupe dispatched Juan Diego to a bishop, with the request to construct a church in her honor on the hillside where she appeared. She miraculously emblazoned her image on Juan Diego's poncho, and the sight of it convinced the bishop that Juan Diego spoke the truth. This miracle led to the subsequent construction of the church and inspired the conversion of large numbers of native peoples in Mexico. When **Father Hidalgo** uttered Our Lady of Guadalupe's name as he rallied Mexicans to fight for independence in 1810, with his *Grito de Dolores*, Our Lady of Guadalupe was transformed into an emblem of Mexican nationalism. Catholics have embraced the saint as their own. Many maintain that she is not the Virgin Mary at all, and they forgo the Festival of the Immaculate Conception of the Virgin Mary for the Feast of Our Lady of Guadalupe.

During the Christmas season, Mexican Americans commonly observe *Las Posadas*, celebrated on the nine days before Christmas, when mass is held at sunrise each day and celebrants reenact Mary and Joseph's journey to Bethlehem and their search for shelter at an inn (*una posada*) before the birth of Jesus. *Las Posadas* culminates with *Misa de Gallo*, Midnight mass on Christmas Eve. On Christmas Day, Mexican Americans customarily remain at home and partake of traditional Mexican Christmas fare. Christmas is a time for *tamalada*, the making of steamy tamales, corn dumplings stuffed with various meat or vegetable fillings, including chicken, pork, turkey, squash blossoms, and even shrimp, and wrapped in corn husks or banana leaves. *Tamalada* is a collaborative effort, and several generations might gather in the kitchen to make the fluffy corn masa, or dough, and the fillings; to soak the husk or leaf wrappers; and to construct, wrap, tie, and steam the tamales, the centerpiece of the Christmas meal. In some homes, in keeping with tradition, children do not receive presents until January 6, *El Día de los Reyes Magos* (Three Kings' Day), which heralds the arrival of the Magi to Bethlehem, bearing gifts for the baby Jesus.

Every autumn in Santa Fe, New Mexico, on the weekend following Labor Day, the Burning of Zozobra, otherwise known as Old Man Gloom, kicks off the Fiestas de Santa Fe, the oldest continuously celebrated festival in the United States. (It was first celebrated in 1712 to commemorate **Diego de Vargas**'s reoccupation of Santa Fe in 1692, twelve years after the Popé Rebellion, when Native Americans in the Spanish province of New Mexico revolted and drove out the Spanish.) During the festival, Old Man Gloom, a fifty-foot marionette, taller than most buildings in the town, is set ablaze and turned to ash, an act signifying the obliteration of the previous year's travails. Just before "Gloom" is ignited, a box of items gathered from celebrants, items that include legal documents (even divorce decrees), letters, and photos, all representative of the past year's worries, is placed inside him. After Old Man Gloom has been consumed by fire, celebrants dance in the streets, shouting, *"¡Viva la fiesta!"*

The Santa Fe Fiesta also features a pet parade (*desfile de los niños*); a pontifical mass; a historical parade (*desfile de la gente*), for which marchers dress as conquistadores and Spanish ladies; and lots of mariachi performances; all culminating in a mass of thanksgiving and a candlelight procession on the final evening. All throughout the festivities, the Santa Fe Fiesta song is on everyone's lips: "*Santa Fe, tus fiestas de septiembre / Se celebran en la capital / Con Zozobra quemando las penas / Ya las fiestas van a comenzar.*" (The English version of the song begins: "In Old Santa Fe, we have La Fiesta / 'Tis the time for singing, dance and play /

On this day we do not take la siesta / While Zozobra burns the gloom away.")

Why do Mexican Americans celebrate Cinco de Mayo?

Cinco de Mayo (the Fifth of May) commemorates Mexico's resistance to, and ultimate liberation from, the French military occupation of the 1860s, the brainchild of **Napoléon III**. On this day in 1862, Mexican forces overpowered the better-armed French occupiers in the Battle of Puebla. While the French went on to defeat Mexican government forces and to install the Hapsburg archduke **Ferdinand Maximilian** of Austria as emperor of Mexico in April 1864, the victory at Puebla emboldened Mexico's freedom fighters, who refused to recognize Maximilian's government and continued to battle the French occupation. Up against Mexican resistance and U.S. opposition to French meddling in Mexico, Napoléon III pulled his forces out of Mexico in 1866 and urged Maximilian to leave the country. Maximilian refused to relinquish power, and in 1867 he was captured in Mexico and executed by a firing squad. It should be added that Cinco de Mayo has nothing to do with Mexican independence from Spanish rule, a feat that is celebrated on September 16.

Cinco de Mayo is a minor holiday in Mexico, but in the United States, it is the biggest Mexican American secular celebration of the year. On Cinco de Mayo, Mexican Americans in towns and cities with sizable Mexican American communities showcase their cultural heritage at fiestas featuring mariachi bands, folk dancing, parades, traditional arts and crafts, and Mexican food and drink. Since the mid-1980s, this holiday has rapidly gained in popularity among all Americans, and just as everyone is Irish on St. Patrick's Day, on Cinco de Mayo, Anglos turn Mexican overnight and join in the revelry. Since taking office, **President George W. Bush** has celebrated Cinco de Mayo at the White House each year, testimony to the fact that this holiday has taken root in mainstream America.

What's a charreada?

A *charreada* is a Mexican rodeo, one that is typically more dangerous than its American descendant, the Western rodeo. (Incidentally, *rodeo* is a Spanish word meaning "a gathering place for cattle.") Mexico's national sport and one quite popular among Mexican Americans, the Mexican *charreada* sprung from both the Spanish tradition of *charrería*, horsemanship, which evolved under the hacienda system in Mexico, and the Spanish *charreada*, which originated in Salamanca, Spain, in the sixteenth century and made its way to Mexico. Mexican *charreadas* were first held in the United States in the 1950s and have grown steadily in popularity. By the mid-1990s, more than eighty-four *charro* federations sponsoring *charreadas* were in operation across the nation.

In the Mexican and Mexican American *charreada*, two or more teams of *charros*, or cowboys, compete against one another in scored riding and roping events. Traditionally, men compete in nine events, including *el paso de la muerte* (the pass of death), in which a *charro* riding bareback, with reins, first tries to leap from his horse onto the back of a wild horse—which is being whipped into a frenzy by three other *charros* on horseback—and then attempts to stay atop the horse, without reins, until it stops bucking. In another men's event, *jineto de toro*, (bull riding), which closely resembles the American rodeo version, *charros* ride bucking bulls. Three of the nine traditional men's events involve horse tripping, where *charros* lasso the legs of a moving horse, causing it to fall or roll to the ground and sometimes seriously or fatally wounding it. These three horse-tripping events were outlawed in several states, including California and New Mexico, in the mid-1990s.

Women on both sides of the U.S.-Mexico border compete in just one event, *escaramuza* (the skirmish), in which teams of eight to twelve women, dressed in Adelita costumes and riding sidesaddle, perform precision riding maneuvers.

What are mariachis?

Since 1979, when the first International Mariachi Conference took place in San Antonio, Texas, mariachi music has evolved into a symbol of Mexican culture in the United States. Mariachi music, a dance music, originated in the Mexican state of Jalisco and includes traditional *sones jaliciences*, *corridos*, *rancheras*, boleros, and much more. Mariachi musicians, known as mariachis, perform in groups of at least seven members, and typically twelve, and play the Spanish guitar, trumpet, violin, *vihuela* (a five-string guitar), and *guitarrón* (a six-string guitar). Dressed in the traditional costumes of Jalisco, which are adorned with sequins, tiny mirrors, glass, and other shiny materials, and sporting large-brimmed, richly decorated sombreros, these roving musicians serenade the crowd with traditional romantic songs, like the old standard *"Cielito lindo,"* in restaurants and at weddings, birthday parties, fiestas, and other public events.

In recent years, the popularity of mariachi has skyrocketed, and more and more Mexican American parents nowadays are signing their children up for mariachi lessons as a way of keeping them in touch with their roots. In the United States (but not in Mexico), increasing numbers of girls and women are taking part in mariachi, historically a male-dominated tradition. The most famous of all is Mexican-Cuban American **Nydia Rojas**, who performed for **President Clinton** at his Hispanic Presidential Inaugural Gala. First performing at the age of nine in Los Angeles–area Mexican restaurants, she honed her skills as a featured vocalist with the all-female band Mariachi Reyna de Los Angeles. Rojas then signed a solo contract with Arista Latin, and in 1996, at age sixteen, she released her self-titled debut album, which showcases boleros, *cumbias*, and *rancheras*, along with typical mariachi numbers. Before long, this talented musician was branching into Latin pop, and in 2001 she cut her first Latin pop album, entitled *Nydia*. In 2005 she changed her stage name but has not released any new works.

What's a piñata party?

Piñata parties are held on children's birthdays and on other special occasions in Mexican American communities and beyond. The piñata, from *piño*, meaning "pine tree," is a hollow straw, clay, or papier-mâché sculpture of a donkey or other animal, a star (the traditional shape in Mexico is a seven-pointed star, representing the seven deadly sins and the devil), or another shape that is decorated with brightly colored paper and sequins. The piñata is filled with toys and candies and then is suspended from the ceiling. Once the party gets going, blindfolded children take turns whacking the piñata with a long stick until it breaks, releasing the surprises hidden inside. The best part is scrambling for the goodies strewn on the floor. It is widely believed that the Spanish introduced the piñata to Mexico, but archeological evidence also suggests that the indigenous peoples of Mexico enjoyed a similar custom at the time of the Spaniards' arrival.

Did Montezuma II eat tacos?

Montezuma II and the Aztec people savored versions of some of the same delicious dishes served today in the thousands of Mexican restaurants and *taquerías* (taco places) all across America. Among the marvelous fare **Hernán Cortés** and his men discovered on Montezuma's lavish table were tomatoes, avocados, chiles, corn, coconuts, papayas, tamales, tortillas, turkey, duck, pork, and, much to the disgust of the Spanish, little hairless dogs. Traditional Mexican cuisine, like Mexican culture, is an amalgam of native, Spanish, and, to a lesser extent, African ingredients and methods. However, the ingredients prized by the native peoples dwelling in Mexico and what is now the American Southwest when the conquistadores made landfall are still at the heart of Mexican and Mexican American cooking to this day.

Are tacos, burritos, gorditas, and fajitas the Mexican national dishes?

No way. All of the above are generally regarded as *antojitos* (little whims), hors d'oeuvres, or in more contemporary parlance, fast food. Unfortunately, very few Mexican restaurants in America serve anything but *antojitos*, and Americanized versions at that. Real Mexican cooking can be found only in Mexican American communities. For instance, in authentic *taquerías* in America, tacos and burritos are stuffed with any one of a vast selection of meats, such as marinated pork, grilled beef, tripe, tongue, and stewed pork brains, which are sliced or diced to order and then folded into warm homemade corn or flour tortillas. Diners then dress their order with any one of an assortment of salsas, such as tomatillo salsa or tomato-cilantro salsa (*salsa fresca*).

In recent times, more and more full-scale restaurants serving authentic Mexican fare have opened in America. In these establishments, some of which specialize in regional Mexican cooking, diners can sample everything from *cabrito al horno* (roasted baby goat) and *pollo pibil* (a Yucatecan dish of chicken baked in banana leaves) to *pescado a la veracruzana* (fish cooked in a sauce of tomatoes, capers, and green olives). A common item on the menu is the national dish of Mexico, *mole poblano*, slices of turkey or chicken smothered in a scrumptious sauce made from chiles, nuts, seeds, onions, garlic, tomatoes, bread, cinnamon, cloves, coriander, and the secret ingredient: unsweetened chocolate.

Is chocolate really Mexican?

The Aztecs were the first to husk, roast, and grind cocoa beans, or cacao. They mixed the ground cocoa beans with spices for an unsweetened drink called *xocolatl*, meaning "bitter water." **Montezuma II** believed that *xocolatl* was an aphrodisiac, and he supposedly drank many cups of the elixir each day. Spanish explorer **Hernán Cortés** took cocoa beans back to the Old World, where tamer versions of hot chocolate were concocted with the omission of the spices in the Aztec recipe and the addition of sugar. Eventually, Europeans developed the expertise to create all sorts of confections out of cocoa. For that reason, most people think of Belgium and Switzerland—not Mexico—when they hear the word "chocolate."

Back in Mexico, Montezuma's elixir evolved but never lost its spice. Nowadays Mexicans and Mexican Americans make the drink with steamed milk, sugar, vanilla extract, and lots of cinnamon.

How is New Southwestern Cuisine different from traditional Mexican cooking of the Southwest?

If you have ever tried a dish called anything like "curried chicken tortilla with coconut rice, cucumber raita, and spicy peanut sauce," you know the difference. New Southwestern Cuisine involves blending ingredients from the world's pantry (Asian and French elements dominate) with Mexican staples such as tortillas and chiles, to create ingenious, tasty, and ofttimes whimsical dishes. New Southwestern Cuisine was all the rage among culinary aficionados in the 1990s and early 2000s.

What are pulque, mescal, and tequila?

Distilled spirits are as popular north of the U.S.-Mexico border as south of it. Pulque, the fermented juice of a succulent (an agave, to be precise) called the maguey or the century plant, is brewed like beer and has a sweet, buttermilk-like flavor. The drink has ancient roots: in pre-Columbian times, it was imbibed during religious rituals. Since pulque does not store well, it is rather hard to come by in the United States. Mescal is a liquor made from a variety of agaves and has a smoky, bitter-almond flavor. A good number of mescals are packaged *con gusano*, that is, with a worm in the bottle, which supposedly enhances the flavor of the spirit.

Tequila is the most prized of the mescals, one derived only from the juice of the blue agave, the *agave azul*. First distilled in the sixteenth century, tequila earned its name from its place of origin: Tequila, a town in the western Mexican state of Jalisco. Nowadays tequila—which is never bottled *con gusano*, has a spicy flavor with a hint of sweetness, is classified by how long it has aged, and can be called tequila only if it is manufactured in Mexico—enjoys global popularity. Premium tequilas are distilled from 100 percent blue agave juice and fetch a high price. (Tequilas must contain by law at least 51 percent blue agave juice.) Tequila is highly regarded as a chaser to cool down food spiced with hot chiles.

CUATRO

Puerto Ricans

What is Puerto Rico?

Quick, name a place that's erroneously called a country; whose residents are American citizens but are barred from voting in U.S. presidential elections, do not pay federal income tax, and yet can be drafted by the U.S. military; whose capital city is nearly a hundred years older than Jamestown; whose currency is the U.S. dollar; and whose people are totally fluent in Spanish—and in many, many cases, in English—and are fiercely proud of their land and their rich African, native, and Spanish heritage.

If you answered, "Puerto Rico," you're familiar with some of the numerous contradictions that characterize the history and political status of this earthly paradise, an unincorporated, organized U.S. territory known officially as the Commonwealth of Puerto Rico, which lies approximately one thousand miles southeast of Miami and is comprised of the island of Puerto Rico, measuring about one hundred miles long and thirty-five miles wide, and the offshore islets of Vieques, Mona, and Culebra.

EARLY HISTORY

Why do Puerto Ricans call their island Borinquen?

Borinquen, which means "the land of the brave lord," is the name given Puerto Rico by its indigenous inhabitants, the Taino, who were a subgroup of the Arawak, the collective name of the Amerindians inhabiting the West Indies (the islands in the Caribbean Sea, which are divided into the Lesser Antilles, Great Antilles, and the Bahamas). The Taino, a seafaring people, inhabited not just Puerto Rico, but the other islands of the Greater Antilles (Cuba, Jamaica, and Hispaniola), as well as the Bahamas and some of the islands of the Lesser Antilles (an island group to the east and south of Puerto Rico.) In actuality, the native peoples of Puerto Rico did not call themselves Taino before the Spanish conquest of the Americas. **Christopher Columbus** christened this subgroup of Arawak Indians Taino, meaning "peace," because it was the first word they uttered when they laid eyes on the conquistador.

The Taino were peaceful people, indeed. They fished, hunted, and gathered pineapples and other fruits in their land of plenty. They slept in *hamacas*, a word that entered the English language as "hammock." Another word with Taino roots is "hurricane," from *huracán*, the god of ferocious winds, whom the Taino understood no one would ever tame.

Incidentally, in addition to "Puerto Rican" and *puertorriqueño*, Puerto Ricans call themselves *boricua* (from Borinquen), especially on the U.S. mainland, to reinforce cultural ties and reaffirm ancient roots.

How did San Juan come to be called Puerto Rico, and Puerto Rico, San Juan?

It all began on November 19, 1493, when **Christopher Columbus**, back in the New World on his second voyage, made landfall on Puerto Rico. Columbus was impressed with the wealth of Borinquen, with its lush vegetation and more than two hundred species of birds. He immediately took possession of the island in the name of **Isabella I** and **Ferdinand II** of Spain, calling it San Juan Bautista, after **John the Baptist**, and Isabella I and Ferdinand II's son, **Juan**. At first the island of San Juan Bautista was ignored, for the most part, by the Spanish, who had bigger fish to fry in Mexico and Peru. As for Columbus, he was more interested in Hispaniola and did not settle Puerto Rico.

That job was left to the Spanish conquistador **Juan Ponce de León**, who, in 1508, was dispatched with a crew of fifty to explore the island and determine whether it harbored any gold. There was very little of the precious metal to speak of, as the Spanish discovered later, but the minute Ponce de León glimpsed the bay at San Juan, he exclaimed, *"¡Ay, que puerto rico!"* ("Oh, what a rich port!"). From that moment on, the island was known as Puerto Rico, and the port where Ponce de León anchored, as San Juan (short for San Juan Bautista). San Juan, of course, was designated the capital of Puerto Rico and remains so to this day. The Spaniards quickly gained control of the island, and in 1509 Ponce de León was appointed the first governor of Puerto Rico, serving at that post until 1512. The island's second largest city and the hometown of thousands of mainland Puerto Ricans still bears his name—Ponce.

Why did Ponce de León bring African slaves to Puerto Rico?

The Taino welcomed the Spanish conquistadores with open arms, believing them to be gods. However, they soon regretted having rolled out the welcome mat. The Spanish began their quest for gold by enslaving the native people, confiscating their lands, and appropriating them as a workforce. In exchange for mining the small deposits of placer gold found on the island and tending the fields to feed the conquistadores, the Taino were given lessons in Catholicism and Spanish history and culture. Under these oppressive conditions, hundreds of Taino died of exhaustion, malnutrition, and maltreatment. Others perished because they had no defenses against the European diseases that the Spanish soldiers brought with them. In desperation the Taino rebelled in 1511, after their pleas for better working conditions went unanswered. **Ponce de León** responded by having six thousand Taino shot on the spot. Those who survived the slaughter took to the mountains or rowed away to other islands.

With the Taino labor pool swiftly dwindling, Ponce de León asked Spain's **Ferdinand II** for permission to bring slaves from Africa to the island to work in agriculture and thus keep Puerto Rico's plantation economy afloat. The Spanish were not the first to engage in the transatlantic African slave trade. To cope with a labor shortage in Brazil, in 1502 the Portuguese brought the first African slaves to the Americas. In 1513 the first shipload of African slaves arrived in Puerto Rico. With them also came smallpox, which took thousands of Taino lives. By 1515 fewer than four thousand Taino remained in Puerto Rico, just a fraction of the population **Columbus** had encountered.

Having given up on gold, Ponce de León turned his hand to transforming the island into an agricultural paradise. In 1515 he introduced sugarcane, and the Spanish government funded the construction of sugar mills by the dozens. The African slaves and the few remaining Taino were put to work cultivating and harvesting the crop by hand from dawn till dusk under the scorching tropical sun. The Africans proved sturdiest of all, and their population increased, while the Spanish and native populations dwindled. By 1531 the Spanish in Puerto Rico numbered 426, and the Africans, 2,264. Before long, land was parceled out to Spaniards desiring to settle in Puerto Rico. Each settler who agreed to farm the land (or, more accurately put, to oversee the slaves who farmed the land) and to remain for more than five years was granted between 200 and 1,400 acres. Soon coffee and spices were cultivated in addition to sugarcane, as these luxury items were in great demand back in Europe. By the seventeenth century, tobacco and ginger emerged as the principal crops. With the wealth amassed on the backs of the Taino and African slaves, Puerto Rico thrived. Spain looked anew at its colony in the Caribbean and decided that, indeed, it was a "rich port," a good place to settle, farm, and grow wealthy.

African slavery persisted in Puerto Rico until **Amadeo I**, the king of Spain, abolished the institution there in 1873. By then the Africans, who believed that their ancient Yoruban deities had followed them to Puerto Rico, had grown deep roots in the fertile tropical soil of the island and felt quite at home there. By then also, racial integration, an intermingling of the Taino, Africans, and Spanish of Puerto Rico, had taken root, giving rise eventually to a largely mestizo population. Recent genetic research has uncovered matrilineal indigenous ancestry in 61 percent of Puerto Ricans and patrilineal European ancestry in 75 percent, which means that the majority of Puerto Ricans are mestizos, overturning the prevailing judgment that Puerto Rico's population is comprised of a white majority, smaller mestizo and African segments, an Asian minority, and no Taino.

What do Puerto Ricans mean when they say *negro*?

The word *negro* is Spanish for "black." Black color. Black race. Black sky. Puerto Ricans, whose complexions range from black to fair, have a variety of words to describe skin color. But *negro* is really not one of them. *Negro* and *negrito* are strictly terms of endearment and are used when addressing anyone, even those with flaxen hair and blue eyes.

A dark-skinned or black Puerto Rican is usually referred to as *de color*, meaning "of color." However, an African American in the United States with identical skin color is called *moreno*, or "brown." A person with light brown skin is called *trigueño*, meaning "brunette" or "swarthy." *Blanco* (white) is used for light-skinned persons, and *Indio* refers to a person with native features.

How did Sir Francis Drake get his comeuppance in Puerto Rico?

In 1588, the year England defeated the Spanish Armada, owing to the maritime skills of English mariner **Sir Francis Drake**, the Spanish colonies in the Caribbean, Puerto Rico included, were under assault by the English. It seems that Puerto Rico had yielded little gold, but that San Juan had proven quite valuable to the Spanish as a stopover for galleons laden with treasure that were heading from Mexico and Peru to Spain. However, the galleons anchored in San Juan Bay were sitting ducks for raiders, pirates, and privateers after treasure. Sir Francis Drake, a state-sanctioned part-time privateer, was a pro at raiding Spanish caches in the New World. (Cash-strapped Elizabethan England could not afford a naval reserve, and it was too weak and vulnerable to engage in open aggression against the Spanish. Hence it looked to privateers to act as a naval reserve and engage in private wars and raids on enemy caches, with the state getting a share of the plunder.)

In the last of his marauding expeditions, Drake set sail for Puerto Rico in 1595 with twenty-seven ships and 4,500 troops. By then the Spanish had cottoned on to Drake's antics, and by the time his fleet sighted Puerto Rico, 1,500 Spanish sailors had joined the 300 stationed on the island. The Spanish purposely sank two of their own ships to block Drake's entrance into San Juan Bay. When Sir Francis Drake and his men finally reached

San Juan on November 22, 1595, they were met by an unceasing blast of artillery from the Spanish. The English fleet swiftly withdrew out to sea and then circled the island, searching for a point of entry. But the Spanish were too well fortified to be penetrated. After another unsuccessful sea assault on Puerto Rico in 1596, Sir Francis Drake finally admitted defeat and, as fate would have it, shortly thereafter died of dysentery and was buried at sea.

However, another Englishman, **George Clifford**, third Earl of Cumberland, and a naval commander and courtier to **Queen Elizabeth I**, managed to capture La Fortaleza, the first fortress built to protect San Juan, and to wrest control of San Juan from the Spanish for five months in 1598. It seems a smallpox epidemic had stricken the Spanish soldiers on the island, and they did not have the strength to keep the English at bay. The peoples of Puerto Rico did their best to make life miserable for the English conquerors, who, succumbing to smallpox, fled. The Dutch invaded in 1625 and even burned San Juan, but the Spanish fended off these attackers, too.

IMPORTANT DATES

November 22, 1595	Sir Francis Drake, the English mariner, explorer, and privateer, sails into San Juan Bay.
December 10, 1898	By the Treaty of Paris ending the Spanish-American War, Puerto Rico is ceded to the United States.
April 12, 1900	The United States declares Puerto Rico an unconsolidated U.S. territory under the Foraker Act.
March 2, 1917	President Woodrow Wilson signs the Jones Act, granting all Puerto Ricans U.S. citizenship.
July 25, 1952	The Commonwealth of Puerto Rico is proclaimed.
November 14, 1993	In a nonbinding referendum, the people of Puerto Rico vote in favor of preserving commonwealth status.
December 13, 1998	In another referendum on the island's status, the people of Puerto Rico again elect to remain a commonwealth.

April 1999	Angry protests erupt on the island of Vieques after a Puerto Rican security guard is killed by errant bombs during U.S. Navy bombing practice there.
January 3, 2001	Sila María Calderón is sworn in as governor of Puerto Rico. She is the first woman ever elected to that post.
May 2003	The U.S. Navy halts all training operations on the island of Vieques.

Who was Field Marshal Alejandro O'Reilly?

By the mid-eighteenth century, illegal commerce was thriving in Puerto Rico as Puerto Ricans traded with European buccaneers and privateers behind Spain's back. What's more, the islanders were farming only 5 percent of the land. As a result, trade between Spain and Puerto Rico came to a virtual standstill. Spain was vexed because Spanish taxes were supporting the island, and yet the Spanish were getting little in return. In 1765 the Spanish king sent **Field Marshal Alejandro O'Reilly**, a brilliant soldier and civic planner, to Puerto Rico to overhaul the system of government, enhance profitability, and bolster the colony's defenses by establishing an organized militia.

Alejandro O'Reilly formulated a plan known as the O'Reilly Report, which is considered one of the most important documents Spain issued to its colonies, because for the first time, the colonists' needs, not just the Spanish crown's interests, were recognized. O'Reilly devised a way of legalizing trade between the Spanish colonies and other European nations that was beneficial to Spain. He also laid the groundwork for a system of land distribution in Puerto Rico, whereby new Spanish settlers were given agricultural acres for free if they were willing to farm them. Through O'Reilly's efforts, new schools were opened and new towns were constructed in Puerto Rico. Houses built in the Spanish style, with thick stone walls that kept the interiors cool, sprang up from coast to coast. Spain's revived interest in Puerto Rico also served to enrich the island's cultural life. Puerto Rico's first painter, and one of its most distinguished, **José Campeche**—who was born in San Juan on January 6, 1751, to an African freed slave from Puerto Rico and a Canary Islander, and who received training from **Luis Paret**, a court painter banished from Spain—did his work during this progressive era.

A GROWING NATIONAL IDENTITY

How did Puerto Ricans feel about Spanish rule?

By the advent of the nineteenth century, an appreciable proportion of Puerto Rico's citizenry was convinced that it was time to leave "home" (Spain) and start a household of their own (sovereignty). By then a cultural and national identity distinct from Spain had arisen in Puerto Rico. In striving for autonomy, Puerto Ricans demanded educational reform; the formation of labor unions; less taxation and more representation; and the appointment of Puerto Ricans, not Spaniards, to local government posts, which at the time were strictly off-limits to all criollos.

Admiral Ramón Power was among the first Puerto Ricans to press for greater representation. In 1810 he was elected to represent Puerto Rico at the Spanish parliament, or *Cortes*. Before the Spanish *Cortes*, he argued that as part of the Spanish empire, Puerto Rico should enjoy the same rights granted to Spain's provinces. Power succeeded in securing both a more liberal constitution for Puerto Rico and Puerto Ricans' right to Spanish citizenship. His provisions for greater self-rule, including the distribution of land to natives and freedom from taxation for those willing to work the land, were contained in the *Ley Power* (the Power Act) and later in the *Real Cédula de Gracias*, issued by **Ferdinand VII** of Spain in 1815. Spanish leniency vis-à-vis Puerto Rico did not last long. When prominent Puerto Rican leaders championed complete autonomy for Puerto Rico, Spain responded by dispatching despotic military governors to the island, who demanded greater allegiance to the mother country and higher taxes from the Puerto Ricans. From 1837 to 1864, the governors denied islanders a voice in their own affairs and persecuted many Puerto Rican leaders, sending some into exile.

One such leader was physician and patriot **Ramón Emeterio Betances**, who called for an end to slavery in Puerto Rico, which, in spite of being officially abolished, was in full swing. He also demanded freedom of speech and freedom of religion for the people of the island. In the late 1860s, Puerto Rico's governor expelled Betances from the island for his revolutionary ideas. Betances sought refuge in the Dominican Republic and in the United States, where with other Puerto Rican freedom fighters, among them **Segundo Ruiz Belvis**, he formed in January 1868 the *Comité Revolucionario de Puerto Rico* (the Revolutionary Committee of Puerto Rico), which planned an armed revolt for Puerto Rican independence. On September 23, 1868, thousands of Betances supporters, heeding his call for independence, marched into the small town of Lares, in western Puerto Rico, wielding firearms and machetes. They set up a provisional government and declared the island the Republic of Puerto Rico. This revolt, which the Spanish easily squelched, became known as *El Grito de Lares*, (the Cry of Lares). Since 1969, September 23 has been a national holiday commemorating *El Grito de Lares*, both on the island and the mainland.

Who was Luis Muñoz Rivera, and why is he called the George Washington of Puerto Rico?

In the aftermath of *El Grito de Lares*, Puerto Ricans demonstrated an unshakable resolve to achieve self-determination and move Puerto Rico forward. They gained some ground in 1887, when **Román Baldorioty de Castro**, an advocate of Puerto Rican autonomy, together with **José de Diego**, organized Puerto Rico's reform-minded liberals under the banner of a political party, the Autonomist Party. After Baldorioty's death in 1889, Puerto Rican journalist **Luis Muñoz Rivera** took control of the Autonomist Party and proposed that it and other splinter parties form a coalition with Spain's *Partido Liberal-Fusionista* (Fusionist Liberal Party), which he believed would cut a deal for Puerto Rican independence.

Was Puerto Rico really free for only a week?

As it turned out, **Luis Muñoz Rivera** was correct in his assumption. In 1898 **Práxedes Mateo Sagasta,** of Spain's controlling Fusionist Liberal Party, granted Puerto Ricans the same privileges that all Spanish citizens enjoyed, as well as the right to elect a Puerto Rican governor general to head a provisional assembly in Puerto Rico that would have full control over local taxes, budgets, and education, and would elect representatives to the Spanish parliament, or Cortes. Luis Muñoz Rivera won the election for governor general, becoming the first Puerto Rican governor of Puerto Rico on July 24, 1898—a giant step toward full sovereignty for the island. A week earlier, on July 17, 1898, the autonomous parliament of Puerto Rico had assembled for the first time. But Puerto Ricans would enjoy the first taste of freedom for only one week. On July 25, in the final phase of the Spanish-American War, U.S. military forces landed at the small port of Guánica, in southwestern Puerto Rico, and occupied the island, with minimal resistance.

What was the Monroe Doctrine?

When **James Monroe** was elected president of the United States in 1817, at the age of fifty-eight, he had a lengthy and distinguished political career behind him, which included service as secretary of state, governor of Virginia, and, most notably, an engineer of the Louisiana Purchase. With Monroe in the White House, U.S. industry prospered, and Manifest Destiny reared its head well beyond the nation's borders.

On December 2, 1823, President Monroe delivered his seventh annual message to Congress, in which he declared that the United States would not tolerate European intervention and expansion in the Americas: ". . . the American continents, by the free and independent condition which they have assumed and maintain, are henceforth not to be considered as subjects for future colonization by any European powers . . ." The issuance of this declaration, which became known as the Monroe Doctrine, was motivated by concern that certain European nations were planning to use military force to restore to Spain the Spanish colonies that had recently gained their independence. There was also concern that England was flexing too much muscle in the hemisphere (having seized territory by nibbling off Belize and the Mosquito Coast of Nicaragua), and that France, under **Napoléon III**, had designs on Mexico and intended to turn it into a client state by imposing a Hapsburg prince on a briefly restored Mexican throne. The Monroe Doctrine sent a clear message to the empires of Europe to cease and desist.

However, the Monroe Doctrine did not contain any language about the United States doing the same, that is, refraining from interfering in colonies and nations in the Americas that were not its own. In fact, the Monroe Doctrine clearly implied that the United States had designated itself the protector of the Americas. Thus, while it appeared, at first glance, to be a straightforward exercise in isolationism and a good-neighbor policy toward the fledgling new republics to the south, such as Mexico, the Monroe

Doctrine actually paved the way for the free ride U.S. imperialism was to take throughout the Western Hemisphere during many decades to come. Puerto Rico was one of the stops along the way.

What was the Spanish-American War all about, and why is it called the first media-staged war?

According to the political rhetoric of the time, Americans fought in the Spanish-American War of 1898 to help liberate Cuba from Spanish domination. Of course, no attention was paid to the fact that Cuban freedom fighters (*libertadores*) **José Martí** and **Antonio Maceo y Grajales**, along with others, had already made great strides toward liberating their country on their own. (By then Cuba and Puerto Rico were the only Spanish colonies left in the Western Hemisphere.) The United States found the perfect excuse to declare war when, on February 15, 1898, the American battleship USS *Maine*, which was sitting in Havana Harbor to keep an eye on the Spanish in case they went too far with the Cubans, was blown up and sunk, with a loss of 266 seamen. The word was that the Spanish had blown the *Maine* to smithereens.

It has been widely speculated that American forces, in search of a reason to go to war—not the Spanish—were the ones responsible for the demise of the *Maine*. The United States sought a military conflict with Spain because a victory over that nation and "necessary" intervention in Cuba and Puerto Rico would ensure the expansion and protection of U.S. foreign markets in lush lands rich in sugar, coffee, tobacco, and minerals. At first **President William McKinley** was reluctant to wage war against Spain, but the United States, by and large, had succumbed to overwhelming imperialistic sentiment. Riding that wave of pro-war sentiment were certain influential politicians and bigwigs in the media. **Henry Cabot Lodge**, the powerful Republican senator from Massachusetts, and his close friend **Theodore Roosevelt**, who was then assistant secretary of the navy, both lobbied intensely for U.S. military involvement in the Caribbean. In 1897 Roosevelt supposedly declared in correspondence to a friend, "In strict confidence . . . I should welcome almost any war, for I think this country needs one."

Newspaper barons **William Randolph Hearst** and **Joseph Pulitzer** were both staunch supporters of a war. They had learned from the American Civil War that wars sell papers and thus boost profits. The Hearst and Pulitzer papers began running stories (many of them true) about the atrocities that the Spanish were committing against the Cubans and urging the president to intervene. William Randolph Hearst is said to have dispatched artist/correspondent **Frederic Remington** to Cuba in 1897 to send back sketches of bloody atrocities. When Remington couldn't find anything truly dreadful to paint, he sent a cable to Hearst in 1898, asking for permission to return home. Hearst was furious. "Please remain," he cabled back. "You furnish the pictures, and I'll furnish the war!"

Who were Teddy Roosevelt's Rough Riders, and how did they help him win the U.S. presidency?

On April 25, 1898, the United States declared war on Spain and soon after launched a naval and ground assault against Cuba, with **Lieutenant Colonel Teddy Roosevelt** and his men of the First United States Volunteer Cavalry, called the Rough Riders, in the vanguard. Roosevelt was declared a hero after he led a daring charge up Kettle Hill (incorrectly called San Juan Hill), near the city of Santiago de Cuba, in eastern Cuba, on July 1, 1898, a battle heavily publicized in the American press. While the United States was conducting naval and ground operations in Cuba, it was also targeting Puerto Rico. On May 12, 1898, U.S. ships bombarded San Juan; on June 25, the USS *Yosemite*, a merchant steamer, blocked San Juan Harbor; and then, on July 25, the U.S. general **Nelson Appleton Miles** led sixteen thousand American troops into the small port of Guánica. It was no contest. Spain—a dwindling empire on its last legs—soon surrendered. On October 18, 1898, the last Spanish troops retreated from Puerto Rico, the transfer of the island's sovereignty to the United States was carried out, and the American flag was hoisted over public buildings.

All in all, the Spanish-American War, what **Secretary of State John Hay** described as a "splendid little war," lasted only a few months, and most of it was actually fought at the bargaining table. Still, U.S. forces suffered over 5,000 casualties. Of these, only 379 were battle casualties; the rest were caused by yellow fever, malaria, and other tropical diseases. Secretary of State Hay helped negotiate the Treaty of Paris of 1898, which brought the brief conflict between Spain and the United States to a formal end. With the Treaty of Paris, signed on December 10, 1898, the United States found itself in possession of Cuba, Puerto Rico, Wake Island, Guam, and the Philippines—in other words, Spain's remaining colonies. You might say Spain was forced to throw in everything but the kitchen sink, and the United States emerged a world power with a lot of land on its hands.

Puerto Rico, which had savored relative freedom for seven days after Spain had voluntarily granted the island many autonomous rights, suddenly found itself a U.S. protectorate. At the time, most Puerto Ricans believed that the U.S. presence in Puerto Rico would be transitory and was simply a formal way of capping 405 years of Spanish domination. Little did they know that they were witnessing the beginning of a tumultuous marriage—called by different names over the years—which prevails to this day. Elsewhere, Cuba remained a U.S. protectorate until 1902, when it declared itself a free and independent nation; and the Philippines won independence in 1946. Guam and Wake Island remain under direct U.S. control.

Meanwhile, Teddy Roosevelt garnered great popularity from his daring feats in the Spanish-American War and was elected governor of New York in 1898. Soon he was off to the White House: In 1900 **President McKinley** won reelection, with Roosevelt as his vice president. On September 6, 1901, before the regular session of the Senate had opened, McKinley was shot by an anarchist, **Leon Czolgosz**, and died days later, on September 14. Teddy Roosevelt succeeded him as president of the United States. Three years later, he still enjoyed popularity and was elected to the presidency in his own right by a resounding majority.

What was the Roosevelt Corollary?

The ink had hardly dried on the Treaty of Paris ending the Spanish-American War when the issue of European intervention in the Western Hemisphere again took center stage. As the twentieth century dawned, European governments began to exert pressure on several Latin American countries to repay their debts. For instance, after the Venezuelan government, plagued by civil discord and gross mismanagement, defaulted on loans to foreign bondholders in 1902, the British, Italians, and Germans dispatched a joint naval expedition to Venezuela, which blockaded and shelled the country's ports. Concerned that the blockading powers were ignoring the Monroe Doctrine's message and were competing with the United States for dominance in the Western Hemisphere, and invariably emboldened by the recent American victory against Spain and the acquisition of its remaining colonies,

President Teddy Roosevelt unveiled, in his annual address to Congress in 1904, the Roosevelt Corollary, which served as an amendment to the Monroe Doctrine and went one step further—some say, one step too far.

While the Monroe Doctrine was meant to curb European intervention in the Western Hemisphere, the Roosevelt Corollary outlined the active role that the United States—and no other nation but the United States—was obliged to play in the region. In this document, President Roosevelt first dismissed any charge that the United States was suffering from "land hunger" or entertaining "any projects as regards the other nations of the Western Hemisphere save such as are for their welfare . . ." The key phrase here is "save such as are for their welfare," for Roosevelt then declares that the United States has every right to act as "an international police power" wherever "chronic wrongdoing, or an impotence which results in a general loosening of the ties of civilized society . . . ultimately require intervention by some civilized nation . . ."

In other words, the United States had the right to intervene unilaterally in the affairs of any country in the hemisphere because it, the United States, was "civilized" and the rest of the nations in the region were not. In the century that lay ahead, this belief in American supremacy and exceptionalism would precipitate more U.S. intervention in Latin America, involving even the overthrow of governments deemed harmful to American investments and the installation of puppet rulers who would follow the policies outlined by Washington. To many Latin Americans at the turn of the century, the Roosevelt Corollary packed a wallop. U.S. imperialism had reached its zenith and was quite a force to be reckoned with.

Who was Eugenio María de Hostos, and why is a college in New York City named after him?

Eugenio María de Hostos was a Puerto Rican journalist, philosopher, educator, writer, and freedom fighter. Born in Mayagüez, Puerto Rico, in 1839, he studied law and education in Spain, where he worked alongside other students for the cause of Puerto Rico's and Cuba's liberation from Spanish rule. In 1869, after Spain's Republicans were victorious over the monarchy but then refused to fulfill their promise of autonomy for Puerto Rico and Cuba, Hostos left Spain and took up temporary residence in New

York City, where he published a prominent revolutionary newspaper, *La América Ilustrada*. In 1875, after participating in efforts by Cubans to secure their independence from Spain, Eugenio María de Hostos went to the Dominican Republic, where he continued his fight for self-determination for the Spanish Caribbean colonies of Puerto Rico, Cuba, and the Dominican Republic, publishing the newspaper *Las Tres Antillas*, which was devoted to the issue. Hostos favored an Antilles confederacy, in which the three colonies would be united as a kind of commonwealth.

When the Spanish-American War erupted, Hostos returned to Puerto Rico, where he organized the League of Puerto Rican Patriots and steered a commission that presented **President William McKinley** with a plan that would afford Puerto Ricans the right to decide, by means of a plebiscite, whether they wanted independence or annexation by the United States. However, when U.S. ambassadors met with Spanish delegates to negotiate the end of the Spanish-American War and the fate of Spain's colonies, the few Puerto Rican officials whom Hostos had convinced the United States to invite to the table were granted no say in the final outcome. With the Treaty of Paris of 1898, ending the Spanish-American War, Puerto Rico became a U.S. protectorate, with fewer rights to self-government than it had enjoyed in recent years under Spain. His dream of independence dashed, in 1900 Hostos left Puerto Rico.

Aside from his political and journalistic career, Hostos dedicated himself to pedagogical pursuits, believing that only through educational opportunity could an oppressed people rise and be liberated. In 1879 he founded the first normal school in the Dominican Republic, where he inherited the title *El Maestro*, "the Teacher" or "the Master." Later, after he migrated to Chile, he was named president of the Chilean Athenaeum, headed two schools, taught constitutional law at the Universidad de Chile in Santiago de Chile, and fought for women's right to equal access to that very same institution of higher learning.

A prolific writer, Hostos penned approximately fifty volumes in the course of his lifetime, including the 1863 sociopolitical novel entitled *La Peregrinación de Bayoán* (The Pilgrimage of Bayoán) and the 1887 political treatise *Lecciones de derecho constitucional* (Lessons on Constitutional Rights). Eugenio María de Hostos died in the Dominican Republic in August 1903, one year after Cuba gained its independence. He never saw his dreams for an independent Puerto Rico realized. Eugenio María de Hostos

Community College in the Bronx, New York, which was formed in 1968 at the urging of Puerto Rican and other Latino leaders, is named in Hostos's honor and holds fast to the philosophy of "progress through education," which he so vigorously espoused.

How did Puerto Ricans react to becoming a U.S. protectorate?

Puerto Rico's transition to a U.S. protectorate, on the heels of Spain's cession of the island to the United States at the end of the Spanish-American War, was rather difficult for most islanders. Puerto Ricans did not believe in the Roosevelt Corollary; that is, that it was the duty of the United States to instruct them in how to conduct themselves like citizens of a progressive, civilized nation. The language barrier, which necessitated the use of interpreters and translators so that Puerto Rican leaders and American military authorities could communicate, created tensions and misunderstanding. The cultural barrier, which caused Americans to question even the most minute details of the Puerto Rican legal system and economic system, and of Puerto Rican public finance and public administration, was even harder to overcome.

On April 2, 1900, almost two years after officially assuming control of Puerto Rico, the United States passed the Foraker Act, which made the island an unincorporated territory of the United States. According to this piece of legislation, Puerto Ricans were neither American citizens nor citizens of an independent nation. A civilian government replaced the transitional military government and allowed for the popular election of Puerto Ricans to both houses of the Puerto Rican legislature, where they could implement laws related to internal affairs. However, the United States retained the authority to appoint a governor, and that governor, who was empowered to veto any legislation and had the final say, was to be an American, not a Puerto Rican. The Foraker Act also put an extra economic squeeze on Puerto Rico by imposing a heavy tariff on the island's exports, the aim of which was to protect American sugar and tobacco interests from Puerto Rican competition.

Puerto Ricans were not terribly pleased with the Foraker Act and their political status. In an open letter to **President McKinley** in the very first issue of the *Puerto Rican Herald*, the bilingual newspaper he launched in 1901 in New York City, **Luis Muñoz Rivera**, by then Puerto Rico's leading statesman (he would represent the island in Congress from 1910 to 1916), wrote that the Foraker Act was "unworthy of the United States which imposes it and of Puerto Ricans who have to endure it." Disenchantment over the state of affairs on the island led to the formation of the Unionist Party of Puerto Rico. The party's platform repudiated U.S. domination and supported any of three options for Puerto Rico: statehood, nationhood, or semi-independence under American protection.

Puerto Ricans remained noncitizens of the world, as dictated by the Foraker Act, until the gathering threat of World War I, as well as unremitting pressure from the islanders, prompted **President Woodrow Wilson** to sign the Jones Act on March 2, 1917. With one sweep of the pen, the president granted U.S. citizenship to all Puerto Ricans. Puerto Ricans had the right to refuse U.S. citizenship, but few did so since refusing citizenship meant relinquishing many civil rights. (Only 288 individuals passed up the initial offer of citizenship; many of these opted for citizenship later on.) The Jones Act also stipulated that a non–Puerto Rican governor appointed by the U.S. president would continue to rule over the island's internal affairs and its new American citizens. As it turned out, Puerto Ricans did not inherit all of the fundamental rights of U.S. citizenship (such as the right to vote in U.S. presidential elections), but they instantly acquired most of the obligations of U.S. citizenship (one exception was they were exempted from filing federal income taxes), including serving in the military if conscripted. (During World War I, about eight thousand Puerto Ricans were drafted into the U.S. armed forces, and the Puerto Rican people donated hundreds of thousands of dollars to the war effort. In World War II, the number of Puerto Ricans who fought alongside their fellow Americans rose significantly, to sixty-five thousand.)

During the 1920s, Puerto Ricans continued to demand greater autonomy in local affairs. Their demands intensified when the Great Depression hit in 1929, sending the sugar economy into a nosedive. Puerto Rican workers found themselves teetering on the edge of starvation. During his tenure as governor of Puerto Rico, from 1929 to 1932, **Theodore Roosevelt Jr.**, **Teddy Roosevelt**'s son, seeking to alleviate the suffering of the Puerto Rican people, launched several economic and cultural programs favorable to Puerto Ricans and spoke of greater self-government for the people. His efforts were not enough.

In 1930, as the Depression raged, **Pedro Albizu Campos**

assumed the leadership of the Puerto Rican Nationalist Party (PNP), which was formed in 1922, and transformed it into a dominant force in Puerto Rico's struggle for independence. He took up the cause at every turn, as in 1934, when nationalists rushed to support thousands of *jíbaros*, or farmworkers, who had walked off the sugarcane fields in a wildcat strike. Concerned that a mass revolutionary movement was forming, Puerto Rican local authorities lashed out at the nationalists, killing some members. On March 5, 1936, Albizu Campos and other leading nationalists were officially charged with conspiring to overthrow the U.S. government. At their trial, the jury, seven of whose twelve members were Puerto Rican, refused to convict, so the authorities handpicked a new jury. Ten of the jurors on this new jury were Anglo Americans, and, consequently, this new jury had no difficulty reaching a guilty verdict. Albizu Campos and other nationalists received prison sentences of six to ten years; Albizu Campos served six years, from 1937 to 1943.

The nationalists would not be stopped in their campaign to bring independence to Puerto Rico. In 1937 the PNP organized a march to commemorate the abolition of slavery in Puerto Rico. It was to take place on Palm Sunday, March 21, 1937, in the city of Ponce. The local authorities granted permits for the event but then revoked them. PNP members took to the streets of Ponce, anyway, and the police opened fire on them, killing twenty-two and wounding over one hundred. In this atmosphere of "unanticipated" violence, two bills recommending independence for Puerto Rico were introduced in the U.S. Congress. Both bills succumbed to stiff opposition, with the opposers arguing that the island's social and economic conditions had to improve before independence could be seriously considered.

Who was the first elected Puerto Rican governor, and what did he do that was so important?

In 1946 the United States appointed **Jesús T. Piñero**, fresh from his post as resident commissioner of Puerto Rico (a nonvoting member of the U.S. House of Representatives), the first native Puerto Rican governor of the island. Then, one year later, Congress passed the Elective Governor Act, according Puerto Ricans the right to choose their own governor and granting said governor full authority to appoint all officials, except the auditor and members of the Supreme Court. In 1948 **Luis Muñoz Marín**, the son of the early patriot **Luis Muñoz Rivera** and leader of the majority Popular Democratic Party (PDP), became the first native son elected governor of Puerto Rico by the Puerto Rican people. Born on February 18, 1898, just as the winds of the Spanish-American War were stirring, Muñoz Marín was first exposed to American politics while a teenager: His father's tenure as resident commissioner of Puerto Rico in the U.S. House of Representatives from 1911 to 1916 took the family to Washington DC. There Muñoz Marín attended Georgetown Preparatory School and then, in 1915, entered Georgetown University's law school. With the death of his father in 1916, he returned to Puerto Rico, interrupting his studies.

Muñoz Marín later returned to the United States, settling in New York City, where he began a life as a writer, penning articles about the American domination of Puerto Rico for the *New Republic*, the *Nation*, and the *American Mercury*. After returning to Puerto Rico in 1931, he worked on *La Democracia*, the newspaper his father had founded, joined the Liberal Party, and was elected to the Puerto Rican Senate in 1932, the same year **Franklin Delano Roosevelt** assumed the U.S. presidency. Among Muñoz Marín's scores of friends and supporters was **Eleanor Roosevelt**. After surveying the rural areas of Puerto Rico in 1933, the First Lady voiced grave concern over the poor state of Puerto Rican farming and the island economy, and lobbied for change. At her bidding, President Roosevelt denounced the "hopeless drive to remodel Puerto Ricans so that they should become similar in language, habits, and thoughts to continental Americans."

As senator, Muñoz Marín drafted with **Carlos Chardón**, then the chancellor of the University of Puerto Rico, a long-term economic plan known as the Chardón Plan, which became the scaffolding for the Puerto Rican Reconstruction Administration, launched in 1935. In 1938 Muñoz Marín organized the PDP, and in 1940 he was reelected to the Senate, serving in that body until 1948, when he was democratically elected governor of Puerto Rico. After World War II ended, and with **Harry S. Truman** in the White House, Muñoz Marín would see to it that Washington supported him in his efforts to revitalize the Puerto Rican economy. He adopted a program based on economic reform and expansion that before long would bring industry to the island and raise the per capita income. Gradually, a new era was dawning for Puerto Rico.

How did Puerto Rico become a commonwealth? And what's a commonwealth, anyway?

As the economic situation improved in Puerto Rico, **Luis Muñoz Marín,** by then governor, turned his attention to questions of the island's status. Earlier in his career, he had rejected the notion of establishing a "commonwealth state," known as the "Irish solution," because it was patterned after Ireland's union with Great Britain (which ended when the Irish Free State was established in 1922). He argued that commonwealth status would amount to nothing more than freedom "on a very long chain." But with Puerto Rico's economy then on the mend, severing ties with the United States would mean relinquishing no-tariff status and other perquisites, which had created a building boom and a strong tourist economy, and were keeping the island's industries percolating. Statehood was another option, and although Muñoz Marín might have opposed it in principle, he was a very practical person. He reasoned that it would take the United States too long to accept his Latin island as another state and declared, "If we seek statehood, we die waiting for Congress." So his PDP decided to adopt what was termed the "intermediate solution," namely, commonwealth status.

Luis Muñoz Marín was so popular in Washington that when he spoke, politicians listened. In 1950 the U.S. Congress passed Public Law 600, which called for an election in Puerto Rico in which the people would determine whether commonwealth status, what Muñoz Marín called the "free associated state," *estado libre asociado*, would be adopted. Muñoz Marín had created the term "free associated state" to please adherents of all three dominant political philosophies. To those who sought independence, the word "free" looked promising. To those in favor of some association or dependence, the word "associated" sounded encouraging. And, finally, for those who advocated U.S. statehood, the word "state" struck a chord. As far as Luis Muñoz Marín was concerned, commonwealth status granted Puerto Rico a significant degree of independence, and it ensured that the island would continue to enjoy the economic and social privileges that ties with the United States provided. Legally, the arrangement was riddled with holes, since it was a unilateral agreement that Congress could abrogate anytime it pleased.

The people of Puerto Rico followed their governor's lead and voted for commonwealth status, which was proclaimed on

July 25, 1952, the same day that Puerto Rico's own constitution was enacted. It was exactly fifty-four years to the day that the United States seized control of Guánica, Puerto Rico. (With the passage of the Puerto Rican Federal Relations Act of 1950, the island had been granted the right to draft and enact its own constitution, whose provisions could not overstep the limitations placed on a U.S. territory. The constitution had been ratified on March 3, 1952, and approved by the U.S. Congress on July 3, 1952.) Luis Muñoz Marín was elected governor of Puerto Rico three more times and would probably have served more terms as governor had he not elected to run successfully for the Puerto Rican Senate in 1964. He passed away in 1980.

Why did Puerto Rican nationalists try to assassinate President Truman?

While commonwealth status afforded Puerto Rico the highest degree of political autonomy it had ever known (or at least had known since the days before the Spanish conquest), it also meant that the island was an unincorporated territory under the jurisdiction of the U.S. government (and remains so to this day). Members of **Pedro Albizu Campos**'s Puerto Rican Nationalist Party, which called for nothing short of complete independence from the United States, felt ignored by **Luis Muñoz Marín** and the commonwealth partisans, and disgruntled over commonwealth status.

In an effort to attract attention to their grievances, members of the party launched a terrorist attack on Blair House, the official state guesthouse of the president of the United States, on November 1, 1950, with the aim of assassinating **President Harry Truman**. The president emerged unscathed from the incident, but one Secret Service agent lost his life, as did one of the assailants. Then, on March 1, 1954, Puerto Rican nationalists **Andrés Figueroa Cordero**, **Rafael Cancel Miranda**, **Irving Flores Rodriguez**, and their leader, **Lolita Lebrón**, opened fire on legislators from the visitors' gallery of the U.S. House of Representatives, wounding five congressmen. One of them, **Congressman Alvin M. Bentley** (R-Michigan), sustained near-fatal injuries. The four coconspirators were sent to prison, and until **President Carter** pardoned all but Andrés Figueroa Cordero in 1979, they worked for Puerto Rican independence behind bars.

Nowadays the *Partido Independentista Puertorriqueño* (Puerto

Rican Independence Party), which was founded in 1946, is a major voice for Puerto Rican independence. It does not advocate domestic terrorism or any form of violence.

Who are Los Macheteros?

The machete is the traditional tool that Puerto Rico's *jíbaros* use to cut cane. In the 1970s and 1980s, members of *Los Macheteros*, "the Machete Wielders," a notorious Puerto Rican terrorist organization founded by **Filiberto Ojeda Ríos**, carried out attacks on the U.S. mainland and in Puerto Rico in an effort to draw attention to their fight for Puerto Rico's independence from the United States. *Los Macheteros* bombed government and military installations, robbed and assassinated law-enforcement officers, and even were responsible for one of the largest robberies in U.S. history, the theft of $7 million from a Wells Fargo depot in West Hartford, Connecticut, on September 12, 1983.

When angry protests over U.S. military training operations on Puerto Rico's Vieques Island erupted in April 1999, after a Puerto Rican civilian guard was killed on a U.S. military range by errant five-hundred-pound bombs, *Los Macheteros* emerged from a decade underground to take up their cry for independence. On September 23, 2005, Ojeda Ríos, who had been on the lam since jumping bail in 1990, while awaiting trial for the Wells Fargo armed robbery, died in a shootout with FBI agents in Hormigueros, Puerto Rico, outraging Puerto Ricans and causing many to speculate that his death might unify and bolster the splintered Puerto Rican independence movement.

Is Puerto Rico still a commonwealth?

Yes, but Puerto Ricans have been afforded numerous opportunities since the 1960s to change the island's status as a commonwealth in free association with the United States. Back in 1964, the United States–Puerto Rico Commission on the Status of Puerto Rico decided that both commonwealth status and statehood were viable options for Puerto Rico, and that Puerto Ricans had to determine which way they wanted to go. In 1967 **Luis Muñoz Marín**, who favored commonwealth status, and **Luis Ferré**, a politician in support of statehood, went back to the polls to try to resolve the issue. In the end, 61 percent of the people voted for continued commonwealth status, while 39 percent chose statehood. In 1968 Luis Ferré was elected governor of the island. While his election might have appeared to signal a desire for statehood on the part of Puerto Ricans, the island remained polarized on the question, and no action was taken to bring the matter before Congress for quite some time.

Apparently concerned that the United Nations was going to officially accuse the United States of colonialism in Puerto Rico, **President Jimmy Carter** called for another referendum on Puerto Rico's status in 1978. The referendum never took place. **President George Bush** (senior) took up the issue in 1989, in his first speech before Congress, declaring that he favored statehood. No progress was made to resolve the question of statehood until November 1992, when Puerto Ricans elected **Pedro Roselló** as governor. Roselló, a strong advocate of statehood, announced soon after becoming governor that a plebiscite to decide the status of Puerto Rico, organized by the Puerto Rican legislature, would be held. The three choices on the ballot were commonwealth status, statehood, and independence. On November 14, 1993, the people of Puerto Rico went to the polls in unprecedented numbers; 48.6 percent voted to retain commonwealth status, 46.3 percent selected statehood, and only 4.4 percent chose independence. It was a very close vote in which none of the options won an absolute majority, and thus it affirmed Puerto Rico's ambiguous relationship with the United States.

The most recent nonbinding referendum on the issue of statehood took place in 1998. As in the past, Puerto Ricans again voted to preserve the status quo, with 50.3 percent choosing the "none of the above" option; 46.5 percent, statehood; 2.5 percent, independence; and 0.1 percent, commonwealth. In 2004 **Aníbal Acevedo-Vilá**, a supporter of commonwealth status, became governor of Puerto Rico after defeating two-term governor Pedro Roselló at the polls, which might have been an indication of Puerto Rican satisfaction with commonwealth status were it not for the fact that Acevedo-Vilá won by only about 3,500 votes in a disputed race. Governor Acevedo-Vilá declared that he would allow Puerto Rico's voters to decide whether to call a constitutional convention on the island's status or to ask Congress to permit a plebiscite on the issue. At the end of 2005, the Bush administration's Task Force on Puerto Rico's Status recommended that Congress set a date for another referendum to decide Puerto Rico's future or, at a minimum, hold hearings on the issue.

Commonwealth vs. statehood: What's the big deal?

The question of commonwealth status versus statehood is a *very* big deal. First of all, as a commonwealth, Puerto Rico is under the control of Congress, which has the discretion to curtail the high degree of local autonomy the island currently enjoys and to replace Puerto Rico's elected governor and legislature with another kind of government. If Puerto Rico was granted statehood, Congress would no longer retain ultimate authority, and the island would possess permanent status. Secondly, with commonwealth status, Puerto Rico elects only a nonvoting resident commissioner to the U.S. House of Representatives: the island has no voting representation in Congress, a privilege afforded only to states. If Puerto Rico ever does become a state, it would send two senators to the Senate and seven or eight members to the House of Representatives, and it would have nine electoral votes, which could certainly impact the Democrat-Republican balance of power on Capitol Hill. Thirdly, the citizens of the Commonwealth of Puerto Rico are allowed to vote in presidential primaries, but they do not have the constitutional right to vote for president. (Puerto Ricans who move to the U.S. mainland gain this right; mainlanders who move to the island relinquish it.) If Puerto Rico was a state, islanders would gain the presidential vote and, consequently, would emerge as a powerful Latino political voice in the nation. And Puerto Rico would be the only state in which the overwhelming majority of residents speak only Spanish (one reason why some Americans oppose statehood for Puerto Rico). With a Spanish-speaking state, America would become an officially bilingual nation, in the way of Canada, and would move one step closer to *hermandad*—brotherhood and sisterhood—with all the Spanish-speaking countries in the hemisphere.

However, as a state, Puerto Rico would lose many of the advantages of commonwealth status. For one, Puerto Ricans' sense of national identity, some argue, would be eroded by the nation's English-speaking majority if Puerto Rico was the fifty-first state. And with statehood, the island would have to forfeit its Olympic team, a potent symbol of Puerto Rican national pride. If they were residents of a state, Puerto Ricans would have to pay federal income tax, from which they are currently exempt. And without commonwealth status, Puerto Rico could lose the tax incentives that have encouraged U.S. companies to invest heavily in the island since the 1950s, perhaps causing the island's economy to go from bad to worse.

What happened on Vieques island in 1999 that really got Puerto Ricans' goat?

The Puerto Rican island of Vieques, which is really only an islet, lies just six miles off the southeast coast of mainland Puerto Rico and is home to fewer than ten thousand residents. Between 1941 and 1950, the U.S. Department of the Navy purchased a total of twenty-two thousand acres on the western and eastern ends of the island, and in the 1940s U.S. naval and other military forces began to use the eastern tip for training operations, involving bombing by naval aircraft, ship-to-shore gunnery practice, and marine amphibious landings. When the U.S. Navy halted its military activities on Culebra, another of the three islets belonging to Puerto Rico, in 1975 in response to local opposition, dissatisfaction over military training operations on Vieques grew. Puerto Ricans and critics of the navy's activities voiced concern over safety issues; over toxic materials from the navy's operations, which they claimed were detrimental to the health of Viequenses and damaged the environment and archeological/historic sites; over noise, especially from ship-to-shore gunfire; and over the economic toll of an absence of tourism and fishing on Vieques. The navy countered that its activities posed no danger and that Vieques was essential to national security as the only site where air, land, and sea exercises could be conducted simultaneously.

Anger over the navy's use of Vieques boiled over in April 1999, when a Puerto Rican civilian employed as a security guard on the island was killed by a pair of off-target five-hundred-pound bombs. Very soon after, dozens of protesters swarmed the U.S. naval training range on Vieques, forcing a stoppage of live-fire training. On January 31, 2000, with the protests still raging, **President Bill Clinton** announced that he and then-governor of Puerto Rico **Pedro Roselló** had agreed to a plan to resolve the dispute over Vieques. The plan called for a referendum of Vieques voters, which was scheduled for November 6, 2001, and then rescheduled for January 2002. Voters would be given the choice of either ending the military's use of Vieques no later than May 2003 or allowing the military to continue its operations indefinitely beyond that date (with an extra $50 million in economic assistance to sweeten the deal). The Clinton-Roselló plan was quite controversial, and protests continued at the Vieques naval base, at least until May 4, 2000, when U.S. federal marshals removed the protesters peacefully. The navy then resumed its bombing practice, but with inert bombs in place of live ammunition.

Dissatisfaction with the Clinton-Roselló plan indisputably contributed to Governor Pedro Roselló's defeat in his bid for re-election in 2000. The winner of that election was **Sila María Calderón**, the former mayor of San Juan, who, incidentally, is a graduate of Manhattanville College in Westchester County, New York. During the campaign for governor, she pledged to take immediate action to halt all war games on Vieques. In April 2001, Governor Calderón introduced a noise prohibition bill, signed into law that month, which was meant to challenge navy ship-to-shore shelling off Vieques. On April 24, 2001, Puerto Rico filed a federal lawsuit to end U.S. military operations on Vieques, arguing that such operations threatened public health and violated the island's 2001 Noise Prohibition Act and the 1972 federal Noise Control Act, but a federal judge dismissed the lawsuit, citing a lack of jurisdiction. All the while human rights activists, actors, politicians, and ordinary folks continued to protest U.S. military exercises on Vieques. **Al Sharpton** and **Robert F. Kennedy Jr.** were among the protesters, and both spent time behind bars for the part they played.

Then in June 2001, before the referendum of Vieques voters called for in 2000 could take place, the Bush administration announced, in an act of reconciliation, that it would halt all military training operations on Vieques by May 2003. In the years since the navy withdrew, the island has gone from a military training site to a pristine and secluded beach resort, some fifteen thousand acres of it now under the control of the Department of the Interior's Fish and Wildlife Service, which has turned those acres into the Vieques National Wildlife Refuge, one of the Caribbean's largest natural preserves.

Why isn't Puerto Rican migration considered immigration, and how did it get started?

Since all Puerto Ricans are U.S. citizens—no matter if they dwell in San Juan or San Francisco—and not foreigners, they can travel freely back and forth between the island and the mainland

United States without passports or visas. In other words, their movement constitutes the internal migration of Americans, not immigration. Confusion abounds in mainstream society about Puerto Ricans' citizenship status. Most Puerto Rican mainlanders have a story or two to tell about the time they were asked about their green card or Puerto Rico's currency or Puerto Rico's president, and more than one media pundit has pontificated on national television about the issue of illegal Puerto Rican immigrants in America!

Puerto Ricans first came to the United States in the 1860s. After Puerto Rico was ceded to the United States at the end of the Spanish-American War, more Puerto Ricans began making their way to the United States—and after 1917, when they were given U.S. citizenship, to the U.S. mainland—to settle or to sojourn, an experience fraught with risks, uncertainty, and obstacles, including a language barrier, poverty, social isolation, and overt discrimination. In the early days, the majority went to Florida and New York to labor in cigar-making shops. Forty percent of those who arrived between 1890 and 1910 eventually returned to Puerto Rico.

The first great wave of migration from Puerto Rico to the mainland United States took place only in the aftermath of World War II and lasted until 1967. The reasons were many, but they essentially boiled down to one issue: economics. During World War II, about one hundred thousand Puerto Ricans served in the U.S. armed forces. Military life exposed these islanders to the superior quality of life on the mainland, fueling their desire to move north. In addition, Puerto Rico's population doubled in size to two million during the first quarter of the twentieth century and continued to grow at a rapid pace due to improvements in medical services. With so many more people on the island, the standard of living did not rise substantially, and the unemployment rate soared. By contrast, jobs on the mainland were plentiful. New York City was a major destination for these Puerto Rican workers, who found low-paying, labor-intensive jobs in the manufacturing sector—which eagerly hired unskilled and semiskilled workers—making apparel, shoes, toys, novelties, and electrical goods, and assembling furniture and mattresses. They also went to work in the food and hotel industries, the meatpacking and baking industries, distribution, laundry service, and domestic service. About half of all these workers were women.

Since 1967 Puerto Rican islanders have settled on the mainland in spurts, depending on the health of the U.S. economy and the mainland job market. Those who went to New York City in the 1960s generally wound up in manufacturing, even though this sector had already begun a gradual decline as early as the 1950s. Then in the 1970s, New York City was gripped by a major fiscal crisis as businesses packed up and headed south and overseas in search of low-wage, nonunion labor. This shrinking of the manufacturing sector had a devastating effect on New York City's Puerto Ricans, who generally did not have the formal education needed to fill the white-collar jobs that were opening in the city's growing service sector.

It should be added that for many decades Puerto Rican migrant workers, about whom most Americans are not even aware, have worked on a seasonal basis harvesting potatoes on Long Island, fruits and vegetables in New Jersey and New York State, tobacco in Connecticut, and sugar beets in Michigan.

How many Puerto Ricans are there, and where do they live?

Puerto Ricans numbered 3,794,776 on the U.S. mainland in 2005, almost as many as lived on the island that year, according to the Pew Hispanic Center tabulations of the Census Bureau's 2005 American Community Survey. Census 2000 tallied 3,406,178 mainland Puerto Ricans, which represents an increase of 28 percent over the 2,651,815 counted in 1990. In the year 2000, New York was the state with the largest Puerto Rican population, with 1,050,293 counted. While New York City's Puerto Rican population fell from 896,763 in 1990 to 789,172 in 2000, its first decline in sixty years, the city has remained the hub of Puerto Rican culture in the continental United States. Puerto Rican New Yorkers, who call themselves Nuyoricans, are concentrated in the South Bronx, East Harlem, the Lower East Side, and Sunset Park, with Spanish Harlem, which Nuyoricans call El Barrio, at the very core, as it has been for decades. Puerto Ricans remain the largest Latino group in New York City, but they are no longer the majority that they once were. According to Census 2000 figures, Nuyoricans comprise about a third of the city's total Latino population.

The reasons behind this decline in Puerto Rican numbers in

New York City include a shrinking birth rate, the aging of the population, and return migration to the island of Puerto Rico by retired Puerto Rican New Yorkers. Another factor at play is Puerto Ricans' migration out of the city, owing largely to its out-of-reach housing prices, to destinations in New York State; to nearby states, such as New Jersey and Pennsylvania; and south to Florida, the state with the second-largest Puerto Rican population (482,027 in the year 2000). The states with the third- and fourth-largest Puerto Rican populations are, not surprisingly, New Jersey and Pennsylvania, respectively. New Jersey saw its Puerto Rican population jump by 15 percent between 1990 and 2000, from 320,133 to 366,788, while Pennsylvania witnessed a 53 percent increase in that time period and counted 228,557 Puerto Ricans in 2000. Census 2000 also tallied a significant number of Puerto Ricans in Massachusetts (199,207), Connecticut (194,443), and Illinois (157,851) in 2000.

How are mainland Puerto Ricans doing?

Puerto Ricans have historically been the most socially and economically disadvantaged of all Latinos. In 1998, for instance, a full 30.9 percent of mainland Puerto Ricans lived in poverty, and 43.5 percent of Puerto Rican children were below the poverty line, and in 2000 approximately 40 percent of New York City's Puerto Ricans had slipped to or below the poverty line. The depressed economic status of mainland Puerto Ricans has been attributed to a number of phenomena, such as the disproportionate number of poor Puerto Rican migrants settling stateside as compared to immigrant groups, owing to the fact that Puerto Ricans' U.S. citizenship removes all obstacles to entering the mainland United States. Low levels of educational attainment, limited job skills, disease disparities (including a high incidence of diabetes, high blood pressure, and depression in the Puerto Rican community), and drug abuse have also been frequently cited as reasons for the economically underprivileged class of Puerto Ricans on the mainland. Some social observers have suggested that the culprits underlying all these social circumstances are rampant ethnic and racial discrimination; the language barrier; and the process of transculturation, of straddling two cultures and two languages, which is commonly accompanied by a disorienting sense of being neither here nor there.

In explaining Puerto Ricans' socioeconomic plight, others, such as **Linda Chavez**, author of *Out of the Barrio: Toward a New Politics of Hispanic Assimilation* (1991), the former head of U.S. English, Inc., a citizens' action group that advocates making English the official language of the United States, and the current chair of the Center for Equal Opportunity, have also pointed a finger at the breakdown of the Puerto Rican family unit, as evidenced by the high rate of female family headship among Puerto Rican mainlanders. And others point to the fact that many Puerto Ricans who migrated to New York City between the 1940s and the 1970s ended up in the manufacturing sector, which in the 1950s began a long, nearly total decline, the effects of which were felt long after.

However, it is also important to point out that the socioeconomic status of mainland Puerto Ricans is advancing at a steady pace. Large numbers of mainland Puerto Ricans hold professional, managerial, technical, and administrative support jobs, which are cornerstones of economic well-being. Interestingly, Puerto Rican mainlanders who live outside of the Northeast have shown better socioeconomic outcomes than their counterparts in the Northeast, owing to their human capital and labor market characteristics.

PUERTO RICAN CULTURAL LIFE

What's a santo?

A *santo* is a saint in the Roman Catholic tradition. But for those many Puerto Rican mainlanders and islanders who are followers of *Santería*—a New World faith centered in Cuba that emerged when the ancient Yoruban religions that West African slaves brought to the Caribbean blended with the Roman Catholic beliefs of the Spanish—*santos* also have counterparts among West African deities. For example, the Catholic St. Barbara is the equivalent of the Yoruban god Chango, the Catholic *Virgen de las Mercedes* is also the Yoruban goddess of the waters, Yemaya, and so on. This practice of worshipping saints and Yoruban deities is just one example of the kind of syncretism that occurred when the Africans brought to the Caribbean came in contact with the Spanish colonizers there.

What's a botánica?

Botánicas, which abound in every Puerto Rican neighborhood in America, are shops that sell herbs and "natural" medicines, as well as religious items for followers of *Santería*: everything from candles, incense, and potions to bead necklaces, religious medals, and statues. Most *botánicas* are owned by a *santero* or *santera*, a priest or priestess of *Santería*, who gives consultations to followers of the religion on everyday problems, such as marital discord, love lost, stress, and health complaints.

How do Puerto Ricans observe
St. John the Baptist Day?

The Puerto Rican calendar is filled with many holidays, from **Eugenio María de Hostos**'s birthday on January 11 to Constitution Day on July 25 and the commemoration of *El Grito de Lares* on September 23. One of the most unusual Puerto Rican holidays is St. John the Baptist Day, *El Día de San Juan Bautista*, which falls in June. At the stroke of midnight on this holiday, Puerto Rican mainlanders and islanders immerse themselves in a body of water to cleanse themselves of bad luck and to invite good luck. This ritual has its roots in the southern Spain of more than a millennium ago, when pagan rites related to the summer equinox blended with Christian observances of Jesus's baptism by St. John, giving way to a practice of immersion in the Mediterranean Sea. This ritual later traveled to the Caribbean, where it took on native and African elements, such as burning candles in honor of Yoruban gods, and so it is the result of a syncretism, in the way of *Santería*. Nowadays in Puerto Rico, folks spend the eve of St. John the Baptist Day picnicking on the beach, waiting until midnight to pitch themselves backward into the ocean to be cleansed. In New York City, where the tradition has fewer adherents, especially among the mainland born, Nuyoricans flock to Coney Island, Far Rockaway, the East River, Orchard Beach, and other watery places to either immerse themselves or to pour a pail of water over their heads, washing away bad luck and inviting good luck.

LATINO HEARTTHROBS OF ALL TIME

1. Marc Anthony   This Puerto Rican pop singer has a passion for salsa, has sold more than ten million albums worldwide (as of 2006), and has appeared in several Hollywood films, including *Bringing Out the Dead* (1999) and *Man on Fire* (2004).

2. Mariah Carey   This pop and R & B singer and songwriter and actress is of Afro-Venezuelan and Irish descent, has several multimillion-selling albums to her name, has earned a handful of Grammys, and was the best-selling female artist of the 1990s.

3. Julie Carmen   This actress first won accolades for her performance in the 1988 film *The Milagro Beanfield War* and has since starred in numerous films, including the Emmy-nominated *Drug Wars: The Cocaine Cartel* (1992) and *King of the Jungle* (2000).

4. Vikki Carr   Since catapulting to fame with her 1966 song "It Must Be Him," this platinum-selling singer and entertainer of Mexican ancestry has won three Grammys, has earned a star on the Hollywood Walk of Fame, has performed for the queen of England and five U.S. presidents, and much more.

5. Gloria Estefan   After crossing over to an English-speaking audience with her 1984 song "Dr. Beat," this Cuban American singing sensation single-handedly brought Latin music into the mainstream in a big way by fusing the Latin sound with R & B and pop. She has millions of fans the world over.

6. Emilio Estevez   One of Martin Sheen's sons, this highly acclaimed actor and director is a top box-office draw. He has starred in such Hollywood hits as *St. Elmo's Fire* (1985), *The Breakfast Club* (1985), and *The Mighty Ducks* (1992) and has directed such noteworthy films as *Bobby* (2006), about the assassination of Robert F. Kennedy.

7. Andy Garcia	This celebrated Cuban American actor has starred in such superb films as *The Untouchables* (1987), *The Godfather: Part III* (1990), *Steal Big Steal Little* (1995), *Ocean's Eleven* (2001), and *The Lost City* (2005), which he also directed and co-produced.
8. Jennifer Lopez	This multitalented superstar achieved fame with her starring role as the singer Selena in the 1997 film *Selena* and with her performance in *Out of Sight* (1998). She later performed on the big screen in such films as *Enough* (2002) and *Border-town* (2006). In 1999 she released her debut album, *On the 6*, which was followed by *J to Tha L-O!: The Remixes* (2002), the best-selling remix album of all time in the world, and others.
9. Ricky Martin	This talented Puerto Rican actor and musician played on the television soap *General Hospital* in 1994 and 1995 and took the Broadway stage in *Les Miserables* in 1996. He launched a solo music career in 1989 and has since released a spate of albums, among them *Sound Loaded* (2000), *La Historia* (2001), *Almas del Silencio* (2003), *Life* (2005), and *MTV Unplugged* (2006).
10. Ricardo Montalbán	This Mexican American actor starred as the unforgettable Mr. Roarke in the 1978–84 TV series *Fantasy Island*, as the evil Khan in the motion picture *Star Trek: The Wrath of Khan* (1982), and in countless other television shows, commercials, and films.
11. Esai Morales	This Puerto Rican actor has starred in such films as *La Bamba* (1987), *My Family*, *Mi Familia* (1995), and *Fast Food Nation* (2006). For eight seasons, he played the role of Lieutenant Tony Rodriguez in the television police drama *NYPD Blue* (1993–2005).
12. Ramón Novarro	This Mexican American heartthrob was cast as a "Latin lover" in silent films and

	talkies. His first starring role was in *The Prisoner of Zenda* (1922), but he gained worldwide acclaim with his performance in *Ben-Hur* (1926).
13. Rosie Perez	This actress and choreographer of Puerto Rican descent has appeared on the small screen and the big screen, in such motion pictures as Spike Lee's *Do the Right Thing* (1989), *White Men Can't Jump* (1992), *Fearless* (1993), and *Riding in Cars with Boys* (2001).
14. Selena Quintanilla	This Mexican American superstar, known simply as Selena, put Tejano music—a blend of Mexican *ranchera*, country, polka, pop, Colombian *cumbia*, and reggae—on the map. In 1995, just as she was about to make her English-language debut, she was gunned down by the president of her fan club.
15. Chita Rivera	After taking the Broadway stage for the first time in 1957, this celebrated Puerto Rican and Scottish stage actress and dancer won a Tony in 1984 for her performance in *The Rink* and one in 1993 for her acting in the Broadway hit *Kiss of the Spider Woman*. In 2002 she became the first Latina to receive the prestigious Kennedy Center Honors award.
16. César Romero	From the 1930s to the 1960s, this popular Cuban American actor played leading men as well as villains, including the Joker in the hit TV show *Batman*, which first aired on January 12, 1966.
17. Linda Ronstadt	America's greatest female pop star of the 1970s, she has been entertaining audiences, recording albums (including some inspired by her Mexican ancestry), and winning Grammys for over four and a half decades.
18. Jon Secada	This Grammy-winning Cuban American pop idol got his start as a backup vocalist in Gloria Estefan's Miami Sound Machine and catapulted to stardom in 1992, with

the release of his multiplatinum album *Jon Secada* and its Spanish-language version, *Otro Día Más Sin Verte*. He has since released three albums: *Heart, Soul, and a Voice* (1994), *Amor* (1995), and *Same Dream* (2005).

19. Charlie Sheen — One of Martin Sheen's sons, he has appeared in more than forty feature films, including the highly acclaimed motion pictures *Platoon* (1986), *Wall Street* (1987), and *Being John Malkovich* (1999), and in the television sitcoms *Spin City* (1996–2002), for which he garnered a Golden Globe Award in 2002, and *Two and a Half Men* (2003–present).

20. Ritchie Valens — This 1950s singer of Mexican ancestry, whose professional career lasted for less than a year, was the first to fuse rock and roll and Latin rhythms. The 1987 film *La Bamba* recounts his rise to fame and his tragic early death in a plane crash in 1959. In 2001 he was inducted into the Rock and Roll Hall of Fame.

21. Raquel Welch — This actress, dancer, and model with Bolivian roots was pigeonholed as a sex symbol in the 1960s and 1970s and was finally recognized as a serious performer in the 1980s. In more recent years, she has appeared on the big screen in *Tortilla Soup* (2001), *Legally Blonde* (2001), and *Forget About It* (2006).

What is one of the biggest Puerto Rican parties of the year?

Puerto Ricans customarily celebrate at home or at social clubs, but they also take their partying out into the street. The biggest Puerto Rican street party of all—over two million people gather—is the National Puerto Rican Day Parade in New York City, held annually along Fifth Avenue on the second Sunday in June, when *comparsas* (carnival dancing groups) and marching bands follow the floats, which are in turn followed by politicians looking for votes. A few big-name Puerto Rican stars usually participate in the forty-two-block parade each year, too. In 2006 **Jennifer Lopez**, **Marc Anthony**, **Rosie Pérez**, and salsa king **Willie Colón** all marched to the Latin beat up Fifth Avenue. In recent years, the National Puerto Rican Day Parade has attracted larger crowds than the Saint Patrick's Day Parade, and it now ranks as the biggest outdoor event celebrated in the United States.

What's compadrazco?

Compadrazco, Spanish for "coparenting," is a critical feature of the Puerto Rican social structure and is also prevalent among other Latino groups. Essentially, it's a social network of extended families, which are linked together by friends who select each other to act as second parents, *madrinas* and *padrinos* (godmothers and godfathers), to their children. The *madrinas* and *padrinos* provide their godchildren a great deal of social support, to the extent that the *madrina* is often the one who buys the wedding ring for her godchild. Close friends often refer to each other as *compadre* and *comadre* as a way of affirming these ties they have forged together, which are nearly as strong as those in extended biological families.

What is Puerto Rican cooking like, and what's the Puerto Rican national dish?

Mainland Puerto Ricans (and islanders, too) love typical American fare, but they also have a delectable tropical cuisine all their own. Among the best known Puerto Rican culinary delights are *pasteles* (a kind of tamal made with plantains and such tubers as yuca and *yautía*, not corn, and stuffed with meat), *lechón asado* (roast suckling pig), and *arroz con gandules* (rice and pigeon peas). *Asopao*, a fragrant, soupy chicken and rice stew, could perhaps be called the national dish of Puerto Rico, owing to the fact that a pot of it is often found simmering on the stove in many a Puerto Rican household. Among favorite traditional desserts on the mainland and the island are cream cheese flan, coconut flan, "milk" flan (*flan de leche*), rice pudding, coconut bread pudding, and *tembleque*, a coconut milk custard.

Spanish, African, and Taino elements are clearly visible in

Puerto Rican cuisine. Puerto Rican cooks use achiote (annatto seeds), which was an essential Taino ingredient, to impart an orange tinge and a subtle flavor to the oil in which foods are sautéed. Many Puerto Rican dishes, such as paella and *caldo gallego* (a rich bean soup), are straight from the Spanish kitchen, but with a tropical twist. Others, such as *mofongo*, "meatballs" made with crushed fried plantains, garlic, and chunks of pork or pork crackling or other meats, are clearly of African origin.

Two critical ingredients in Puerto Rican cooking cannot go without mention. One, called *adobo*, is a seasoning composed of garlic, oregano, crushed peppercorns or ground pepper, salt, and a bit of lime juice or vinegar. *Adobo* is rubbed into meat, poultry, and fish, imparting a marvelous flavor. The other must-have ingredient in the Puerto Rican kitchen is *sofrito*, a marinade or sauce made of onions, garlic, green and red bell peppers, sweet red chiles, cilantro, *recao* (a rather strong-smelling herb available in Puerto Rican and Asian markets), oil, and sometimes tomatoes, all of which are pureed together. *Sofrito* is the foundation for sauces, soups, and stews, including *asopao*, and is also used as a condiment at the table. Many Puerto Rican cooks keep a batch of *sofrito* tucked away in the refrigerator or freezer, since so many island dishes call for it.

CINCO

Cuban Americans

BEFORE THE *CUBA LIBRE* WAS INVENTED

What was Cuba like before Fidel Castro?

On October 28, 1492, soon after making landfall on Cuba, the largest and westernmost island of the Antillean archipelago, **Christopher Columbus** wrote this in his journal: "[I have] never seen anything so beautiful . . . The singing of small birds is such that it seems as if one would never desire to depart. Flocks of parrots darken the sun. There are trees of a thousand species, each has its particular fruit, and all of a marvelous flavor."

The Taino and Siboney, two Arawak tribes, inhabited the island and lived by fishing, hunting, and farming. They grew corn, sweet potatoes, yuca (a tuber that is still immensely popular among Cubans and Cuban Americans), tomatoes, pineapples, and other fruits, and were also skilled at numerous crafts, including woodwork, ceramics, and textile production. Out of wild cotton and palm fibers, they made hammocks, fishing lines, and an array of other useful tools. Columbus observed in one of his letters that the women seemed to work more than the men, but he was unsure whether they were permitted to own property.

Although the exact number of Taino and Siboney inhabiting Cuba when Columbus arrived on the scene is not known (some sources estimate one hundred thousand), it is certain that within a few decades after the explorer stepped foot on the island, European diseases and the hard labor the Spaniards imposed on the native peoples had nearly decimated their population. Another Arawak tribe, known as the Mayari, also inhabited Cuba before the Spanish *conquista*, but, as with the Siboney and Taino, few traces of them remain.

Did the Siboney and Taino invent Cuban cigars?

You could say so, since they cultivated tobacco extensively and taught **Columbus** and other conquistadores how to roll and smoke cigars. The word "tobacco" comes from the Taino *tabaco*. Curiously, the process of rolling these popular leaves has not changed much over the centuries.

What did the Spanish want with Cuba, and why was it so important?

At first, as was their custom, the Spanish prospected for gold. Spanish conquistador **Diego de Velázquez**, who had settled in Hispaniola (an island that now comprises the Dominican Republic and Haiti), was sent to Cuba by the Spanish crown in 1511 to secure the island and establish settlements for the purpose of mining gold. Between 1512 and 1515, Velázquez founded the Cuban settlements of Baracoa, Bayamo, Trinidad, Sancti Spiritus, Havana, Puerto Principe, and Santiago de Cuba. Gold was ultimately discovered in the central highland region of the Sierra Maestra, a mountain range on the western part of the island (the very mountain range from which **Fidel Castro** would launch his 1959 revolution), but the amount was insignificant. Cuba's wealth really lay in its strategic location and fertile soil.

Flanked by the Gulf of Mexico and the Caribbean Sea, Cuba lies at the crossroads of three main maritime routes: the Straits of Florida to the north, the Windward Passage to the east, and the Yucatán Channel to the west. For this reason, the island was the perfect pit stop for Spanish conquistadores exploring other corners of the Americas. However, this easy access to maritime routes also rendered Cuba vulnerable to foreign aggression—namely, English, Dutch, and French pirates and privateers stalking Spanish galleons en route from Mexico and Peru, their holds filled with gold and other valuables. From the early days of the Spanish conquest, Spain valued Cuba for its location. When African slaves were brought to the island by the thousands to work in the fertile fields and Cuba prospered from its agricultural pursuits, Spain viewed this as a handsome side benefit.

How did Havana come to be swapped for Florida?

In the British and French hostilities of the Seven Years' War (1756–63), the Spanish came to the aid of the French, and consequently, Britain vowed to seize control of Spain's New World colonial possessions. In 1762 the British decided that Cuba, where sugarcane, coffee, and tobacco grew in abundance and the trade winds always blew in the mariner's favor, would make a nice little colony. They struck Havana Harbor and seized control of the city. Some good came of the British occupation for Cuba's criollos (those of pure Spanish blood who were born in the Spanish colonies, as opposed to in Spain), who until then had been forced to trade almost exclusively with Spain or else deal in the black market with other European powers. For instance, trade taxes were abolished, and the island was thrown wide open to commerce with merchants and traders from Great Britain and the American colonies. All at once Cuba saw that it had great prospects for a thriving economy. But the British occupation was short-lived, lasting only ten months, since Spain could not bear to lose its Caribbean jewel. In 1763 the Spanish convinced the British to swap Cuba for Florida (which was practically unfit for habitation).

What part did the British play when it came to African slavery in Cuba?

The Spanish had not opposed African slavery (in fact, they were among the first to engage in the slave trade); they just never saw a great need for it in Cuba. The British, however, realized that an effective way to tap Cuba's potential in agriculture was to introduce slave labor. Encouraged by the British, slave traders from around the globe descended on Cuba for a share of the newly opened market. In the ten months of British rule in Cuba, over ten thousand African slaves were brought to the island—many more than would ordinarily have entered Cuba under Spain over a period of ten years or more. With the influx of African slaves, sugarcane, tobacco, coffee, and other crops flourished on the island. The British favored the cultivation of sugarcane, and thus it became Cuba's principal crop. Cuba's reliance on a single-crop economy, which has been both the joy and the bane of the island's existence to this day, had begun. In 1779 Cubans were given authorization to conduct free trade with North America and were granted exemptions from start-up taxes for new sugar mills. As a result, sugar plantations sprouted all over the island, and more slaves were brought over to keep up with the demand from international markets. Cuba was transformed overnight; that transformation brought growth. By the end of the eighteenth century, Havana ranked as one of the largest cities in the New World.

The African slaves in Cuba were treated better than those in other Spanish colonies. For instance, the number of "free colored" people in Cuba was higher than elsewhere. This was due to the fact that white Spanish slaveholders customarily freed their many illegitimate children, and that slaves in Cuba had the right to purchase their freedom and that of their children, an arrangement called *coartacíon*. They paid their owners a down payment and then a fixed sum in installments. *Coartación* was possible because the Spanish looked upon the Africans not as a people they were born to possess, but merely as a commodity, a source of cheap labor.

Did the Africans in Cuba rebel?

The Africans longed for their homelands in West Africa (as many of their soulful ballads remind us), they longed for freedom, and, of course, they very much minded being exploited. And exploited they were, especially in remote areas of Cuba, where slaveholders paid less heed to the laws of *coartación*. Consequently, there were thousands of *cimarrones*, or runaway slaves, and numerous slave uprisings occurred in Cuba in the eighteenth and nineteenth centuries. In 1727 three hundred slaves rebelled on one Havana plantation alone. Four years later, another slave revolt closed down the copper mines of Santiago de Cuba.

These uprisings ultimately gave way to a more organized emancipation movement. In 1811 a free African Cuban carpenter named **José Antonio Aponte** organized a large-scale revolt in Havana, demanding that all the slaves be set free. In this atmosphere of rebellion, fair-minded intellectuals awoke to the injustices of slavery and lent their support, along with free Africans and slaves, to Aponte's cause. Aponte's revolt, as well as hundreds of others throughout the island—in Matanzas, Holguín, Puerto Principe, Manzanillo, and almost every village and hamlet in Cuba—engendered not only a new social awareness, but also a terrible backlash by criollo and Spanish-born slave owners. In retaliation for their insurrection, African Cubans were tortured and slaughtered. An uprising in Matanzas province in the early nineteenth century, involving more than three hundred slaves from fifteen sugar plantations, ended when a local squadron of Spanish lancers attacked and dispersed hundreds of brave fighters, killing many in the process. However, the slaves' struggle was not in vain. In the 1870s, an African Cuban was to emerge a leader in the fight for slave emancipation and Cuban independence. His name was **Antonio Maceo**, and it is thanks to him and three other prominent revolutionaries, **Carlos Manuel de Céspedes**, **Máximo Gómez**, and **José Martí**, that Cuba won its independence from Spain.

Why did it take Cubans so long to gain their independence from Spain, and how was slavery a key factor?

Whereas the rest of Latin America (except Puerto Rico) had gained its independence from Spain by the mid-nineteenth century, Cuba remained a Spanish colony until the Spanish-American War of 1898. Numerous factors contributed to this delay in fulfilling the dreams of generations of Cuban criollos who had envisioned a nation separate from Spain since the mid-eighteenth century. One faction of society that dragged its feet when it came to Cuban independence was the Cuban criollo elite, who owned the sugar and tobacco plantations. Members of the elite sought reforms that would benefit them, while they flagrantly disregarded the needs of the Cuban people as a whole. While they wanted lower tariffs and freer trade with the rest of the world, they feared that independence from Spain might be bad for business.

By 1817 Great Britain, which had eradicated the slave trade in its own territories in 1807, was pressuring Spain to abolish the African slave trade in its colonies. Britain's efforts were in vain, as evidenced by the fact that between 1821 and 1831, more than three hundred transatlantic expeditions brought an estimated sixty thousand African slaves to Cuba. Finally, in 1845, the Spanish acquiesced and enacted the Law of Abolition and Repression of the Slave Trade, which declared that all slaves brought to Cuba after 1820 were in illegal bondage and were entitled to their freedom. The Cuban criollos openly defied the law, refusing to manumit slaves already in Cuba and even bringing more to the island. In fact, from 1845 to 1850 an average of ten thousand slaves arrived in Cuba annually, the same number that had been brought to Cuba annually in the years 1830–45. This defiance of the Law of Abolition and Repression of the Slave Trade constituted an odd sort of insurrection by the criollo landed gentry, who decided it was best to be independent of Spain but did not advocate freedom for all.

However, the Law of Abolition and Repression of the Slave Trade certainly made doing business and growing sugarcane in Cuba a lot more expensive. For one, slave mortality, which previously had caused plantation owners little concern, now presented a problem. Before, African slaves could be replaced at the drop of a sombrero and for the cost of one, but once the slave trade was made illegal, their price skyrocketed. Between 1800 and 1820, the price of a male slave dropped from three hundred pesos to sixty, but by the 1860s a slave cost as much as fifteen hundred pesos.

IMPORTANT DATES

1763	Spain hands Florida to the British in exchange for Cuba.
May 19, 1895	José Martí, who fought for Cuba's freedom, dies at the Battle of Dos Rios.
May 20, 1902	Cuba wins its independence and elects its first president, Tomás Estrada Palma.
January 1, 1959	Fulgencio Batista flees Cuba in the early dawn for safety in Spain. Fidel Castro takes control of Cuba.
February 7, 1962	President Kennedy imposes a total embargo of Cuba.
October 22, 1962	President Kennedy announces that Russian atomic-missile sites are being built in Cuba, a threat to the region's security. He calls for a blockade of Cuba and demands the withdrawal of all offensive weapons from the island.

March 12, 1996	The Helms-Burton Act is signed into law. It strengthens sanctions against the Cuban government and authorizes U.S. nationals whose property was confiscated in Cuba to file suit in U.S. courts against foreign firms that might be using that property.
April 22, 2000	Heavily armed INS agents seize Elián González at gunpoint from his uncle's house in Little Havana.
January 18, 2006	Representing the state of New Jersey, Robert Menendez (D) becomes the first U.S. senator of Cuban American descent.

How was Cuba almost annexed to the United States in the 1840s?

When the Spanish enacted the Law of Abolition and Repression of the Slave Trade in 1845, the Cuban criollo elite—the landowners, not the intellectuals—who depended on African slaves to work their plantations, felt disaffected from Spain. It occurred to members of the Cuban elite that if the United States annexed Cuba, they could preserve slavery and sell their sugar, tobacco, and coffee to North America duty free. The annexation of Texas, which was permitted to join the Union as a slave state, was the perfect example of the kind of arrangement the elite envisioned for Cuba.

Just as the Cuban criollo elite was following events in the United States, during the nineteenth century, the Americans were intensely eyeing Cuba, owing to the island's proximity, strategic location, mineral wealth, and rich soil. The notion of Manifest Destiny had excited Americans' imagination, and Cuba seemed like an ideal piece of real estate. In an 1823 letter to U.S. minister to Spain **Hugh Nelson**, then secretary of state **John Quincy Adams** voiced America's conviction that the annexation of Cuba was something of a natural law: "But there are laws of political as of physical gravitation," wrote Adams, "and if an apple severed by a tempest from its native tree cannot choose but fall to the ground, Cuba, forcibly disjoined from its own unnatural connection with Spain, and incapable of self-support, can gravitate only towards the North American Union, which by the same law of nature cannot cast her off from its bosom." An operative phrase in Adams's letter is "incapable of self-support." Over this idea alone, wars have been fought.

Adams never managed to secure Cuba for the United States, but his aspirations concerning the island were never forgotten and had a profound impact on future generations in Washington. As annexation fever grew among the Cuban criollo elite in the 1840s, the U.S. government bolstered its efforts to obtain Cuba. First, **President James Polk** offered Spain $100 million for the island in 1848, but the Spanish declined. Then, in 1854, **President Franklin Pierce** upped the ante to $130 million, but again Spain turned down the offer. On October 8, 1854, American ministers to Spain, England, and France met in Ostend, Belgium, and proclaimed loudly and publicly that the United States wished to purchase Cuba. Ten days later at Aix-la-Chappelle, they crafted the Ostend Manifesto, a document that contained a warning to the Spanish that if they did not acquiesce, then "by every law, human and divine, we shall be justified in wresting it [Cuba] from Spain if we possess the power." Anyone with a little foresight could have predicted that sooner or later, a Spanish-American War would be fought.

But the United States suddenly became involved in domestic affairs that pivoted on the issue of slavery. Within a decade, the nation was embroiled in the Civil War, which brought activity on the international front to a virtual halt. At the same time, Cuban criollos with justice on their minds were becoming more organized, inspired by Latin American leaders such as **Simón Bolívar** and **José de San Martín**, who were forging independent democratic republics in South America.

What was the Grito de Yara, and why did Cuban landowners change their minds about slavery and independence from Spain?

In May 1865, Cuba's Reformist Party, which was composed mainly of the criollo elite, directed a memorandum to the Spanish Parliament with four basic demands: that Cubans be represented in the parliament, the tariff system be completely reformed, criollos be afforded the same rights as *peninsulares* (those born in Spain), and that slavery be permanently abolished in Cuba, with compensation. Several factors contributed to the Cuban criollo elite's sudden about-face on the issue of slavery. First, it was clear that slavery had to end sooner or later. Second, Cuban planters had found other groups of laborers to work in their fields. Between 1840 and 1870, about 125,000 Chinese men and women became indentured workers in Cuba. At the same time, poor or displaced Spanish workers, primarily from the Canary Islands, Galicia, and Asturias, who were bearing the brunt of a crumbling economy at home, were pouring into Cuba. These white immigrants went to work at *ingenios* (sugar mills), *cafetales* (coffee plantations), and other places where Africans traditionally toiled.

With its economy in the throes of a depression caused by the loss of its New World colonies and mishaps at home, Spain tightened the screws on Cuba and, in the view of many patriots, hammered the first nail into its imperialist coffin on the island. Instead of letting the Cubans be, the Spanish augmented the authority of their military tribunals, denied Cubans any parliamentary voice, banned political meetings, raised taxes a whopping 6 percent, and imposed protectionist duties on all foreign products. In response to the latter, the United States raised tariffs on Cuban goods by 10 percent. Cuban producers were caught in the middle, squeezed from both sides, with ever-diminishing profits and foreign markets. Within a couple of years, cattle barons from Camagüey, sugar landlords from Oriente, and members of the Cuban elite from all over the island convened in the town of Yara to plan a mass rebellion against Spain. Whites, African Cubans, small farmers, free men and slaves, and people of all classes joined in the rebellion. The gathering on October 10, 1868, known as *El Grito de Yara* (the Cry from Yara), proclaimed Cuban independence and the establishment of a provisional republic. The protesters decried unfair taxation and called for free trade with all nations, a freely elected representative government, and "universal manhood suffrage." Not surprisingly, women were excluded from voting (it was not until the 1930s that Cuban women won the right to vote), but in the context of the times, it was clearly a step toward greater equality.

This first cry for independence escalated into a bloody civil war against Spain that is known as the Ten Years' War. The Spanish, seeing their prized colony slipping away—a colony they had previously dubbed "Cuba most faithful" because it had remained loyal while Mexico, Venezuela, and other colonies were severing their ties with Spain—took no prisoners. They destroyed the sugar mills, torched the land, and perpetrated mass executions. When the conflict ended in defeat for Cuba in 1878, the island was left in a state of utter desperation. Spain simply took up where it had left off, forbidding the Cubans from having any say in government and imposing steep taxes.

How did U.S. business interests profit from Cuba's Ten Years' War?

Devastated by the war, many Cuban growers relinquished their ownership positions in the *ingenios* and *cafetales*, trading their property titles for stock options in the U.S. corporations that took over their land. In effect, Cuban growers became administrators of companies owned by U.S. corporations. Some U.S. corporations, such as E. Atkins & Company in Boston, foreclosed on estates to which they had loaned money for agricultural operations and, as a result, acquired vast sugar properties and other holdings from insolvent Cuban landlords. By 1895 less than 20 percent of mills in Cuba were owned by Cubans. Almost immediately, 95 percent of all Cuban sugar exports found their way to the United States. The island had a single-crop economy and a single country to which to sell. The stage was set for what would eventually become one of Cuba's greatest tragedies.

Who was José Martí?

José Martí y Pérez was Cuba's **George Washington** and **Thomas Jefferson** all rolled into one. Born in Havana to Spanish parents on January 28, 1853, Martí is remembered throughout the Spanish-speaking world not only as a brilliant political leader, but also as a great poet. He was the founder of the *modernismo* literary style in Cuba—the precursor of the symbolist movement, which stressed simplicity and directness, in a departure from the florid style of the nineteenth century. Among Martí's literary works are the books of poetry *Ismaelillo* (1882) and *Versos sencillos* (Plain Verse, 1891) and the short story collection *La edad de oro* (The Golden Age, 1898).

José Martí answered the call to rebellion against the oppressive Spanish regime early in life. At the tender age of sixteen, he was arrested for sedition and sent into exile. He spent his first period of exile (1871–78) in Spain, Mexico, and Guatemala, where he penned his famous poem "La Niña de Guatemala." The second time he was exiled from Cuba, Martí went to England and the United States, where he lived from 1880 until 1895. For several years, he resided in New York City—on Water Street, near the Fulton Fish Market. There he wrote some extraordinary political prose, which decades later became the blueprint of the unofficial constitution of anti-Castro Cuban Americans in Miami. Martí's writings have also served **Fidel Castro** well in his political speeches and proclamations.

Who wrote the song "Guantanamera"?

"*Guantanamera / Guajira guantanamera . . .*" The song, made popular by the late 1940s–1950s American folk music group the Weavers, is based on a traditional Cuban ballad (sung to a *guajira*, a farm girl, from Guantánamo) and contains lines from a famous poem by **José Martí:** "*Yo soy un hombre sincero / de donde crece la palma / y antes de morirme quiero / cantar mis versos del alma*" ("I am an honest man / from the land where the palm tree grows / and before I die I want / to sing the poems in my soul").

What role did José Martí play in Cuba's second bid for independence?

While in the United States, **José Martí** was instrumental in planning Cuba's second struggle for independence. He studied the Ten Years' War and another failed war, called *La Guerra Chiquita* (the Small War), and concluded that Cuba had failed in its efforts toward self-determination for lack of organization. In 1882 he wrote: "The revolution is . . . a detailed understanding based on advanced planning and great foresight." Martí also understood that independence was merely a first step toward the creation of a thriving nation. In 1892 he proclaimed: "Our goal is not so much a mere political change as a good, sound, and just equitable social system without demagogic fawning or arrogance of authority. And let us never forget that the greater the suffering, the greater the right to justice, and the prejudices of men and social inequities cannot prevail over the equality which nature has created." Martí also addressed concerns about the control of wealth by a few and devised a sophisticated democratic philosophy, writing: "A country with a few rich men is not rich—only the country where everyone possesses a little wealth is rich. In political economy and good government, distribution is the source of prosperity."

Just after war between the Cubans and the Spanish broke out

in Cuba in 1895, José Martí returned to the island, with the intent of leading the fight for liberation. For Martí, as for the revolutionaries at his side, liberation meant freedom from oppression, racism, and all foreign domination, whether by the empire across the Atlantic or the empire to the north. He believed that "to change masters is not to be free." José Martí would not live to witness the outcome of Cuba's quest for freedom. He died while fighting the Spanish at the battle of Dos Rios on May 19, 1895, about three years before the United States got involved in the war.

So why did the United States fight the Spanish-American War?

The United States had been itching to gain control of Cuba for most of the nineteenth century. When the Cuban criollos proved mighty, and it became evident that Cuba would soon not only be free from Spanish domination, but would attain sovereignty, the U.S. government decided that unusual measures were needed if it was to seize control of Cuba. After overcoming his initial reluctance to wage war against Spain, **President William McKinley** found the perfect excuse to get involved in the Cuban war of independence when, on February 15, 1898, the American battleship the USS *Maine* was blown up in Havana Harbor. In his message before Congress on April 11, 1898, President McKinley prepared the way for direct U.S. involvement in Cuba. "I ask Congress," he said, "to authorize and empower the President to take measures to secure a full and final termination of hostilities between the Government of Spain and the people of Cuba, and to secure in the island the establishment of a stable government . . . and to use the military and naval forces of the United States as may be necessary for these purposes." As it turned out, the U.S. government would find it most necessary to use its military and naval forces for these purposes.

The Spanish-American War, in which the United States sought to end Spain's domination of Cuba (and other Spanish colonies) and to acquire some of this territory for itself, was declared and then won by the Americans in a matter of ten weeks. American motion-picture producers, along with the American press, did their part in drumming up popular support for the war, igniting the patriotic fervor of audiences at vaudeville and variety stage venues with films of events in Cuba and of ships, cavalry, and **Teddy Roosevelt** in Washington DC. In the fallout of the Spanish-American War, the United States acquired Puerto Rico (see chapter 4), the Philippines, Guam, and the Wake Islands. The United States also took control of Cuba but held on to it only until 1902.

Is it true that the Cuban revolutionaries would have won the war without American intervention?

Yes. Guided by **José Martí**, the Cubans had mounted a carefully planned war of insurrection, and as 1898 dawned, they were in complete control of the countryside and were already marching into several urban centers. The Spanish knew that they were no match against the Cuban rebels, who had popular support, and that it was just a matter of time before they would have to lay down their arms. Cuban independence and Cuban self-rule were destiny manifest.

If lust for Cuba was the reason the United States went to war with Spain, how come Cuba got its independence by 1902?

The Cuban rebels had carefully studied **President McKinley**'s declaration of war, and having been forewarned by **José Martí** about America's determination to acquire Cuba, they mounted an unprecedented public-relations campaign to ensure that the United States would agree to recognize *Cuba libre*—an independent Cuba. A substantial number of Americans, journalists and liberal politicians among them, supported Cuba's bid for independence. However, President McKinley and others on Capitol Hill opposed it, and in the end, the hawkish president and the more liberal wing of government reached a compromise: the United States did not have to recognize Cuban independence outright as long as there was some sort of disclaimer. That disclaimer is Article IV of the American War Resolution, known as the Teller Amendment, which reads as follows: ". . . the United States hereby disclaims any disposition or intention to exercise sovereignty, jurisdiction, or control over said Island except for the pacification thereof, and asserts its determination, when that is accomplished, to leave the government and control of the Island to its people."

What's a Cuba libre?

Cuba *libre* means literally "free Cuba" and is a phrase taken from the nineteenth-century Cuban revolutionary cry *"¡Viva Cuba libre!"* A *Cuba libre* is a popular cocktail that is one part rum and two parts Coca-Cola. The implication is obvious: Cuba became free, thanks to one part Cuban effort (rum, the Cuban national beverage) and two parts U.S. muscle (Coca-Cola, the quintessential American soft drink). The irony of it did not escape Cubans. Until the death in 1997 of **Roberto C. Goizueta**, a Cuban American who fled **Castro**'s regime and settled in the United States, where he served as the chief executive officer of the Coca-Cola Company, it looked as if the *Cuba libre* was mostly Cuban American. Incidentally, under the direction of Roberto Goizueta, the Coca-Cola Company grew by leaps and bounds, opening whole new markets, including the vast one of China.

What was the Platt Amendment, and why did it open a bucket of worms that helped fuel the 1959 revolution led by Fidel Castro?

The Teller Amendment clearly stated that the United States would not attempt to take over Cuba, but interpreted another way (the way the U.S. government interpreted it), it did not preclude the United States from "protecting" Cuba from itself and helping the island along. Thus, in 1900 the McKinley administration selected Cuban candidates whom it believed Cubans should elect to public office, but the Cuban people refused to elect those candidates. This uppity attitude enraged **President McKinley** and many members of Congress, who decided that Cubans were unwise and thus unable to rule themselves.

Finally, U.S. secretary of war **Elihu Root** drafted a proposal, later christened the Platt Amendment, that advocated letting Cubans go their own way as long as "the Government of Cuba consents that the United States may exercise the right to intervene for the preservation of Cuban independence, [and] the maintenance of a government adequate for the protection of life, property, and individual liberty . . ." The proposal also stipulated that "the Government of Cuba shall never enter into any treaty or other compact with any foreign power or powers which will impair or tend to impair the independence of Cuba." It stated, too, that "the Government of Cuba will sell or lease to the United

States lands necessary for coaling or naval stations." Translation? The United States had the right to instruct the Cuban people on how to govern themselves, to interfere in Cuba's foreign policy when it deemed necessary, and to establish naval stations on the island.

Despite the fact that the Platt Amendment was approved in June 1901, Cuba tried its utmost to go about its business. The Cuban people assembled their own government and, in 1902, elected their first president, **Tomás Estrada Palma**. But the United States was clearly in the picture. In 1903 the U.S. government installed a naval base at Guantánamo Bay and proceeded to closely monitor Cuban affairs. At the same time, American business interests invested heavily in sugar, coffee, tobacco, and other crops on the island. The Cuban economy flourished as never before. Cuba's place as the chief supplier of sugar to America was firmly established, but it was precisely this one-crop economic system that later caused so much distress.

The idea that Cubans were not the masters of their fate, owing to the Platt Amendment, remained a thorn in the side of Cuban patriots. That thorn caused a great deal of irritation on three separate occasions: in 1906, 1912, and 1917, when U.S. military forces invaded Cuba and took provisional charge of its government to protect American interests from internal political unrest and corruption. In the wake of those invasions, Cuban presidents and representatives ran on anti–Platt Amendment platforms, promising to have this piece of legislation repealed. That would not happen until 1934, when **Ramón Grau San Martín**, Cuba's great democratic president (1933–34, 1944–48), proclaimed the abrogation of the Platt Amendment on the day of his inauguration. The United States, however, did get to retain its lease of Guantánamo Bay. After **Fidel Castro** seized power in 1959, he reminded the Cuban people that they had been under U.S. imperialist domination ever since the day the Platt Amendment took effect. The Platt Amendment had become such a symbol of oppression in the minds of Cubans that the mere mention of it was enough to get governments elected and new dictators cheered into office.

What's Guantánamo Bay?

Guantánamo Bay is a large, deep bay on the southeastern shore of Cuba. Covering thirty square miles, it is one of the best-protected bays in the world. The British captured the bay in 1741, during the War of Jenkins's Ear (1739–48); renamed it Cumberland Bay; and established the island's first naval station there during their brief sojourn in Cuba. Then in 1903, the U.S. government secured a perpetual lease on Guantánamo Bay as stipulated in the Cuban-American Treaty, which was renewed in 1934 and which cannot be annulled unilaterally. The U.S. military presence on what **Fidel Castro** and other Cubans consider Cuban territory has long been a source of disagreement between the two nations. American naval operations there also serve to remind Castro's government just how close the United States is.

Who was Fulgencio Batista?

Fulgencio Batista y Zaldívar was the most powerful political figure in Cuba from 1933 to 1944. As an army sergeant, Batista participated in the 1933 ouster of **Gerardo Machado y Morales**, a much-hated dictator who ruled Cuba by graft, corruption, and nepotism (at one point during his regime, almost everyone in high office was related to him). That same year, Batista orchestrated a coup that led to the overthrow of the provisional government of **Carlos Manuel de Céspedes** (a direct descendant of the great nineteenth-century revolutionary by the same name), which had been put in place by the United States. But Batista managed to gain the confidence of the U.S. ambassador to Cuba, who secured him the unconditional backing of the United States. From 1933 to 1940, Batista ruled Cuba from behind the scenes; then, in 1940, he was elected president of Cuba. Of mixed native, African, and Spanish descent, Batista came from humble beginnings—a first for a Cuban president, since those who preceded him belonged to the ruling white elite. He remained in office until his term ended in 1944. In free elections that year, **Ramón Grau San Martín** emerged the victor and ruled Cuba until 1948.

Batista retired to Florida in 1944, but in 1952 he returned to Cuba, with the intent of reestablishing his rule. This time he led a bloodless coup d'état, seizing the reins of government from the democratically elected president, **Carlos Prío Socarrás**. Batista's disregard for the democratic process infuriated Cubans, but he placated the populace with promises of free elections. He did hold presidential elections in 1954 and 1958, but he won handily through graft and ballot fixing. Over time Batista grew from a corrupt, Latin American–style dictator into a power-hungry, ruthless politico who stuffed his pockets and crushed dissent. As **Fidel Castro** and other opposition leaders decried his dictatorship, Batista intensified his efforts to create a police state in Cuba, sending countless members of the opposition to jail or to their deaths.

When he could not eradicate the opposition, Batista bought their favor. After taking money for himself from the proceeds of the national lottery and other sources, Batista doled out the rest in exchange for political backing. In 1957 *Revista Carteles*, a weekly Cuban newsmagazine, disclosed that twenty officials in the Batista government possessed numbered Swiss bank accounts, each with deposits of over $1 million. Batista also gave $1.6 million to the Roman Catholic Church; $5 million to labor unions; and, unbelievably, $1 million a month to newspaper editors and reporters in exchange for their silence. It was no wonder that somewhere in the Sierra Maestra of Oriente Province, a revolution was brewing.

In spite of the undeniable corruption of Batista's dictatorship, on the surface Cuba's economy appeared to be thriving. The island enjoyed one of the highest per capita incomes in Latin America (second only to oil-rich Venezuela) and one of the region's highest standards of living. Havana was as sophisticated and cultured a city as any European capital. By 1957 there were more television sets in Cuba (one per twenty-five inhabitants) than in any other Latin American country. And Cuba was first in telephones, automobiles, and railroads. The island was extolled by many nations aspiring to such creature comforts and general economic well-being.

If Cuba was doing so well, how come a revolution was waiting in the wings?

In the 1950s, Cuba was a mass of contradictions. Yes, the economy was among the strongest in Latin America, but Cuba's economy was tied not to other Latin American countries, but to the United States, which exerted enormous influence on the island. Cuba subsisted almost exclusively on U.S. imports and paid U.S. prices for them, a trend that only intensified over time. For instance, in 1950 Cuba imported $515 million worth of goods from the United States, but by 1958 that figure had risen to $777 million. During the same period, the island's per capita annual income was a mere $374, compared to $2,000 in the United

States. To add insult to injury, in the mid-1950s, the price of sugar, that old reliable crop that ensured Cubans' survival, suddenly plummeted in markets around the world. **Fulgencio Batista** imposed no tariff protection and thereby discouraged the development of any other national industries, since they would not be able to compete against American-made goods.

Then, too, a seemingly unbridgeable chasm yawned between the haves and the have-nots. Although 1950s Havana was one of the world's most expensive cities, with the largest per capita number of Cadillacs, the vast majority of Cubans lived in poverty. Out of a population of almost 6 million, only 620,000 were considered middle class, 200,000 were civil servants, and another 200,000 were service workers, just slightly below the middle class. The rest of the population was comprised of peasants and agricultural workers, large numbers of unemployed, and the very rich, who accounted for a slight percentage of Cubans.

The vast *latifundios*, or agricultural estates, were owned by a handful of wealthy Cubans, as well as by American syndicates, who held 25 percent of all the land in production. The American syndicates often kept the land idle, awaiting a sudden demand for sugar in the world market before bothering to plant or harvest the crop. As a result, the 25 percent of the Cuban people who were employed as sugar workers could only find work an average of one hundred days a year. These workers' daily wages declined sharply during the 1950s, and so did social services. The disparity in the standard of living between the rural and urban populations of Cuba intensified. For instance, while 80 percent of city dwellers had electricity and running water, only 15 percent of rural folk could count on such amenities. In Havana, the ratio of doctors to patients was 1 to 227, while in Oriente (Cuba's easternmost province, where Castro comes from), the ratio was a dismal 1 to 2,423. Illiteracy was on the rise, as fewer children attended school in the 1950s than had done so in the 1920s.

To make matters worse, most of Cuba's wealth was being siphoned out of the country by U.S. companies that took their profits home or by wealthy Cuban nationals, who, fearing a debacle in their very unstable society and an economic depression, courtesy of Cuba's single-crop economy, put their money to work elsewhere—primarily in American real estate, banks, and investment institutions. In the meantime, the Cuban middle class, one of the strongest in Latin America, watched its buying power dwindle and its pool of white-collar jobs evaporate. Middle-class

Cubans, as well as the rural poor, were unable to improve their lot, since they lacked the wherewithal to take their meager savings out of the country or to invest them in a safe vehicle, such as Cuban real estate, which, in a matter of years, had tripled in price as a result of inflation.

Compounding the social and economic disparities and the dire consequences of an almost exclusive dependence on sugar was the deep moral malaise that afflicted the people of this beautiful island. Casinos, controlled by American organized crime and sanctioned by Batista (who took a hefty cut of the profits), were a thriving industry. Illegal drugs were sold openly. Pornography clubs, as well as brothels, became attractive employers for thousands of Cuban women from rural areas who could find no other means of supporting their families. By the end of 1958, an estimated 11,500 women earned livings as prostitutes. In addition, hundreds of underage girls and some boys, as young as eight or nine, were kidnapped into prostitution. Grinding poverty forced many to abandon their newborn babies at the doorsteps of local orphanages. Juvenile delinquency, hopelessness, and suicide had become the norm. The vast majority of the hardworking poor and middle class were caught in an unbearable vise.

While Cuba was falling apart in the 1950s, an idealistic Cuban political leader named **Fidel Castro** was organizing an army of revolutionaries, calling for a clean sweep of government corruption and inefficiency, and promising to end the U.S. economic domination of Cuba and the foreign exploitation of Cuban women and minors. In the cities and throughout the countryside, the people revolted; they gathered at mass demonstrations, planted bombs in movie theaters and other public places, and demanded that the dictator leave at once. Seeing his control slipping, Fulgencio Batista instituted a Gestapo-like police force, which conducted witch hunts and executed citizens en masse.

The foreign press—particularly the American press—was well aware of the Batista regime's human rights violations. Articles in foreign newspapers shed light on one significant fact: the weapons that Batista used to carry out his atrocities were being furnished by none other than the United States of America. **President Dwight Eisenhower** found himself in a very serious dilemma: although Batista's government protected the interests of U.S. companies and investments on the island and cooperated when it came to U.S. military operations in Cuba, Batista's totalitarian measures were completely at odds with America's fundamental principles. And although **Earl T. Smith**, the U.S. ambassador to Cuba, warned Eisenhower that Castro was an alleged communist (a word that made Americans shudder in those tense Cold War years), the American president felt he could no longer justify supplying arms to Fulgencio Batista.

Toward the end of 1958, the United States suspended the sale of tanks and other weapons to Batista's regime. In the dawn of January 1, 1959, the dictator, seeing the writing on the wall, fled Cuba for Spain, where he died a rich man in 1973. At about the same hour, Fidel Castro, **Che Guevara**, **Raúl Castro**, **Camilo Cienfuegos**, and a host of other revolutionaries began their long descent from the Sierra Maestra toward the Cuban capital. They rode in open jeeps, sporting their trademark beards and khaki uniforms, greeting the droves of cheering, hopeful Cubans along the highways and byways, who believed that at last, democracy and basic morality would be restored in their beloved country.

Who is Fidel Castro, and what happened to his idealistic revolution, which sent scores of Cubans fleeing to Miami?

Fidel Castro Ruz, better known as Fidel to friend and foe alike, was born in Oriente, the easternmost province of Cuba, on August 13, 1926. He attended Jesuit schools in Santiago de Cuba, Oriente's capital city, and in Havana, and in 1950 he graduated from the University of Havana with a degree in law. In 1948 Castro married **Mirta Diaz Balart de Nuñez**. While he was in exile in Mexico in 1955, she divorced him, and in the wake of the revolution, she and members of her family declared themselves loyal anti-Castro democrats and fled to the United States. Fidel's nephew **Lincoln Diaz-Balart**, who was just four years old when he left Cuba in 1959, has represented the state of Florida in the U.S. House of Representatives since 1992. And another of Fidel's nephews, **Mario Diaz-Balart**, who is Lincoln Diaz-Balart's brother, has represented Florida in the House since 2002. Fidel's eldest son, **Fidel Castro Diaz-Balart**, who was born in 1949, has remained loyal to his father. A nuclear physicist, he served as head of Cuba's atomic energy commission from 1979 to 1992.

Fidel Castro was a political animal from an early age. In the late 1940s and early 1950s, he was a member of the *Partido Ortodoxo*, which was organized in 1947 around the issue of government corruption and the need for reform. Castro opposed **Batista**'s regime from the start, and on July 26, 1953, he launched a daring attack on the Moncada barracks in Santiago de Cuba, with the intent of seizing arms for his guerillas and igniting a popular revolt. This assault against Batista's regime failed, and Castro was sentenced to fifteen years in prison, but his daring maneuver earned him instant recognition. From prison he wrote his famous "history will absolve me" defense speech, in which he presents his anti-imperialist, reformist, and nationalistic ideals. At the time, Castro did not reveal that he was a Marxist-Leninist or propose outright a communist agenda. In 1955 Batista's government granted Fidel Castro amnesty, under the condition that he leave Cuba for good.

Castro went into exile in Mexico, where he founded the Twenty-sixth of July Movement (a date celebrated in Cuba today with as much fanfare as the Fourth of July in the United States) for the purpose of overthrowing the Batista dictatorship. In December 1956, Castro and eighty-one other rebels, including his brother **Raúl Castro** and the Argentine revolutionary **Ernesto "Che" Guevara**, made their way surreptitiously by boat to Cuba. Only twelve rebels, including the Castro brothers and Che Guevara, survived a botched landfall, and they immediately set up military headquarters in the westernmost part of the Sierra Maestra, in Oriente Province. From there Fidel Castro and his followers organized a revolution against the Cuban government, recruiting thousands of disgruntled peasants in Cuba's interior and exciting the imagination of millions of Cubans of all social and economic classes, who viewed Castro as a New World messiah with the vision to bring sanity, law and order, and economic well-being to Cuba. By 1957 Castro had garnered the backing of foreign countries, owing in part to an interview he'd given in his Sierra Maestra headquarters early that year to American journalist **Herbert Matthews** from the *New York Times*, which painted a portrait of him as a courageous, romantic figure whose sole aim was to hold free elections in Cuba and restore the Cuban Constitution of 1940. By 1958 many of Cuba's opposition groups had thrown their support behind Castro, and that very year Castro and his guerilla forces seized command of numerous cities. Batista knew his days were numbered.

When Fidel Castro took control of Cuba in 1959, his revolutionary regime welcomed middle-of-the-road politicians and citizens, a large number of whom viewed him as a democratic reformer with an honest, clear-cut agenda to rein in the widespread corruption and mismanagement in Cuba's government and get on with the island's constitutional democracy. In a matter of months, however, Castro began implementing socialist reforms, which included the confiscation of privately owned land and industries. As early as 1961, he publicly declared, "I have been a Marxist-Leninist all along and will remain one until I die." Castro proceeded to align himself with the Soviet Union, both economically and politically, in effect handing the island over to Soviet premier **Nikita Khrushchev**.

At home Castro put members of the Communist Party of Cuba and party sympathizers in charge of the media, the schools and universities, and every other important institution. In the way of all communist leaders, he could neither tolerate nor afford dissent, and he established organizations to monitor the Cuban people, stifling any opposition. For instance, every district formed a Committee for the Defense of the Revolution, which made an inventory of each resident's personal property and recorded his or her activities. In those days, it was hard to know whom you could trust; neighbors and even friends betrayed each other. Those who strayed from communist doctrine or defied the regime were dealt with harshly. Thousands upon thousands of Cuban nationals who opposed Castro's government were executed or incarcerated in concentration camps. Castro's puritanical regime also sent gay men and lesbians, no matter their political bent, to a concentration camp known as Guanahacabibes. Writers, filmmakers, singers, composers, and artists were put on notice: Let your art reflect communist ideology or else.

As early as 1959, Cuba's political elite, mainly Batista supporters, *Batistianos,* who knew Castro wanted them dead, fled the island. Then hundreds of thousands of Cubans who had believed Castro to be a quintessential democratic leader awoke to the realization that they had exchanged one dictator for another, and that their island had become a perilous beachhead for the Soviet Union, where any minute a nuclear war between the superpowers could explode in their midst. By 1960 a large wave of Cuban immigration to the United States had been unleashed. Upper-, middle-, and lower-middle-class Cubans fled the island for the United States, in particular Miami, where the U.S. government welcomed them as political refugees.

What's a gusano?

Gusano, Spanish for "worm," is a derogatory term Castro Cubans use for Cuban exiles and Cuban Americans. Latinos also might call Cuban Americans *gusanos*—sometimes in jest and sometimes not. Another name Latinos have for Cuban Americans (particularly those who came in the 1960s) is *los tenía*, literally "the I-used-to-have people," because Cuban Americans often reminisce about all they used to have back in the old country.

Who was Che Guevara?

Ernesto "Che" Guevara was born in Argentina on June 14, 1928. His nickname, Che, translates loosely as "Hey, buddy!" and is a vernacular phrase Argentineans use when addressing one another. Although he was trained as a physician, Che Guevara was first and foremost a student of Marxist-Leninist ideology and a revolutionary. In Argentina, where he was a member of the Communist Party, he led revolts against **President Juan Perón** (**Evita**'s husband) in 1952, and in 1953 he went to Guatemala, where he joined the leftist regime of **Jacobo Arbenz Guzmán**. After Arbenz was overthrown in 1954, Che Guevara joined **Fidel Castro** in Mexico to help plan the communist revolution in Cuba. When Castro's rebels invaded Cuba in 1956, Guevara performed superbly and became one of Castro's most trusted comrades. Although Che Guevara held many important posts in the Castro government, such as minister of industry (1961–65), his campaign to transform Latin America into a communist playground took precedence. In 1965 he embarked on a secret mission to Bolivia to train a guerilla force. Two years later, Bolivian government troops captured Guevara near Santa Cruz and executed him.

Che Guevara is remembered for his goatee and his black Argentine beret, as well as for his guerilla training manuals and Marxist-Leninist revolutionary books, including *Guerrilla Warfare* (1961) and *Man and Socialism in Cuba* (1967). Hollywood turned his life story into the feature film *Che!* (1969), in which **Omar Sharif** plays Guevara, and **Jack Palance**, Castro.

What has Fidel done for Cuba?

Aside from aligning Cuba with the Soviet bloc as the Cold War raged, assisting Marxist-Leninist revolutions around the globe (most notably in Angola, where hundreds of Cuban soldiers perished), and violating Cuban citizens' human rights for nearly half a century now by denying them freedoms of speech, assembly, association, movement, and the press and subjecting them to intense surveillance, detention, house arrest, arbitrary searches, the confiscation of their possessions, severe travel restrictions, dismissals from employment for political reasons, desperate living conditions, and much worse, **Fidel Castro**'s greatest claims to fame are undoubtedly the successful consolidation of a communist regime within ninety miles of American shores and the establishment of the longest dictatorship in history.

During his dictatorship of over forty-seven years, Castro has invested much effort into education—stressing technology and science, in the way of most communist regimes, including the former Soviet Union—and as a result, Cuba enjoys the highest literacy rate in Latin America. One of Castro's early revolutionary aims was to transform Cuba's economy from one based on a single crop to one that was technology and service oriented. In reality he has not succeeded any more than his predecessors in bringing Cuba out of its single-crop economic nightmare. He simply found another buyer for Cuban sugar. Whereas previous Cuban governments sold sugar to the United States, Castro sold it to the Soviet Union—at least until that country collapsed in 1991, sending the Cuban economy, which had come to rely on Soviet subsidized trade and billions of dollars in Soviet aid to sustain it, into an even steeper decline.

Castro's government also initially placed great emphasis on cradle-to-grave social services that were called "achievements of the revolution." As a result, Cuban nationals have had access to health care and other social welfare benefits that were denied them during the Batista years. However, Cuba has been in such desperate economic straits that medical equipment and supplies, including basic medicines, are scarce, and Cubans suffer needlessly. Furthermore, many of the illnesses that Cubans contract are the direct result of poor nutrition and a lack of preventive care, for which only the Castro regime is to blame.

What happened at the Bay of Pigs, and why did Cuban Americans blame President Kennedy?

The mass exodus of Cubans from the island that commenced in 1959, as well as **Fidel Castro**'s ceaseless tirades against the United

States, put the U.S. government on notice. When, soon after seizing power, the fatigue-clad Cuban dictator brokered international agreements with the Soviet Union and other communist countries, and completely nationalized all U.S. businesses and commercial properties on the island—in effect declaring an ideological war against his nearest and most powerful neighbor—the U.S. government was forced to take action. In 1960, **President Dwight Eisenhower** gave the CIA the go-ahead to recruit, train, and equip Cuban exiles in the United States for operations against Castro's regime. By then the CIA had a successful track record of toppling foreign leaders, among them Guatemalan president **Jacobo Arbenz Guzmán** in 1954. Amid rapidly worsening relations between the United States and Cuba, on January 3, 1961, just before leaving office, President Eisenhower severed diplomatic relations with Cuba.

By early April 1961, **Allen Dulles**, who had been serving as director of the CIA since 1953, and his aides were putting the finishing touches on Operation Zapata, a plot to secretly invade Cuba and oust Castro, with the aid of U.S. Brigade 2506, which was comprised of newly trained Cuban exiles. Dulles persuaded **President John F. Kennedy**, then newly elected, to move ahead with the invasion of Cuba and ignite a carefully orchestrated popular revolt in Cuba, with the assistance of anti-Castro agents strategically positioned on the island. A facet of Operation Zapata, which was not revealed to the public until a Senate investigation of President Kennedy's assassination brought it to light years later, was the CIA's plan to assassinate Fidel Castro, with the help of the Mafia, namely, **Sam Giancana** and **John Roselli**'s hit men. Giancana was murdered before he could tell the Senate the inside story; Roselli testified, but his decomposed body was found floating in an oil drum in Florida shortly thereafter. Kennedy agreed to the CIA plan but wanted the impending operation to appear as a preemptive strike against Cuba in response to its recent arms buildup, which posed a threat to U.S. security.

U.S. Brigade 2506 initially received President Kennedy's full backing, but the Cuban invasion was ill conceived from the start. First of all, the 1,400 middle-class Cuban exiles of Brigade 2506, most of whom had never before held a rifle, had not received enough training and were underequipped. They were also kept in the dark as to what their next move would be once they reached Cuba's shores. Secondly, the U.S. government apparently had vast quantities of misinformation in its files regarding the island's topography and the military installations around the designated landing site, *Bahía de Cochinos* (the Bay of Pigs), on the south coast of Cuba. Cuban exiles who knew the territory well warned U.S. intelligence that treacherous coral reefs at the proposed landing site would jeopardize the mission, but the CIA did not heed their warning. The CIA also failed to notice that Fidel Castro had recently built himself a beach house very near the Bay of Pigs, and thus the whole area was heavily guarded. Also, given the chosen landing site, Brigade 2506 would be unable to establish communications with Cuban rebels poised to join them in the invasion. If that were not bad enough, the so-called secret mission was leaked to the press—and no doubt to Castro's soldiers and loyal militia, who were fully prepared to greet Brigade 2506 with armored tanks and heavy ammunition when it reached Cuba's shores on April 17, 1961.

In planning the invasion, the CIA assured members of Brigade 2506 that the United States would provide full air cover during the entire operation and that should the exiles be captured, the U.S. military would come to their aid. At the last minute, once the invasion was already under way, President Kennedy changed his mind and cancelled U.S air strikes across the island, which had already commenced and had been meant to cripple the Cuban air force and thus provide Brigade 2506 with air superiority. Meanwhile, on April 17, 1961, Brigade 2506 made landfall at the Bay of Pigs, but it did not get the support from the local population that the CIA had expected, in part because Castro had already executed or imprisoned those conspiring with the American invaders. President Kennedy decided against lending Brigade 2506 air support, against launching several combat operations against the Cuban air force, and against sending in the marines, even though U.S. ships had been stationed off the Cuban coast and the troops were poised for action.

President Kennedy's sudden stand-down may have stemmed from concern that the Bay of Pigs invasion would not be interpreted as a preemptive strike against Cuban military installations, but rather as a direct confrontation with a Soviet bloc country, and that it would precipitate the next world war. Whatever President Kennedy's reasons, his decision cost 114 Cuban exiles their lives at the Bay of Pigs. Another 1,189 were taken prisoner as proof positive to the world of the United States' invasion. **Attorney General Robert F. Kennedy** later gave Cuba foodstuffs as ransom to secure the release of the captured exiles. The captives' families in the United States also handed Castro hard cash for the young invaders' release. Some Cuban refugees wired their entire life savings to Fidel in exchange for their sons.

In later years, once their U.S. citizenship papers were in order, the overwhelming majority of Cuban Americans of the first wave registered Republican. Their preference for the Republican Party was founded on the belief that the Republicans were more effective in combating communism and dictatorships in Cuba and around the globe. They were also unwilling to forget the "Kennedy betrayal." Older generations of Cuban Americans in Miami even call a person who is weak-spined and probably leftist a *kennedito* ("little Kennedy"). Anti-Kennedy sentiment was so pervasive in the Cuban American community in the early 1960s that after President Kennedy was assassinated in 1963, some pointed a finger at Cuban Americans as potential conspirators. In his 1991 film *JFK*, **Oliver Stone** explores the possibility of a Cuban American role in the Kennedy assassination. Unfortunately, the director paints a stereotypical picture of Cuban Americans as a devious, power-hungry bunch capable of such a heinous act.

What caused the Cuban Missile Crisis?

Soviet premier Nikita Khrushchev interpreted the United States' abysmal failure at the Bay of Pigs as a sign that the U.S. president was weak. In the summer of 1962, he secretly established a nuclear beachhead in Cuba, right at **President Kennedy**'s doorstep, to deter future U.S. invasions of the island and to guarantee the Soviet Union a more favorable balance of power (a Soviet presence in the Caribbean would offset the U.S. placement of deployable nuclear warheads in Italy, the United Kingdom, and, in particular, Turkey). Khrushchev's clandestine construction of nine launching sites for medium-range nuclear missiles in Cuba took the world by surprise.

Once aerial photographs by U.S. military intelligence uncovered the frightening time bomb at America's threshold and the photographs were shown to President Kennedy on October 16, 1962, the Pentagon advised the president to launch a full-scale surprise attack on Cuba, with the aim of toppling Castro's regime. Instead, Kennedy issued a public ultimatum to the USSR on October 22, 1962: he declared a naval blockade on Cuba and demanded the immediate withdrawal of all nuclear missiles from the island and the dismantling of the nuclear-missile installations. The world held its breath as the superpowers teetered on the brink of nuclear warfare. Finally, on October 28, Khrushchev acquiesced to Kennedy's demands and agreed to remove the nuclear missiles and dismantle the missile installations in Cuba in exchange for reassurances that the United States would refrain from intervening militarily or politically in Cuba's affairs. While the Kennedy administration gave such reassurances, it proceeded to impose an economic embargo against Cuba in 1962, which remains in effect to this day.

The Cuban Missile Crisis ushered to a close a very long chapter in history for most Cuban Americans. Although many still hoped against hope that they would return to their beloved homeland, the vast majority acknowledged that the United States was home and that Castro's downfall might take quite a number of years. No one measured Castro's dictatorship in decades, let alone half centuries. Given that U.S. foreign policy largely focused on preventing nations from falling to communism—the geopolitical concept of falling dominoes—Cuban Americans, and all Americans, never imagined that a communist regime would be allowed to exist only ninety miles from Florida, but as Bob Dylan's popular 1964 ballad proclaimed, the times they were a-changing. And President Kennedy had another war to wage with the Communists just then—this time in Asia, in a country called Vietnam.

How many Cubans fled Cuba in the 1960s and 1970s, and how did they fare?

In the early days of the mass exodus from Cuba, Cubans were free to board any of the Pan American flights departing the island for Miami. **Fidel Castro** considered this a surefire method of purging the country of enemies of the state. Those Cubans who left after the spring of 1961 were forced to hand over all their life savings and possessions to the Cuban government, except for five dollars and one outfit of clothing. Despite the terrific losses, about two thousand Cubans fled Cuba each week. Then, during the summer of 1961, in the aftermath of the Bay of Pigs invasion, Castro made emigration a kind of roulette: he punished some for merely applying to leave, while granting permission to emigrate to others. After **President Kennedy** imposed a naval blockade of Cuba in 1962, all flights from the island to Miami were canceled, and emigration was outlawed. This ban on emigration lasted until 1965.

Still, in those days about thirty thousand Cubans managed to escape Cuba by sailing or floating across the Straits of Florida, or flying first to Mexico or Spain and then on to the United States.

In 1965, when Castro once again opened the floodgates of emigration, flotillas of Cuban exiles in Florida headed to Cuba to pick up their relatives. The U.S. government also organized an airlift of Cubans, and 3,700 entered the country each month. In 1973 Castro again slammed the doors shut on emigration. For the next seven years, until 1980, virtually the only way to leave Cuba was to steal away on a makeshift raft and sail across the treacherous, shark-infested Florida Straits to Miami and freedom. An untold number of Cubans who attempted the journey died in rough seas along the way or succumbed to exposure or shark attacks.

Those Cubans who came to the United States during the 1960s and 1970s—the first large wave of Cuban refugees—wasted no time in rebuilding their lives in Miami, though a minority settled in New Jersey (where Union City emerged as a Cuban American hub), New York, Washington DC, and Los Angeles (where they settled first in Echo Park and then dispersed throughout the Southland). Many initially received aid in the form of temporary shelter, meals, medical care, and $100 a month from the Cuban Refugee Emergency Center in Miami, but they swiftly gained a footing in their new country. Within a year, some Cuban refugees who had come penniless to American shores owned businesses or held white-collar jobs. Their education, skills, and fervent desire to succeed, as well as the fact that the great majority were Caucasian and did not experience overt racial prejudice, enabled the refugees to quickly establish a thriving Cuban American enclave in Miami. By 1970 Cuban exiles controlled Miami's service sector. In the decades to come, they would transform the city from a retirement beach town built on a swamp to what international bankers, politicians, and businesspeople call the "capital of Latin America."

What is the Cuban Adjustment Act?

On November 2, 1966, the U.S. Congress adopted the Cuban Adjustment Act, which gives all citizens of Cuba admitted or paroled into the United States after January 1, 1959, and present in the country for at least one year, the special status of political refugees, with the right to automatic permanent residence. Under the Cuban Adjustment Act, Cuban refugees face none of the restrictions governing immigration to the United States, such as presenting proof of persecution at home, and are virtually guaranteed permanent resettlement in the United States (unless they are criminals), whether they simply overstay their tourist visas or arrive anywhere on U.S. shores (and not just at designated ports of entry) with no documentation at all. The Cuban Adjustment Act has remained in effect to this day, though it has come under challenge at times from those who believe that Cubans should not be afforded special status.

Who were the Marielitos, and why did so many people despise them?

In the spring of 1980, twelve Cubans, with no legal way of leaving Cuba, crashed through the gates of the Peruvian embassy in Havana, demanding political asylum. A few days later, **Fidel Castro** lifted his seven-year ban on emigration and announced that all Cubans wishing to leave the island should report to the port of Mariel, where Americans could pick them up by boat. Eleven thousand Cubans showed up, unleashing a second wave of Cuban immigration. Castro then flung open the doors of his prisons, and between April 21 and September 26, 1980, he allowed Cuban Americans from Miami to load nearly 125,000 Cubans, approximately 1.3 percent of Cuba's population at the time, onto shrimp boats and other vessels, dubbed the Freedom Flotilla. The Cuban refugees, known as Marielitos because they departed from the port of Mariel, were boatlifted to Key West. On May 11, 1980, alone, 4,588 Cuban refugees sailed to the United States, breaking the record for the most arrivals in a single day. **President Jimmy Carter** gave the okay to take in the refugees for humanitarian and political reasons. The Marielitos were granted parole status, which meant that they could live in the United States, but they were not considered to have officially entered the country. (Essentially, they occupied a legal no-man's-land, an odd status.) Under the Immigration Reform and Control Act of 1986, most of the Marielitos eventually were given permanent resident status.

There was only one problem with the whole operation: while the vast majority of Marielitos had been law-abiding citizens in Cuba or legitimate political prisoners (whose only crime had been to oppose the communist regime), some were mentally ill (about six hundred), and some were suspected of being common criminals whose offenses were serious enough to warrant detention and then removal from the United States. Others were also targeted for detention and removal for such reasons as committing a crime on American soil before their parole status was adjusted to permanent resident. When it became clear that some of the refugees were part of a dastardly ruse played on an amiable President Carter by Fidel Castro to get rid of his Cuban undesirables, Americans were up in arms. Cuban Americans in Miami, who had rushed to the aid of the new arrivals with the full weight of their highly organized private charitable organizations, were horrified. They feared that this wave of Cubans would tarnish the stellar image they had worked so hard to build in America. Many criticized President Carter's decision to let the Marielitos enter the United States in the first place.

The U.S. government initially detained 22,000 of the original 125,000 Mariel Cubans, but most of the detainees were found to have committed only political crimes in Cuba and were set free. In the end, only some 3,700 Mariel Cubans were deemed excludable aliens by the U.S. Immigration and Naturalization Service. Excludable aliens, unlike illegal aliens, are not considered persons under the U.S. Constitution and, therefore, have no rights. However, Cuba refused to repatriate its nationals who had fled, and so 2,300 of the excludable aliens were simply shipped to two U.S. penal institutions, one a regular prison in Oakdale, Louisiana, and the other a maximum-security prison in Atlanta that had once housed **Al Capone**. (Unfortunately, these few bad apples gave all Marielitos a bad name, as evidenced by the 1983 motion picture *Scarface*, in which Al Pacino plays a cocaine-addicted, violent Cuban Mariel, and they would fight for decades to reverse this negative stereotype.) The excludable Marielitos remained behind bars, with no right to legal counsel, for seven years, until 1987, when a sudden change in U.S.-Cuba relations brought the whole matter to a head.

In November 1987, the United States and Cuba reached an agreement aimed at controlling the flow of Cubans into the United States. The agreement established an annual quota of twenty thousand Cuban immigrants as long as Castro agreed to take back the Mariel excludable aliens whose names had been put on a list in 1984. In the immigration process, the United States gave priority to former Cuban political prisoners and their relatives. Those who saw no way out of Cuba or could not bear to wait were forced to take to the seas in small boats. Upon learning that they were going to be returned to Cuba, the imprisoned Marielitos rioted. In the riot negotiations, the Department of Justice promised "fair and equitable" hearings to review each case and release those deemed harmless to society. Thousands were set free, but many others continued to languish behind bars.

On January 12, 2005, almost twenty-five years after the Marielitos fled to the United States, the U.S. Supreme Court ruled in *Clark v. Martinez* that Marielitos **Sergio Suarez Martínez** and **Daniel Benítez** and similarly situated persons, who have been deemed inadmissible aliens and are subject to removal, but cannot be removed, can only be detained for a period of six months, a reasonable period of time to execute their removal from the United States. With the Supreme Court's decision that the continued detention of Marielitos was illegal, U.S. immigration officials began quietly releasing some of the approximately 750 Marielitos still incarcerated in American prisons. In the case of many of the Marielitos freed from Alabama prisons, government officials simply gave them an immigration card and little else and dumped them at a Salvation Army.

FILMS ABOUT LATINOS

1. *West Side Story* (1961)

2. *Alambrista!* (1977)

3. *Zoot Suit* (1981)

4. *The Ballad of Gregorio Cortez* (1982)

5. *El Norte* (The North, 1983)

6. *Scarface* (1983)

7. *Crossover Dreams* (1985)

8. *La Bamba* (1987)

9. *Born in East L.A.* (1987)

10. *Stand and Deliver* (1988)

11. *The Milagro Beanfield War* (1988)

12. *The Mambo Kings* (1992)

13. *American Me* (1992)

14. *El Mariachi* (1992)

15. *Mi Vida Loca* (My Crazy Life, 1993)

16. *A Million to Juan* (1994)

17. *I Like It Like That* (1994)

18. *Desperado* (1995)

19. *My Family, Mi Familia* (1995)

20. *Lone Star* (1996)

21. *Star Maps* (1997)

22. *Selena* (1997)

23. *Before Night Falls* (2000)

24. *Maid in Manhattan* (2002)

25. *Real Women Have Curves* (2002)

26. *Chasing Papi* (2003)

27. *Boricua* (2004)

28. *Maria Full of Grace* (2004)

29. *Spanglish* (2004)

30. *The Motorcycle Diaries* (2004)

31. *Maid in America* (2005)

32. *Carlito's Way: Rise to Power* (2005)

33. *The Lost City* (2005)

34. *Ask the Dust* (2006)

35. *Bordertown* (2006)

36. *Nacho Libre* (2006)

37. *Quinceañera* (2006)

38. *El Cantante* (2007)

What is the 1992 Cuban Democracy Act?

The 1992 Cuban Democracy Act, also known as the Torricelli law, because it was the undertaking of **Congressman Robert Torricelli** (D-NJ), was the first significant piece of legislation related to the U.S. embargo of Cuba since **President Kennedy** imposed comprehensive sanctions against the island in 1962. The Cuban Democracy Act was meant to strengthen the economic restrictions on Cuba and further isolate **Fidel Castro** in the aftermath of the Soviet Union's collapse by prohibiting any foreign-based subsidiaries of U.S. companies from engaging in trade with the island. Additionally, the Cuban Democracy Act prohibits entry into the United States of any vessel loading or unloading freight that has engaged in trade with Cuba in the last 180 days.

What was the 1994 rafter refugee crisis, and why did it unleash something of a challenge to the Cuban Adjustment Act of 1966?

In 1994 a crisis erupted when forty thousand Cubans in a flotilla of small, barely seaworthy boats headed en masse to Florida's shores. Alarmed that **Fidel Castro** would unleash a mass emigration from Cuba and that Florida would be inundated, **President Bill Clinton**, after consulting with Cuban American **Jorge Mas Canosa**, who was one of the most powerful lobbyists in America at the time, refused the Cuban rafters (*balseros*) permission to enter the United States. Instead, they were interned along with Haitian boat people at the American military base at Guantánamo Bay and at the base in Krome, Florida. Clinton also severed all flight service between Miami and Cuba for family members, made it unlawful for U.S. residents to send cash remittances to relatives in Cuba, and expanded Radio Martí—a kind of Voice of America station whose broadcasts are aimed at Cuba. (Some critics argue that President Clinton acted so swiftly and decisively because his brother-in-law, **Hugh Rodham**, is married to **Maria Victoria Arias**, a Miami lawyer who shares Jorge Mas Canosa's sentiments about Cuba.) Some in the Cuban exile community were up in arms over the way the Cuban rafters were treated, and ultimately, the Clinton administration allowed the Cubans at Guantánamo Bay to enter the United States as refugees.

In the aftermath of the Cuban rafter refugee crisis, the Clinton administration and members of Congress considered ways to avert a similar outflow of Cuban rafters in the future and to promote an orderly, safe migration of Cubans. One proposal put forward was to abandon the Cuban Adjustment Act of 1966, which grants all Cubans seeking asylum in the United States the special status of political refugees and stipulates that once they have been physically present in the United States for at least one year, they may been afforded permanent resident status. In the end, the Cuban Adjustment Act was not repealed.

What is the wet-foot/dry-foot policy?

Instead of repealing the Cuban Adjustment Act of 1966 in the wake of the 1994 Cuban rafter refugee crisis, **President Clinton** signed migration accords with Cuba that same year that grant the United States the right to return to Cuba all Cubans picked up at sea—even if they are found just a few meters from U.S. shores—by the U.S. Coast Guard (those who reach dry land are exempt and are given special refugee status) in exchange for allowing twenty thousand Cubans to immigrate to the United States annually through a legal visa lottery system in place in Cuba. Approximately half of those Cubans who obtain such visas are admitted as "parolees" through the parole authority vested in the U.S. attorney general, which means that they are eligible for refugee benefits, while the other half are treated as immigrants with no special refugee benefits.

The so-called wet-foot/dry-foot policy—that is, the extension of special refugee status only to those Cubans who flee Cuba and actually touch American soil (dry foot) and not to those floundering miles or even just meters offshore (wet foot)—has made the prospect of finding freedom across the Florida Straits much more remote for Cubans. The policy has also angered and frustrated many in the Cuban American community and beyond, who deem it barbaric. The occasional national television coverage of desperate, dehydrated Cubans floating or swimming just off the Florida coastline, struggling to outwit U.S. Coast Guard boats pursuing them as they attempt to touch dry land, underscores the poignancy of the situation.

The debate over wet-foot/dry-foot turned especially bitter in early 2006, when the U.S. government deported fifteen Cubans who had fled Cuba and on January 4, 2006, had made it as far as some pilings of an abandoned, partially collapsed bridge in the Florida Keys, as their small boat filled with water. The U.S. government concluded that since pieces of the bridge were missing and it no longer connected to land, its pilings did not count as "dry land." Had the fifteen Cuban migrants made it to the new bridge, a hundred yards away, the U.S. government would have in all probability allowed them to remain in the United States. In February 2006, a federal judge ruled that the U.S. government's conduct concerning the fifteen Cubans had been unreasonable, and it ordered the government to make every effort to bring the Cubans back to the United States, something **Fidel Castro** is unlikely to permit.

Hoping to improve their chances of touching American soil and obtaining asylum, Cubans have increasingly turned to people-smuggling operations in South Florida to provide them passage across the Florida Straits. In a way, the smugglers have made the journey from Cuba a bit safer for those fleeing the island, because they travel by speedboats, not by rickety rafts and makeshift boats. Since 2001 an increasing number of Cubans have forsaken the heavily patrolled Florida Straits altogether and have attempted to reach Puerto Rico, a U.S. territory with commonwealth status, by first flying to the Dominican Republic and then making the voyage by boat from there to Puerto Rico. The same voyage is taken each year by thousands of Dominicans seeking to enter the United States illegally.

As far as the goal of issuing twenty thousand visas annually to Cuban "lottery winners" is concerned, the United States has kept up its part of the agreement—but not without some interference by the Cuban government. In the periodic meetings on migration that have taken place between U.S. and Cuban officials since the 1994 migration accords, the United States has voiced concern over such Cuban practices as demanding high fees from those seeking to leave Cuba and denying exit permits without reasonable cause to particular individuals.

What happened to Brothers to the Rescue in 1996?

Ever since the Bay of Pigs invasion ended in disaster, the U.S. government has refrained from lending official military backing to Cuban American schemes to oust **Fidel Castro** from power. However, to this day the United States continues to condemn Castro's dictatorship and impose the trade embargo against Cuba that **President Kennedy** ordered. Washington has also looked the other way whenever Cuban American exile groups in South Florida plan and execute attacks against Cuba.

One such group is Brothers to the Rescue (*Hermanos al Rescate*), which several pilots organized in May 1991, after hearing of the death of a fifteen-year-old Cuban boy, **Gregorio Pérez Ricardo**, who had fled Castro's Cuba on a raft and had perished from severe dehydration in the Florida Straits. The mission of Brothers to the Rescue is "to promote and support the efforts of the Cuban people to free themselves from dictatorship through the use of active nonviolence." The organization concentrates much of its efforts on finding and saving Cubans fleeing Cuba on makeshift rafts, whose lives are in peril in the Straits of Florida, and on aiding the families of Cuba's political prisoners. It has also air-dropped emergency food and water supplies to Cuban rafters stranded on uninhabited Bahamian islands and has made regular deliveries of food, medicine, and clothing to a Cuban refugee camp in Nassau, Bahamas. As of 2007, Brothers to the Rescue had conducted over 2,400 humanitarian missions, saving the lives of over 4,200 Cubans in desperate need in the Florida Straits, from a five-day-old newborn to a seventy-nine-year-old man.

On these aerial search-and-rescue missions, pilots from Brothers to the Rescue have penetrated Cuban airspace from time to time. On February 24, 1996, a Cuban MiG-29 flying over international waters shot down two unarmed civilian aircraft, Cessna 337s, operated by Brothers to the Rescue, killing four fliers on board. Castro, who personally gave the order for the brutal attack, alleged that the fliers had violated Cuban airspace. The Cuban government defended its harsh actions by claiming that earlier in the year Brothers to the Rescue had twice dropped anti-Castro leaflets over Havana, forcing Cuba to issue a warning that in the future it would shoot down any aircraft violating Cuban airspace. The Cuban American community expressed outrage over the incident, as summed up in the remarks of congresswoman **Ileana Ros-Lehtinen** (R-FL), a Cuban American, who was quoted as saying, "I think this is an act of aggression, of terrorism."

President Clinton denounced Castro for shooting down planes that posed no threat to Cuba's security and declared the act a clear violation of international law. To punish Cuba, the Clinton administration imposed tighter political and economic sanctions, including suspending charter flights (the only passenger air service in place) between the two countries; lent greater financial backing to Radio Martí; and compensated each of the victims' families with a portion of frozen Cuban assets. The president also abandoned his opposition to the Helms-Burton bill and pledged to work with Congress to secure its passage.

What exactly is the Helms-Burton Act, and which Cuban Americans cosponsored it?

The Helms-Burton Act is one of the two most important pieces of Cuba-related legislation of the 1990s (the other was the 1992 Cuban Democracy Act). The purpose of the Helms-Burton Act, which was introduced in 1995 by South Carolina senator **Jesse Helms** and Indiana congressman **Dan Burton**, both Republicans, and was signed into law by **President Clinton** on March 12, 1996, was to further tighten the comprehensive sanctions against Castro's repressive communist regime; to outline U.S. policy toward, and assistance to, a transition from communism to a stable, democratic form of government in Cuba; and to authorize U.S. nationals and companies to sue in U.S. Federal Court any person, company, or government conducting business in Cuba who traffics in American property confiscated by the Cuban government. In terms of the latter, the Helms-Burton Act, also known as the Cuban Liberty and Democratic Solidarity Act or the Libertad Act, grants U.S. presidents the authority to suspend lawsuit provisions for periods of six months if such an action is in the best interest of the United States and expedites a transition to democracy in Cuba. President Clinton suspended the lawsuit provisions throughout his years in office due in part to threats of economic retaliation from the international community, and thus far **President George W. Bush** has followed this pattern.

Among the cosponsors of the Helms-Burton bill were the three Cuban Americans in the U.S. House of Representatives at the time, namely, **Lincoln Diaz-Balart** (R-FL), **Ileana Ros-Lehtinen** (R-FL), and **Robert Menendez** (D-NJ), all of whom continue to serve in Washington. In addition to his dedication to the Helms-Burton Act and other Cuba-related legislation, as well as to his constituents and the larger Cuban American community, Congressman Lincoln Diaz-Balart, who was elected to the House from Florida's Twenty-first Congressional District in 1992, has done much on behalf of all Latinos. He participated in the successful campaign to reinstate Social Security benefits and food stamps for legal immigrants denied access to such aid by the welfare reform law of 1996. And, the congressman was the chief initiator of the Nicaraguan Adjustment and Central American Relief Act of 1997, which extended legal residency to hundreds of thousands of U.S. immigrants. In 2000 a poll conducted for *Hispanic* magazine (September 2000 issue) ranked Congressman Diaz-Balart among the nation's ten most influential Hispanics. That same year he was reelected to Congress without opposition.

In 2002 Congressman Lincoln Diaz-Balart was joined in the House by his brother, **Mario Diaz-Balart**, who represents Florida's Twenty-fifth Congressional District. In 2004 Mario Diaz-Balart was reelected to a second term without opposition. In 2006, he (and his brother) supported President Bush's efforts to craft a more comprehensive immigration bill, one that would grant work permits to undocumented immigrants and make it possible for the undocumented in the United States to gain green cards and eventually U.S. citizenship after a requisite number of years.

Congresswoman Ileana Ros-Lehtinen, who has represented Florida's Eighteenth Congressional District since 1989, is the first Latina ever elected to the U.S. Congress. Like her Republican Cuban American colleague with some seniority in the House, Congressman Lincoln Diaz-Balart, she has also accomplished much on behalf of her constituents, all Cuban Americans, all Latinos—and the peoples of Latin America. As the first Latina to chair a House subcommittee and the first woman to chair the Subcommittee on International Operations and Human Rights, Congresswoman Ros-Lehtinen has played a pivotal role in shaping U.S. foreign policy, particularly in Latin America.

Robert Menendez—who was born in New York City on New Year's Day, 1954, to Cuban parents who had left Batista's Cuba in 1953, and who grew up in a tenement building in Union City, New Jersey—represented New Jersey's Thirteenth Congressional District from January 3, 1993 to January 17, 2006, as the lone

Cuban American Democrat in the House of Representatives. While in the House, he served as the vice chairman of the Democratic Caucus. In 2002 he was elected chair of that organization, making him the highest-ranking Latino in the House at the time. Menendez resigned from the House in January 2006, after Governor-elect **Jon S. Corzine** of New Jersey appointed him to fill the U.S. Senate seat Corzine made vacant by resigning from the Senate to serve as governor of New Jersey. Upon his swearing in on January 18, 2006, Robert Menendez became New Jersey's first minority senator and the third Latino in the U.S. Senate. In the November 2006 elections, he held on to his Senate seat. For his unwavering commitment to human and civil rights, and for his vast accomplishments, Robert Menendez was awarded the Ellis Island Medal of Honor in 1988 and the Medallion of Excellence for Leadership by the Congressional Hispanic Caucus Institute in 1999.

Who is Elián González?

On Thanksgiving Day, 1999, Americans in a fishing boat plying the Straits of Florida came upon a small Cuban boy clinging to an inner tube. The boy, six-year-old **Elián González**, was one of only three survivors among fourteen Cubans who were attempting to sail to Florida and freedom when their rickety boat capsized. Elián's mother, **Elizabet Brotons**, was one of those who had perished. After his dramatic rescue at sea, Elián was lovingly cared for by his great-uncle, **Lazaro González**, his cousin **Marisleysis González**, and other Miami relatives. During his stay in their modest white stucco home in the Little Havana neighborhood of Miami, he was adopted by the Cuban American community as a symbol of defiance and resentment of **Castro**.

Had his mother survived the perilous crossing to freedom in the United States, Elián González would have been granted special refugee status automatically and permanent residency after remaining in the United States for one year, in keeping with the 1966 Cuban Adjustment Act. (Cuban Americans argue that Elián should have been granted special refugee status since the Cuban Adjustment Act does not make exclusions for minors.) Since Elián's mother did not survive, a months-long legal battle over custody of the little boy ensued between his Miami relatives, who made every effort to keep Elián in Miami, and the boy's father, **Juan Miguel González**, whom Fidel Castro eventually shipped to the United States to await a verdict in the case. All the while,

Castro waged a public-relations war to have Elián returned to Cuba, and the **Clinton** administration put up little resistance to the Cuban dictator. The Elián González case made it all the way to the U.S. Supreme Court, which declined to intervene.

When the Clinton administration then called upon Elián's Miami relatives to turn over the boy, they refused. In response, heavily armed INS agents under the command of then–attorney general **Janet Reno** (a Miami native) stormed the González house in a predawn raid on April 22, 2000, seizing at gunpoint a terrified Elián from the arms of one of the fishermen who had rescued him, a horrifying moment preserved forever in a Pulitzer Prize–winning photograph. Federal officials claimed that the raid was justified because they had received a tip about ammunition stored at a neighboring house to be used in the event of such a raid. In response to the violent raid, Lazaro González and his family filed a lawsuit contending that their constitutional rights had been violated.

In June 2000, in the company of his father, Elián was flown back to Cuba, to a hero's welcome orchestrated by Castro. Since Elián's return to Cuba, the González family has reaped rewards for its display of loyalty to the Cuban dictator: Juan Miguel González has stood at Castro's side at important events, was awarded Cuba's highest civilian decoration, and was promoted to leader of the local Communist Party organization. The family has also received scarce consumer goods, including a new television set. As for Elián, he apparently is under surveillance to "protect" him from journalists and others curious about his fate.

What impact did the Elián affair have on the 2000 U.S. presidential election and on the Cuban American community?

In the 2000 presidential election, **Vice President Al Gore** and the Democratic Party paid an enormous political price for the **Clinton** administration's **Elián** policy. Gore, the incumbent, lost by the slimmest margin—and one highly contested—to **George W. Bush**. As fate would have it, the election boiled down to the Florida vote—and dimpled, hanging, and pregnant chads—and thus the convictions of Florida voters, a significant percentage of whom are Cuban American. In the aftermath of Elián's return to Cuba, many Cuban Americans vowed that they would never again vote for another Democrat. They kept their word in 2000. According to a Miami-based pollster, President Clinton garnered 35 percent (others say 40 percent) of the Cuban American vote in Florida in 1996, while in 2000 Gore captured less than 20 percent in what Cuban Americans call *el voto castigo*, "the punishment vote." Thus it appears the Clinton administration's handling of the Elián case cost Al Gore Cuban American votes and, ultimately, the presidency, a sentiment **Geraldo Rivera** voiced on his television program *Rivera Live*, on December 18, 2000, when he declared that Elián González won the 2000 presidential election for the Republicans and George W. Bush.

The Elián affair, like the failed Bay of Pigs invasion, represents catastrophic loss and crushing disappointment for Cuban Americans and is a defining moment in Cuban American history. Many Cuban Americans were angered that communist dictator **Fidel Castro** was able to use the custody battle over Elián as a propaganda tool to rally the Cuban people, and that the dictator succeeded in his campaign to have Elián returned to Cuba, thanks to the full cooperation of the Clinton administration. Many believe that had the Republicans commanded the White House at the time, Elián would not have been sent back to Cuba.

Cuban Americans were also painfully aware that the Elián affair had not only heightened ethnic and racial tensions in Miami-Dade County, but had done extensive damage to the Cuban American community's reputation across the nation. It was clear to most that the scenes of Cuban Americans waving the American flag upside down and committing acts of civil disobedience in their effort to keep the little boy in America had created the perception that Cuban Americans were a bunch of right-wing radicals. In fact, a Florida International University poll taken in 2000 found that 82 percent of the 1,975 Cuban American respondents in Miami-Dade County felt that the Elián affair had hurt the interests of Cuban Americans.

Have Cubans defected while on U.S. soil?

Ever since **Fidel Castro** imposed his communist regime on Cuba, Cubans with the opportunity to travel abroad, including Cuban ballet dancers and ballerinas, singers, surgeons, and baseball players, have defected while on U.S. soil and have sought political asylum in the United States. For instance, in October 2003, **Gema Diaz** and **Cervilio Amador** of the Ballet Nacional de Cuba defected in Miami, during a U.S. tour, and a week later, in New York, three of their fellow dancers followed suit.

How do Cuban Americans feel about Castro and the trade embargo against Cuba?

Cuban Americans generally have nothing good to say about **Fidel Castro**, the dictator who stole their country, forced them into exile, and caused them incalculable suffering and pain. They call him *el tirano* (the tyrant), *el diablo* (the devil), *la bola de churre* (the grime ball), and other choice names. Driving down the streets of Miami, one cannot help but notice bumper stickers proclaiming "No Castro, No Problem." As for the U.S.-sponsored embargo against Cuba, the majority of Cuban Americans are of the conviction that the only strategy for bringing an end to Castro's totalitarian regime, and at the same time protecting the international community from potential acts of terrorism (especially bioterrorism, given that Cuba has invested heavily in biotechnology), armed subversion, and international drug trafficking by Cuba, is a continued economic blockade of the island. (Incidentally, the issue of Cuba and bioterrorism came to the fore in 2002, when the **Bush** administration accused Cuba of producing deadly pathogens, such as anthrax, that can be used in biological warfare and called the country a serious threat to national security.)

While the majority of Cuban Americans support the U.S. embargo of Cuba, there was a time not so long ago when almost everyone in the community was behind it. With the passing away of the old guard, the historic leaders of the exile opposition to Castro; the rise to positions of power in the Cuban American community of a younger generation of Cuban Americans with fresh approaches; and the influx of Cubans from 1990 to the present, including the twenty thousand "lottery winners" per year, willing to engage in a dialogue with Fidel Castro (a willingness the majority of more recent Cuban immigrants have expressed), Cuban American attitudes about Cuba and the U.S. embargo have become less monolithic.

In fact, since 1990 there has been a dramatic rise in the number of Cuban Americans who oppose the embargo, as evidenced by the results of Florida International University's Cuba Poll 2000. The poll, conducted in September and October 2000, found that 33 percent of Cuban American respondents were against the embargo, triple the number who opposed it in 1991.

The poll also found an increase in the percentage of Cuban Americans in support of sales of medicine and food to Cuba. A total of 43.1 percent strongly agreed that medicine should be sold to Cuba, up from 28.1 percent in 1997. And over 37 percent were strongly in favor of allowing food to be sold to the island, up from 20.3 percent in 1997.

Those Cuban Americans who believe that the embargo should be lifted argue that it harms innocent Cuban citizens, the victims of Castro's regime, and that it creates a negative image of the United States as a bully pushing around an impoverished nation, which serves only to bolster Castro's communist regime. Furthermore, they contend that with the Cold War's end and the dissolution of the Soviet Union (and its financial aid package to Cuba), Castro's dictatorship no longer poses a military threat, which renders the embargo obsolete. And they maintain that the embargo represents failed U.S. policy, because although punitive sanctions have been in place for over four and a half decades, they have yet to stimulate democratization and economic liberalization in Cuba.

The diversity of opinions over the embargo in the Cuban American community is reflected to some degree in its powerful political lobbying group, the Cuban American National Foundation (CANF), where change has been afoot since at least 2001. CANF was founded by the late **Jorge Mas Canosa**, a charismatic Cuban American megamillionaire who was CEO of Church & Tower, a Miami construction company, whose clients include Southern Bell and all of Miami-Dade County. In his day, Mas Canosa was the biggest individual Latino contributor to candidates for national office and, according to Washington insiders, the most important lobbyist in Washington after the American Israel Public Affairs Committee.

As chairman of CANF, Jorge Mas Canosa did not waver in his commitment to the promotion of a free, democratic Cuba through the strict enforcement of the U.S. embargo, and he was greatly responsible for keeping the embargo in place. In 1998 Mas Canosa's son, **Jorge Mas Santos**, a highly successful businessman who transformed a telephone cable–laying company his father had started into the telecommunications enterprise MasTec Inc., the largest Latino-owned business in the United States, took over as chair of CANF. Mas Santos and other more moderate CANF leaders, in something of a departure from Mas Canosa's approach, have advocated maintaining the trade embargo and at the same time sending humanitarian shipments of medicine and food to Cuba, extending U.S. government assistance to Cuba's political dissidents and small entrepreneurs, and arranging academic exchanges between American and Cuban universities—all steps that would aid the Cuban people without providing Castro the means to bolster his repressive communist regime and that the U.S. government has sought to take.

Despite this opposition to the trade embargo of Cuba, the (George W.) **Bush** administration, the majority of Cuban Americans, and CANF are convinced that the only way to effect a peaceful transition to democracy in Cuba is to preserve the status quo, that is, maintain pressure on Cuba's communist government for change via the embargo. The Bush administration reiterated its position on Castro and the trade embargo of Cuba on the heels of former president **Jimmy Carter**'s call for an end to the embargo in the context of his historic trip to Cuba in May 2002, the first by a former or current U.S. president since Fidel Castro's 1959 revolution. In a speech before an audience of Cuban Americans at the White House on May 20, 2002, President Bush declared: "Well-intentioned ideas about trade will merely prop up this dictator, enrich his cronies, and enhance the totalitarian regime. It will not help the Cuban people."

What will happen to Cuba after Castro falls?

For decades now, Cuban Americans have pondered this question, sometimes halfheartedly, thanks to **Fidel Castro**'s uncanny powers of self-preservation. But ever since the news broke on the night of July 30, 2006, that Castro had undergone emergency surgery for intestinal bleeding and had temporarily ceded power to his younger brother, **Raúl Castro**—sending Cuban Americans into the streets of Miami in celebration, shouting, *"¡Cuba sí, Raúl no!"*—conversations have been quite animated on both sides of the Florida Straits as to what exactly is ailing Castro (it remains a state secret), when he will meet his demise, and what will happen to Cuba in the aftermath of his death. After a brief fainting spell during a speech on June 23, 2001, Castro had made it clear that with his departure, Raúl Castro would take over and predicted that Cuba would stay its present course. As first vice president of Cuba, minister of defense, and second secretary of the Cuban Communist Party (PCC), Raúl Castro has been preparing the foundation for his succession since the early 1990s by reinforcing three institutions that might ensure a seamless transition after Fidel's death, namely, the PCC, the Revolutionary Armed Forces, and the central government bureaucracy.

Cuban Americans naturally have a different view of a Cuba without Fidel and hold fast to the belief that Castro's death will usher in the complete demise of his communist regime and a new era of democracy, human dignity, opportunity, plenty, and prosperity for Cuba—brought about with the help of Cuban Americans. This sentiment is echoed by influential Miami businessman **Jorge Mas Santos**, who chairs the Cuban American National Foundation (CANF), the Cuban American community's most powerful political lobbying organization. He once described CANF as a "think tank in waiting," poised to relocate to Havana after Castro and help transform Cuba into "the diamond of this hemisphere." Also poised to aid in Cuba's transformation are South Florida's Cuban American business leaders. An executive poll commissioned by *South Florida CEO* magazine and conducted by Bendixen & Associates in 2006 showed that a substantial number of South Florida business leaders would seek to expand their enterprises in a post-Castro democratic Cuba, lending significant resources and their business acumen to the endeavor. In the poll, 70 percent of Cuban American business leaders cited their Cuban heritage and a "sense of duty" as major reasons to invest their personal assets in a post-Castro Cuba.

What plans has the U.S. government made for a post-Castro Cuba?

Over the decades, the U.S. government has also contemplated Cuba's future without **Fidel Castro** and has taken action to facilitate the future establishment of a democratic society and a market economy in Cuba. Specifically, the United States Agency for International Development (USAID), as mandated by the Helms-Burton Act, has been awarding grants since its inception in 1996 to promote a democratic transition in Cuba by forging ties with the island's human rights activists, providing a voice for Cuba's independent journalists, aiding in the development of independent Cuban nongovernmental organizations (NGOs), offering direct outreach to Cubans, defending Cuban workers' human rights, and planning a program of assistance to a future transitional Cuban government.

And in October 2003, **President Bush** created the Commission for Assistance to a Free Cuba, an intergovernmental agency over-seen by the U.S. State Department for the purpose of speeding Cuba's peaceful transition to a free and democratic society. In 2006 the commission issued its second report, stating that the United States must be prepared to assist Cuba within weeks of Fidel Castro's death. The commission also recommended creating a two-year, $80 million democracy fund to boost internal opposition to Castro and earmarking $20 million a year to fund democracy programs "until the dictatorship ceases to exist." On August 4, 2006, right after Castro ceded power temporarily to his brother and it looked as if his regime might unravel, **Secretary of State Condoleeza Rice** released a brief message to the Cuban people, in which she reiterated the United States' commitment to a free Cuba: "All Cubans who desire peaceful democratic change can count on the support of the United States. We encourage the Cuban people to work at home for positive change, and we stand ready to provide you with humanitarian assistance, as you begin to chart a new course for your country."

HAVANA, U.S.A.: THE LAND OF THE FIESTA, BUT NOT THE SIESTA

How many Cuban Americans are there, and where do they live?

According to the Pew Hispanic Center tabulations of the Census Bureau's 2005 American Community Survey, 1,462,593 Cuban Americans and Cuban-born residents lived in the United States in 2005. Census 2000 counted 1,241,685 Cuban Americans and Cuban-born residents, and in 1990, 1,053,197 were tallied. According to Census 2000 data, the five states with the greatest number of Cubans in 2000 were Florida (833,120), New Jersey (77,337), California (72,286), New York (62,590), and Texas (25,705). The Cuban population figures for New Jersey and New York actually represent a decline in numbers. Areas of the country that experienced the highest growth in the number of Cuban Americans in the 1990s were the South and the West, as evidenced by California, which in the 1990s pulled ahead of New York to earn the ranking of third among states with the highest number of Cuban Americans.

Most of the 833,120 Cuban Americans counted in Florida in 2000—a significant increase from the 674,052 tallied in 1990—call Miami-Dade County home. And, at the very heart of that home is *Calle Ocho*, Eighth Street, in Miami's Little Havana.

What's Little Havana, and why isn't it so Havana anymore?

Little Havana, just west of downtown Miami, was the primary enclave of the first wave of Cuban exiles in the 1960s and 1970s and is still the capital of Cuban America. *Calle Ocho*, Eighth Street, runs through the heart of Little Havana, and all along it are Cuban restaurants (as many as you'd find in four districts in Havana, Cuba), including the landmark Versailles; stands selling Cuban sandwiches, *café cubano*, and *batidos* (tropical-fruit milk shakes); botanicas; supermarkets; and every conceivable type of Cuban shop.

Along Little Havana's streets, which sport more signs in Spanish than in English (some even say "English Spoken Here"), and in parks, like the famous Máximo Gómez Park, Cuban American men, especially old-timers, gather around small card tables, smoking cigars, sipping *cafecitos*, and playing dominoes, a favorite island pastime for Cubans, as well as for Puerto Ricans and Dominicans. While the men scramble the dominoes, they talk politics, ponder just how much longer **Fidel Castro**'s regime will last and if he might already be dead, and perhaps put down a bet on *la bolita*, an illegal lottery that no one cares to crack down on.

But that's the old Little Havana. It's still there, filled with melancholy warriors of a bygone era and plenty of Anglo tourists, who come down to savor the flavor and visit a "foreign country" without having to trouble with a passport. (Actually, Miami residents themselves joke that the reason they live in Miami is because it's so close to the United States.) But the more recent generations of Cuban Americans have left Little Havana for the elegant suburbs of Coral Gables, Hialeah, Coconut Grove, Key Biscayne, and South Beach, the trendy art deco enclave of heavenly beach that Jewish retirees from points north developed and made famous in the 1950s. Even as they have fanned out over Miami and have joined the mainstream, Cuban Americans have remained faithful to their heritage, and Cuban flavors nowadays permeate all of Miami.

Little Havana, Cuban Americans say, is neither so little nor so entirely Havana anymore. Little Managua, a growing community of Nicaraguan immigrants, is gradually blending with the old Little Havana, and these days the newer Spanish-speaking arrivals serve the food and even run some of the shops that younger generations of Cuban Americans left behind. Residents with roots in the Dominican Republic, Colombia, Honduras, El Salvador, and other Central and South American countries, lured by the Latin climate Cubans have created, can also be found strolling the streets of Little Havana and Greater Miami.

Why is Miami called the capital of Latin America?

Behind Little Havana, and miles from the comfortable suburbs where many of Miami's more than half a million Cuban Americans make their homes, looms the city's thriving commercial center, with its tall glass buildings and hundreds of international banks. This is also part of the city that Cuban Americans are rightly credited with transforming. Since the 1960s, Cuban Americans, many of whom are top-notch entrepreneurs and are well versed in both American and Latin ways, have served as liaisons between U.S. corporations and Latin American companies eager to do business with the United States. The natural synergism and desire for enterprise between Cuban Americans and their contacts to the south and north turned Miami—which had been an alligator-infested swamp until the 1920s and a retirees' colony from the 1950s to the 1970s—into the thriving "capital of Latin America," as Cuban American **Xavier Suarez**, a former mayor of Miami, called the city.

Cuban Americans are not only at the helm of international trade and banking in this cosmopolitan city, they also predominate in the top leadership positions in politics and education in Miami and all throughout Miami-Dade County. For instance, the mayor of Miami, **Manny Diaz**, who in 2001 defeated former six-term mayor **Maurice Ferre**, a Puerto Rican, and was reelected in 2006, is Cuban American. (Incidentally, Diaz served as the lawyer for **Elián González**'s Miami relatives. See chapter 8.)

Since Cuba is only ninety miles from Florida, do Cuban Americans visit?

For most of the nearly five decades that **Fidel Castro** has governed Cuba, the island has been off-limits, with some exceptions, to Cuban Americans and U.S. permanent residents—and all American citizens, for that matter—in keeping with regulations issued in 1963 by the U.S. Department of the Treasury as part of the trade embargo against Cuba. According to these regulations, Americans are expressly forbidden from traveling to Cuba unless they obtain a special license from the Department of the Treasury. The catch is that only a select few may apply for these licenses, namely, Cuban Americans and permanent resident aliens visiting immediate family members (only one two-week visit every three years is permitted); U.S. and foreign government officials traveling on official business; journalists employed by a news reporting organization (and supporting technical and broadcasting personnel); full-time professional researchers engaged in noncommercial, academic research; full-time professionals attending professional conferences or meetings set up by an international professional organization or institution; undergraduate or graduate students enrolled in an academic program and teachers teaching in one; persons engaging in permitted export sales, such as the sale of medicines; and just a few others.

Tourist travel and business travel in Cuba by Americans (other than that related to allowed export sales) are not permitted under U.S. law. Anyone caught violating this travel ban could face civil penalties and criminal prosecution upon returning to the United States. Nonetheless, over the years Cuban Americans and American tourists without a license have routinely visited Cuba via third countries, such as Mexico or Canada. For decades, the U.S. government rarely imposed civil penalties on nonauthorized travelers to Cuba or pursued criminal prosecution (most of the civil actions initiated each year involved contraband), but since mid-2006, U.S. law enforcement authorities have been dealing more harshly with those who fail to comply with U.S. Department of the Treasury regulations regarding travel to Cuba, imposing fines averaging $7,500.

U.S. citizens and U.S. permanent resident aliens licensed to travel to Cuba must adhere to a travel per diem allowance. For example, persons traveling to Cuba to visit immediate family members are allowed to spend up to fifty dollars per day on non-transportation-related expenses and up to fifty dollars *per trip* for transportation. (U.S. citizens and permanent resident aliens are barred from using credit cards in Cuba and may only carry forty-four pounds of luggage.) In addition to the per diem allowance, licensed travelers, except for children under age eighteen, may carry (or send) to Cuba family remittances totaling no more than $300 per household in any consecutive three-month period, no matter how many relatives in Cuba will receive the funds and provided the recipient is not a "prohibited official of the Government of Cuba," such as an employee at the Ministry of Defense or an editor at a Cuban state-run media organization.

In January 1998, the **Clinton** White House temporarily lifted the U.S. travel ban for Cuba so that American Catholics could go to the island for the visit of **Pope John Paul II**. Over one thousand Cuban Americans, in what was described as the largest mass return of Cuban exiles to the island in history, made the trip to Cuba. Not all Cuban Americans were in favor of easing travel restrictions for the pope's visit. Many, including Cuban American congresswoman **Ileana Ros-Lehtinen**, would have preferred all Cuban Americans to stay home and watch the papal festivities on television. Those opposed to the pilgrimage (and to all travel to Cuba by U.S. citizens), and there were many, were concerned that it would send a message of support to Castro and lend credibility to his tyrannical regime.

What's a YUCA?

Yuca, or cassava, a starchy, fibrous tuber with a flavor as mild as a potato, was once cultivated by the Siboney and Taino of Cuba. Nowadays, it is a fixture at the Cuban American table and is commonly served fried, like french fries, or boiled until tender and then bathed with *mojo*, olive oil flavored with garlic and citrus juice. Note that yuca must not be consumed raw: in its raw state, the tuber contains cyanogenic glucosides, which are converted to cyanide when the raw plant is chewed or ground. Exposure to this cyanide usually results in chronic toxicity, not death, in humans.

A YUCA, a term coined in 1988, is a Cuban American yuppie—a young, upwardly mobile Cuban American. YUCAs, who were born in the United States and have seen Cuba only in their parents' and grandparents' photographs of palm trees and the Malecón wall in Havana, are a bilingual, bicultural, and economically successful lot. They speak both English and Spanish flawlessly (with no accent) and are likely to lapse into one or the other without realizing it. YUCAs are mostly Caucasian and considerably more liberal in their attitudes than their elders. They prefer to listen to *Cadena Azul, La Cubanisima,* and *Radio Mambí* (Miami Spanish-language news and music stations) than to Radio

Martí. Unlike their parents and grandparents, who are largely Republican, YUCAs have tended to vote Democrat—though the trauma of **Elián González** has changed that somewhat. As a group, they are eager to help the millions of people in Cuba who are in dire straits as a result of the disintegration of the Soviet Union in 1991 and **Castro's** failed policies, but the majority have no desire to return to Cuba to live when Castro's authoritarian regime disintegrates.

Are all Cuban Americans rich?

Cuban Americans' very enterprising nature has led many to stereotype them as *los ricos*, "the rich kids." While Cuban Americans as a group are wealthier than other Latinos, when it comes to finances, they mirror to a great extent non-Latino whites in the general population. Their income about equals the national average.

What's Santería?

Santería is a New World religion or way of worship that emerged when the ancient Yoruban religions that West African slaves brought to the Caribbean blended with the Roman Catholic beliefs of the Spanish colonizers. The gods, or orishas, of *Santería* fused with the Catholic saints, called *santos*, in a phenomenon known as religious syncretism. So for instance, the African god Babalú-Ayé is also the Catholic St. Lazarus, and Yemaya, the African goddess of the waters, is the Catholic *Virgen de las Mercedes*. Practitioners of *Santería*, the "religion of the saints," not only worship a pantheon of deities, they also consult *santeros* and *santeras*, male and female priests, who dispense ritual paraphernalia, such as candles, beads, and ointments, as well as advice on how to solve any problem imaginable—including relationship, money, and health concerns—which usually involves strengthening the individual's connection with the orishas.

Early on in Cuba, *Santería* was practiced in secret to conceal it from the Spanish, who sought to eradicate such "primitive" and "superstitious" practices. Despite the secrecy, *Santería* grew very popular in Cuba, and among its followers were not only slaves and their descendants, but also Cubans with no African blood. In the 1950s, it was recorded in a government gazette that Cuban president **Carlos Prío Socarrás**, a white, democratically elected president, donated government money to both the Catholic Church and the *Santería* religion.

Nowadays *Santería* is practiced in Miami, New York, and virtually every city and town with a sizable Cuban, Puerto Rican, or Dominican community, but it is difficult to estimate the number of adherents. Most assert that their religion is misunderstood and thus seldom discuss their beliefs with outsiders. Mainstream America has, in fact, been known to condemn *Santería*, partly because one of its rituals involves animal (not human) sacrifice to honor the gods. In 1993 the U.S. Supreme Court ruled that a 1987 ban on animal sacrifice in Hialeah, Florida, violated the First Amendment right to religious expression for Cuban American followers of *Santería*. Cuban Americans and other Latinos, even those who did not practice *Santería*, viewed this high-court decision as a victory for ethnic understanding.

What's a fiesta de quince?

It is the equivalent of a sweet sixteen party or bat mitzvah, only it's for *quinceañeras*, fifteen-year-olds. *Fiestas de quince* are very popular in Miami, and in the way of debutante balls, they are often held in large ballrooms or at country clubs and end up costing Cuban American parents thousands of dollars and taking months of planning. Other Latino groups also celebrate girls' coming-of-age with *fiestas de quince*. The Hollywood feature film *Quinceañera* (2006), about a Mexican American girl's coming-of-age in Los Angeles' Echo Park neighborhood, offers marvelous and poignant commentary on this rite of passage.

What foods are found on the Cuban American table?

Cuban Americans have a great fondness for the flavors of the old country. Unlike other Latin American cuisines, such as Mexican and Guatemalan, Cuban cooking is not spicy. Garlic, onions, citrus juice, and olive oil—not chiles—impart flavor and aroma to Cuban dishes. Among popular Cuban main entrées are *lechón asado* (juicy, garlicky roast suckling pig), *picadillo* (a ground meat stew studded with green olives, capers, and raisins), *ropa vieja* (a stew of shredded flank steak, tomatoes, peppers, and onions, whose name translates literally as "old clothes"), *camarones enchilados* (shrimp in a creole sauce), and Cuban-style paella. Main dishes are usually accompanied by copious amounts of *tostones* (fried green plantains), *plátanos maduros fritos* (fried ripe plantains), or *yuca con mojo* (yuca served with garlic-flavored oil), and by *moros y cristianos* (black beans cooked with rice) or white rice and black beans served separately. For dessert, some Cuban favorites are *arroz con leche* (rice pudding), *flan de leche* ("milk" flan), *flan de coco* (coconut flan), and bread pudding, usually followed by a cup of *café cubano* or *café con leche*.

Cuban Americans love to snack on sandwiches, such as the *media noche*—a Cuban version of the multilayered Dagwood sandwich—featuring slices of roast pork, ham, cheese, and pickles stacked on sweetened egg bread, and commonly served with a side of *mariquitas*, plantain chips deep-fried like potato chips. Cuban sandwiches, and other fast foods, are sold at little stands and restaurants all over Miami and in other cities and towns with substantial Cuban American communities.

SEIS

Dominican Americans

EARLY HISTORY

Is the Dominican Republic an island?

Sort of. The Dominican Republic and Haiti actually share the Caribbean island of Hispaniola, which is the second-largest island of the Greater Antilles (Cuba, Puerto Rico, Hispaniola, and Jamaica). The eastern two-thirds of Hispaniola constitutes the Dominican Republic, and the western one-third, Haiti. To the northwest of Hispaniola lies Cuba, and to the east is Puerto Rico.

When did the Spanish colonize Hispaniola?

Christopher Columbus made his first landfall on Hispaniola on December 5, 1492. There he established the very first Spanish colony in the New World, which he named La Isla Española for Spain itself. At some point, historians are uncertain exactly when, the island earned a second name, Hispaniola. (In Spanish, the island is nowadays known as both La Isla Española and Hispaniola;

however, internationally, it is called only Hispaniola.) Columbus was delighted when the Taino, the native peoples of Hispaniola, who were a subgroup of the Amerindian group called the Arawak, welcomed him bearing masks and amulets made of gold, for he supposed that the island harbored great riches. In fact, Columbus was so taken with Hispaniola that he made it his main base for exploration of the region. Incidentally, Dominicans claim Columbus as a virtual native son and allege that he was buried in the oldest cathedral in the Americas, the Cathedral of Santa María la Menor, which was completed in 1520 in Santo Domingo, the capital of the Dominican Republic. The Spanish refute this claim and maintain that the conquistador's remains are in Seville, Spain.

The Spanish crown was eager to settle Hispaniola and to establish gold mining on the island, and so in 1496 Columbus's brother, **Bartolomeo Columbus**, founded Santo Domingo. The Spanish colonizers were merciless in their exploitation of the native peoples as a labor force, and the Taino swiftly succumbed to overwork and disease. In just five years, the Taino population plummeted from around one million to approximately five hundred. Beginning in 1503, the colonizers brought African slaves to the island to replenish the labor pool. By 1543 the Spanish had mined all the gold in Hispaniola and turned their attention to Mexico and Peru, which held great promise.

The Spanish colonizers who ventured to Hispaniola gravitated to the eastern part of the island, where they established plantations. They neglected the island's western third and in 1697, under the Treaty of Ryswick, ceded it to the French, who christened it Saint-Domingue. The French colonists who settled in Saint-Domingue imported thousands of African slaves to work the land. Then, in 1795, the Spanish ceded the eastern two-thirds of Hispaniola to France. Nine years later, in 1804, the African slaves in Hispaniola revolted against the French and declared the western region of the island an independent nation called Haiti. The Spanish colonists of Santo Domingo, as the remainder of the island was by then called, were also disheartened by the way in which France handled their affairs, and in 1808 they rebelled against the French and reestablished rule.

After the inhabitants of Santo Domingo ousted the Spanish in 1821, the two halves of Hispaniola duked it out, each battling for hegemony over the island as a whole. In 1822 the Haitians invaded and conquered Santo Domingo. Santo Domingo's Spanish-speaking inhabitants swiftly grew quite discontented with Haitian rule, and on July 16, 1838, **Juan Pablo Duarte**, considered the Dominican Republic's greatest national hero, and other Dominican freedom fighters organized *La Trinitaria*, an underground dissident society, with the aim of throwing off the yoke of the Haitian occupiers. By 1843 Duarte was exiled to Caracas for engaging in insurgent activities, but the Santo Domingo independence movement gathered momentum nonetheless, and in 1844 Santo Domingo's Spanish-speaking inhabitants rose up against Haitian domination and emerged victorious, proclaiming their independence on February 27, 1844, and establishing a separate nation called the Dominican Republic.

Duarte had envisioned a peaceful democracy for the Dominican Republic. However, blinded by idealism, he procrastinated in taking control of the new nation and, consequently, did not fare well in the political free-for-all that followed independence in 1844. As it turned out, the Dominican Republic's independence was not lasting. In 1861 the nation submitted to Spanish rule once again in an attempt to ward off the Haitians, who had annexation on their mind. A war of independence from Spain soon erupted, however, and the Dominican Republic declared victory in 1865.

A TIME OF TROUBLES

Why did the United States intervene in the affairs of the Dominican Republic?

From 1865 to 1899, two political factions controlled the Dominican government: the Reds, led by **Buenaventura Báez**, and the Blues, who after 1878 were commanded by **General Ulises Heureaux**. The ruthless Heureaux eventually seized the reins of power and imposed a dictatorship in the Dominican Republic—complete with bribery, murder, secret police, and informants—that endured from 1882 to 1889, though he was actually in office from September 1882 to September 1884, from January 1887 to February 1889, and from April 1889 until his assassination on July 26, 1899. (He maintained an iron grip on power between his terms in office and achieved reelection through electoral fraud.) Heureaux used his office to enrich himself and his cronies at the country's expense, mixing up his private accounts and the state's finances. When Heureaux could no longer run his police state, owing to the mounting public debt, he arranged secret loans from sugar planters, local merchants, and the Santo Domingo Improvement Company. In 1897, with the Dominican Republic on the verge of bankruptcy, he printed $5 million in unsecured paper money, debasing the currency and sending a large number of merchants to their ruin. On July 26, 1899, **Ramón Cáceres**, a member of the revolutionary organization *Junta Revolucionaria de Jóvenes* (Young Revolutionary Junta), which had been laying the foundation for a revolt against the dictator, took matters into his own hands and fatally shot Heureaux as he was passing through the town of Moca.

After the dictator was gone, those in power were unable to resuscitate the flatlining Dominican economy. Faced with a mounting foreign debt, in 1904 the Dominican Republic went bankrupt. European nations threatened to intervene in the island's affairs in order to collect their debts. Seeking to preclude such European involvement, **President Teddy Roosevelt** added the Roosevelt Corollary to the Monroe Doctrine as part of his annual message to Congress in 1904. The Roosevelt Corollary proclaimed that the United States reserved the exclusive right to intervene in the internal affairs of nations in the Western Hemisphere. In other words, the nations of Europe had no right to meddle in the Western Hemisphere. In accordance with a treaty signed in 1905 with the Dominican Republic, the United States, in keeping with the Roosevelt Corollary, exercised the right to partial control of the island to sort out claims by European governments and to protect American investments.

From 1906 to 1911, **Ramón Cáceres** served as president of the Dominican Republic, and the country, though still plagued by moments of unrest, experienced a period of modernization and reform. On November 19, 1911, Cáceres was assassinated, unleashing another wave of extreme violence and fiscal chaos. In 1916 **President Woodrow Wilson** felt he had no other recourse than to invade the Dominican Republic (U.S. Marines and all) to restore peace. After the invasion, the United States imposed a military government, which carried out numerous institutional reforms, including building a national road system and sanitation facilities; reorganizing the tax system and the public administration system; and expanding primary education. Still, the U.S. occupation embittered a great number of Dominicans. The marines were not withdrawn until 1924, when Dominicans democratically elected **Horacio Vásquez** president. In 1927 Vásquez extended his term from four to six years with the approval of the U.S. Congress, even though the Dominican constitution of 1924 did not allow for such an extension. Amid brewing discontent with Vásquez's unconstitutional expansion of his power, **Rafael Estrella**, a lawyer, organized a rebellion in February 1930, driving Vásquez, then ailing, into exile. Estrella was named provisional president, but his days in office would be few.

Who was Rafael Trujillo, and what were his passions?

Ironically, the U.S. occupation forces in the Dominican Republic helped the Dominicans organize a new national guard, which they eventually placed under the command of **Rafael Leónidas Trujillo**, a brigadier general and commander-in-chief of the Dominican army. Generalissimo Trujillo used his domination of the military to steal the presidential election in 1930, essentially overthrowing provisional president **Rafael Estrella**. This marked the onset of one of the longest, most brutal dictatorships in history, lasting until Trujillo's assassination in 1961. It was also one of the richest dictatorships in history. In the 1950s, Rafael Trujillo, the son of a lower-middle-class postal clerk, ranked among the world's wealthiest people. By the time of his death, he had amassed a net worth of $800 million, and he and his family owned about half of the arable land in the Dominican Republic. According to *Time* magazine, he invested $100 million of that wealth in the United States and Puerto Rico alone. Besides money, the dictator had a passion for erotic poetry, and it is said that his minions leafed through medical journals in search of information on the latest stimulants and enhancers of virility.

Trujillo, who patterned his uniforms after those of the dictator **Heureaux**, also had a passion for control and cruelty. He controlled the press and the schools with an iron fist, and, thus, the minds of the Dominican people. He quelled dissent through torture and genocidal massacres of the opposition, through the close monitoring of each and every citizen, and by instilling fear in all. For instance, every Dominican had to carry not only a personal identity card at all times, but also a certificate of good conduct issued by the police. By 1957 Trujillo had six domestic spy operations in place, which supplied him with an endless stream of information on "unreliables" and ordinary citizens. Dominicans soon learned that a neighbor or even a trusted friend might be a spy, and they became paranoid of one another, heeding the proverb *"En bocas cerradas no entran moscas"* ("Flies do not enter closed mouths").

For over thirty years, Dominicans endured Trujillo's reign of terror. Throughout most of this period, the United States did not balk at the state of domestic affairs in the Dominican Republic, as Trujillo made certain to pander to the U.S. government. For instance, during World War II he was a ready supplier to the American market of coffee, tobacco, sugar, and cocoa, products sorely needed in the United States, and when the Cold War raged, he was one of few Latin American leaders to vehemently condemn communism. By the mid-1950s, however, the United States could no longer ignore the brutality and mass repression in Trujillo's Dominican Republic.

One event that precipitated the U.S. government's reevaluation of the Dominican dictator happened far from the Dominican Republic. On the night of March 12, 1956, just after teaching a graduate seminar, a Columbia University lecturer named **Jesús de Galíndez** vanished on the streets of New York City. During the Spanish civil war, Galíndez, a Basque, had fought on the side of Spain's Loyalists, and against the Nationalists, who were led by Franco. With Franco's victory in the war, and the fierce retaliation against the Loyalists that it engendered, Galíndez fled first to France and then, in 1939, to the Dominican Republic. Settling in Santo Domingo (which Trujillo had by then renamed Ciudad Trujillo, literally, "Trujillo City," in his own honor), Galíndez, a lawyer, took a teaching post and also dispensed legal advice to Trujillo's government. The reality of Trujillo's murderous rule soon became obvious to him, and by 1946 he was very active in the anti-Trujillo underground. Upon securing a visa to travel to the United States, Galíndez made his way to New York City, where, in an apartment on lower Fifth Avenue, he compiled a scathing account of Trujillo's regime, which he transformed into a 750-page dissertation on the dictator for his PhD degree from Columbia University; wrote articles denouncing Trujillo for U.S. and Mexican magazines; and even penned a novel about the dictator.

Trujillo got wind of the dissertation, which was entitled *The Era of Trujillo*, and unable to abide such criticism, ordered the kidnapping of Galíndez in New York. Apparently, Trujillo's henchmen found an American, **Gerald Lester Murphy**, a young employee at an air-taxi company in Miami, who, for a nice profit, was willing to rent a small aircraft and pilot it from the United

States to the Dominican Republic. On that flight, Murphy unwittingly transported Galíndez to the Dominican Republic. The details of what happened next to Galíndez are rather murky, but according to several accounts, he was brought before Trujillo, who ordered him to literally eat his words, and was then brutally murdered. As for Murphy, according to a February 25, 1957, article in *Time* magazine, he then went to work as a copilot for the Dominican national airlines, a job Trujillo himself arranged. On December 3, 1956, Murphy quit his job with the airlines and began packing his bags to leave the Dominican Republic. However, the next day, his abandoned Ford was found by the sea in Santo Domingo, and he was never seen nor heard from again. According to the *Time* article, Dominican officials asserted that in a suicide note he'd left in a Santo Domingo prison cell, a Dominican airline pilot, **Octavio de la Maza**, had confessed to pushing Murphy off a cliff and into the shark-infested sea below. The U.S. chargé d'affaires concluded, upon an examination of the evidence, that La Maza could not have committed suicide, which meant his supposed suicide note was bogus.

Many members of Congress were appalled by the "disappearance" of both Jesus de Galíndez and Gerald Murphy at the hands of Trujillo. Events in 1959 and 1960 were the straw that broke the camel's back. On June 14, 1959, Dominican exiles staged an invasion of the Dominican Republic, with the intent of overthrowing the Trujillo regime. Trujillo's forces swiftly crushed the invasion, and those exiles taken captive were tortured and then murdered, on Trujillo's orders. In 1960, after it found Trujillo guilty of attempting to assassinate **President Rómulo Betancourt** of Venezuela, who had sharply criticized the Dominican dictator, the Organization of American States (OAS) imposed economic and diplomatic sanctions on the Dominican Republic. Trujillo's days were numbered.

The sanctions threw the Dominican economy into a nosedive. Dominicans could endure no more. On the night of May 30, 1961, Rafael Trujillo was gunned down along Santo Domingo's waterfront by disillusioned former minions. His reign of terror ended as abruptly as it had begun.

Who were the Butterflies?

Patria, **Minerva**, and **María Teresa Mirabal**, three sisters from a prominent Dominican family, engaged in acts of resistance to undermine **Rafael Trujillo**'s ruthless dictatorship and bring justice and democracy to their nation. They were known by those around them as Las Mariposas (the Butterflies), which was the code name Minerva Mirabal used in her secret anti-Trujillo activities. As highly visible political activists, the three sisters met with fierce retaliation from the regime. They, along with their husbands, were incarcerated numerous times before Trujillo's henchmen brutally murdered them on a remote mountain road on November 25, 1960.

In the aftermath of Trujillo's assassination, the Mirabal sisters emerged as national heroines and emblems of feminist resistance in the Dominican Republic. A fourth Mirabal sister, **Dedé**, who had been too frightened to join Patria, Minerva, and María Teresa in their defiance of tyranny, turned the family home, located in the town of Ojo de Agua, into a museum in honor of her three sisters. Their tragic story is also poignantly told by **Julia Alvarez** in her best-selling novel *In the Time of the Butterflies* (1995), which in 2001 was made into a film by the same name, starring **Salma Hayek**, **Edward James Olmos**, and **Marc Anthony**. The sisters have been further memorialized by UNESCO, which designated November 25, the anniversary of their deaths, as International Day for the Elimination of Violence Against Women.

In a marvelous act of final justice, a mural depicting Patria, Minerva, María Teresa, and Dedé Mirabal was painted on the *Obelisco del Malecón*, a 137-foot obelisk that Trujillo had built to himself in Santo Domingo, and in 1997 the monument was rededicated to the sisters. The mural was painted in pastel colors as a way of undercutting Trujillo's code of machismo gone awry. The sisters' heroism and commitment to political activism live on in the next generation of Mirabals: Dedé Mirabal's son, **Jaime David Fernández Mirabal**, served as vice president under democratically elected president **Leonel Fernández** when he was in office from 1996 until 2000.

Why did the United States get involved in the Dominican Republic in the 1960s?

After the assassination of **Rafael Trujillo**, the Dominican Republic experienced a power vacuum as the dictator had never designated a successor. Members of the Trujillo family became locked in a power struggle, but in November 1961 they were driven into exile in France. **Vice President Joaquín Balaguer**, a conservative, took over the presidency, but he was forced to share power with a Council of State, which was established on January 1, 1962, to oversee the Dominican Republic's transition from dictatorship to democracy. This arrangement had been in effect for only sixteen days when Dominican air force general **Pedro Rodríguez Echavarría** overthrew the council and sent Balaguer into exile. However, Rodríguez could not hold on to power, and the Council of State was reinstated, but without Balaguer. The council steered the government until December 1962, when Dominicans held their first free elections in forty years and elected "leftist" populist reformer and returned exile **Juan Bosch** by a comfortable majority.

As a result of the Dominican Republic's efforts to establish a democracy, on January 4, 1962, the OAS lifted the sanctions it had imposed in the last days of the Trujillo regime, and support began to pour in from the United States. However, Washington grew concerned when Bosch entertained establishing diplomatic ties with **Fidel Castro**'s Cuba. Right-wing opposition to Bosch soon grew intense in response to reforms he proposed, such as civilian control of the military and land redistribution, and he was ousted by a right-wing military coup in September 1963. A supposedly civilian triumvirate, essentially a dictatorship, ruled the country until April 24, 1965, when Bosch supporters, who called themselves Constitutionalists because they advocated a constitutional government, staged a coup in an attempt to reestablish Bosch's control of the country.

With both sides heavily armed, the chaos swiftly escalated into a bloody civil war. **President Lyndon B. Johnson**, at the request of the anti-Bosch army, once again sent in the marines (and then airborne units), initially to evacuate U.S. citizens and foreign nationals in harm's way, a military intervention known as Operation Power Back. Under the pretext that American interests in the Dominican Republic were being threatened and that the island nation might morph into a "second Cuba," President Johnson then gave U.S. military forces the order to restore peace. The OAS called for a cease-fire and organized a peacekeeping force, which gradually replaced the U.S. troops. In September 1965, the two warring factions in the Dominican Republic reached a compromise agreement and recognized **Hector García-Godoy**, former foreign minister under Bosch, as provisional president under OAS auspices. He remained at the helm until a new constitution was written and elections, supervised by the OAS, were held in

June 1966. Juan Bosch and Joaquín Balaguer, who had the support of U.S. interests, were the leading candidates, and the latter emerged the victor.

As fate would have it, Joaquín Balaguer ruled the Dominican Republic for the next dozen years—a period known as "the Twelve Years"—with the same spirit of authoritarianism as Trujillo, though he was not a bloodthirsty dictator. He enjoyed the backing of the military, the right, and the Church, and during his rule the Dominican Republic experienced relative political stability and an economic miracle, thanks to a dramatic rise in the price of sugar on the world market, foreign investment, and an increase in tourism. Balaguer used the revenues to build schools, hospitals, roads, dams, and bridges, to the delight of the Dominican people, who reelected him in 1970 and 1974. With a sharp decline in world demand for sugar, coffee, and cocoa in the mid-1970s, the Dominican economic boom went bust, and support for Balaguer waned. In the 1978 election, **Antonio Guzmán Fernández**, of the opposition Dominican Revolutionary Party, defeated Balaguer, who, refusing to concede, ordered the military to destroy the ballot boxes and declared himself the victor. Only after the U.S. government threatened to withdraw foreign aid did Balaguer back down. Low sugar prices continued to hamper the Dominican economy, which was battered further in 1979, when two ferocious hurricanes destroyed the homes of two hundred thousand inhabitants and caused $2 billion in damage. Guzmán decided against running for a second term in 1982. That same year, he committed suicide: apparently, he was overwrought about allegations of nepotism and corruption in his government.

How did Joaquín Balaguer assume power a second time?

Salvador Jorge Blanco won the elections held in 1982, but he was no better at coping with the Dominican Republic's mounting debt or the decline in the demand for sugar than his predecessors. When, in 1984, Blanco tried to turn the economy around by implementing austerity measures in cooperation with the International Monetary Fund, such as raising the price of basic foodstuffs, Dominicans rioted in the streets, and the police and military were called in to restore order. In 1986 the disillusioned people of the Dominican Republic voted **Joaquín Balaguer**, by then elderly and legally blind from glaucoma, back into office by the narrowest margin. Counting the ballots took weeks. A narrow margin and a long wait for a vote count usually mean one thing in Latin America: In a close election, extra votes can always be found.

Balaguer, who was reelected in 1990 and 1994, despite accusations of electoral fraud, would run the country until 1996. He achieved a narrow victory in the 1994 election, which was mired in unrelenting violence, in part by accusing his Afro-Dominican opponent of being in cahoots with the Haitians, an effective ploy given that many Dominicans harbored concerns that an overpopulated Haiti would invade. During Balaguer's terms in office, economic conditions continued to deteriorate, and hyperinflation, unemployment, a collapsing infrastructure, a shortage of hospitals and educational institutions, pollution, and emigration became the norm. In 1990 over half of the Dominican Republic's seven million people lived in poverty. Though he was ninety, blind, and partially deaf by the time he stepped down, Balaguer did not wish to relinquish power but was forced to because of a constitutional amendment and pressure from the United States. Just months after leaving office, he was accused of ordering the assassination of three political opponents and of misappropriating at least $740 million in government funds.

When did the Dominicans finally experience democratic elections?

Not until 1996, when Dominicans democratically elected **Leonel Fernández**, a young, vigorous man, into office by a narrow margin. It would be the first time in history that the entire island of Hispaniola would have democratically minded leaders. While Fernández's pro-investment policies and privatization of state-run industries had a beneficial effect on the Dominican Republic's economy, ushering in a period of sustained economic growth beginning in the late 1990s, a phenomenon unheard of in Dominican history, they did not have a serious impact on the country's high poverty rate, to the profound despair of the Dominican people. The Dominican constitution did not permit Fernández to run for a second term, and in 2000 **Hipólito Mejía**, whose campaign slogan was "People First" and who promised to tackle the country's most pressing issues, namely, poverty and corruption, won the presidential election, defeating **Danilo Medina** of the ruling Dominican Liberation Party and former president **Joaquín Balaguer**, who, amazingly, ran again.

During his four years in office, Mejía launched a number of initiatives to improve the lot of the poor, including the installation of water lines and the construction of paved roads in rundown neighborhoods and rural villages, and a land reform program that placed property in the hands of one hundred thousand farmworkers. In the latter half of his term in office, however, he faced a disintegrating economy, precipitated in large measure by his efforts to address banking fraud and government corruption scandals, especially the 2003 collapse of Banco Intercontinental (Baninter), the Dominican Republic's second largest privately held commercial bank. Though he was not obliged to, Mejía guaranteed all US$2.2 billion in unbacked Baninter deposits. The bailout led to a fiscal shortfall, which, in turn, triggered massive inflation (42 percent) and a 65 percent devaluation of the Dominican peso.

Public outrage over Mejía's handling of the 2003 economic crisis, coupled by chronic electricity shortages, translated into his defeat in the 2004 presidential elections. His predecessor, former president Leonel Fernández, whose campaign theme was "Return to Progress," emerged the victor in the race, vowing to foster fiscal austerity, to battle corruption, and to address the people's social concerns. Since Fernández's reelection, inflation has fallen. The people of the Dominican Republic appeared to reward his efforts to resuscitate the economy when Fernández's Dominican Liberation Party captured a majority of seats in the upper and lower houses of the Dominican Congress in 2006, signifying a major shift in power among the main political parties in the country. Still, Fernández is not without his critics, who accuse him of trampling on Dominicans' civil rights and freedom of expression and devoting too much energy to technological development, to the detriment of such critical issues as the food supply, public health, and public education.

LIFE IN DOMINICAN AMERICA

What brought Dominicans to American shores, and where have they settled?

Before 1960 few Dominicans made their way to the United States: Trujillo's ironfisted regime maintained strict control over visas and travel abroad. After Trujillo's assassination in 1961, and fueled by the 1965 civil war, Dominican immigration rose to significant levels and then remained steady through the 1970s. Then in the 1980s, when economic depression plagued the Dominican Republic, immigration soared. In that decade alone, 250,000 Dominicans entered the United States legally, constituting the second-largest national group of immigrants from the Western Hemisphere, with Mexicans being the largest. The 1990s and the early years of the new century also saw an unprecedented number of Dominicans immigrating to the United States, due to enduring social injustice and a continued lack of economic opportunity in the Dominican Republic.

According to the Pew Hispanic Center tabulations of the Census Bureau's 2005 American Community Survey, there were 1,135,756 Dominican Americans and Dominican nationals in the United States in 2005, a significant rise from the 764,945 tallied in Census 2000 and more than double the 520,151 counted in 1990. Census 2000 figures reveal that the five states with the largest Dominican population in 2000 were New York (455,061), New Jersey (102,630), Florida (70,968), Massachusetts (49,913), and Rhode Island (17,894). In 2000 Dominicans were the largest foreign-born contigent in New York, New Jersey, and Connecticut, surpassing all other immigrant groups.

Miami; Providence, Rhode Island; Lawrence, Massachusetts; and some small towns in Michigan boast sizable Dominican communities, but the place with the greatest concentration of Dominican Americans and Dominican nationals by far is New York City, which in 2005 was home to 532,000, according to the Census Bureau's 2005 American Community Survey, an increase over the 332,977 counted by Census 2000 (which might have undercounted Dominicans). (The 2005 figure above is an estimate. The American Community Survey was not intended to provide an actual population count, but rather to measure characteristics.) Washington Heights, Hamilton Heights, and Inwood in Manhattan, as well as Corona in Queens, are the very heart of Dominican life in New York City. Washington Heights has the largest Dominican community in the nation; Dominican Americans refer to it as Quisqueya Heights, after the native name for Hispaniola.

In addition to Dominicans who enter the country through legal channels and secure U.S. citizenship, there is also a sizable undocumented Dominican population in America. No reliable data on this population's size have been published, but many researchers assert that as many as three hundred thousand undocumented Dominicans have settled in the United States. One way that Dominicans enter the United States illegally is by paying a small fortune, often an entire year's wages, to smugglers to transport them across the shark-infested Mona Passage, the eighty-mile stretch of turbulent sea separating the Dominican Republic and Puerto Rico. This perilous journey, undertaken in small, rickety boats or on rafts, costs thousands their lives each year. If they make it across the Mona Passage and succeed at dodging the U.S. Border Patrol agents combing the western coastline of Puerto Rico, a U.S. territory with commonwealth status, Dominicans customarily work until they have enough money to travel to the U.S. mainland. They either hop a plane from Luis Muñoz Marín International Airport in San Juan to the mainland, usually to New York, with false documents, pretending to be Puerto Ricans, who are American citizens, and thus needing no visa or passport, or they board container ships sailing to mainland ports, sometimes paying crew members to look the other way. Naturally, it was much easier for Dominicans to travel illegally from Puerto Rico to the U.S. mainland before September 11, 2001, and the establishment of the U.S. Department of Homeland Security.

Who are the retornados?

The *retornados*, or returned immigrants, are Dominicans who have spent some time in the United States and then have returned to the Dominican Republic, either to establish businesses with capital earned abroad or for personal reasons. There is no reliable data indicating just how many Dominicans have gone to America and then returned to their homeland, but their number must be significant as companies and organizations that serve *retornados'* special needs have cropped up in the Dominican Republic.

How have Dominican Americans fared?

Although clearly defined Dominican communities first appeared in the United States over forty-five years ago, Dominican Americans have always been the invisible Latinos, especially in comparison to Mexican Americans, Puerto Ricans, and Cuban Americans. And since a large percentage of Dominican Americans are of mixed African, native, and Spanish descent, they have encountered the same prejudice and racial discrimination that African Americans have suffered in America. Operating under the false belief that Dominican immigrants represent the poorest, most disenfranchised members of Dominican society, some Americans have argued that these immigrants burden the nation's social service system. While Dominicans do dominate the ranks of the small percentage of Latinos receiving public assistance, the truth is that the vast majority of Dominican Americans are extremely hardworking people who have never been on welfare or received food stamps or workers' compensation. What's more, as a group, Dominicans who come to the United States are more highly educated than those on the island, and a good number among them are professionals.

Unfortunately, too many Dominican immigrants end up in low-wage, low-status blue-collar jobs. Based on the U.S. Census Current Population Survey for 1998 and 2000, the Lewis Mumford Center for Comparative Urban and Regional Research at the University of Albany estimated that in 2000 the mean earnings of employed Dominicans was just below $8,000 and that 36 percent of the population lived in poverty. In New York City, where Dominicans endure the highest poverty rate of all New Yorkers, a large number of Dominican women make a meager living working in the garment industry (and enjoy little job protection), while Dominican men work for modest pay in manufacturing, in the restaurant and hotel industry, or as livery drivers. No matter how scant their earnings, a good number of Dominicans send a significant portion of their paycheck to relatives back in the Dominican Republic.

Little by little, Dominicans in New York, with the support they get from their strong, close-knit community, have been working their way up. Some have launched new small businesses or revamped preexisting ones, particularly bodegas, supermarkets, diners, family-style restaurants, travel agencies, and taxicab companies. As an example of just how invisible Dominican Americans are, Dominican restaurateurs in New York City are apt to describe their fare as Spanish and American, which is what Cuban and Puerto Rican cooking in America used to be called in the old days. Thus many of their patrons, both Latinos and non-Latinos, have the false impression that they are being served dishes made by Cuban and Puerto Rican chefs. Dominican restaurateurs fear that if they told the "whole truth," their non-Dominican clientele, unfamiliar with Dominican flavors, would shy away.

What event constitutes perhaps the greatest tragedy for the Dominican community in America?

On November 15, 2001, American Airlines Flight 587, bound from New York's JFK airport for Santo Domingo, crashed shortly after takeoff, in the Belle Harbor section of Far Rockaway, Queens, killing all 260 passengers and crew on board. A great percentage of those on the flight were Dominicans from Washington Heights; many were looking forward to reunions with relatives on the island. The crash, which came just two months after the September 11 terrorist attacks, in which at least 41 persons of Dominican descent perished, was another devastating blow to Dominican Americans and Dominican nationals in New York and across the nation.

Among those lost on Flight 587 were radio personality **Papi Lafontaine** and the daughter and grandchildren of famous Dominican merengue singer **Cuco Valoy**, also known as El Brujo. Other victims were U.S. Navy petty officer **Ruben Rodriguez**, who had just completed a seven-month tour of duty on the USS *Enterprise* and was headed to the Dominican Republic to be reunited with his wife and children, and **Feliz Sanchez**, a Merrill Lynch banker who had survived the attacks of September 11 and was bound for Santo Domingo to meet with **Sammy Sosa** and other major league baseball players about investment in the Dominican Republic.

The crash of American Airlines Flight 587, coming so close on the heels of the September 11 terrorist attacks, shook the entire nation. For a time, people across America were certain that terrorists had downed Flight 587, though this proved not to be the case. With so much attention focused on Flight 587 in the days after the crash, many in New York City's Dominican enclaves expressed the sentiment that in the midst of so much tragedy, which was so difficult to bear, at least the rest of the nation might finally be made aware of their existence.

Who are some prominent Dominican Americans?

One of the leading voices in American literature of the day is Dominican-born writer **Julia Alvarez**, who took the literary world by storm in 1991 with the publication of her first novel, *How the García Girls Lost Their Accents*. Her other works of fiction, including *In the Time of the Butterflies* (1994), *¡Yo!* (1997), *In the Name of*

Salomé (2000), and *Saving the World* (2006), have also earned kudos for the author.

Oscar de la Renta, one of the most recognizable names in the world of haute couture and ready-to-wear, was born in the Dominican Republic on July 22, 1932. After an apprenticeship with Spanish couturier **Cristóbal Balenciaga** in Spain and a stint as a couture assistant at the house of Lanvin in Paris, De la Renta made his way to New York City in 1963 to design for **Elizabeth Arden**. Two years later, he launched his own ready-to-wear label and, in ensuing decades, created what is now a billion-dollar international fashion business.

Born in the Dominican Republic on August 19, 1971, tennis star **Mary Joe Fernández** played at Wimbledon, her first Grand Slam tennis match, in 1986, at just fourteen years of age. She went on to become one of the world's leading doubles players, capturing nineteen career doubles titles, two in Grand Slam events, before retiring from the tour in 2000. At the 1992 Summer Olympics, Mary Joe won gold with doubles partner **Gigi Fernández** (no relation) after defeating the Spanish doubles pair **Arantxa Sánchez Vicario** and **Conchita Martínez** in the finals before the king and queen of Spain. Fernández and Fernández repeated their stellar performance by capturing doubles gold at the Summer Olympics in Atlanta in 1996.

The Dominican Republic has contributed immensely to the American sport of baseball. Here are just a few noteworthy Dominican "boys of summer," not all of them U.S. citizens. After being selected to pitch for the San Francisco Giants in 1960, **Juan Marichal**, who was born in Laguna Verde, Dominican Republic, on October 20, 1937, and resides in Santo Domingo, would win 191 games during the 1960s, outperforming all other National League pitchers. In 1983 he was inducted into the National Baseball Hall of Fame, the first Dominican to be bestowed that honor, and in 1999 the *Sporting News* ranked him seventy-one on its list of one hundred greatest baseball players. In 2005 a statue of Marichal, one of three statues honoring the Giants' all-time greats (the others are of **Willie Mays** and **Willie McCovey**), was unveiled at the Giants' baseball stadium, AT&T Park (at the Lefty O'Doul entrance gate).

Baseball superstar **Sammy Sosa**, who played for the Chicago Cubs from 1992 until early 2005, when he was traded to the Baltimore Orioles, grew up in poverty in the Dominican Republic. As a youngster, he resorted to fashioning a makeshift baseball out of a sock wrapped in tape and a glove out of milk cartons so that he could play *pelota*, as baseball is known on the island. Sosa made major league history in 1998, when he (along with **Mark McGwire**) beat **Roger Maris**'s record, set in 1961, of sixty-one home runs in a single season. That year he was also named the National League's Most Valuable Player and became a star overnight. In 1999 Sosa made baseball history as the only player to hit sixty home runs in two seasons, and in 2000 he led the majors with fifty home runs and joined **Babe Ruth** and Mark McGwire as the only players to hit fifty homers in three different seasons. The year 2001 was another stellar one for Sammy Sosa: he again topped sixty home runs and led the major leagues in RBIs. In late 2005, Sosa was granted free agency, and sadly, in 2006, his career reached its final inning.

Pitcher **Pedro Martínez**, who was born on October 25, 1971, in the Dominican Republic, is known as the Strikeout King. He is such a dynamo on the mound, thanks to his complete command of the fastball (his travels at around 95 mph), the slider, and the changeup. While with the Montreal Expos in 1997, Martínez won the Cy Young Award, but the Expos did not have the funds to retain him, and so he was traded to the Boston Red Sox. In 1999 Martínez won his second Cy Young Award, this time by a unanimous vote, a feat he repeated in 2000 (as the first player to win the award unanimously in consecutive seasons), after he went 18-6, had an extraordinary 1.74 ERA, and led the league in strikeouts and shutouts. A rotator cuff injury plagued Martínez in 2001, but he bounced back and finished his career with the Red Sox in 2004 with a 117-37 record, the highest winning percentage for a pitcher in baseball history, and a World Series victory, one that ended eighty-six years of drought for the Red Sox. Martínez signed on with the New York Mets in 2005 and became a career two-hundred-game winner in 2006.

Manny Ramirez, considered one of the best right-handed hitters in baseball today, is another Dominican dominator. Born in Santo Domingo on May 30, 1972, Ramirez moved with his family to New York City when he was thirteen and grew up in the Washington Heights section of the city. His major league baseball career began in 1993 with the Cleveland Indians. In the 1999 season, Ramirez was the talk of all baseball as he chased **Hack Wilson**'s record, set in 1930, of 191 RBIs in a single season. While he didn't shatter that record, he drove in an impressive 165 runs, hit .333, and slammed 44 homers. In 2000 Ramirez sat out for forty-four games but still racked up 122 RBIs, hit a career-high .351, and led the American League in slugging percentage (.697) for the second consecutive season. Since 2001 Ramirez has worn a Boston Red Sox uniform. In 2005 he became one of only forty-five players in the four hundred home run club and hit his twentieth career grand slam (only **Lou Gehrig** hit more, with twenty-three).

What is the favorite pastime of Dominican America?

Baseball, of course, the national sport of the Dominican Republic. Baseball superstars **Manny Ramirez** and **Pedro Martínez** represent only the tip of the iceberg when it comes to baseball talent currently taking the field in the Dominican Republic and Dominican America. In fact, Dominicans represent a large, inexpensive labor pool for major league baseball: the average signing bonuses for Dominican players totaled $30,000 in 2006, about half of the amount American players received.

Of course, Dominican Americans are also proud of their national music and dance, merengue, which, together with Puerto Rican salsa, is número uno among Latinos in New York City and elsewhere. The Dominican community in America is also proud of *bachata*, an energetic guitar-based blues that emerged in the Dominican Republic's dance halls and brothels and was long criticized as a musical style of the poor. With the large wave of Dominican immigration to the United States in the 1980s, *bachata*—and its bitter lyrics about gloom, despair, betrayal, shattered love, and loss—leapt the class chasm and became a potent symbol of Dominican culture.

What kinds of foods do Dominican Americans like?

Dominican Americans are fond of typical American fare, but they also have a love of traditional island cooking. The traditional Dominican culinary repertoire, like the Puerto Rican and Cuban, features chicken, pork, goat, beef, fish, and seafood dishes mildly flavored with garlic, onion, and citrus juice, and accompanied by rice, beans, fried plantains, and tropical tubers, such as yuca and yautia. Of the three Caribbean cuisines, Dominican cooking has the most pronounced African elements. The flavors of Africa are readily apparent in Dominican *sancocho*, a savory stew made with beef, chicken, goat, or pork (and occasionally all four), to which chunks of West African yam, yautia, and yuca are added. A dish of *sancocho* adorned with avocado slices and rice is a quintessential Dominican meal in both Santo Domingo and Washington Heights. And a memorable one, too.

To tell you the truth, the hardest thing coming to this country wasn't the winter everyone warned me about—it was the language. If you had to choose the most tongue-twisting way of saying you love somebody or how much a pound for the ground round, then say it in English. For the longest time I thought Americans must be smarter than us Latins—because how else could they speak such a difficult language . . . I guess for each one in the family it was different what was the hardest thing. For Carlos, it was having to start all over again at forty-five, getting a license, setting up a practice. My eldest, Carla, just couldn't bear that she wasn't the know-it-all anymore. Of course, the Americans knew their country better than she did. Sandi got more complicated, prettier, and I suppose that made it hard on her, discovering she was a princess just as she had lost her island kingdom. Baby Fifi took to this place like china in a china shop, so if anything, the hardest thing for her was hearing the rest of us moan and complain.

Julia Alvarez, from *¡Yo!*

239

SIETE

Americans of Central and South American Descent

Who are the Latinos with roots in Central and South America?

Latinos with roots in Central America include Salvadoran Americans, Guatemalan Americans, Nicaraguan Americans, Honduran Americans, Panamanian Americans, and Costa Rican Americans. (Americans with roots in Belize, which was a British colony until achieving independence in 1981, are not counted as Latinos.) While Central Americans began entering the United States in small numbers as early as the nineteenth century, immigration from Central America to the United States did not reach significant levels until the late twentieth century, and so Latinos with roots in Central America are truly newcomers. They are such newcomers that in 2000, 34.5 percent of the foreign-born population in the United States was from Central America, according to March 2000 U.S. Census Bureau data. Scourges of every kind—from military dictatorships, right-wing death squads, and guerilla insurgencies to grinding poverty and hunger—are what triggered the movement north of peoples from most Spanish-speaking

Central American countries. In the 1990s, with democracy in place in Central American nations, economic chaos was the primary factor motivating Central Americans to head north to the United States. Economic upheaval continues to drive Central American immigration to this day.

A significant percentage of the Central American population in the United States has relatively low levels of educational attainment. Among the foreign born aged twenty-five or older, only 44.3 percent have at least a high school diploma, according to Census 2000 data. The high school graduation rate is lowest among those born in El Salvador, Guatemala, and Honduras and highest among those born in Costa Rica and Panama. As a consequence, the overwhelming majority of Central Americans are employed in low-paying jobs, and a good number live in poverty.

Latinos of Spanish-speaking South American ancestry include Colombian Americans, Ecuadoran Americans, Peruvian Americans, Argentinean Americans, Chilean Americans, Venezuelan Americans, Bolivian Americans, Uruguayan Americans, and Paraguayan Americans. (Americans with roots in Guyana, French Guiana, Suriname, and Brazil—which were British, French, Dutch, and Portuguese colonies, respectively—are not considered Latinos.) Although they began immigrating to the United States in small numbers as early as the nineteenth century, South Americans, like Central Americans, are relatively new to the American scene. The vast majority of Spanish-speaking South American immigrants came to the United States after 1960, and a large percentage arrived after 1980. In the year 2000, 6.6 percent of the foreign-born population in the United States was from South America.

Most Spanish-speaking South Americans have come to the United States in search of greater economic opportunity, although some, such as Colombians and Chileans, have also sought shelter from war, military dictatorships, and political instability. In recent times, the people of South America have experienced the most trying period in their history since the days of military dictatorship almost two decades ago. Unraveling economies, rampant unemployment, escalating crime, and social turmoil—as well as inept rule, abuse of power, and large-scale corruption—have not only fueled popular protests that have toppled governments, but have also stimulated immigration to the United States.

Latinos with roots in Spanish-speaking South America belong largely to the middle and upper-middle classes and reside primarily in urban areas. In 2000 they were most concentrated in the New York–New Jersey metropolitan region, Los Angeles, Washington DC, and the Miami–Fort Lauderdale area. As a group, they are generally well educated. For this reason, they are employed in large numbers in the managerial and professional sector. Very few are employed in agriculture.

How reliable are Census 2000 figures when it comes to Americans with roots in Spanish-speaking Central and South America?

Not very. As with the Dominican population, Census 2000 data portray the Central and South American populations in the United States as much smaller than experts estimate. Some attribute this to a trend among Latinos of relinquishing national self-identification and embracing a pan-Latino identity. Many others, however, attribute the undercount to the fact that the Census 2000 form provided specific boxes designating ethnicity only for those with Mexican, Puerto Rican, and Cuban roots, while all other Latinos had to check the generic "other Hispanic" box and write in details about their ancestry. The problem is that the Census 2000 form did not include examples of possible ethnic descriptions to guide those filling it out, such as "Salvadoran" or "Nicaraguan," terms that appeared on the 1990 census form, and a great many simply identified themselves in general terms, such as "Hispanic." Based on the U.S. Census Current Population Survey for 1998 and 2000, the Lewis Mumford Center for Comparative Urban and Regional Research at the University of Albany estimates that the actual size of the various subgroups of Spanish-speaking Central and South Americans in the United States was much larger in 2000 than Census 2000 indicates.

SALVADORAN AMERICANS

When did the Spanish conquer El Salvador?

Launched in 1524, the Spanish conquest of El Salvador changed forever the course of the country's history. At the time Spanish conquistador **Pedro de Alvarado** stepped foot in what is now El Salvador, it was inhabited by five Mesoamerican groups, one of which was the Pipil, an industrious people closely related to the

Aztecs, who called their homeland Cuscatlán, meaning "Land of the Jewel." The Pipils fiercely defended themselves from the Spanish onslaught, and Alvarado and his soldiers were forced to retreat to Guatemala. But four years later, the Spanish invaders, who couldn't get precious metals off their minds, managed to subdue the Pipils. The Spanish christened their colony El Salvador (the Savior) and incorporated it into the province of Guatemala.

The Spanish unearthed little silver and gold in El Salvador, and so they turned to agriculture, providing fourteen families, known as *los catorce grandes*, with enormous tracts of land. *Los catorce grandes* put the native peoples to work cultivating cacao, indigo, and, later, coffee. On September 15, 1821, nearly three centuries after the Spanish first set foot in the region, El Salvador, along with Guatemala, Nicaragua, Honduras, and Costa Rica, announced an end to Spanish domination. Believing that strength lay in unity, these five Central American colonies joined together as the United Provinces of Central America on July 1, 1823, but this union completely fell apart just fifteen years later, in 1838. In the 1840s and 1850s, each of the colonies declared itself a republic independent of Spain as well as the United Provinces of Central America. Still, they expressed hope for Central American reunification, and between 1838 and 1965, countless unsuccessful attempts at a reunion were made.

Changes over the years in El Salvador's political status brought little relief to the subjugated native peoples and mestizos, and eventually, they took matters into their own hands and rebelled. One of their most famous uprisings took place in 1833, when **Anastasio Aquino** rallied thousands of natives and mestizos under the banner "Land for those who work it!" Conditions did not improve in the aftermath of the uprising, but the stage was set for events that would rip the nation apart at the seams.

When Did El Salvador declare its sovereignty?

In 1856 El Salvador officially proclaimed itself a sovereign nation. The governments that would steer the country until the end of the nineteenth century were determined to develop a strong economy by supplying international markets with coffee. These governments were essentially oligarchies controlled by *los catorces grandes*, which by this time actually numbered around two hundred and possessed most of the land and wealth of El Salvador.

Los catorces grandes were able to produce high yields of coffee by exploiting the native and mestizo workers, who they forced to labor on the plantations and prohibited from acquiring parcels of their own to farm.

As the twentieth century dawned, El Salvador was one of the most prosperous nations in Central America, owing to its leading export crop—coffee. Coffee made it possible for railways to be constructed, highways to be paved, and the cities to grow. In this atmosphere of prosperity, the nation enjoyed relative stability, but it was only skin-deep. Discontent was growing among the exploited poor, and the tiny ruling oligarchy did nothing to defuse the mounting pressure, which would bring much heartache to the country in 1932.

What is La Matanza?

La Matanza, meaning "the Slaughter," of 1932 marks one of the low points in El Salvador's tumultuous history. When the Great Depression (1929–41) rocked world markets, the price of coffee plummeted, and the already poor workers of El Salvador suffered wage cuts or lost their jobs altogether. As a result, the political situation became extremely unstable in El Salvador. In 1930 **Arturo Araujo**, who favored land reform and social democracy, was elected president, to the great shock of the Salvadoran oligarchy and military. After Araujo announced that he would permit the communist party to take part in municipal elections, the military tossed him out of office and put a right-wing general, **Maximiliano Hernández Martínez**, in his place.

When Hernández Martínez did nothing to alleviate the peasants' suffering, rebel forces headed by university student **Agustín Farabundo Martí** formed a communist party called the Farabundo Martí National Liberation Front (FMLN). The FMLN exerted pressure on the Hernández Martínez government to reform the country's system of land ownership, which had left the people desperately poor, with power and wealth concentrated in the hands of a few. When their cries went unanswered, the rebels organized a two-day revolt by the farmers in 1932. In response, the military, under orders from Hernández Martínez, executed Farabundo Martí and slaughtered thirty thousand insurrectionists, many of them natives.

Who Was José Napoleón Duarte?

For the next four decades, the people of El Salvador endured ever-worsening economic conditions and continued to cry for the fair redistribution of the land. But the government, which remained under the coffee elite's control, refused to institute reform and called on the armed forces to suppress the masses. Finally, in 1972, it seemed that El Salvador was on the brink of change when **José Napoleón Duarte**, a moderate reformist candidate who had founded the Christian Democratic Party, appeared to have won a majority in the presidential election. Before a victory could be announced, however, the government had Duarte imprisoned, tortured, and exiled.

After Duarte was sent into exile, violence and repression became endemic in El Salvador. Civil disorder continued to escalate as conditions worsened for the poor peasants, and guerilla groups grew in number and daring. The government's response to this increased dissent was to organize death squads, which hunted down, tortured, and exterminated thousands of citizens thought to be sympathetic to the reform cause. (Women clad in blue jeans were highly suspect.) Those who perished came to be known as *los desaparecidos*, or "the disappeared ones," because military and paramilitary forces denied any involvement in their fate.

The situation came to a head in 1977, when government forces murdered **Father Rutilio Grande**, a rural pastor. San Salvador's **Archbishop Oscar Romero**, a beloved religious leader, lashed out at the regime for its brutality, ushering the Catholic Church into the struggle. In 1979 reformist officers led a successful coup and installed a junta, run by both the military and civilians, which promised an end to the violence and sweeping land reforms. José Napoleón Duarte returned to El Salvador from exile, and the people thought that maybe, just maybe, change was on the horizon.

Why did civil war break out in El Salvador, and when was peace finally restored?

The civilians in the junta, which **Duarte** headed, objected to the military's unceasing efforts to crush dissent, and they soon threw up their hands and resigned. All power was once again concentrated in the hands of the military, which lashed out at the

rebels—and at anyone suspected of belonging to the opposition—with a vengeance. Countless Salvadorans were tortured and
murdered by death squads. The FMLN fought back, and in 1980
a civil war erupted in El Salvador. One fateful event that sparked
the civil war was the assassination on March 24, 1980, by government forces, of **Archbishop Romero**, who had again openly criticized the Salvadoran government for its draconian rule.

The United States, fearful that an FMLN victory in the civil
war might foster the spread of communism in Central America,
lent massive economic and military aid to the Salvadoran government, ignoring its horrendous human rights violations. By the
mid-1980s, the **Reagan** administration was dispatching a whopping $1.2 million a day to bolster the Salvadoran government in
its fight. (Between 1978 and 1993, the United States would give
El Salvador a grand total of $1.1 billion in military aid.) Although
it did not go as far as deploying U.S. troops in El Salvador to fight
the FMLN rebels, the U.S. government supplied cutting-edge
weapons, such as M60 machine guns and M16s, and also helped
train and maintain Salvadoran army battalions.

One American-trained battalion, the Atlacatl Battalion, was
responsible for one of the largest massacres in twentieth-century
Latin American history. In Operation Rescue, conducted in late
1981, the Atlacatl Battalion slaughtered one thousand civilians in
an attempt to loosen the rebels' hold on the region of Morazán.
When the news broke, Salvadoran and American officials denied
that any such massacre had occurred. The Reagan White House
was in the middle of negotiating with Congress for continued aid
to El Salvador, and verification of the massacre would have un-
dermined its argument that the Latin American nation had
stepped up its efforts to protect human rights.

In 1984 José Napoleón Duarte was elected president of El
Salvador, finally realizing his dream of leading the nation. Duarte
tried to restore harmony, but the ongoing civil war, economic
hardship brought on by his fiscal austerity measures, and accusations of corruption on the part of his government left the door
open for a wealthy coffee grower, **Alfredo Cristiani**, of the right-
wing National Republican Alliance (ARENA), to prevail in the
1989 presidential election. In September 1989, the Cristiani government and FMLN rebels finally sat down at the negotiating table. At the last minute, the FMLN launched a final offensive but
failed to garner enough popular support to overthrow the government. During the fighting that ensued, an army-sponsored

death squad broke into a Catholic university and brutally murdered six Jesuit priests, their housekeeper, and her daughter. This incident stunned the world, and the United States reacted by withdrawing aid from the Salvadoran government, forcing it to return to the negotiating table with the FMLN. The Commission on the Truth for El Salvador, appointed by the United Nations in 1992 to get to the bottom of the most atrocious breaches of human rights in El Salvador, revealed that the Salvadoran minister of defense, **René Emilio Ponce**, had ordered the massacre of the Jesuit priests.

For two long years, the opposing sides negotiated under the supervision of the United Nations, and finally, in January 1992, they signed historic peace accords. Under the accords, the Salvadoran government agreed to institute extensive reforms, among them the redistribution of land, the downsizing of the military, the creation of a civilian-controlled police force, and a purge of its most notorious human-rights violators. The government also guaranteed the FMLN political freedom. In return, the FMLN agreed to throw down its weapons.

The pace of reform was slow at first, and El Salvador struggled to resuscitate its economy. Twelve years of civil war had had a devastating effect on the nation; over seventy-five thousand people had lost their lives, and hundreds of thousands had been uprooted. But ARENA enthusiastically embraced democracy and the free market concept, and the FMLN dissolved its guerilla forces and became a legal political party. With democracy building a reality, the World Bank and international investors were more than happy to aid El Salvador in its reconstruction. By the late 1990s, the nation's economy had improved, but the welfare of a large segment of the Salvadoran population had not, owing to the concentration of wealth in the country. Still, there has been some progress: in 1991, 66 percent of the population lived in poverty, but by 2004 the poverty rate had dropped to 34.6 percent.

How many Salvadoran Americans are there, and when did Salvadorans start coming to America in large numbers?

In 2005, 1,240,031 Salvadoran Americans and Salvadoran nationals called the United States home, according to the Pew Hispanic Center tabulations of the Census Bureau's 2005 American

Community Survey, up from the 655,165 counted by Census 2000. (The actual count in 2000 was probably higher, given that Census 2000 did not take into account the unknown number of Salvadorans who did not specify their Salvadoran origin on the census form and the hundreds of thousands of undocumented Salvadoran refugees in America.)

Emigration from El Salvador was just a trickle until the turbulent decade leading up to the civil war, when about 34,000 Salvadorans came to America. Among those immigrants were many members of the ruling class who had already experienced American life (a large percentage had been educated in American universities), and they settled legally in the United States. After the civil war erupted in 1980, untold numbers of Salvadorans received death threats or orders to join the army, and they watched in horror as death squads killed family members, friends, and neighbors. In response, a stream of terrorized Salvadorans, mainly of the middle and lower classes, without so much as a suitcase, rushed for the border. In the 1980s alone, approximately 214,000 Salvadorans entered the United States via legal channels. An unknown number of mostly poor Salvadoran peasants crossed into the United States illegally, making their way to American soil through Mexico by using counterfeit papers or by bribing officials manning border control posts.

Some were also led or transported north and over the U.S.-Mexico border by smugglers, called coyotes, who demanded large sums of money for the risky, arduous trip. Abuse at the hands of the coyotes was commonplace, and stories abound of coyotes dumping Salvadorans in the middle of the desert in Arizona or California, without food, water, or directions on how to reach civilization. A good number of Americans, particularly those who deplored the United States' use of El Salvador as a battleground on which to fight the Soviet Union, sympathized with the desperate Salvadorans and other Central Americans crossing the border. In the early 1980s, an American named **Jim Corbett**, along with several others, and aided by about three hundred religious congregations, organized the sanctuary movement, a network of safe houses for people escaping Central America. Their work shined the spotlight on the plight of Central Americans fleeing war and extreme hardship.

In the 1990s, even with civil war a thing of the past, Salvadorans continued to face economic upheaval at home, and they do so to this day. The only way for struggling families to survive has been to send members north to work in the United States. Like the refugees of the civil war, many Salvadoran immigrants of the 1990s (and those from other Central American countries) trekked through Mexico to the United States, a practice that continues. Since the 1990s, the journey has been especially fraught with danger. As they pass through Mexico, which they call "crossing the beast," Central American immigrants, who the Mexican government has classified as felons, are routinely assaulted, raped, or robbed by hoodlums, including by members of a branch of the Los Angeles–based gang Mara Salvatrucha, and are hunted down by soldiers and the police, who strip them of their belongings and money and sometimes shoot to kill. And many would-be immigrants are taken into slavery or dumped back over the Mexico-Guatemala border. As **Gustavo Arellano**, a columnist for the *Orange County Weekly* once noted, Central American immigrants are "the Mexicans of Mexico," for they are treated as badly in Mexico as Mexicans are in the United States.

Some critics claim that the United States fosters this situation because it expects Mexico to act as a filter for immigrants headed north from Central America. As a result, Mexican immigration agents are especially tough on Central Americans trying to squeeze through. Mexico has taken steps to ameliorate the situation by setting up roadblocks along its southern border and along well-traveled corridors so that Central Americans will find it difficult to even step foot on Mexican territory. In 2001 Mexico and Guatemala launched a joint repatriation project, funded in part by the United States, to transport Central American migrants captured in Mexico back to their country of origin, rather than simply depositing them on the Guatemalan side of the Mexico-Guatemala border, where most simply turn around and trek north once again. Those who are returned to their home countries are less likely to try again, given the longer road and higher costs. For the Mexican government, this project is part of *Plan Sur* (Plan South), which was launched in 2001 to tackle the organized crime and corruption feeding off the illicit smuggling of migrants along Mexico's southern border. Human rights groups have contended that *Plan Sur* merely forces Central American migrants to pay more to migrant smugglers and to choose more remote, and thus more perilous, routes north. The beefing up of the U.S.-Mexico border since the September 11, 2001, terrorist attacks has made the trek across the border even more perilous, and as with Mexicans crossing illegally into the United States, the death toll is high for Salvadorans.

What is the status of Salvadoran refugees in America?

Most of the legal and undocumented Salvadoran refugees of the civil war period sought political asylum once in the United States, but only about 3 percent of applicants were granted that status. Unable to produce documents to prove "a well-founded fear of persecution," the others were deemed ineligible for political asylum and placed in deportation. In fleeing for their lives, most had not paid any attention to gathering paperwork. But the truth of the matter is that no documentation in the world would have sufficed, because the refugees were pointing a finger at the Salvadoran government as the source of their anguish, the very government the United States had been nurturing with aid. (If the U.S. government had granted the Salvadoran refugees political asylum, it would have faced the unsavory task of justifying the position it took in El Salvador's civil war.)

Those considered ineligible for political asylum or whose cases were still pending (that is, most Salvadorans) were stamped economic refugees, which meant that they could be deported at the drop of a hat. Fearing deportation, the Salvadoran refugees (along with refugees from Nicaragua, Guatemala, and Honduras who were in the same boat) filed a class-action suit in 1985, alleging that the U.S. Immigration and Naturalization Service (INS) had discriminated against them and had wrongly dismissed their appeal for political asylum. In 1990 the INS agreed to a settlement that guaranteed all members of the class-action suit a fair hearing and the right to live and work legally in the United States while their asylum claims were pending.

Between 1986 and 1990, one hundred thousand undocumented Central Americans who had arrived before 1982 received the good news that their status had been changed to that of legal immigrants, thanks to the amnesty provisions of the Immigration Reform and Control Act of 1986. But by 1996 the INS still had not addressed the remaining asylum claims of Salvadorans and other Central Americans. Many of the refugees whose status was still pending concluded that they were eligible for suspension of deportation (which leads to permanent residency), since enough time had elapsed for them to meet the requirement of seven years' residency. (The other requirements were good moral character and proof that the refugee and his or her parents, spouse, or children who were legal U.S. residents would suffer exceptional hardship were the refugee deported.)

However, in 1996 the U.S. Congress passed a sweeping immigration law, the Illegal Immigration Reform and Immigrant Responsibility Act (IIRAIRA), which was lauded as legislation that would control illegal immigration. Instead, the IIRAIRA, which is still in effect (as of 2007), has led to high levels of deportation (in the years 1996–2006, nearly 1.4 million immigrants were deported) as well as—by making detention mandatory for those awaiting deportation—the large-scale detention of undocumented immigrants, asylum seekers with improper documentation, and other noncitizens, who are denied due process and can be held indefinitely. The IIRAIRA ignores the role of the courts as defenders of people up against an overzealous government. For example, U.S. Citizenship and Immigration Services (CIS) agents at the border, even those at a low level, have the right to deport individuals summarily and ban them from reentering the United States for up to ten years if there is suspicion of fraud. In terms of undocumented immigrants, if the CIS (which replaced the INS) catches them, they can also be deported and barred from reentering the United States for up to ten years—even if it means they are torn from their families.

The IIRAIRA has also made suspension of deportation harder to obtain. Refugees have to show ten years of residency, as well as proof of good character and hardship to their family to ward off deportation. (The refugees' hardship is no longer considered.) However, much of the time that refugees rack up in the United States is not permitted to count toward the ten years, and quotas are set on the number of refugees who can be granted suspension of deportation in any given year. As a result of the IIRAIRA, the approximately three hundred thousand Central American refugees whose status was still undecided in 1996 remained in limbo.

Before long, Congress recognized the deleterious effect of the IIRAIRA on so many Central American immigrants' lives and passed the Nicaraguan Adjustment and Central American Relief Act of 1997 (NACARA). Until it expired on March 31, 2000, the NACARA gave permanent residency (the first step toward citizenship) to undocumented Nicaraguans (and Cubans) continuously present in the United States since December 1, 1995. However, the NACARA did not provide Salvadorans, Guatemalans, and Hondurans with the same opportunity to adjust (legalize) their status, even though they had fled armed conflicts, poverty, and natural disasters of the same or of an even greater magnitude. The NACARA merely provided certain individuals of these subgroups with two traditional forms of relief—suspension of deportation and cancellation of removal—that were in place prior to the enactment of the IIRAIRA.

As a result of the inconsistency in the way the NACARA treats the various Central American subgroups, an unknown number of Salvadorans (as well as Guatemalans and Hondurans) with undocumented status have had no means by which to regularize their immigration status. In March 2001, the **Bush** administration sought to alleviate some of their suffering by suspending the deportation of Salvadorans in the aftermath of destructive earthquakes that hit El Salvador earlier that year. Undocumented Salvadorans were granted Temporary Protected Status (TPS) for a period of eighteen months, permitting them to live and work temporarily in the United States without fear of detention or deportation. Some 250,000 Salvadorans residing in the United States before the earthquakes hit were awarded TPS. TPS, however, is not a path to permanent residency, and those awarded it have had to spend hundreds of dollars to renew it. In 2006 a few refused to spend the money to reregister, believing that immigration reform was just around the corner, and that they should save their hard-earned dollars to cover the cost of citizenship. But such reform has not manifested itself, and hundreds of thousands of Salvadorans still live in legal limbo.

Where do Salvadoran Americans live, and how are they doing?

The five states with the largest Salvadoran population in the nation in 2000 were California (272,999), Texas (79,204), New York (72,713), Virginia (43,653), and Maryland (34,433). However, the miscalculations by the U.S. Census Bureau in 2000, stemming from the wording on the census form, must be kept in mind. For instance, the 2000 census surely miscalculated the number of Salvadorans in California, the group's number one destination. The 1990 census counted approximately 339,000 Salvadorans in the state. It seems implausible that California's Salvadoran community could have shrunk in the 1990s, given the visible signs of growth in the community over the decade, especially in the greater Los Angeles area, with its large Salvadoran population.

Despite the fact that almost 25 percent of Salvadoran immigrants in the United States have attended college and that many among them are professionals, over half of employed Salvadoran immigrants work long hours at low-paying jobs. This is invariably a reflection of their undocumented status in the United States and their fear of deportation. Salvadorans have a very strong work ethic and have been doing their utmost to forge a new life in the United States and join mainstream society. In preparing for citizenship, many have taken advantage of the English-language classes and American history lessons offered by a network of social service agencies, such as the Central American Resource Center (formerly the Central American Refugee Center) in Los Angeles, which Salvadoran refugees founded in 1983.

What are remesas?

Once Salvadoran immigrants settle into their new lives in the United States, most begin to send payments, known as *remesas*, or remittances, back home to alleviate the financial distress and meet the basic needs of family members left behind. While in 1980 Salvadorans sent home just $10 million in remittances, in 2005 that figure had grown to $2.8 billion, according to Central Bank estimates, making Salvadoran workers in the United States the largest source of foreign exchange revenue in El Salvador. Salvadorans also contribute to the welfare of those back home by investing in business opportunities in their homeland that provide jobs locally. And, Salvadorans participate in fund-raisers sponsored by the more than one hundred Salvadoran hometown associations in the United States. The funds collected are essentially development aid for El Salvador; they go toward bankrolling such community projects as Red Cross clinics, ambulance services, road construction, and schools.

Family remittances and hometown fund-raisers are so critical to El Salvador's welfare that fostering close ties with Salvadorans in the United States is a high priority of the Salvadoran government. In fact, Salvadoran diplomats in the United States often serve as mediators between the hometown associations and officials back in El Salvador, identifying potential contributors and eliminating bureaucratic obstacles. Dollars—which account for most of the money in circulation in El Salvador—are of such critical importance in keeping the country's troubled economy growing that on January 1, 2001, El Salvador adopted the U.S. dollar as its official currency. (While the colón remains legal tender, colones are no longer printed.) A major concern of the Salvadoran government is that the United States will take a tougher stance on Salvadoran immigration and, consequently, remittances will fall.

Salvadorans in the United States are proud of their status as major investors and bankrollers in El Salvador and of the good works they are able to do, but remittances come at a steep price. A fair number of Salvadorans work long hours at more than one or even two jobs so that they can send funds home on a regular basis. The monies they send could be used to improve the quality of their own lives and their children's lives in America. Some in the United States argue that the downside of remittances is that they encourage immigration, by reinforcing the notion that wealth is easily attained in *el norte*. Others contend the opposite, that remittances prevent massive emigration to the United States by providing income to those who would otherwise head for the border and by strengthening democratic institutions in El Salvador. Some in El Salvador are concerned that remittances have given rise to a culture of dependency, arguing that Salvadorans find it easier to rely on dollars sent home than to work at a job. Others in El Salvador counter that employment opportunities are scarce, making such dollars their only lifeline.

GUATEMALAN AMERICANS

How resistant were the native peoples of Guatemala to Spanish rule?

Extremely resistant. Spanish conquistadores, led by **Pedro de Alvarado**, first set foot in what is present-day Guatemala in 1522. They ruthlessly pursued their mission to "bring light to those in darkness, and also to get rich," as one of Alvarado's men wrote. This mission directly involved the Maya of Guatemala, who, as with the native peoples in Spain's other colonies, were forced to convert to Catholicism and were driven into slave labor. But of all the native peoples in Central America, the Maya put up the greatest resistance to subjugation. That many Guatemalans—and Guatemalan Americans—today partake of Mayan religious practices is testimony to their success. Still, Spanish rule took its toll on the Maya: Before the sixteenth century was over, about 80 percent of the one million Maya who inhabited the Guatemalan highlands had lost their lives fighting the Spanish or their European diseases.

Who was Mariano Gálvez, and why was he such an Anglophile?

Guatemala, El Salvador, Nicaragua, Honduras, and Costa Rica declared their independence from Spain in 1821, and two years later they formed a federation called the United Provinces of Central America. Just before the federation was dissolved in 1838, a liberal named **Mariano Gálvez** emerged as the leader of Guatemala. Gálvez created an export-driven economy, and to fuel it, he made room for the cultivation of more crops by auctioning off lands held by the Church, groups of native peoples, and mestizos. The leading export was cochineal (a crimson or carmine dye derived from the cochineal insect, a native of tropical and subtropical South America and Mexico), and the major buyer was England, which had an expanding textile industry in the early nineteenth century. Consequently, 90 percent of the products that Guatemala imported were British, and the Guatemalan economy became closely tied to Britain's. Gálvez turned out to be more of an Anglophile than anyone could have guessed. He lured English settlers to Guatemala with promises of land grants, and he attempted to replace the Spanish legal system with a British-inspired one.

How was coffee king in nineteenth-century Guatemala?

While **Mariano Gálvez**'s reforms made Guatemala richer, they inspired the wrath of the native and mestizo peasants, who saw little of the wealth and wanted their land back. In 1838 a poor criollo peasant named **Rafael Carrera** led a guerilla insurgency that toppled the Gálvez government. Carrera would, for the most part, rule Guatemala from 1839 until his death in 1865. He gave the Church back its real estate and its authority to dictate family life and education. A conservative leader, Carrera also showed concern for the native and mestizo masses. When coffee took the place of cochineal as Guatemala's major export, Carrera did not appropriate native and mestizo lands to grow coffee beans.

After Rafael Carrera's death, Guatemala experienced rebellion, which was orchestrated by **Serapio Cruz** together with liberals and planters in the western highlands, setting the stage for the rise to power in 1873 of **Justo Rufino Barrios**, the first of several liberal military dictators to rule the country. In the name of economic growth and modernization, Barrios passed anticlerical legislation; expanded the public education system (to the benefit of the middle and upper classes); attracted foreign investors, especially British and German businessmen, to build the nation's infrastructure; and encouraged the formation of banks and other financial institutions. While he was most certainly a reformer, Barrios also expanded the coffee industry by expropriating native and mestizo lands and taking advantage of the workers. He also fortified the military, which became a tool of repression under his leadership.

What effect did the Depression have on Guatemala?

Two other liberal leaders governed Guatemala after **Justo Rufino Barrios**, adhering to his blueprint for running the country. Then in 1898, **Manuel Estrada Cabrera** took office, and during his tenure, which lasted until 1920, Guatemala saw sustained economic growth as coffee exports expanded. By the 1920s, the United States was heavily invested in Guatemala, replacing the Germans and the British, and thus exerted an enormous influence on Guatemalan internal affairs. The Great Depression (1929–41) caused the value of Guatemalan coffee beans to nosedive, which translated into increased unemployment and poverty for Guatemalans. The people grew restless, and Guatemala was racked by a series of revolts.

A general named **Jorge Ubico** managed to restore stability to the nation, and in 1930 he was overwhelmingly elected to the presidency. By squelching all opposition, including the Communist Party, through the use of military force, Ubico remained at the helm until 1944. During his years in office, he formulated myriad regulations that promoted the agenda of wealthy landowners and foreign investors, especially the United States. For instance, he forced the native peoples to carry passbooks that proved they had worked for at least 150 days in a given year. In order to obtain such proof, many natives had to go to work for wealthy landowners.

Why did the United States invade Guatemala over bananas?

During World War II, **General Ubico**, in collaboration with the United States, seized German property in Guatemala and permitted the U.S. military to station troops on Guatemalan soil. In so doing, Ubico lost the support of the coffee elite. Wartime inflation caused Guatemala's middle class immense hardship, setting the stage for demonstrations against Ubico's dictatorship. In 1944 a reformist alliance of Guatemalans, composed of students, professionals, and soldiers—who wanted the Americans out of Guatemala and a better life for the people—forced Ubico, who got no help from the coffee elite, to relinquish the presidency. That same year, **Juan José Arévalo**, a university professor who had been exiled to Argentina, was voted into office. Arévalo set to work building democracy in Guatemala; his efforts were sustained by his successor, **Colonel Jacobo Arbenz Guzmán**, who became president in 1950. Arbenz's greatest contribution was his agrarian reform program, which returned 1.5 million uncultivated acres on large plantations to the native peoples and the mestizos. The big landowners who lost some acreage were reimbursed for their losses, but they were nonetheless infuriated.

One of them was the United Fruit Company (UFCO), an American enterprise that cultivated tropical fruit, primarily bananas and pineapples, on huge tracts of land in Guatemala and elsewhere in Latin America. Called *la frutera* ("the fruit company") and *Mamita Yunay* (Mommy United) in Central America, the company was king of the banana trade in that part of the world for much of the twentieth century. Under Arbenz's land reform program, about 234,000 acres of the UFCO's land were expropriated, and the UFCO went kicking and screaming to **President Dwight Eisenhower**. Several individuals in the Eisenhower administration had close links to the UFCO, and they beseeched the president to take retaliatory action. So President Eisenhower, to protect the interests of American industry, announced that Guatemala had forged an alliance with the Soviet Union (Arbenz supported Guatemala's Communist Party) and thus was no friend of the Americans. On June 18, 1954, the United States traded bananas for bullets when two hundred

American troops and six aircraft, under the direction of the CIA, invaded Guatemala from Honduras. The U.S. government then vowed to bomb Guatemala City if the Guatemalan military did not withdraw its support from Arbenz.

Arbenz fled the country, and the U.S. ambassador to Guatemala, **John Puerifoy**, handed the Guatemalan government over to **Colonel Carlos Castillo Armas**, who had the backing of Guatemalan businesses, the right wing, and the CIA. Armas reversed Arbenz's agrarian reforms, handing acreage back to the big landowners, among them the UFCO. He also reinstated military rule and had no qualms about using force to achieve his aims—which included demolishing any opposition from leftist organizations, such as student groups, labor unions, and political parties. Soon Armas intensified his efforts to quell dissent by torturing, imprisoning, or condemning to death thousands of Guatemalans whom he considered suspect. But in making so many enemies, Armas jeopardized his rule—and his life.

In 1957 a palace guard from the opposition killed the dictator. What followed was three decades of rule by American-backed military dictatorships, which crushed popular resistance with violence. In the 1970s, guerilla forces in Guatemala set about recruiting native peoples of the highlands in large numbers. The Guatemalan government reacted by forming death squads, which combed the country in search of rebels, whom they slaughtered by the thousands. In the 1980s, the situation worsened when the government gave villagers the choice to join the army and fight the rebels or be killed. Hundreds of thousands died, and many thousands fled to the highlands or across the border. This cycle of violence continued virtually unchecked until the mid-1980s, when the United States, which could no longer reconcile all of the human rights abuses in Guatemala, withdrew much of its support from the Guatemalan government.

When was democracy given another chance in Guatemala?

Democracy was given another chance in Guatemala in 1986, when the military allowed **Marco Vinicio Cerezo Arévalo**, a civilian and the leader of the Christian Democratic Party, to take office. However, during his five-year rule, Cerezo's hands were tied, since he knew the military would do away with him if he strayed too far from its objectives. He did not dare negotiate with the guerillas, who wanted lands returned to the natives and mestizos, better health care, higher wages, and a voice in politics for the people.

In 1993 **Jorge Serrano Elías**, a center-right businessman, orchestrated a coup and seized control of the country, but the United States responded by cutting off economic aid to Guatemala, and within one month Serrano was history. Serrano had initiated peace talks with the major guerilla group in Guatemala, the Guatemalan National Revolutionary Unity (URNG), and his successor, **Ramiro de León Carpio**, took over where Serrano left off, on June 5, 1993. (On April 17, 2002, he would be found dead in a Miami apartment; his death was attributed to a diabetic coma.) De León Carpio ultimately called general elections, and in 1996 the reform-minded **Alvaro Arzú**, of the National Advancement Party, was elected president. Under his administration, the peace talks that had begun between the government and the URNG in 1991 accelerated. In December 1996, the two parties signed peace accords brokered by the United Nations, ending Guatemala's thirty-six-year civil war, one of the bloodiest in Latin America. By war's end, some two hundred thousand civilians, mostly peasants, had been killed or had "disappeared," and 80 percent of Guatemala's eleven million people lived in poverty, amid rampant crime and other forms of social violence. By signing the accords, which made constitutional reforms internationally binding, Guatemalans prepared the ground for the first seeds of democracy to be sown.

President Alvaro Arzú's government failed to implement key reforms that were tied to the peace accords and intended to remedy the political, social, and economic problems that had fueled the war (such as the redistribution of land, one of the war's main causes). Meanwhile, the crime rate in Guatemala rose, and attention to human rights lagged. In this atmosphere, **Alfonso Portillo**, of the opposition Guatemalan Republican Front, a party with links to the atrocities committed during the civil war, enjoyed a landslide victory in the 1999 presidential elections, which were deemed free and fair by international observers.

Portillo promised his countrymen that he would forge ahead with the peace process, pursue the continued liberalization of the economy, and preserve strong links to the United States. Still, not all of his policies, including his fiscal austerity measures, were popular with Guatemalans, who continued to endure widespread poverty. In 2000 over 57 percent of the Guatemalan people were categorized as poor; and 27 percent, as extremely poor. Under Portillo, democracy in the country remained fragile, and in 2003 former Guatemala City mayor **Óscar Berger**, who had the backing of the country's sugar and coffee farmers and banking bigwigs, won the presidency, defeating former Guatemalan dictator **Efraín Ríos Montt**, whose candidacy was controversial, to say the least, owing to the human rights abuses his military regime (1982–83) had perpetrated, including a genocide against Guatemala's native people.

When did Guatemalans start coming to America in large numbers?

In 1954, when **President Arbenz** fled Guatemala, many Guatemalans—mostly intellectuals, political activists, union leaders, and university students—were either forced into exile or left their homeland out of fear of persecution and settled in the United States. The majority of Guatemalans in this early immigration made California their new home. The Guatemalan government's campaigns of terror during Guatemala's thirty-six-year civil war, which ended in 1996, forced a large number of Guatemalans to immigrate. As with Salvadorans, they either entered the United States through legal channels or made their way north through Mexico and over the border as undocumented aliens. *El Norte*—a film cowritten by **Gregory Nava**, **Anna Thomas**, and Guatemalan American **Arturo Arias** and nominated for an Academy Award for Best Screenplay in 1982—depicts the arduous journey north of two youths, a sister and brother, who flee violence in Guatemala for refuge in Los Angeles.

As with Salvadoran refugees, the lives of undocumented Guatemalan immigrants in the United States were made more difficult with the passage of the Illegal Immigration Reform and Immigrant Responsibility Act of 1996. And like Salvadorans, they were not among those groups afforded the opportunity to regularize their immigration status with the passage of the Nicaraguan Adjustment and Central American Relief Act of 1997. For this reason, undocumented Guatemalans live in the shadows, dodging the CIS and hoping for immigration reform, just like their Salvadoran counterparts.

In 2005, 780,191 Guatemalan Americans and Guatemalan nationals called the United States home, according to the Pew

Hispanic Center tabulations of the Census Bureau's 2005 American Community Survey. This represents a sizable increase over the 372,487 Guatemalan Americans and Guatemalan nationals counted in Census 2000 (which was probably an undercount) and the 268,779 tallied in 1990. California boasts by far the largest Guatemalan population in the nation—143,500 Guatemalan Americans and Guatemalan nationals were counted in the state in 2000—and Los Angeles has the largest Guatemalan community outside of Guatemala. Guatemalans in Los Angeles are concentrated in the Pico Union section of the city. Runners-up to California in 2000 were New York, with 29,074 Guatemalans counted; Florida, with 28,650; Illinois, with 19,790; and Texas, with 18,539. New York City, Chicago, Houston, and Washington DC, in particular have attracted Guatemalans. So, too, have the farm belts of California, Texas, and Florida, where Guatemalans are employed as seasonal migrant farmworkers to pick crops.

The tendency among the many Guatemalans who are in the United States illegally is to try to blend into the Central American crowd, at least in the big cities, rather than sticking together in a large community, and so they risk losing touch with their roots. Like Salvadorans in America, Guatemalan Americans and Guatemalan refugees have little or no formal education and tend to toil at low-paying jobs, such as in restaurants, factories, domestic service, and gardening. Despite their generally modest standard of living, Guatemalans in America are optimistic that the future will be gentler and kinder.

NICARAGUAN AMERICANS

How did Nicaragua make the transition from a Spanish colony to a sovereign nation?

The first Spanish conquistador to step foot in what is present-day Nicaragua was **Francisco Fernández de Córdoba**, who arrived there in 1523. Shortly after, he quite literally lost his head when he went against the wishes of his superior, **Pedro Arias de Ávila**, and tried to make Nicaragua a separate Spanish province. Arias de Ávila served as governor of Nicaragua from 1526 to 1531, and during that time he subdued the Nicarao Indians and other indigenous tribes with a vengeance. The Spanish did not relent in their subjugation of the native peoples, and by 1650 the native population had been reduced to one-third of its original size. Just as in El Salvador and Guatemala, those who survived were forced to abandon their traditions, relinquish any claim to the land, and provide free labor for the Spanish.

When Nicaragua, along with El Salvador, Guatemala, Honduras, and Costa Rica, declared its independence from Spain in 1821, it became part of Mexico. This alliance lasted only a year, until Nicaragua joined the United Provinces of Central America, uniting with El Salvador, Guatemala, Honduras, and Costa Rica. In 1838 Nicaragua left the United Provinces due to irreconcilable differences over whether an interoceanic canal should be built through the country. Although it declared itself a sovereign nation, Nicaragua lacked a national government, and each village and city oversaw its own affairs. This worked to the advantage of those living in rural areas, because their rights to the land were not interfered with, and they were able to grow enough food to support their families.

How did an American end up as Nicaragua's first president and English as the country's official language?

Most Nicaraguan leaders agreed that if Nicaragua was to engage in international trade, like a respectable nation, it would need a national government to regulate the use of the land and natural resources. However, they could not agree on how to set up such a government. Two camps emerged: one, based in León, which became known as the Liberal Party, and the other, centered in Granada, called the Conservative Party. The Conservative Party, with **Fruto Chamorro** as its leader, established the Republic of Nicaragua in 1854 and was pretty much in charge. The liberals were intent on wresting control away from the conservatives, and so they invited an American named **William Walker** to León to seek his counsel on how to accomplish this feat.

In 1855 Walker arrived in Nicaragua with his own notions about the country's future. Soon he took command of the liberal military, and thousands of Americans, with Manifest Destiny on their minds, joined up in hopes of obtaining land grants and other perks in Nicaragua. In 1856 Walker went so far as to proclaim himself president of Nicaragua. He ruled the country for one year, during which he declared English the official language,

sold or contributed parcels of land to American companies, legal-
ized slavery, and even attempted to incorporate Nicaragua into
the United States. In the face of this act of American imperialism,
the armies of Central America united and battled Walker and his
forces. The American admitted defeat in 1857 and left
Nicaragua. A central government was then formed, and from
1857 to 1893, it was headed almost solely by conservatives. The
conservative leaders created an atmosphere of political stability in
Nicaragua, but they also passed laws that made it easy for coffee
planters, who by then had whole markets abroad to supply, to
seize land from the native and mestizo peasants. With no parcels
of their own to farm, the peasants were left with no means to support themselves and their families.

Why did the United States become embroiled in Nicaragua's affairs?

The United States wanted the rights to build a canal through
Nicaragua to connect the Pacific and the Atlantic oceans. **José
Santos Zelaya**, an ironfisted liberal dictator who took over
Nicaragua in 1893, was apprehensive about foreigners having any
say about a canal on Nicaraguan territory. Zelaya had made a lot
of enemies among the conservatives, and so the United States,
with its own interests very much at heart, encouraged the conservatives to stage a revolt against the dictator. When Zelaya's forces
executed two American adventurers who had tried to blow up
two Nicaraguan ships, the U.S. government decided it had the
perfect excuse to take matters into its own hands and sent in
the marines.

Despite U.S. participation in the conservative revolt commanded by **Juan Estrada**, Zelaya hung on to leadership until
1909, when another liberal, **José Madriz**, stepped into office. The
U.S. government, in keeping with its role as "international police
power" (as spelled out in the 1904 Roosevelt Corollary to the
Monroe Doctrine), forced Madriz to resign his post, and the
Nicaraguan Congress named Juan Estrada president in 1911.
Estrada refused the leadership, to protest the United States' extensive involvement in Nicaraguan affairs, and **Vice President
Adolfo Díaz**, a conservative, assumed office. The U.S. government
bankrolled Díaz $14 million (in the form of loans from American
banks) to pay off European creditors banging at the door, but only
after he agreed to allow the United States to supervise Nicaragua's

financial matters until 1925, the year the debt was scheduled to be repaid.

Nicaraguans voiced despair over this arrangement, which essentially transformed their country into a U.S. protectorate, and the United States sent in the marines once again to restore peace. In 1916 the Nicaraguan government, now beholden to the Americans, granted the United States exclusive rights to build a canal through its territory, but in the end the U.S. government found Panama more suitable for a canal. The United States was also given the go-ahead to set up military bases in Nicaragua, which it did, and the marines were a constant presence until 1933.

In the late 1920s, rebel forces banded together in opposition to the pervasive U.S. presence in Nicaragua and what they perceived as excessive American meddling in their nation's affairs. They found a leader in **General Augusto César Sandino** and called themselves Sandinistas in his honor. Although they were greatly outnumbered, the Sandinistas waged a successful guerilla campaign against the marines.

What was the Somoza dynasty?

In 1933 the United States withdrew its forces from Nicaragua after Nicaraguan leaders promised to do their utmost to encourage order. Just to help matters along, the U.S. government arranged a Nicaraguan presidential election in 1932, a year before American troops were pulled out. **Juan Bautista Sacasa**, a former rebel, was sworn in as president, and the United States organized the Nicaraguan National Guard to help him preserve order. A Nicaraguan named **Anastasio Somoza García** was chosen to head the National Guard. President Sacasa and General Somoza did not get along. They disagreed on a whole host of issues, including what to do about **General Sandino** and the Sandinistas. In 1934 General Somoza took matters into his own hands and engineered the assassination of Sandino by the Nicaraguan National Guard. Realizing that the situation had spun out of control, President Sacasa tried to curb Somoza's powers, but it was too late. In 1936 Somoza swooped down on Sacasa, forcing him to resign. The next year found General Somoza president of Nicaragua, the result of fraudulent elections.

The Somoza clan, which included family members and trusted friends, would steer Nicaragua for the next forty-two years—and would accumulate enormous personal wealth in the process. Control was concentrated in the clan's hands, and those who challenged its absolute rule were intimidated or killed by the National Guard. In 1947 General Somoza handed the presidency over to a friend, but in 1950 he took the helm once again. By now the people of Nicaragua, who had lived so long in panic and poverty, were summoning their courage, and social unrest grew. In 1956 a young poet named **Rigoberto López Pérez** assassinated General Somoza at a ball in León. The reins of power were transferred to Somoza's eldest son, **Luis Somoza Debayle**, who ruled Nicaragua until his death from a heart attack in 1963. A confidant of the Somoza family then assumed the presidency, but he died in office in 1966. Another of General Somoza's sons, **Anastasio Somoza Debayle**, subsequently took over as president and governed with the same brutality as his father. While Somoza Debayle's riches multiplied, the people's plight grew more desperate. By the time Anastasio Somoza Debayle was reelected in 1974, 60 percent of Nicaraguans were suffering from malnutrition, and the middle and upper classes were in deep despair.

What was the Sandinista National Liberation Front?

In the early 1960s, the Sandinista National Liberation Front (FSLN), modeled after **General Augusto César Sandino**'s guerilla forces, was founded. The FSLN sought to eliminate government corruption and to lift the Nicaraguan people out of grinding poverty and despair. Even though the Somoza government had imprisoned or murdered numerous FSLN leaders over the years, the FSLN managed to become the largest and most influential opposition group in Nicaragua. In the 1970s, the FSLN brought numerous diverse groups into its fold, including student organizations and trade unions, and by 1978 it was clear that it had wrested control of the country away from its leader. But **Anastasio Somoza Debayle** would not relinquish the last vestige of power until 1979, when he fled first to the United States and then on to Paraguay, where he was later assassinated.

Who were the Contras?

With **Somoza Debayle** out of the way, the FSLN set up a government with distinct Marxist components. A nine-member national directorate took over the decision making, and the people voiced their opinions through the various organizations that were formed for peasants, workers, women, and other groups. At first the FSLN turned to the United States and the West for financial support, but by 1980 the Sandinistas had established close diplomatic and trade ties with the Soviet Union and Cuba. The Cold War was still raging, and this alliance rattled the nerves of the United States. In 1980 Republicans in the United States condemned the "Marxist Sandinista takeover of Nicaragua." To protect U.S. interests in the region and halt what it perceived as the spread of communism in Latin America, the **Reagan** White House cut off aid to Nicaragua and ensured that the World Bank and the International Monetary Fund followed suit. In 1981 President Reagan, certain that the Sandinistas would permit the USSR to erect military bases on Nicaraguan territory, secretly gave the CIA permission to fund opponents of the Sandinistas. These opponents, or counterrevolutionaries, who disagreed with the FSLN's agenda, became known as the Contras.

The Contras waged guerilla warfare throughout Nicaragua, forcing the Sandinistas to turn to the Soviet Union for military aid in the form of weapons, tanks, and aircraft. The International Court of Justice and the U.S. Congress condemned the fighting and the Reagan administration's support of the Contras, but the White House simply took the matter underground and diverted profits from the illegal sale of arms in Iran to the Contras. At the same time, President Reagan put the squeeze on the Sandinista government by imposing an economic embargo on Nicaragua, which would last until 1990 and would force the country to depend even more heavily on the Soviet bloc.

The actions of the United States and the Contras dealt the FSLN a crippling blow and upset its social agenda. The FSLN had to channel an enormous amount of money, which had been earmarked for health care and education, into fighting a war against the Contras. The U.S.-imposed embargo only made the people's situation worse. By 1988 Nicaragua was in desperate financial straits. Unemployment had skyrocketed to a whopping 35 percent, and inflation had soared to an unbelievable 33,000 percent. When the 1990 national elections rolled around, Nicaraguans voiced their desperation at the polls. Sandinista **Daniel Ortega Saavedra**, a fervent Marxist, who had been elected president of Nicaragua in 1984 and had fought tooth and nail against the U.S.-backed insurgency, was defeated, and **Violeta Barrios de Chamorro**, the leader of the opposition coalition, walked away the victor. Once she declared an end to the fighting and her intentions to establish a free market economy and to democratize Nicaragua, **President George Bush** lifted the embargo and promised to lend financial support.

Even after its defeat, the FSLN remained the most popular party in Nicaragua and retained both strong representation in the national assembly and command of the labor unions and the armed forces, even though they were greatly reduced. Annoyed that Chamorro did not strip the FSLN of all its power and that the economy was not being privatized at a swift pace, Washington reduced its aid package to Nicaragua. As a result, the Chamorro government had trouble jump-starting the Nicaraguan economy. The Contras, by then called *recontras*, were also miffed about FSLN participation in the Chamorro government, and they reacted with outbursts of violence against demobilized Sandinistas, known as *recampas*. Nevertheless, the two sides managed to sit down at the bargaining table and hammer out a peace agreement in 1994. During her seven years in office, President Chamorro took significant steps toward consolidating democratic institutions, stabilizing the economy, decreasing human rights violations, and advancing national reconciliation.

Though peaceful, Nicaragua nonetheless, remained politically polarized. In the 1996 presidential elections—judged free and fair by international observers—former Managua mayor **Arnoldo Alemán**, the leader of the center-right Liberal Alliance (which later became the Liberal Constitutionalist Party) was declared the winner, but Daniel Ortega of the FSLN, who was seeking reelection, accused Alemán of voter fraud. Alemán achieved some success in liberalizing the economy and improving the country's infrastructure, but charges of corruption marred his administration. In peaceful elections held on November 4, 2001, Nicaragua's fourth free and fair elections since 1990, Constitutionalist Liberal Party candidate **Enrique Bolaños**, who at one time was imprisoned by Ortega's regime, was elected president. Bolaños promised to continue President Alemán's efforts at democracy building, but he confronted daunting challenges, such as a faltering Nicaraguan economy, $4 billion in foreign debt, and widespread poverty. In the 2006 presidential election—which former president **Jimmy Carter** declared clean and fair after monitoring it—Daniel Ortega, the former Marxist president of Nicaragua and Cold War foe of the United States, staged a comeback, beating out five opponents. There was much speculation over whether Ortega had truly metamorphosed into the more pragmatic leftist he claimed to be. Only time will tell. Upon assuming the presidency, Ortega promised to tackle Nicaragua's poverty and to encourage foreign investment, which is crucial to the country's well-being, since its economy is heavily dependent on exports to the United States and foreign markets.

How many Nicaraguan Americans are there, and where do they live?

Nicaraguans—primarily professionals, intellectuals, labor leaders, political dissidents, and university students—began entering the United States in the 1930s to escape persecution at the hands of **General Somoza**. The 1940s brought Nicaraguans in search of opportunity to America's shores; a good number of them actually returned later to Nicaragua to join the emerging entrepreneurial class. In 1979, which marked the onset of war between the Sandinista government and the Contras, Nicaraguans began fleeing en masse across the border. Between 1982 and 1992, one out of ten Nicaraguans sought refuge in a foreign country. The majority of Nicaraguans who entered the United States in this ten-year period did so illegally, typically by crossing Honduras, Guatemala, and Mexico, and then the U.S.-Mexico border.

In contrast to Guatemalan and Salvadoran refugees, Nicaraguans received preferential treatment when they applied for political asylum in the 1980s and early 1990s, because they fled a communist government (not a U.S.-backed one) that the United States had tried desperately to topple. Undocumented Nicaraguans were also the only Central Americans to receive permanent residency under the Nicaraguan Adjustment and Central American Relief Act of 1997 until it expired on March 31, 2000. Nicaraguans continue to come to America to this day, but for economic reasons and in fewer numbers.

According to the Pew Hispanic Center tabulations of the Census Bureau's 2005 American Community Survey, in 2005, 275,126 Nicaraguan Americans and Nicaraguan nationals lived in the United States. In 2000 the U.S. Census Bureau counted 177,684 people of Nicaraguan descent, a decrease of 12 percent from the 202,658 tabulated in 1990. (The decline in numbers is certainly due to the confusion over the 2000 census form.) Census 2000 data indicate that the five states with the largest Nicaraguan population in 2000 were Florida (79,559), California (51,336),

New York (8,033), Texas (7,487), and New Jersey (4,384). The majority of Nicaraguan nationals and Nicaraguan Americans in Florida live in Miami, where they have formed a thriving enclave called Little Managua.

As a group, Nicaraguans are more educated than Salvadorans and Guatemalans in the United States and are not in the same legal limbo regarding their immigration status. Thus they have generally avoided the low-paying-job trap. About one-third of all Nicaraguan Americans hold white-collar positions, and another third of the Nicaraguan American community is blue collar. They own a great number of businesses in Miami-Dade County, including restaurants, automotive repair shops, and money transfer agencies. Nicaraguans in the United States cultivate close ties with their homeland. Many send home a good chunk of their earnings, in the form of remittances, and some have invested in real estate and businesses back in Nicaragua.

HONDURAN, PANAMANIAN, AND COSTA RICAN AMERICANS

How many Honduran Americans are there, and where do they live?

According to the Pew Hispanic Center tabulations of the Census Bureau's 2005 American Community Survey, in 2005 the United States was home to 466,843 Honduran Americans and Honduran nationals. By comparison, the U.S. Census Bureau tallied 217,569 Honduran Americans and Honduran nationals in 2000, up from 131,066 in 1990. The five states with the largest number of Honduran Americans and Honduran nationals in 2000 were Florida (41,229), New York (35,135), California (30,372), Texas (24,179), and New Jersey (15,431). An appreciable number of Honduran nationals, many of whom are undocumented, and Honduran Americans work as migrant farm laborers in America's agricultural belts.

Hondurans settled in the United States as early as the late eighteenth century. Since then there has been a very small but steady flow of Hondurans to America, though the number of immigrants rose in the 1980s and 1990s, when civil wars in neighboring countries created political unrest and greater economic woes in Honduras. (The borderlands of Honduras were a training ground for Nicaraguan Contras fighting the Sandinista government.) Honduras's troubles intensified in October 1998, when Hurricane Mitch ravaged the country, killing five thousand people and displacing 1.5 million. Honduras remains one of the least developed and poorest nations in Latin America, with an economy dependent on coffee and bananas, a reality that feeds emigration.

What about Panamanian Americans?

While there were many Panamanians among the Central Americans who made their home in the United States in the 1970s, they have arrived in much-reduced numbers since then. Pew Hispanic Center tabulations of the Census Bureau's 2005 American Community Survey indicate that in 2005, 141,286 Panamanian Americans and Panamanian nationals resided in the United States. In 2000 the U.S. Census Bureau counted 91,723 persons of Panamanian ancestry (probably an undercount), a very slight decrease from the 92,013 tallied in 1990. The five states with the highest concentration of Panamanian Americans and Panamanian nationals in 2000, according to census data, were New York (20,055), Florida (15,117), California (10,688), Texas (7,076), and Georgia (3,745).

How are Costa Rican Americans different from other Americans of Spanish-speaking Central American ancestry?

Pew Hispanic Center tabulations of the Census Bureau's 2005 American Community Survey show that in 2005, the United States was home to 111,978 Costa Rican Americans and Costa Rican nationals, a large increase over the 68,588 persons of Costa Rican descent counted in Census 2000 (probably an undercount). The reason that the Costa Rican community in America is so diminutive is that ever since its birth as a nation in 1821, Costa Rica has known political stability and democracy for the most part: the only instability was a failed dictatorship in 1917–18 and an attempted revolution in 1932. In fact, the country has been so stable that it earned the title "the Switzerland of Central America." Thus the Costa Rican people are distinct from other

Central Americans in that they have never had to flee their home-land due to political oppression or economic hardship. Most Costa Ricans chose to settle in America either because they married a U.S. citizen, they attended an American university and then found a desirable job in the United States, they decided to pursue a particular career path, or they took advantage of opportunities for research or professional advancement that are nonexistent in Costa Rica.

The five states with the greatest concentration of Costa Ricans in 2000 were California (13,232), Florida (11,248), New Jersey (11,175), New York (7,845), and Texas (3,302). Rather than residing in their own neighborhoods, Costa Rican Americans and Costa Rican nationals are either very much a part of the American mainstream or they move in circles of other Latinos.

COLOMBIAN AMERICANS

What were the Spanish seeking in Colombia?

Christopher Columbus, who explored the mouth of the Orinoco River in 1498, was probably the first Spaniard to step on what is now Colombian soil. In the early sixteenth century, many Spanish conquistadores trekked through Colombia in their quest for the mythical city of El Dorado, a place supposedly resplendent with gold and precious stones. While the Spanish never located El Dorado, they did found the city of Cartagena on Colombia's Caribbean coast, which evolved into a major port for ships sailing to Spain laden with gold and other New World treasures.

Why did the United States pick a fight with Colombia?

After 1740 a good deal of present-day Colombia belonged to New Granada, a territory that also encompassed Ecuador, Panama, and Venezuela. In 1819 Spain relinquished its control of New Granada, which was then renamed Greater Colombia. By 1830 Ecuador and Venezuela had seceded, and the remaining territory—namely, Colombia and Panama—was renamed the Republic of New Granada. (In 1886 it underwent another name change, this time to the Republic of Colombia.) In the 1830s, two rival political parties dominated the political scene in the Republic of New Granada: the Conservative Party, which favored a strong central government, and the Liberal Party, which wanted power split between a weaker central government and regional governments. Their various efforts to consolidate power kindled unrest for most of the century, culminating in a ferocious civil war waged from 1899 to 1902. By the time the civil war ended, one hundred thousand had died, the conservatives were in control, and the Republic of Colombia was a wreck.

The United States took advantage of Colombia's vulnerability. In 1902 Washington flexed its muscles in the region by laying claim to the zone where the Panama Canal was being constructed. The U.S. government tried to persuade Colombia to sign a treaty that officially gave the Americans full authority in the canal zone, but the Colombians refused. To make doubly sure that the United States understood their position, the Colombians sent troops to Panama to protect what was theirs. With a little nudging from the U.S. government, the Panamanians fought off the Colombian forces and declared their independence in 1903.

What was La Violencia?

For the next four decades, peace reigned supreme in Colombia. Then, in 1948, the rivalry between the Conservative Party and the Liberal Party escalated again to civil war, which lasted until the mid-1960s in the countryside. Anywhere from two hundred thousand to three hundred thousand Colombians perished during this period, known as *La Violencia*. In 1953 a military coup in Colombia brought the downfall of **Laureano Gómez**, who had tried to create a fascist state ever since being elected president of Colombia in 1949, and put **General Gustavo Rojas Pinilla** in command. When the economy worsened, liberals and conservatives banded together in opposition to Rojas, and in 1957 he fell from power. A year later, the two parties forged a coalition government, known as the National Front. With the National Front at the helm, the Colombian government began to put its shattered nation back together again. In 1966 **Carlos Lleras Restrepo** was named president, and until the end of his rule in 1970, he made efforts to diversify Colombia's economy, halt inflation, and institute land reforms.

How did the drug trade engulf Colombia?

Elections in 1974 heralded the end of the National Front–led government. The rift between the haves and the have-nots had grown wide in Colombia, perfect conditions for a Marxist, antigovernment guerilla movement. During the late 1970s, the Colombian economy, which had known growth for many years, went into a tailspin due to a mountain of foreign debt. Colombia was besieged by guerilla unrest, as well as violence from drug traffickers, who were consolidating their operations in cartels, and Colombians fled en masse over the border to safety in Venezuela. The Colombian government attempted to eradicate the drug trafficking, *el narcotrafico*, but it was met with stiff resistance, owing to the fact that the illegal drug trade supplied income to many Colombians. The drug cartels gradually took control of Colombian life. Their acts of terrorism—including massacres; car bombings; and abductions and assassinations of journalists, foreigners, public officials who refused to take bribes, and others— amounted to what acclaimed Colombian writer **Gabriel García Márquez** calls a "biblical holocaust," in *News of a Kidnapping* (1977), his nonfiction work about Colombian **Pablo Escobar**, kingpin of the Medellín cartel.

In 1989, with Colombia reeling out of control, **President Virgilio Barco Vargas** attempted to crack down on the drug cartels, and again Colombia's drug lords responded with violence. During the 1990 presidential election campaign, the drug cartels assassinated candidates they deemed a threat, but still **César Gaviria Trujillo**, a politician who just said no to drugs, managed to survive and win the election. Trujillo gave the drug cartels a bad time, encouraged pluralism, and made way for native peoples and former guerillas to participate in the nation's political life. He also revived the economy somewhat by negotiating with foreign creditors to bring down Colombia's debt.

Despite the efforts of Trujillo and other leaders, guerilla warfare and the drug trade dominated the headlines in Colombia throughout the 1990s, and continue to do so to this day, though the current Colombian president, **Álvaro Uribe**, who was elected in 2002, has made some strides in reducing violence and retaking rebel-held urban areas. The war waged between the guerillas and the Colombian armed forces, which are backed by illegal right-wing paramilitary groups hired by big landowners and merchants to defend their property from guerilla incursions, has displaced over a million people since 1985 and generated an unending epidemic of torture, murders, kidnappings, rapes, and massacres of civilians caught in the cross fire. The paramilitaries are known to commit atrocities on behalf of the Colombian army. The guerillas are heavily involved in drug activities; they act as bodyguards for *los narcos*, the narcotics traffickers, who are equally violent. In 1999 the guerillas held sway in about 40 percent of the nation—the part with abundant oil and coca bushes—and the narcotics traffickers controlled 80 percent of the world's cocaine production.

Since 1989 the United States, in the name of the "war on drugs," has supplied the Colombian government with funds and equipment for its antidrug operations—to the tune of $2.2 million per day in 2001, making Colombia the world's third largest recipient of U.S. aid, after Israel and Egypt. The U.S. government has also trained Colombian soldiers, provided the Colombian government with intelligence information, and deployed special operations forces to Colombia. Some critics argue that escalating military aid and involvement will only lead to bogging the United States down in an armed conflict against Colombian guerillas, and that the introduction of weapons from the United States simply leads to more human rights violations, murders, and displacement in Colombia.

What brought Colombians to America, and where have they settled?

A handful of Colombians settled in the United States in the nineteenth century, along with other South Americans. Colombian immigration picked up after World War I, when Colombian professionals came to America in a small but steady stream. Most settled a short subway ride away from their Manhattan workplaces, in the Jackson Heights section of Queens, a middle-class neighborhood, which became known as *El Chapinerito*. (Chapinero is a suburb of Bogotá.) The civil war of 1948 inspired Colombians to relocate to the United States in greater numbers in the 1950s, and this emigration continued unabated in the 1960s and 1970s, owing not to violence, but to economic chaos in Colombia. Since the Immigration and Nationality Act of 1965 established a strict quota for immigration (not political asylum) from the Western Hemisphere, very few Colombians, and only the most desirable, were allotted visas. With little chance of establishing legal residency, most Colombians who came to the United States during these decades planned to remain only a short while to earn money. Of course, scores of Colombians stayed on without permanent residency.

By 1990 the Colombian population in the United States had risen to about 378,726, as Colombians fled the violence perpetrated by guerillas, narcotics traffickers, paramilitaries, and other criminal elements in Colombia. In the 1990s, the exodus of Colombians from their homeland continued unabated due to the ongoing and increasingly destructive civil conflict: According to U.S. government estimates, 800,000 people, or 2 percent of Colombia's population, fled the country between 1996 and 2000. As the 1990s drew to an end, they sought entry to the United States in record numbers: While 150,514 applied for nonimmigrant visas in 1997, 366,423 did so in 1999. Large-scale emigration from Colombia has continued in the first decade of the new millennium. By 2005 approximately one of every ten Colombians lived abroad.

The Pew Hispanic Center tabulations of the Census Bureau's 2005 American Community Survey indicate that in 2005 there were 723,596 Colombian Americans and Colombian nationals living in the United States. In 2000 the U.S. Census Bureau counted 470,684 persons of Colombian ancestry residing in the United States. Given that the first decade of the twenty-first century has seen little abatement in the long-standing conflict in Colombia, Colombians will undoubtedly continue to seek refuge in America in large numbers.

In the 1960s and 1970s, those Colombians with means settled in Jackson Heights, while others moved to burgeoning New York City enclaves in Rego Park, Flushing, Elmhurst, and Woodside. A small number chose Los Angeles, Houston, Washington DC, and Chicago. Miami, with its gentler climate, Latin flavor, and status as the business capital of Latin America, has attracted the majority of immigrating Colombians ever since the early 1980s. According to Census 2000 figures, the five states with the greatest concentration of Colombian Americans and Colombian nationals were Florida (138,768), New York (104,179), New Jersey (65,075), California (33,275), and Texas (20,404).

What is one of the biggest obstacles Colombian Americans have faced?

Ever since the 1980s, Colombian Americans have had to fight the pervasive belief that they are a bunch of drug traffickers who have brought violence, corruption, and addiction to America's streets. Nothing could be further from the truth. The overwhelming majority of Colombian Americans are committed professionals, entrepreneurs, or employees in the service industries, and the Colombian American community has done much to enrich American society.

THE OTHER AMERICANS OF SPANISH-SPEAKING SOUTH AMERICAN DESCENT

What brought Ecuadorans to America?

Before the mid-1960s, only a scant number of Ecuadorans found their way to the United States. In 1964 Ecuador passed the Land Reform, Idle Lands, and Settlement Act, which called for the expropriation of land from absentee landlords and its distribution to the poor peasants. Many of the peasants, who had no experience as landowners and no credit, simply could not manage the land, and they were forced to abandon it. Many left the rural areas altogether in search of opportunity in the cities, and some chose to immigrate to the United States. When these Ecuadorans sent money back home, others were encouraged by the economic prospects in America. Since the 1960s, Ecuadorans have entered the United States in a steady stream, owing to periods of economic instability in Ecuador, including the economic and financial crises that befell the country in the late 1990s. In an effort to resuscitate the nation, the Ecuadoran government replaced the sucre with the U.S. dollar as the official currency in January 2000. Thanks to the dollarization of its economy and its supplies of petroleum, Ecuador emerged as one of the fastest-growing economies in Latin America by 2001, but this did not translate into a reduction in poverty. In 2006 an estimated 70 percent of the population lived in poverty, a reality that has fueled emigration.

The Pew Hispanic Center tabulations of the Census Bureau's

2005 American Community Survey indicate that in 2005 there were 432,068 Ecuadoran Americans and Ecuadoran nationals residing in the United States. By comparison, in 2000 the U.S. Census Bureau counted 260,559 Ecuadoran Americans and Ecuadoran nationals. The five states with the highest concentration of Ecuadorans in 2000 were New York (123,472), New Jersey (45,392), Florida (23,939), California (18,115), and Illinois (12,060).

Some Ecuadorans seeking to immigrate to the United States take the legal route and wait in their homeland for a visa. Others head north and cross the U.S.-Mexico border illegally or come by boat from Puerto Rico and live as undocumented aliens, without ever applying for a visa. Most newcomers have one destination in mind: the New York metropolitan area. The Ecuadoran community in America is close-knit and resistant to assimilation, partly because Ecuadorans generally swear allegiance to their home country and plan on returning and thus see no point in wholeheartedly embracing the American way of life. As a result, only a small percentage of those who are eligible for citizenship pursue it, and many do not speak English fluently. While Argentinean Americans, Chilean Americans, and other Americans with roots in Spanish-speaking South America are mostly professionals and entrepreneurs, and Americans of Central American descent are largely working class, Ecuadoran Americans belong to both ranks.

Why are Peruvian Americans called "the children of success"?

Peruvians began immigrating to America in the nineteenth century, but the greatest number arrived after World War II, in response to economic calamity and political violence and instability in Peru. The first to come were upper-class Peruvians. In the 1970s, the number of middle-class Peruvians entering the United States rose significantly. They put their education and business acumen to work and have acculturated to the United States rather easily. For this reason, they are called "the children of success." The 1980s saw an increase in the numbers of lower-class Peruvians coming to America. Their assimilation has been the hardest due to a lack of formal education.

According to the Pew Hispanic Center tabulations of the Census Bureau's 2005 American Community Survey, in 2005, 415,352 Peruvian Americans and Peruvian nationals resided in the United States, up from the 233,926 tallied in 2000. The five states with the largest Peruvian population in 2000 were California (44,200), Florida (44,026), New Jersey (37,672), New York (37,340), and Virginia (10,525).

What is the Argentinean Americans' secret to success?

The Pew Hispanic Center tabulations of the Census Bureau's 2005 American Community Survey reveal that 189,303 Argentinean Americans and Argentinean nationals lived in the United States in 2005. Census 2000 counted 100,864 Argentinean Americans and Argentinean nationals.

The first sizable group of Argentineans to immigrate to the United States arrived in the 1960s. They were mainly highly educated professionals seeking greater economic opportunities. Argentina's Dirty War, which lasted from 1976 to 1983, sent more Argentineans, a good percentage of them Jews, to American shores, as well as to Europe and other Latin American nations. During this "war," the military toppled the country's ineffectual leader, **Isabel Perón**, in a coup; destroyed the small guerilla movement; and abducted, tortured, and murdered at least fifteen thousand people—*los desaparecidos* (the disappeared)—who allegedly had links to the Left or to terrorist groups.

In the early twentieth century, Argentina was one of the world's wealthiest nations and enjoyed an immigration boom from Europe—earning Buenos Aires the title "the Paris of Latin America." In the decade after World War II, Argentina began to hit a few economic bumps in the road, but until the late 1990s, politics and persecution, not economics, fueled Argentinean emigration. For most of the 1990s, Argentina was the economic shining star of Latin America. Then in the late 1990s, the country experienced a severe recession and widespread unemployment. Conditions worsened until Argentina hit rock bottom in 2001, when a mountain of debt caused its economy, currency, banking system, and rule of law to collapse simultaneously—which led to Argentina defaulting on its international loan obligations, the largest sovereign government debt default in history—leaving untold numbers of "Argentines without means" to purchase even basic foodstuffs. The dire circumstances gave way to bloody protests and pillaging, illegal repression and criminal prosecution of demonstrators by the government, and the installation of five presidents in two weeks. The profound economic, political, and social crises that beset Argentina from the late 1990s to early 2002 sent thousands of Argentineans to the United States and to Italy, Spain, and Germany, the very countries their forbears fled in despair at the turn of the twentieth century to seek opportunity in a booming Argentina. In March 2002, Argentina began to pull itself out of the economic morass; since then, its economy has achieved an astounding recovery.

Thanks to their high educational attainment, the majority of Argentinean Americans are professionals, technicians, and skilled workers. They prefer urban areas with Latin spice. New York City is a favorite destination because it is a center of international business and retains an Italian flavor, which Italo-Argentinean Americans appreciate. The five states with the largest number of Argentinean Americans and Argentinean nationals in 2000 were California (23,218), Florida (22,881), New York (14,407), New Jersey (7,795), and Texas (4,711).

What has motivated Chileans to come to America?

First it was gold. The gold rush of 1848 brought Chilean miners to American shores in droves. After gold fever died down, Chilean immigration came almost to a screeching halt, and many Chileans in America also returned home, with stories of hardship rather than fortune. Those who stayed behind settled in San Francisco, in a neighborhood called *Chilecito*, or Little Chile, or in other enclaves in California, known as Chilitowns. Chileans did not come to America in significant numbers again until Chile's civil war of 1891. The mid-1960s saw a wave of Chilean immigration comprised mainly of young, middle- and upper-class Chileans enrolled at American colleges and universities, professionals in search of opportunity, and the Chilean spouses of Americans doing business in Chile.

In 1973 Chilean dictator **Augusto Pinochet** overthrew **President Salvador Allende**—whose socialist policies had given rise to internal dissent among conservatives—in a bloody coup, abruptly interrupting Chile's democratic tradition. Under General Pinochet's martial rule, crimes against humanity—including torture, assassinations, mass executions, and disappearances—were commonplace, and much of the country was plunged into abject poverty. Pinochet's reign of terror sent over one million Chilean citizens, particularly intellectuals, journalists, and other professionals, running for their very lives to Europe, Canada, and other parts of Latin America. A small percentage, about 10 percent, found refuge in the United States, where, without jobs, contacts, and housing, they had a tough time starting anew.

In 1988 a national referendum was held to determine whether General Pinochet's rule should continue. The resounding victory of the "no" vote gave rise to democratic elections in 1989, in which Christian Democrat **Patricio Aylwin** emerged victorious (although Pinochet remained army commander-in-chief until March 1998). With Chile's return to democracy and civilian rule in 1990, President Aylwin encouraged Chileans in exile to return home with promises of financial aid. Thousands went back to a democratic Chile—and to family members they had not seen in aeons. Many took home children who had been born in the United States and spoke poor Spanish. The Chilean government responded by creating Spanish as a Second Language programs in schools. President Aylwin's transitional democracy did economic wonders for Chile. By the time he left office in 1994, President Aylwin had transformed Chile into Latin America's fastest growing economy, and over a million Chileans had moved above the poverty line.

In 2000 **Ricardo Lagos**, a moderate socialist and a prominent former dissident who was in exile during Pinochet's regime in the 1970s, was elected president by a narrow margin. A champion of European-style socialism, he vowed to rid Chile of the economic disparities left by market-oriented economic reform and to transform the nation into a social democracy. With Lagos steering the country, Chile's economy remained a model for all Latin America, despite the problems confronting Chile's neighbors. In the 2006 presidential elections, Chileans selected a woman to lead them: **Michelle Bachelet**. A physician, Bachelet spent two years of her childhood in the United States after her father, a general, was assigned to the Chilean embassy in Washington DC. Soon after assuming office in 1973, Pinochet had her father imprisoned, and after enduring months of torture, he succumbed to a heart attack in prison in March 1974. Months later Michelle Bachelet and her mother were taken prisoner, and she was subjected to physical and psychological torture during her months-long detainment. In 1975 she and her mother went into exile. Upon being elected president of Chile, she vowed to preserve the nation's sizzling economy and its close relationship with the United States.

Thanks to the stability it has enjoyed since President Aylwin's transitional democracy, Chile is the only Spanish-speaking nation in South America to experience little net emigration. The Pew Hispanic Center tabulations of the Census Bureau's 2005 American Community Survey indicate that in 2005, 105,141 Chilean Americans and Chilean nationals resided in the United States. In 2000, by comparison, the U.S. Census Bureau tabulated a mere 68,849 persons of Chilean ancestry. The five states with the largest concentrations of Chilean Americans and Chilean nationals in 2000 were California (13,530), Florida (13,400), New York (9,937), New Jersey (5,129), and Texas (2,934).

What about Venezuelan, Bolivian, Uruguayan, and Paraguayan Americans?

Add 162,762 Venezuelans, 68,649 Bolivians, 51,646 Uruguayans, and a small number of Paraguayans (the Pew Hispanic Center tabulations of the Census Bureau's 2005 American Community Survey provides no data for Paraguayans; Census 2000 counted 8,769) to the Latinos with roots in Colombia, Ecuador, Peru, Argentina, and Chile, and you get a marvelous mosaic of Americans of Spanish-speaking South American descent.

OCHO

La Política

LATINO VOTERS

What is the Voting Rights Act all about?

The civil rights movement launched by African Americans in the 1960s served as a model for Latino activists. For instance, the Brown Berets, the Chicano self-defense group organized in 1967, were modeled on the Black Berets, and African studies programs at America's institutions of higher learning gave rise to Latino studies programs. And, most importantly, the legal actions taken by African American leaders served as a blueprint for Latino leaders eager to rectify political and social injustice.

The first legal battles that Latinos fought to end discrimination took place in New York in the early 1970s, when a Puerto Rican group brought a lawsuit against the state alleging that it discriminated against Puerto Ricans at the polls by providing English-only ballots. The group argued that as native-born Americans whose mother tongue was Spanish, Puerto Ricans had a legal right to ballots in Spanish. The group won its case, and all voting material was rendered bilingual.

On the heels of the Puerto Rican victory, the Mexican American Legal Defense and Education Fund (MALDEF), which was founded in 1968 and is the nation's foremost nonprofit Latino litigation, advocacy, and educational outreach organization, lobbied intensely to ensure that the 1975 amendments to the Voting Rights Act of 1965 would embrace citizens with Spanish last names in the Southwest, where voter discrimination ran rampant. The Voting Rights Act of 1965 prohibits discrimination in voting procedures and practices due to color or race, including the use of literacy tests and poll taxes, which had been employed to limit African Americans' access to the voting booth. Within a decade, Congress recognized that U.S. citizens whose limited English-language reading and oral skills prevented them from participating fully in the political process also needed to be protected. And so the protections of the Voting Rights Act were extended to them in 1975 for a period of seven years (and again in 1982 for another seven years). As a result of these amendments to the Voting Rights Act, the Latino voter base is vastly larger.

Real power or paella in the sky: How much political clout do Latinos really wield?

If political power is measured by the number of Latino and Latina leaders in all levels of government in the first decade of the twenty-first century, the answer to the question is *mucho*.

And if it is measured in terms of the significance of Latino voters to the Democrats and the Republicans, then the answer is again *mucho*, since both parties acknowledge that the days of alienation and so-called "voter apathy" among Latinos are gone. With this in mind, both parties have been courting Latinos, who are considered a swing group, able to be won over by either Republicans or Democrats, due in part to their religious and demographic diversity. What makes Latinos such a sought-after voting bloc is the fact that the Latino population has been growing at a phenomenal rate, and thus with each passing year Latinos constitute a greater percentage of the overall U.S. voting population. (They are projected to represent 14 percent of the electorate by 2010, up from 7 percent in 2000.) Also, a good number of Latinos are recent arrivals with no political allegiances at all (but as naturalized citizens, they have a fervor to vote), and thus their political affiliation is up for grabs. Finally, Latinos are concentrated in a number of key electoral states, including California, Texas, New York, and Florida.

The Republican Party witnessed just how mighty a voting bloc Latinos could be in the 1996 presidential election, when the Latino voter turnout was the highest ever recorded at that point in time, thanks to an aggressive voter registration drive and get-out-the-vote efforts in Latino communities, sparked in part by the harsh anti-immigrant legislation and rampant immigrant bashing of the day, which the Republicans were fueling. The anti-immigrant, xenophobic atmosphere in America instilled fear—and a desire for action—in Latinos. As it turned out, the Latino voter turnout and displeasure with the Republicans played a decisive role in keeping **President Bill Clinton** in office for a second term. In fact, while 72 percent of Latinos were registered Democrats in 1996, an astonishing four out of five Latinos voted for Clinton that year. However, Latinos have not consistently put their voting power to work. Between 1990 and 2000, the number of Latino voters across the nation increased an astonishing 18 percent, from 5 million to 5.9 million, due to two main sources: young people attaining voting age and new Latino citizens. Still, in the 2000 presidential election, the Latino voter turnout, 28 percent, was no higher than in 1996, because Latinos were no longer confronting the virulent nativism and xenophobia that had gripped the nation in the mid-1990s. Still, the 2004 presidential election saw a significant decrease in Latino voter apathy: 48 percent of registered Latino voters made their way to the polls.

Since 1996 a clear shift in Latino political party identification, which historically has been overwhelmingly Democrat, has taken place, causing some to question whether Latinos' long support for the Democratic Party might be evaporating. It appears that Republican efforts to woo Latinos have paid off, and more and more Latinos have gravitated to the Republican Party, in part because of the Republicans' devotion to "family values" (meaning their anti-abortion and anti–gay marriage stances). According to *The 2004 National Survey of Latinos: Politics and Civic Participation*, a report published by the Pew Hispanic Center / Kaiser Family Foundation, a mere 45 percent of registered Latinos identified themselves as Democrats in 2004; 20 percent, as Republicans; and 21 percent, as Independents. Still, the future may see the Latino pendulum swing back in the Democrats' favor given that by 2006 the American electorate, Latinos included, was fast growing weary of the **Bush** administration, particularly its Iraq policy and its assault on the judicial system and civil liberties.

With the ever-increasing number of Latinos in American politics, and the explosive growth in the Latino population and in the number of Latino voters, the possibility of a Latino vice president of the United States—or even a president—no longer looks like paella in the sky.

Is it true that a hefty share of Latino campaign contributions goes to the Republican Party?

Yes, even though in 2006 about half of Latino voters aligned themselves with the Democrats and only about 20 percent called themselves Republicans.

The reason that the Republican Party is a magnet for Latino campaign contributions is that Cuban Americans, who are the most solvent Latino subgroup and the one most involved in mainstream politics, are 52 percent Republican and only 17 percent Democrat (according to *The 2004 National Survey of Latinos: Politics and Civic Participation*) and have voted at least 70 percent Republican in presidential elections in the past two decades, and as much as 88 percent Republican (**Ronald Reagan** in 1984). The only anomaly was the 1996 presidential election, when **Bill Clinton**, a Democrat, captured an unprecedented 40 percent of the Cuban American vote. The Cuban American factor also explains why a disproportionate percentage of Latino political contributions comes from Florida, the home of over eight hundred thousand Cuban Americans. From 1979 to 2000, Cuban Americans made campaign contributions at the federal level of $8.8 million, $3.9 million of which went to federal candidates. (And they gave additional millions in backdoor financing and soft money, which went unrecorded.) The top non-Latino recipients of those particular campaign contributions were, in descending order, **George Bush** (senior), **Bob Graham**, **Paula Hawkins**, **Connie Mack**, **George W. Bush**, and **Dante B. Fascell**. All but Graham and Fascell are Republicans. While this sum pales in comparison to the campaign contributions that some political and business-oriented lobbies made in the same period, it was enough to buy the ear and support of politicians on both sides of the political aisle, as evidenced by the U.S. government's fervent anti-Castro, pro–Cuban embargo stance over the decades.

The four biggest individual Cuban American contributors in

the years 1979–2000 were **Teresa Estrada** and **Alfred Estrada**, head of Pan American Enterprises and *Vista* magazine ($725,310); **Paul Cejas**, former chair and CEO of CareFlorida Health Systems (($411,606); **Domingo R. Moreira**, head of the Free Cuba Political Action Committee and director of CANF, the Cuban American National Foundation ($370,216); and the late **Jorge Mas Canosa**, CEO of Church & Tower, a prominent Miami construction company ($364,670). From January 1, 1999, to February 28, 2002, Cuban Americans made campaign contributions amounting to $1.8 million. A sizable portion of that sum came from the Bacardi **Fanjul** brothers—Alexander, Alfonso, Andres, and José—who are the principal owners and managers of the Flo-Sun Corporation, America's largest sugar producer. (The Fanjul family was Cuba's largest sugar empire for many decades before **Fidel Castro**'s putsch.) The Fanjul brothers have thrown their support, financial and otherwise, to both the Republicans and the Democrats. (Alfonso Fanjul was **Bill Clinton**'s Florida cochair in 1992, and José Fanjul has lent his support to the Republicans.)

As the founder of CANF, whose agenda has long been to oust Fidel Castro and establish a democratic government in Cuba, Jorge Mas Canosa was the second most important lobbyist in America, after Israel. Mas Canosa was a true American success story. He fled Castro's regime in 1960, at age twenty-one, and arrived in Miami a penniless refugee. After working as a stevedore, shoe salesman, and milkman, he purchased a faltering construction company and transformed it into an empire. Until his health suddenly diminished in 1997, many in the Cuban American community and about Washington were confident that Mas Canosa would make a successful bid for the presidency of Cuba when Castro's regime fell.

In the past few decades, other major individual Latino contributors to candidates for national office have been Puerto Rican **Marife Hernández**, a former U.S. Department of State chief of protocol and the former head of the Cultural Communications Group, who has lent support to the Democrats; Cuban American **Roberto G. Mendoza**, who from 1990 to 2000 was vice chairman of J.P. Morgan and Company, the fifth largest U.S. bank; **Arturo Díaz**, a Puerto Rican businessman affiliated with various companies in Rio Piedras and San Juan, Puerto Rico, including Betteroads Asphalt Co.; Mexican American attorney **Earl Luna**, who is based in Dallas; and Cuban American **Roberto C. Goizueta**, who steered the Coca-Cola Company as CEO from 1981 until his death in 1997.

Are there any Latino watchdog organizations?

There are dozens and dozens of such groups out there. Some represent Latinos across the board, while others are devoted to a particular subgroup (Mexican Americans, Puerto Ricans, Dominican Americans, etc.). Among the organizations that have the longest history and have attracted the most widespread attention are the League of United Latin American Citizens (LULAC), the Mexican American Legal Defense and Education Fund (MALDEF), the American GI Forum (AGIF), the National Council of La Raza (NCLR), the ASPIRA Association, and the National Puerto Rican Coalition, Inc. (NPRC).

Established in 1929, LULAC, whose mission is to "advance the economic condition, educational attainment, political influence, health and civil rights of the Hispanic population in the United States," which it does through community-based programs, is the oldest Latino social organization in the United States. The mission of MALDEF, which was formed in San Antonio in 1968 and is the preeminent nonprofit Latino litigation, advocacy, and educational outreach organization in America, is "to foster sound public policies, laws and programs to safeguard the civil rights of the forty million Latinos living in the United States." AGIF, which was founded by Mexican American veterans in 1948, is dedicated to addressing the discrimination and injustices that Latino military personnel and veterans have confronted. Founded in 1968, NCLR is "the largest Latino civil rights and advocacy organization in the United States." Since 1961, ASPIRA has devoted itself to the "education and leadership development of Puerto Rican and other Latino youth." The mission of NPRC, which was incorporated as a membership organization in 1977, is to "enhance the social, political, and economic well-being of Puerto Ricans throughout the United States and in Puerto Rico, with a special focus on the most vulnerable."

Some organizations are committed to addressing the concerns of Latinas, who have suffered double discrimination, based both on gender and ethnicity/race. One such group is 100 Hispanic Women, Inc., founded in 1996, which supports Latinas in their efforts to attain leadership posts that influence public policy and which devises strategies and programs in such areas as legislative action, economic development, and health and education reform to improve Latinas' quality of life and foster their growth. Another is MANA, a national Latina organization established in 1974 by Mexican American women, whose mission is "to empower Latinas through leadership development, community service, and advocacy."

Besides these organizations that work to effect change in the political, economic, and social arenas, there is the Hispanic Association on Corporate Responsibility (HACR), founded in 1986, whose principal directive is to closely monitor the private sector so that large corporations "do the right thing" and reinvest a portion of the money that Latinos spend back into Latino communities by way of employment opportunities, franchise and dealership opportunities, and donations to philanthropies.

LATINO POLITICIANS IN WASHINGTON AND BEYOND

How many Latinos are in elected office?

With each passing decade, the Latino presence at every level of government increases. At the beginning of 2006, 5,132 Latinos held elected posts around the nation, up from 3,743 in 1996, an increase of 37 percent. These Latinos served in a total of forty-three states, but 42 percent of them held office in Texas. While Georgia and New Hampshire had no Latinos in elected office in 1996, in 2006 the Peach State boasted seven, and the Granite State, three. In the same year, Alaska, Kentucky, Missouri, North Dakota, Oklahoma, South Carolina, and Virginia each had one Latino in elected office.

At the onset of 2006, two-thirds of Latino elected officials held posts at the municipal and school board level, but a sizable number were also members of the U.S. Congress, governors, state officials, state legislators, county officials, judicial and law enforcement officials, and special district officials. In 2006 there were twenty-four Latinos in the U.S. House of Representatives, three in the U.S. Senate, and seven in statewide posts.

It should be noted that Latinos have not only been elected to office at every level of government, but they have also received appointments, often to high-ranking posts. One of the most noteworthy Latino political appointees is the current attorney general of the United States, **Alberto Gonzales**, who is the first Latino, and the first Mexican American, to head the Justice Department, the preeminent legal post in the land. Born in San Antonio, Texas, in 1955, Gonzales grew up in poverty, then went on to graduate from Harvard Law School. After working as a corporate lawyer, he served as general counsel to **George W. Bush** in the early days of Bush's Texas governorship. In 1997 Bush named Gonzales Texas secretary of state and then, in 1999, appointed him a justice of the Texas Supreme Court. In 2004 President Bush chose Gonzales, who at the time was the top White House lawyer, to replace **Attorney General John Ashcroft**, and in early 2005 Gonzales's nomination was confirmed. Two years later, Gonzales resigned his post as attorney general amid accusations of firing federal prosecutors for purely political reasons and then perjuring himself during a 2007 congressional inquiry into the matter.

What do Latinos in the U.S. Congress stand for?

Ever since 1928, when Mexican-born **Octaviano Larrazolo**, a Democrat turned Republican from New Mexico, was elected to the U.S. Senate, Latinos have contributed to forging the nation's legislative policy agenda. The overwhelming majority of Latinos in both houses of Congress have been in the past and continue to be Democrats. As of 2006, there are twenty-four Latinos serving in the U.S. House of Representatives, nineteen of whom are Democrats. The priorities of Latinos in the House vary according to the districts and states they represent, and they stand on both sides of the issues.

Historically, Latinos in the House have been united under the banner of what was until 2003 the sole Latino caucus within the U.S. House of Representatives, namely, the Congressional Hispanic Caucus (CHC), a bipartisan group formed in 1976 by five democratic Latino congressmen: **Herman Badillo** (NY), **Baltaser Corrada** (PR), **Eligio "Kika" de la Garza II** (TX), **Henry B. Gonzalez** (TX), and **Edward Roybal** (CA). The CHC was originally established to monitor executive, judicial, and legal actions, to make certain that the Latino community's needs were being met. In its three decades in operation, the CHC has accomplished much on behalf of Latinos, despite efforts over the years to limit government's effective representation of minorities. One of the CHC's crowning achievements was the decisive role it played in the 1992 passage of the Language Assistance Amendments to the Voting Rights Act, also known as the "bilingual voting bill," which increased the number of jurisdictions that must provide language minority populations with language assistance, by making assistance a requirement if a jurisdiction contains at least ten thousand members of a minority group who meet specific criteria. The Language Assistance Amendments have made bilingual voting information readily available to minorities with limited English proficiency, thereby assuring that those in America who speak a language other than English have ready access to the ballot box.

In 2003 the four Latino Republicans in the House, along with **Congressman Devin Nunes** (R-CA)—citing irreconcilable differences with Latino Democrats—formed the Congressional Hispanic Conference as a counterpoint to the Congressional Hispanic Caucus. The Congressional Hispanic Conference is dedicated to promoting policy outcomes that are important to all Latinos and Americans of Portuguese descent, "not just those with liberal politics" as **Congressman Henry Bonilla**, a founding member of the group, declared.

Since the U.S. Constitution went into effect in 1786, only six Latinos have served in the U.S. Senate, and in the years 1978–2004, there were no Latinos at all in the upper house of Congress. In 2006 three Latinos were serving in that body, representing Colorado, Florida, and New Jersey.

Who are the Latinos in Congress?

Among the first Latinos in the U.S. Congress were **Octaviano Larrazolo** (R-NM), the first Latino senator; **Dennis Chávez** (D-NM), who served in both the House and the Senate; **Joseph Manuel Montoya** (D-NM), who also served in both the House and the Senate; **Congressman Henry B. González** (D-TX); **Congressman Edward Roybal** (D-CA); and **Congressman Eligio "Kika" de la Garza II** (D-TX). They should be carved into Mount Rushmore, according to Latinos.

When Dennis Chávez, a Democrat from New Mexico, was elected to the U.S. Senate in 1935, after serving in the U.S. House of Representatives since 1930, he became the nation's second Latino senator, following in the footsteps of Senator Octaviano Larrazolo, who served in the Seventieth U.S. Congress in 1928. Dennis Chávez distinguished himself in the Senate from

1935 until his death on November 18, 1962. During his tenure in both the upper and lower houses of Congress, he fought discrimination by calling for improved public health facilities, federal aid to schools, and greater employment opportunities. For twenty years, he battled for the passage of a Fair Employment Practices Act to eradicate racial discrimination in the workplace. About equality in America, Chávez once said, "Either we are all free, or we fail; democracy must belong to all of us."

With a long tenure in state politics and a seat in the U.S. House of Representatives since 1957, Democrat Joseph Manuel Montoya of New Mexico was elected to the U.S. Senate in late 1964 to fill the unexpired term of Dennis Chávez. He was subsequently reelected and remained in the Senate until January 1977. One of Montoya's most memorable moments on the Hill was his work in 1973 and 1974 on the Senate Watergate Committee, a special committee convened to probe the Watergate break-in and subsequent scandal. Montoya also accomplished much to ensure the safety of the country's food supply, authoring the Wholesome Meat Act of 1967, the Wholesome Poultry Act of 1968, and the Clean Hot Dog Act of 1974, and was a champion of civil rights. Joseph Montoya died on June 5, 1978, in Washington DC, just six months after departing the Senate.

Representative Henry B. González (D-TX), the first person of Mexican American heritage to represent Texas in the U.S. House of Representatives, served in Congress from 1961 until his retirement in 1998. González chaired the powerful House Banking, Finance, and Urban Affairs Committee for three terms and earned a reputation as a champion of the underdog. Known widely as Henry B., he passed away in San Antonio on November 28, 2000. Former San Antonio mayor **Henry G. Cisneros** remembered Henry B. González and his decades of distinguished service with these words: "So many hearts were touched. So many dreams were forged because of Henry González." One of Henry B. González's eight children, **Charlie Gonzalez**, has kept these dreams alive: in 1998 he won his father's seat in the House. He continues to serve in that post. Since 1999 he has chaired the Hispanic Caucus Civil Rights Task Force and has served as a Texas Regional Whip for the Democratic Caucus.

Ed Roybal, who was elected to the House in 1962 and served until his retirement in 1992, provided thirty years of service to the working-class voters of East Los Angeles, never forgetting his commitment to the city's minorities, elderly, and disabled. During his tenure on the Hill, he introduced, with Texas senator **Ralph Yarborough**, the first Bilingual Education Act and served as a member of the powerful House Appropriations Committee. When he passed away in 2005, **Senator Dianne Feinstein**, in a tribute on the floor of the U.S. Senate, remembered the congressman as "a true leader and pioneer for the City of Los Angeles, the State of California, and for the national Latino community." Ed Roybal's commitment to public service lives on. In 1992, the very same year he retired, his daughter, **Lucille Roybal-Allard** (D-CA), was elected to the U.S. House of Representatives. In the decade and a half that she has been in Congress, she has made counterterrorism, U.S. intelligence, underage drinking, domestic violence, and public health issues her priorities.

Elected to represent Texas's Fifteenth Congressional District in 1964, Kika de la Garza enjoyed a distinguished career of thirty-two years in the U.S. House of Representatives. During his House tenure, he was a steadfast defender of farming interests. In 1981 he became the first Latino to chair a standing subcommittee in the House of Representatives when he was selected chair of the House Committee on Agriculture. A strong protector of Latinos' civil rights, from 1989 to 1991 he chaired the Congressional Hispanic Caucus, which he cofounded in 1976. He also fought for better living conditions for the country's poor and low-income citizens, and for access to health care for the elderly and to education for all.

From 1983 to 1997, **Bill Richardson** represented New Mexico's Third Congressional District in the U.S. House of Representatives. In Congress he played a leadership role as Chief Deputy Democratic Whip and also served on the House Commerce, Natural Resources, and Intelligence committees. On February 1, 1997, Richardson became U.S. ambassador to the United Nations. In that post, he took on complex international negotiating challenges, including the crisis over Iraq. On August 18, 1998, Bill Richardson was sworn in as U.S. Secretary of Energy, which made him the highest-ranking Latino in the Clinton administration. In 2002 Richardson was elected governor of New Mexico. As governor he has made economic growth, water issues, military bases, driving while intoxicated, energy, fiscal responsibility, health care, tax cuts, and education his priorities. In 2007 Richardson entered the 2008 Democratic presidential race.

The year 1989 was a historic one for Latinas. That year **Ileana Ros-Lehtinen** became the first Latina and the first Cuban American in the United States Congress, after she was overwhelmingly elected to fill the seat of a popular Democratic congressman from Florida, **Claude Pepper**, after his death. In 1990 Congresswoman Ros-Lehtinen easily won reelection, garnering 60 percent of the vote. Over the years, she has worked tirelessly on issues related to education, the well-being of children and the elderly, women's health, the environment, victims' rights, and others. She has also contributed immensely to shaping U.S. foreign policy, particularly toward Latin America, chairing several International Relations subcommittees, among them the Subcommittee on International Operations and Human Rights (she is the first Latina ever to chair a House subcommittee), on which she was a vocal advocate of human rights and democracy. She currently chairs the Subcomittee on the Middle East and Central Asia.

Another Latina, **Nydia Velázquez** (D-NY), who was born in Yabucoa, Puerto Rico, made history in 1992 by becoming the first Puerto Rican woman to serve in the House. She represents the Twelfth Congressional District of New York, which encompasses sections of Manhattan's Lower East Side, Brooklyn, and Queens. In 1998 she became the first Latina ever to serve as chair or ranking member of a full committee in the House when she was named Ranking Democrat on the Small Business Committee. Over the years, Congresswoman Velázquez has distinguished herself as an advocate for working people and the poor, fighting to secure affordable housing, quality education, and health care for all New Yorkers.

Cuban-born Republican **Lincoln Diaz-Balart**, who is related to **Fidel Castro** and who represents Miami's Twenty-first District, which is 80 percent Cuban American, is another member of the House "class of 1992." In Congress he has supported and initiated legislation of utmost importance to Latinos, including the Nicaraguan Adjustment and Central American Relief Act of 1997, which extended legal residency status to hundreds of thousands of immigrants in America. He has also fought for tax relief for hardworking Americans, for educational reform, transportation funding, and environmental protection. In 2002 his brother, **Mario Diaz-Balart**, who is also a Republican, joined him in the House. In his comparatively brief time in office, Mario Diaz-Balart has helped found the Congressional Hispanic Conference and has pushed for tax relief for working Americans, the elderly, and small businesses; for safeguarding taxpayer money; and for more affordable health care.

From 1992 until 2006, when he filled the seat left vacant in the U.S. Senate by departing New Jersey governor-elect **Jon S. Corzine**, another Cuban American, **Robert Menendez,** served in the U.S. House of Representatives, where he rose through the ranks to become the third-highest ranking Democrat. From 1998 until 2006, he was vice chairman of the Democratic Caucus, which made him the first Latino ever elected to a leadership post in Congress and the highest-ranking Latino among House Democrats. For his unwavering commitment to human rights, Congressman Menendez was awarded the 1998 Ellis Island Medal of Honor.

In 1997 Latinos and all Americans lost a heroic statesman when **Frank Tejeda** (D-TX), another congressman from the "class of 1992," met an untimely death. Tejeda, who transformed himself from a high school dropout into a respected lawyer and the first congressman from the new Latino Twenty-eighth District in Texas, is proof positive that no obstacle in life is insurmountable.

The other Latinos who are currently shaping policy in the U.S. House of Representatives are **Joe Baca** (D-CA); **Xavier Becerra** (D-CA); **Dennis Cardoza** (D-CA); **Henry Cuellar** (D-TX); **Luis Fortuño** (R-PR); **Raúl Grijalva** (D-AZ); **Luis Gutierrez** (D-IL); **Rubén Hinojosa** (D-TX); **Grace Napolitano** (D-CA); **Solomon Ortiz** (D-TX); **Ed Pastor** (D-AZ); **Silvestre Reyes** (D-TX), whom in 2006 **Nancy Pelosi**, as incoming Speaker of the House, selected to chair the House Intelligence Committee; **John T. Salazar** (D-CO); **Loretta Sánchez** (D-CA); **Linda Sánchez** (D-CA); **José Serrano** (D-NY); and **Hilda Solis** (D-CA).

Incidentally, Congresswoman Loretta Sánchez, who is from Orange County, California, achieved a stunning victory in the 1996 election when she upset nine-term incumbent Republican **Robert Dornan** by a slim margin to become the nation's first Mexican American woman in Congress. Dornan contested the election, calling for an investigation into possible voter fraud, but a grand jury investigation into the allegations returned no indictments, and in early 1998 a Congressional task force determined that Sánchez could retain her seat. Over the years, she has focused on issues of economic development, education, crime reduction, and the protection of senior citizens. In 2002 she was joined in the House by her sister, Congresswoman Linda Sánchez, who is the first Latina in history to serve on the House Judiciary Committee. Loretta Sánchez and Linda Sánchez are the first sisters—and the first women related to one another—to serve in the United States Congress.

The three Latinos currently serving in the U.S. Senate belong to a small but distinguished group. The 2005 swearing in of **Senator Mel Martinez** (R-FL) and **Senator Ken Salazar** (D-CO) marked a pivotal moment in Latino history: For the first time since 1977, about a quarter century, Latinos had achieved political representation in the Senate. In 2006 **Robert Menendez** (D-NJ) joined Martinez and Salazar in the U.S. Senate. Together, the three senators represent half of all Latinos who have ever served in the U.S. Senate, joining the ranks of Octaviano Larrazolo, Dennis Chávez, and Joseph Manuel Montoya. Martinez, Salazar, and Menendez also share the distinction of being the first Latino senators in history to represent a state other than New Mexico.

Senator Martinez also enjoys the distinction of being the first Cuban American ever elected to the U.S. Senate. Born Melquiades Rafael Martínez in Sagua la Grande, Cuba, he fled **Castro**'s rule at the age of fifteen under Operation Pedro Pan, a humanitarian effort that facilitated the escape to freedom of over four thousand Cuban children from December 1960 to October 1962. He was placed with foster families, who cared for him until he was reunited with his family four years later. Before taking his seat in the Senate, Mel Martinez served as U.S. secretary of housing and urban development under **President George W. Bush**. In yet another first, Senator Martinez was elected general chairman of the Republican National Committee in early 2007, becoming the first Latino leader of the Republican Party.

The brother of Congressman John T. Salazar (D-CO), Ken Salazar comes from a Mexican American family with a long history of farming and ranching in Colorado's San Luis Valley—since before the state was admitted to the Union in 1876. Before going to the Senate, Ken Salazar served as the attorney general of Colorado from 1999 to 2004. The only Democrat to win an open Senate seat in 2004, he won a tight Senate race against beer baron **Peter Coors**.

Robert Menendez, who was born on New Year's Day, 1954, to Cuban parents who had left **Batista**'s Cuba in 1953, and who grew up in a tenement building in Union City, New Jersey, was the sole Cuban American Democrat in the U.S. House of Representatives from 1993 to 2005. In 2002 he was elected chair of the House's Democratic Caucus, which made him the highest-ranking Latino in that chamber. He resigned from the House in January 2006, after he was appointed to fill the U.S. Senate seat made vacant by governor-elect **Jon S. Corzine** of New Jersey.

Who are some prominent Latino politicians outside of Washington?

New Mexico governor **Bill Richardson** has achieved nationwide recognition. Capitalizing on his clout, he declared in early 2007 that he was running for the Democratic nomination for president in 2008.

Another prominent Latino in elected office outside the beltway is **Manuel "Manny" Diaz**, who has served Miami as its mayor since 2001. Born in Havana in 1954, he arrived in the United States with his mother, their pockets empty, in 1961. Diaz first captured the attention of the nation as a lawyer in the custody battle over six-year-old Cuban refugee **Elián González**, who was rescued from the Straits of Florida on Thanksgiving Day, 1999, after the boat holding him and thirteen others fleeing Cuba, including his mother, capsized en route to Florida. Diaz represented the Miami relatives of Elián in the custody battle—one that escalated into a messy war between **Attorney General Janet Reno** of the **Clinton** administration and Miami's Cuban exile community. In November 2001, in his first campaign for public office, Manny Diaz was easily elected mayor of Miami. For bringing city hall out of virtual bankruptcy in under three years, making a clean break with corrupt Miami politics, and nurturing an urban development boom, Diaz was reelected mayor in 2005, garnering 65 percent of the vote. In 2004 the Manhattan Institute recognized his achievements, awarding Mayor Diaz its Urban Innovator of the Year Award.

Another Latino mayor who has attracted much attention is **Antonio R. Villaraigosa**, a liberal Democrat and a longtime labor organizer. In 2005 Villaraigosa was elected the first Mexican American and first Latino mayor of Los Angeles in well over a century. Born Antonio Ramon Villar Jr. to Mexican immigrants in Los Angeles, he became Antonio Villaraigosa in 1987, when he married **Corina Raigosa** and the two fused their surnames. Villaraigosa entered the political arena in 1994, with his election to the California State Assembly, emerging as majority leader of that body in 1996 and assembly speaker in 1998. In 2001 he ran for mayor of Los Angeles but lost to fellow Democrat **James Hahn**. In 2003 he was elected to the Los Angeles City Council, representing the Fourteenth District. Two years later, in his second bid for the Los Angeles mayoralty, he defeated incumbent mayor James Hahn by cobbling together an electoral coalition that transcended ethnic and racial divides, becoming the city's first Latino mayor since 1872, when **José Cristóbal Aguilar** held that post.

In his years as mayor, Antonio Villaraigosa has committed himself to obliterating cronyism at city hall; revamping the Los Angeles public school system; dismantling gangs; providing for the city's homeless; and fostering public health and safety, economic development, and the greening of Los Angeles, among other issues. Owing to his accomplishments and his enormous visibility on the national political stage, he has graced the cover of *Newsweek* magazine, been touted in *Time* magazine as one of the nation's twenty-five most influential Latinos, and been ranked as one of the fifty most beautiful Latinos by *People en Español*.

Albuquerque mayor **Martin Chavez**, who is currently serving his third term in office, has also achieved much for the city that he serves, New Mexico's largest. Chavez was first elected to the mayor's office in 1993; he dedicated his initial term to cleaning up Albuquerque, lowering its crime rate, and launching a vital water conservation program. Rather than pursue a second term as mayor, Chavez made an unsuccessful run for the governorship of New Mexico. In 2001 he again made a bid for the mayor's office, succeeded, and picked up where he left off, achieving a significant reduction in crime and water usage, and bringing jobs to Albuquerque and the state of New Mexico. Four years later, in 2005, voters expressed their confidence in their mayor, selecting him for a third term.

THE ISSUES

Terrorism: Who is José Padilla, and how did he become a pawn of Al Qaeda's anti-American, anti-Latino, racist network?

In the September 11 attacks on the World Trade Center and the Pentagon, Latinos were killed and injured alongside their fellow Americans. In the aftermath of the attacks, thousands of Latinos heard the urgent call to defend the cause of freedom and the United States. They served with distinction—and continue to serve—in the U.S. armed forces in Afghanistan, Iraq, and in other terrorist hot spots around the globe. They have also served their country in this time of war in other government departments, such as the Central Intelligence Agency and the Department of Homeland Security.

Given Latinos' patriotism and love of America and the American way of life, it came as a shock to the community when in 2002 a thirty-one-year-old Brooklyn-born man of Puerto Rican descent named **José "Pucho" Padilla** was arrested in Chicago and held without charge as an "enemy combatant" of the United States. Padilla grew up in Chicago, where he became a street gang member, and eventually he wound up serving time in a Florida prison as an accessory to a road-rage murder. While in prison, Padilla converted to Islam and changed his name to Abdullah al Muhajir. After his release, he married a Muslim woman and moved to Afghanistan and then Pakistan, where, allegedly, the Al Qaeda terrorist network recruited him to conspire against his own country. About a month before his arrest, Padilla left Pakistan and spent a brief time in Zurich, Switzerland, before heading to Cairo. He remained in Cairo for several weeks, went back to Zurich, and then flew to Chicago, where he was taken into custody at the airport. Padilla was carrying over $10,000 in cash, believed to have come from Al Qaeda and to have been earmarked for scouting locations to detonate "dirty bombs" in the United States. According to FBI sources, Padilla used the Internet at a home in Lahore, Pakistan, to learn how to build a dirty bomb that could spread radioactive material over dozens of city blocks.

Padilla's arrest was the result of a tip given by a high-level Al Qaeda operative interned by the U.S. government at Guantánamo Bay. This fact led many U.S. government strategists and Latino leaders to speculate as follows: Although Padilla might indeed have been a treacherous enemy combatant, he was possibly a low-grade, expendable operative to Al Qaeda and was betrayed by a bigwig for the purpose of making the U.S. government believe that all the information that Al Qaeda captives feed U.S. authorities is true, since the Padilla tip turned out to be a real lead, when, in fact, it is little more than misinformation. Further, by implicating a non-Arab in the Al Qaeda terrorist network and thus creating the impression that Arabs and non-Arab Americans are in cahoots, the bin Laden gang probably hoped to undermine racial profiling as a deterrence tool for U.S. authorities, which would make it far easier for them to perpetrate further mass murder in the United States.

U.S. officials proceeded to hold Padilla, an American citizen, for three and a half years without access to counsel and without any formal charges, essentially depriving him of his human rights. Then, late in 2005, when the U.S. Supreme Court was determining whether or not to review the legality of Padilla's military detention, the government, wanting to keep that issue out of the Supreme Court, abandoned the dirty bomb case against him, and he was transferred to the criminal justice system and charged on counts of providing monetary support to terrorists, making him the only accused terrorist to have his status changed from enemy combatant to criminal defendant. In 2007 Padilla was found guilty in a federal court of terrorism conspiracy charges, despite the controversy over whether the Bush administration had trampled on his rights as a U.S. citizen by detaining him for so long without formal charges.

Why is immigration an issue that is front and center?

The United States has long been a nation conflicted over the issue of immigrants. The tendency has been to demonize new immigrants, blaming them for all of society's ills, and then, with the passage of time, to glorify their contributions to American life. For instance, in the nineteenth century, a period of heavy Irish immigration to the United States, America's Irish faced virulent Celtophobia—overt discrimination and hatred at the hands of the establishment, which believed that they were dull-witted, lazy, and backward. Talk flowed of expelling the Irish from America and halting Irish immigration. Some in the Protestant majority deemed the influx of the Irish Catholics into America a papal conspiracy. Signs in shop windows in cities proclaimed, "No Irish Need Apply," or simply the acronym "NINA." In the 1830s, anti-immigrant mobs even threatened to burn down the first St. Patrick's Cathedral, which still stands on Mott Street in Manhattan and was a religious haven for New York City's Irish Catholics. This period has long been forgiven and forgotten: Irish Americans are lauded for their vast contributions to this nation, and Americans delight in the Kennedy dynasty, the St. Patrick's Day Parade, shamrocks, the wearing of the green, pints of Guinness, and the luck of the Irish.

For centuries, immigrants from Spanish-speaking Latin America, and American-born persons of Spanish-speaking Latin American ancestry alike, have been a major target of nativist bigotry in the United States. This is due to the fact that significant Latin American immigration, especially from Mexico, has been an ongoing process; a percentage of Latin American immigrants cross into the United States illegally; and Latinos have historically been deprived of opportunities for economic advancement and political and social empowerment.

Nativism with regard to immigrants from Spanish-speaking Latin America has been an especially strong political force in the United States in the past decade and a half. For example, in 1994 California Republicans, led by **Governor Pete Wilson** (who was looking for a way to get reelected), sought to put a stop to what they termed the "browning" of California, which they perceived was detrimental to the state's European American inhabitants, by giving illegal immigrants, the overwhelming majority of whom were Mexican, a good reason to return to their home country and by discouraging other Mexicans from entering California. To achieve this end, they championed Proposition 187, a measure aimed at making life exceptionally tough for California's illegal immigrants by excluding them from various federal programs, including Medicaid, welfare, and food stamps, and by denying their children U.S. citizenship even if they were born on American soil, as well as access to public schools and government-sponsored health care, including immunization programs. California Republicans also championed a lesser-known measure, Proposition 209, which would end affirmative action.

Proponents of Prop 187 vilified Mexicans at their rallies to whip up support for the measure among Anglo Californians. They also grossly exaggerated the number of illegal aliens in the state and forgot to mention that 50 percent of illegal aliens were legal aliens who had overstayed their visas. California voters bought their arguments hook, line, and sinker. Prop 187 was approved at the polls by 59 percent of California voters, but there was strong opposition from the state's registered Latinos, 57 percent of whom turned out to vote. The measure also came under legal scrutiny, and the courts ultimately overturned it. The voters' approval of Prop 187 created grave concern among California's two million permanent resident aliens (most of whom were Mexican), who feared that they were next in line for demonization by the state's Republicans. Overnight, the number of persons of Mexican origin enrolled in citizenship classes in California rose exponentially, and the number of applications for U.S. citizenship in the state climbed 500 percent from 1992 levels. Even years later, in the late 1990s, the Los Angeles district office of the U.S. Immigration and Naturalization Service was receiving approximately twenty-five thousand applications for citizenship per month.

The passage of Prop 187 also gave unregistered Mexican Americans, many newly naturalized, the impetus to register to vote. Before Prop 187, many were not sure which party to join. Not surprisingly, after Prop 187, most opted for the Democratic Party. This marked a real shift in allegiance, since before Prop 187 the Republicans could count on up to two-fifths of the Latino vote. And so, the nativistic measure backfired on California's Republicans. However, the fact is that the Republicans were misled. Even if Prop 187 had sent illegal aliens fleeing south over the U.S.-Mexico border, the "browning" of California would not have been stemmed. Illegal aliens or no illegal aliens, the disparity between Latino and Anglo birthrates in California ensures that the state will have a Latino majority by the year 2040.

The support in California for Prop 187, and nativism in general, kept immigration, particularly from Mexico, front and center as a political issue in the United States in the second half of the 1990s, spawning numerous other harsh anti-immigrant laws, including the 1996 Illegal Immigration Reform and Immigrant Responsibility Act (IIRAIRA). The IIRAIRA and a related bill, the Antiterrorism and Effective Death Penalty Act, also of 1996, were supposed to make it easier to control illegal immigration and to root out terrorists in the United States. Instead, they have resulted in the detention, maltreatment, and deportation of large numbers of undocumented immigrants, asylum seekers who lack adequate documentation, and other noncitizens, as those awaiting deportation are subject to mandatory detention. (See chapter 7.)

Since taking office, **President George W. Bush** has pursued a more balanced Latin American immigration policy. For instance, in 2001 the Bush administration sought to address the inconsistency in the treatment of Central American immigrants inherent in the IIRAIRA by granting undocumented Salvadorans Temporary Protected Status (TPS) after devastating earthquakes struck El Salvador. And before the September 11, 2001, terrorist attacks on the United States, President Bush was at work on a Mexican migration accord with Mexican president **Vicente Fox**. The Bush White House was weighing such proposals as granting legal status to the millions of Mexican undocumented immigrants already living in the United States and launching a new temporary worker program for Mexicans who had not yet crossed the border, a program that would not only ensure that temporary workers' legal rights were protected, but would foster a secure, regulated southern border and safe, legal Mexican migration. The terrorist attacks of September 11 diverted attention away from the work on a Mexican migration accord and caused the United States to consider the U.S.-Mexico border chiefly as a security risk rather than a revolving door for workers and goods.

In 2004 President Bush returned to the issue of designing a guest-worker program to stem the flow of illegal aliens across the U.S.-Mexico border and offer a legal migration alternative. In response, Congress began proposing reforms to existing immigration laws, including those contained in H.R. 4437, otherwise known as the Sensenbrenner bill, which was passed in the House at the end of 2005. The bill—which called for increased penalties for illegal immigration and the categorization of all illegal aliens, and those aiding and abetting them, as felons—unleashed widespread protests between February and May 2006, as millions of Latinos and fair-minded non-Latinos took to the streets, demanding both an overhaul of the bill and a path to legalization for America's illegal aliens. The largest protests took place on April 10, 2006, when in each of 102 cities, between a hundred thousand and five hundred thousand protesters marched on behalf of rights for illegal aliens.

While Latinos were protesting in the streets in the spring of 2006 and long into that summer, cries for border security and an end to illegal immigration by anti-immigrant zealots and the uninformed in America reached a feverish pitch, with armed private citizens, calling themselves Minutemen, even taking it upon themselves to fortify the U.S. border with Mexico—a border that runs for 1,951 miles, complete with long stretches of the scorching Sonoran and Chihuahuan deserts, and thus is impossible to secure entirely. The Latino protests and the uproar about the border sent politicians from Washington scurrying to the Sonoran Desert, one of North America's hottest, in the dead of summer for a photo op. With Congress still negotiating an immigration reform package, even President Bush felt compelled to make an appearance at the Arizona-Mexico border and to deploy a limited number of National Guard troops to the border to reinforce the Border Patrol, a drop in a bucket that can never be filled.

President Bush's campaign for immigration reform was stymied in 2007, when the Senate rejected a bill calling for sweeping changes to immigration law. Nativist politicians and pundits, ignoring Mexican laborers' long, courageous history in America—ignoring the Bracero Program, the El Paso Incident, Operation Wetback—and never acknowledging who's doing the gardening, picking the fruit, cleaning the houses, and diapering the Anglo babies of America, continue to depict illegal immigrants from Mexico and other Spanish-speaking Latin American countries as a plague of locusts on the nation. They will do so openly until mainstream America recognizes that these immigrants—vital contributors to the American way of life and a source of cultural enrichment—should be granted the opportunity to earn permanent legal residency and that it is the responsibility of those in Washington both to provide some modicum of security along the nation's borders and to develop a fair legal workers program for the citizens of Latin America desiring to labor in the United States.

Why is redistricting such a hot tamale?

Redistricting, also known as reapportionment, is the process undertaken by states every ten years, based on population changes reflected in the U.S. census, of redrawing judicial, state legislative, and congressional district boundaries. The idea is to redraw district boundaries so that every district has roughly the same number of voters, in keeping with the principle of "one person, one vote." In most states, the party that controls the state legislature is the one that oversees the redistricting process. (In other states, an independent commission directs redistricting.) The party in charge of redistricting does its best to ensure that its incumbents and candidates are (re)elected. Consequently, boundaries are rearranged in ways that create the greatest number of districts that can succeed in voting into office the candidates of the party in charge.

The effects of redistricting are felt at all levels of government, from local school boards to city councils to the U.S. House of Representatives. After the 1930 census, the House put a ceiling on membership at 435 and established the policy, in effect to this day, of shifting congressional seats among states. Thus, as new congressional districts are created, an equal number are lost. (For instance, Census 2000 found that the population growth in the West and South exceeded that in New York, and so New York lost two House seats.) It is no surprise that the whole topic of redistricting can elicit despair among members of Congress.

In the decades before the passage of the Voting Rights Act of 1965, both major political parties created voting districts that diluted the vote of minorities so that they did not possess enough voting power to ensure the election of representatives of their choice—and thus had no voice. One tactic that the parties commonly used was "cracking," that is, spreading over two or more districts voters from minority communities that would have the potential of voting candidates into office if they belonged to a single district, thereby diluting their numbers so that they had no influence on the outcome of elections. Another tactic was "packing," drawing as many members of a minority group as possible into one district in order to eliminate their influence in surrounding districts.

The Voting Rights Act did much to improve minorities' chances of securing representation in government. Section 2 of the Voting Rights Act prohibits minority vote dilution, that is, diluting racial or language minorities' voting strength so that the candidates of their choice are not elected. In 1986 the U.S. Supreme Court ruled in *Thornburg v. Gingles* that a minority community must meet three criteria in order to prove that its vote has been diluted: it must be sufficiently large to constitute a majority in a district, it must be politically cohesive, and it must show that the majority community votes as a bloc to defeat the minority's preferred candidates.

In 1993 defeated candidates and political factions who chalked up their losses to minorities' gains struck back. They challenged two new black majority voting districts in North Carolina in *Shaw v. Reno*, charging that race had been used to draw the district boundaries, which was a violation of the Equal Protection Clause of the Fourteenth Amendment. The U.S. Supreme Court sided with the plaintiffs, basing its decision on the shape of the two districts and not on proof that the plaintiffs had suffered vote dilution or discrimination. *Shaw v. Reno* spawned a series of litigation known as the "Shaw cases," in which plaintiffs challenged majority-minority districts simply by showing that race played a predominant role in the redistricting process. The Shaw cases made it much more difficult to draw district lines in ways that gave racial and ethnic minorities a fair opportunity to elect candidates of their choice.

In 1995 the U.S. Supreme Court held, in *Miller v. Johnson*, that race can be a factor in the redistricting process, but it may not be a predominant one. In 2001 the Court reaffirmed its decision when, in *Hunt v. Cromartie*, it overturned a lower court's decision that race was a predominant factor in the drawing of North Carolina's Twelfth District, establishing that in this district, race and political behavior were closely aligned. This was considered a step forward by those advocating race- and ethnicity-based redistricting, but they are still concerned that in order to avoid a Shaw challenge, those overseeing the redistricting process act to minimize the factors of race and ethnicity.

The issue of minority vote dilution by those redrawing district lines resurfaced again in 2006. That year the U.S. Supreme Court, in *League of United Latin American Citizens v. Perry*, debated whether state legislatures were permitted to reshape voting districts more than once a decade to favor the party in power, and how judges might determine if a state has wrongfully diluted minorities' influence in that process. At the root of the case was the Texas congressional map engineered in 2003, mid-decade, by former House majority leader **Tom DeLay**, in which the state's congressional district lines were adjusted to enable the Republicans, who had achieved a majority in the Texas legislature in 2002, to replace Democratic congressional seats with Republican ones. The tactic proved successful: in the next congressional elections, the Republicans gained six seats in Congress. Democratic challengers argued that splitting up traditionally Democratic voting districts for partisan gain violated the U.S. Constitution and federal voting rights laws, while minority advocates, among them the American GI Forum, emphasized that this partisan gain came at the expense of Latino and African American voters, whose voting blocs had been fractured ("cracking"), thus reducing their voting strength. In its decision, the high court upheld most of Tom DeLay's congressional map, saying that state legislators may redistrict as often as they wish, but not all of the map: it rendered Texas's District Twenty-three invalid, citing racial gerrymandering, a violation of the Voting Rights Act.

Still, political jockeying aside, many have questioned the wisdom of race- and ethnicity-based redistricting. They belong to the melting-pot school, which says that character and ability supersede ethnicity and that minorities should not be ghettoized, but should be part of diverse communities. They argue that boundaries should be drawn so that the Garcias end up in the same district as the Cuomos, the Bloomsteins, the Tates, and the O'Shaughnessys—and not just with the Gonzalezes—and that they should all together be able to elect Ms. Mantenfel or Mr.

Perez to Congress, or whoever happens to be the best person for the job. That's the idea, anyway.

Linda Chavez is one prominent Latino who is against race- and ethnicity-based redistricting. In her 1991 book, *Out of the Barrio: Toward a New Politics of Hispanic Assimilation*, she argues that in order to maintain the political power that redistricting has given many Latinos, they are forced to stay together in the barrio, where they remain part of the poor underclass, a fate political clout was supposed to save them from in the first place. Advocates of race- and ethnicity-based redistricting, such as **Congresswoman Nydia Velázquez** of New York, counter that the "melting pot" concept may be good in principle, but in reality countless Latinos have been deprived of their constitutional rights to adequate housing, health care, social services, education, and economic opportunity because they have been barred from full participation in the electoral process. Unless Latinos can send representatives who are committed to their communities to the state legislatures and to Congress—which race- and ethnicity-based redistricting makes possible—this situation will persist.

NINE LATINAS WHO HAVE MADE A DIFFERENCE

1. Joan Baez	Born in 1941, folk singer and songwriter Joan Baez has been a champion of nonviolence and human rights for over four decades. She was at the forefront of the civil rights movement and the anti–Vietnam War protests. She founded the Institute for the Study of Nonviolence in 1965 and Humanitas International in 1979, and has served on the national advisory board of Amnesty International.
2. Fabiola Cabeza de Baca Gilbert	Born in 1898, Fabiola Cabeza de Baca Gilbert dedicated herself to improving the lives of the people of New Mexico. One of her efforts was helping to introduce modern food preparation systems in the state. She was the first Latina to receive a U.S. government Superior Service Award. She also distinguished herself as a

writer; her best-known work is *We Fed Them Cactus* (1954), a personal chronicle of the Cabeza de Baca family.

3. Linda Chavez   In 1983 Linda Chavez became the first Latina to serve as director of the U.S. Commission on Civil Rights, a post she remained at until 1985, when she was appointed director of the White House Office of Public Liaison, which made her the highest-ranking woman in the White House. In January 2001, President-elect George W. Bush nominated Chavez as his secretary of labor, but with allegations that she had employed an illegal alien as her housekeeper a potential threat to her nomination, she stepped aside. Linda Chavez is currently president of the Washington DC–based Center for Equal Opportunity, "the only think tank devoted exclusively to the promotion of color-blind equal opportunity and racial harmony."

4. Dolores Huerta   The most prominent Chicana labor leader in the nation, Dolores Huerta has fought for fair working conditions for America's minorities, especially migrant farmworkers, for many decades. She played a leading role in the landmark grape boycott of 1968–70, cofounded the United Farm Workers with César Chávez, and served as the organization's vice president from 1970 to 1973.

5. Antonia Novello   In 1989 Antonia Novello became the first Latino and the first woman appointed U.S. surgeon general. While at that post, until mid-1993, she paid special attention to such issues as the health of minorities, women, and children; smoking; underage drinking; and HIV/AIDS. From 1993 to 1996, Novello served as the United Nations Children's Fund (UNICEF) special representative for health and nutrition. In 1996 she was appointed visiting professor

6. Helen Rodriguez-Trias

of health policy and management at the Johns Hopkins School of Hygiene and Public Health, and in 1999 she was named commissioner of health for the State of New York.

A pediatrician with an expertise in maternal and family health, Helen Rodriguez-Trias established Puerto Rico's first center for neonatal care while still a resident at the University of Puerto Rico hospital. In 1970 she relocated to New York City, and in the ensuing decades she emerged as a nationally recognized health-care advocate. Among her many distinctions, she was the first Latina appointed president of the American Public Health Association, the largest and oldest organization of public health professionals in the world. For her efforts on behalf of children, women, AIDS patients, and the poor, she was awarded a Presidential Citizen's Medal in 2001.

7. Josefina Sierro

In the 1930s, Josefina Sierro organized an underground railroad reminiscent of Harriet Tubman's to bring home Mexican Americans who were taken to Mexico against their will during the U.S. government's draconian campaign to deport Mexicans en masse.

8. Emma Tenayuca

From a young age, Emma Tenayuca, who was born in Texas in 1916, fervently championed the rights of Mexicans and women in that state at a time when neither had a voice, earning herself the title *La Pasionaria de Texas* and the status of role model for such activists as César Chávez. Among the many acts of protest and empowerment she engaged in was a strike she organized of twelve thousand Mexican women pecan shellers, in San Antonio in January 1938, in response to a decrease in wages to three cents per day. The strike lasted several months.

9. Elizabeth Vargas	A veteran of television journalism, Elizabeth Vargas, who is of Puerto Rican and Irish American parentage, has been an inspiration for Latinas seeking to break through the glass ceiling. In her illustrious career, she has served as a substitute cohost and anchor of NBC's *Today* show (1993–96), a correspondent for *Dateline NBC* (1993–96), a news anchor for ABC's *Good Morning America* (1996–97), a correspondent and coanchor for ABC's *20/20* (1997–2004 and 2004, respectively), and a host of ABC's *20/20 Downtown* (1999–2002). In the first five months of 2006, she shared (with Bob Woodruff) the anchor desk of ABC's evenings news broadcast, *World News Tonight*—delivering the news solo after Woodruff suffered a serious injury in Iraq on January 29, 2006. Currently, she coanchors ABC's *20/20*.

Does bilingual education mean we'll all be speaking Spanish soon?

Bilingual education got its start in Dade County, Florida, in 1960, when hundreds of thousands of newly arrived Cuban refugee children were enrolled in the county's public schools. The Cuban refugees, holding fast to the belief that **Fidel Castro** would fall from power before long and that they would soon be homeward bound, felt that their children should be taught in both English and their mother tongue. They pushed for legislation that required the public schools to teach the kids a half day in Spanish and a half day in English. The Cuban children, who were mostly middle class and quite motivated, were high achievers overall. In fact, they achieved higher scores than English-speaking children in other schools in Florida.

Impressed by the Cuban refugee children's scholastic achievements, politicians and teachers in the Southwest were champing at the bit to try bilingual education out on their own Spanish-speaking students. And so Texas senator **Ralph Yarborough** introduced a bill in 1967 that called for federal aid for bilingual education in schools that enrolled poor Mexican American children of limited English-speaking ability. Those who testified at the U.S. Senate hearings to examine the proposal insisted that these children, who were both linguistically and socially disadvantaged, would learn more rapidly if they received instruction in both Spanish and English, and that this in turn would build their self-esteem. They also argued that the children performed poorly in school in part because they were cut off from their roots and, consequently, had a "damaged self-concept." To rectify this, they recommended that the schools instruct the children about Mexican American culture. Although Senator Yarborough's bill was geared toward Spanish-speaking individuals, it led to the introduction of thirty-seven other bills, all of which were consolidated into a single piece of legislation, the Bilingual Education Act of 1968, also known as Title VII of the Elementary and Secondary Education Act. The Bilingual Education Act decreed that children should be taught in their native language for one transitional year, during which they honed their English-language skills, but then should transfer over to English-only classes.

The use of bilingual education solely as a short-term remedy to children's limited English-speaking ability was short-lived. In 1974 the U.S. Supreme Court held in *Lau v. Nichols* that in providing non-English-speaking students of Chinese descent instruction in a language they did not understand, the San Francisco school system had denied them the meaningful opportunity to participate in the public education system and therefore had violated the Civil Rights Act of 1964. The San Francisco school system had to agree to provide bilingual education to Chinese, Filipino, and Latino students. With the Supreme Court's decision in *Lau v. Nichols*, bilingual education was transformed from a transitional-year program to a multiple-year one, with an emphasis on teaching children their native tongue first and then English. *Lau v. Nichols*, as well as the Equal Educational Opportunity Act of 1974, gave rise to amendments to the Bilingual Education Act in 1974 and 1978. The 1978 amendments broadened the eligibility requirements for bilingual education programs from limited English speaking ability to limited English proficiency, meaning difficulty in speaking, comprehending, reading, or writing English.

In the 1970s, 1980s, and 1990s, much debate raged over how best to structure bilingual education. Some bilingual educators and politicians favored the immersion method: placing students in English-only classes and then providing them special instruction in their native language after school or at another time. Others advocated the English as a Second Language method, which is identical to the immersion method, with the exception that students are given some support in the native tongue. Others preferred the transitional method: offering students instruction in their native language while gradually replacing it with English-language instruction. And some backed the far less common double-immersion or double-language method: placing English speakers learning Spanish and Spanish speakers learning English side by side in one classroom, with the goal that all students end up bilingual. The double-immersion method caused quite an uproar; some interpreted it as an anti-American plot to make everyone Spanish speaking. A 1996 study conducted by George Mason University on the long-term success of students in bilingual education programs nationwide found that those who were taught by the double-immersion method performed the best academically, followed by those taught by the transitional method.

The proliferation of bilingual education eventually touched off a debate not over how to shape bilingual programs, but whether they should exist at all. Opponents argued that bilingual education merely served as a stumbling block in the path to English-language proficiency. This argument was voiced by influential members of the Latino community, including Mexican American **Richard Rodriguez**, author of such works as *Hunger of Memory: The Education of Richard Rodriguez* (1981), *Days of Obligation: An Argument with My Mexican Father* (1992), and *Brown: The Last Discovery of America* (2003). Opponents of bilingual education also insisted that students who received bilingual instruction were held to a lower standard, a practice, they contended, that put the students' futures in jeopardy because potential employers might decide that those educated in bilingual programs were not as well prepared for the workforce as their peers. Some who were against bilingual education even argued that bilingual programs were a form of insidious discrimination, since many immigrant Latino kids wound up in separate classrooms—and eventually in a separate world. Others opposed bilingual education because it sometimes targeted the wrong students, placing on a bilingual track Latino children born in America, previously taught in English, and having a solid command of English, as if bilingual education were the right of every minority child in America.

Many who opposed bilingual education were as much concerned about the larger question of America's fate as they were about the futures of immigrant children. English-only proponents, essentially nativists, argued that the great influx of Spanish speakers into the United States, who neither immersed themselves in English nor were encouraged to acculturate to the mainstream (and who had no need to do so, thanks to federal and state-sponsored bilingual programs), had created an undeniable Spanish-speaking atmosphere, which threatened the nation's unity. They insisted that without English to hold it together, the nation would break into political, cultural, and social factions, each vying for its own interests. To lend credence to this argument, English-only advocates often quoted **Teddy Roosevelt**, who once said, "The one absolute certain way of bringing this nation to ruin, or preventing all possibility of its continuing to be a nation at all, would be to permit it to become a tangle of squabbling nationalities. We have but one flag. We must also learn one language and that language is English."

In response to growing concern over the fate of the nation, **Senator S. I. Hayakawa** of California introduced a joint Senate resolution in 1981 to amend the U.S. Constitution so that it would read, "The English language shall be the official language of the United States," but the bill went to sleep during the Ninety-seventh Congress. What motivated Hayakawa to introduce such a resolution was those *"Se Habla Español"* signs found everywhere on the American landscape—from classrooms to storefronts. Fifteen years later, politicians had still not laid this issue to rest. In 1996 the Bill Emerson English Language Empowerment bill, a bill to make English the official language of the U.S. government, passed in the House but was not taken up in the Senate. U.S. English, Inc., an organization promoting English only, played a large part in getting the bill through the House. In 2002 U.S. English supported unsuccessful efforts by **Senator Richard Shelby** of Alabama and **Congressman Bob Barr** of Georgia to get official English bills passed in the 107th Congress. At the state level, English-only proponents met with greater success. As of 2006, twenty-seven states, alarmed over the sound of "so much Spanish," had enacted legislation declaring English their official language.

The arguments put forth by bilingual education proponents gained strength in 1997, when the results of a five-year study of the educational progress of immigrant children in bilingual programs in San Diego were released. The study found that the children had quickly become fluent in English and that they actually favored English over their native tongue. The study also showed that they received better grades and dropped out with less frequency than fellow students whose parents were born in the United States. However, opponents of bilingual education were quick to underscore the study's findings that a high percentage of immigrant students favored an ethnic label such as Mexican American over simply American, which, in their estimation, indicated that the country was, indeed, in the process of breaking into factions. And so the debate raged on.

Bilingual education was transformed in 2002, when President Bush signed the landmark No Child Left Behind education law, whose long-term aim is to revamp America's failing schools through curricular reform, enhanced teacher training, and greater accountability. Under No Child Left Behind, federal funds have continued to support English-language programs for non-English-speaking children, but rapid English-language acquisition and accountability are now at the forefront of these programs. Schools must show that their students have made academic progress in English through annual English-language fluency assessment.

Two things are clear in all this. Government and educators have an ethical responsibility to provide equal opportunities for a quality education for all of America's schoolchildren, including the 18.6 percent who (as of 2006) are Latino. Bilingual education has been around for a long time now, and it should be abundantly clear which aspects of it aid children's academic progress and which do not. The future of the country hinges on it.

When was a Latino studies department first established?

In the late 1960s, in response to all the fervor over bilingual and bicultural education at the elementary and secondary levels and at the height of the Chicano renaissance, Mexican Americans sought to establish courses focusing on their own culture at institutions of higher learning in America. The first academic department dedicated to Latinos was the Mexican American studies department established at California State University at Los Angeles in 1968. A year later a historic Chicano conference was held in Santa Barbara, California, where Chicano activists and intellectuals drew up a declaration calling for the formation of Chicano studies programs in higher education institutions throughout

California. Soon colleges and universities around the nation were establishing entire departments devoted to the study of Chicanos, other Latino subgroups, and Latinos as a whole. By the year 2000, there were about four hundred Latino studies (including Chicano studies, Dominican studies, etc.) certificate programs in place at over 250 colleges and universities across the United States. And by 2000 a good number of Latino studies departments had also been established; these continue to increase at a rate of one or two annually.

THE TOP 25 COLLEGES AND UNIVERSITIES FOR LATINOS IN 2006
(According to *Hispanic* magazine)

1. Harvard University

2. Princeton University

3. Amherst College

4. Yale University

5. University of Pennsylvania

6. Stanford University

7. Pomona College

8. Massachusetts Institute of Technology

9. Columbia University

10. Dartmouth College

11. Brown University

12. Rice University

13. University of Notre Dame

14. University of California, Berkeley

15. University of California, Los Angeles

---

16. University of Southern California

17. University of California, San Diego

18. New York University

19. University of California, Santa Barbara

20. University of California, Davis

21. University of Florida

22. University of Texas at Austin

23. University of Miami

24. Rutgers, The State University of New Jersey

25. Texas A&M University

The establishment of a Latino studies curriculum and Latino studies departments on university campuses and increasing Latino visibility have resulted in recent years in the creation of countless corporate grants and fellowships for Latino undergraduate and graduate students and Latino studies departments. Among the myriad fellowships available are the Hispanic College Fund's undergraduate scholarships; the National Association of Hispanic Nurses' nursing scholarships; the Chicana/Latina Foundation's scholarships for Latina undergraduate and graduate students in northern California; and the League of United Latin American Citizens' scholarships for business and engineering majors. These supplement a federal program that contributes many millions a year to bilingual and bicultural secondary and higher education. Latinos have come a long, long way from the meager sums given to enhance their education just three decades or so ago.

NUEVE

Famous Latinos

RITMO LATINO

What is Latin rhythm all about?

Mambo, salsa, samba, conga, *son, son montuno, guaracha,* merengue, *cumbia, bugalu, danzón,* bolero, Afro-Cuban Latin jazz, and even cha-cha (known as *cha cha cha* in Spanish) are all part of what Americans call the Latin beat. Its foundation is African, since the tambour, the conga, and the bongo drums, brought over by African slaves, are the heart and soul of this contagious music.

Over the centuries, the Spanish guitar, fiddle, accordion, trumpet, and saxophone were added to African and Amerindian instruments—such as the marimba (xylophone), the maraca and other rattles, bells, the guiro (a serrated gourd that is played by scraping it with a stick), and the claves, the wooden sticks that keep the beat. The result is a distinctive sound that defies even the tin-eared to sit still.

In the United States, where Latin music thrives, hardly a nightclub, ballroom, disco, television show, ice-skating rink, or dance company has not felt the impact of that irrepressible Latin beat. It seems that the rhythm has infected the whole world, since nowadays Latin music has fans all around the globe. Salsa, conga, *guaracha*, merengue, and Latin jazz bands play to full houses in Amsterdam, Paris, London, Moscow, and Montevideo. Even Japan boasts numerous all-Japanese salsa bands, one of which is the popular *Orquesta de la Luz*.

The Latin beat is but one of myriad Latino sounds heard in America. Another important style that has crossed over to mainstream America, thanks to Mexican American music legend **Selena**, is Tejano—a blend of Mexican *ranchera*, country, polka, pop, Colombian *cumbia*, and reggae—which is especially popular in Texas. Tragically, Selena was murdered by the president of her fan club in 1995, on the eve of her English-language debut. Her death shocked the entire nation, Anglos and Latinos alike, and also fostered a greater appreciation of the richness of Mexican American culture.

Is the tango considered Latin rhythm?

Not really. The tango is a Latin dance and song style. It became popular in turn-of-the-century Buenos Aires and within two decades had spread throughout Latin America, Europe, and the United States. The tango is derived from the *milonga*, a sexy Argentinean dance, and the habanera, a graceful dance that originated in Cuba. (The habanera achieved popularity far beyond Cuba's shores. For instance, in **Georges Bizet**'s 1875 opera, *Carmen*, the title character sings a habanera aria.) By the 1920s, the tango had evolved into an elegant, stylized dance with long, gliding steps and dips, accompanied by melancholic music and songs. Legendary Argentinean singer and actor **Carlos Gardel** popularized tango songs in the World War I era and put Argentina on the musical map. Incidentally, **Evita Perón** (of *Evita* fame), the wife of Argentinean president **Juan Perón** (1946–55, 1973–74) and an influential, albeit informal, member of his government, is said to have been a big tango aficionada.

Was Desi Arnaz responsible for bringing Latin rhythm to the United States?

Cuban-born actor and musician **Desi Arnaz** was certainly responsible for introducing mainstream America to the sounds of

African Cuban drums, with his famous rendition of **Margarita Lecuona's** 1941 song "Babalú" on the hit television show *I Love Lucy*, which first aired in 1951. Incidentally, "Babalú" is a song to the Yoruban deity Babalú-Ayé, a much beloved *santo* of the *Santería* religion.

But even before *I Love Lucy* was first beamed into America's living rooms, Spanish violinist, bandleader, and composer **Xavier Cugat**, who had once lived in Cuba and Mexico, helped popularize Latin rhythms in America as leader of the orchestra at the Waldorf-Astoria hotel in New York City beginning in 1933. In 1934 Cugat's orchestra, along with **Benny Goodman**'s and **Ken Murray**'s, signed on to the NBC coast-to-coast radio show *Let's Dance*, a show that Nabisco sponsored to advertise the Ritz cracker. Before long, Cugat was much sought after by Tinseltown, and his orchestra starred in numerous popular films of the 1930s and 1940s, which served to further acquaint Americans with Latin rhythms. Cugat was not new to Hollywood: before he had even formed his first band, in 1928, he had worked his Latin magic behind the scenes as a sound mixer and film producer for several of **Charlie Chaplin**'s pictures.

A Latin musician who, like Desi Arnaz, made a huge splash among 1950s Anglo audiences was Cuban orchestra leader **Dámaso Pérez Prado**, who mixed *guaracha* rhythms with jazz elements to create mambo. Prado and his orchestra spread the mambo craze to all corners of America with their 1951 West Coast tour. One of Prado's biggest hits was "Cherry Pink and Apple Blossom White," which hovered at number one on the U.S. charts for ten weeks after its 1955 release. At around the same time, Mexican American **Ritchie Valens**, the first Latino rock star, was breaking new ground by fusing R & B–styled rock and roll with traditional Spanish and Mexican folk sounds. He was just starting to make waves in the mainstream, with songs like "Come On, Let's Go," "Donna," and his rock and roll rendition of the traditional Mexican song "La Bamba," when he, along with **Buddy Holly** and **J. P. Richardson** (also known as the Big Bopper), perished in a plane crash during a snowstorm on February 3, 1959, forever commemorated by rock fans as "the day the music died."

Ritchie Valens paved the way for every Latino rock star that followed. His life story is chronicled in the 1987 motion picture *La Bamba*. After the film's release, the traditional Mexican folk song that Valens popularized was on everybody's lips: Even those who couldn't say, *"Para bailar la bamba se necesita . . ."* would hum,

"*La la la la la Bamba la la la la la. . . .*" As a tribute to his accomplishments, Ritchie Valens was honored with a star on the Hollywood Walk of Fame in 1990. In 1993 the U.S. Postal Service issued a Ritchie Valens stamp, and in 2001 the singer was inducted into the Rock and Roll Hall of Fame.

In the 1960s, Puerto Rican conga player and bandleader **Joe Cuba**, whose parents left Puerto Rico in the 1920s and settled in Spanish Harlem, mixed Latin music with rhythm and blues to create *bugalu*, which was all the rage from 1966 to 1968. Cuba is perhaps best known for his *bugalu* tune "Bang Bang," which was an overnight hit in 1967 and crossed over from the Latin to the Anglo charts. By then Mexican American singer **Trini López** was skyrocketing to fame with his single "If I Had a Hammer," which hit number one in twenty-five countries, and the "king of Latin music," **Tito Puente**, the great Puerto Rican bongo player, orchestra leader, and composer, was catching on among Anglos. During an illustrious career spanning six decades, Tito Puente shaped Latin music into its present-day amalgam of salsa, Afro-Cuban sounds, and Latin jazz. In those six decades, he recorded over one hundred albums; performed at the White House; received five Grammys; was honored with a star on the Hollywood Walk of Fame in 1990; played in the 1992 film *The Mambo Kings* (and even performed some of his own music), which brought him Hollywood fame and broad recognition; and accomplished much, much more. He died on May 30, 2000, but his memory will live on forever in his music.

Some of that music he recorded with singer and composer **Celia Cruz**, the "queen of salsa," who began her singing career in Cuba in the 1940s, not long after winning a radio talent contest. She joined Cuba's most popular band, *La Sonora Matancera*, in 1950, headlining at the Tropicana, Havana's legendary nightclub, and settled in New York in 1961 on the heels of **Castro**'s takeover of Cuba. A musical powerhouse, she launched her solo career in 1965. Before long, her strong, metallic, very African rhythms, from *Santería* religious chants to cha-chas, mambos, and salsa—punctuated with shouts of "*¡Azúcar!*"—had made her the idol of Latinos all over America, catching on a bit later among Anglos. In the course of her stellar career, Celia Cruz recorded more than seventy albums, twenty-three of which went gold; appeared in theater productions and in motion pictures, including *The Mambo Kings* (1992); and was honored with a star on the Hollywood Walk of Fame, two Grammys, and even a statue in the Hollywood Wax

Museum. In 1995 **President Clinton** presented Celia Cruz with the National Medal of Arts, making her the first Latino pop singer to earn that distinction. Celia Cruz passed away on July 16, 2003, marking the end of an era for Cuban exiles. In May 2005, the Smithsonian Institution's National Museum of American History launched an exhibit entitled *¡Azúcar!* The Life and Music of Celia Cruz, paying tribute to the queen of salsa.

Three Mexican American performers whose careers were launched in the mainstream in the 1960s eventually made it into the pantheon of America's greatest performers of the twentieth century. The first is platinum-selling singer and entertainer **Vikki Carr**, whose career took off in 1961 with her hit song "He's a Rebel," which was soon followed by her smash hit "It Must Be Him." In the course of her illustrious career, she has performed for soldiers in Vietnam, the queen of England, five U.S. presidents, and zillions of fans; has released fifty-nine best-selling recordings; has been honored with a star on the Hollywood Walk of Fame; and has won three Grammys: in 1985 for Best Mexican-American Performance for *Simplemente mujer*, in 1992 for Best Latin Pop Album for *Cosas del amor*, and in 1995 for Best Mexican-American Performance, Vocal or Instrumental, for *Recuerdo a Javier Solis*.

The second is America's "queen of folk," **Joan Baez**, who is also a great humanitarian and was actively involved in the civil rights movement and the Vietnam War protest. She first captivated a widespread audience with the release in 1960 of her debut album, *Joan Baez*, a collection of traditional songs. From then until this day, she has released dozens of recordings, and fans have flocked to festivals, political events, and concerts to see her perform. In the early seventies, young Americans sang along to her smash hit "The Night They Drove Old Dixie Down," which was a top Billboard hit in 1971. The third is **Linda Ronstadt**, who everyone thought was Anglo until she crossed over (or back) to her Mexican roots and recorded an album in Spanish. Her versions of **Roy Orbison**'s "Blue Bayou" and Buddy Holly's "It's So Easy" made her America's greatest female pop rock star in the 1970s. Linda Rondstadt has been one of the nation's most esteemed performers for over four and a half decades—during which she has created more than thirty recordings, from her 1967 debut album, *Evergreen*, to her 2006 *Adieu False Heart*, for which she teamed up with Cajun folk traditionalist **Ann Savoy**; and has won pop, rock, country, and Latin music Grammys.

In the late 1960s, Puerto Rican crooner **José Feliciano**, who has a string of gold- and platinum-selling albums, wooed audiences with his suggestive single "Light My Fire," which he included on his 1968 album *Feliciano!* and which reaped two Grammys in 1968, one for Best Contemporary Male Pop Vocal Performer and one for Best New Artist. Around the same time, Mexican American singer/guitarist **Carlos Santana** was hypnotizing millions with his *"Oye como va,"* from his album *Abraxas*. With the dawning of the new millennium, this Rock and Roll Hall of Famer is as popular as ever: his 1999 album, *Supernatural,* which some consider his greatest work and which garnered him a record-breaking eight Grammys, including Album of the Year, has sold over twenty-five million copies.

In the 1970s, along came Mexican American **Freddy Fender**, who was born Baldemar Huerta, to migrant workers in a Texas border town, and renamed himself after the brand of his guitar. A three-time Grammy winner, Freddy Fender captivated audiences with his country-style and Latin-tinged songs, such as his 1975 hit "Before the Next Teardrop Falls." He passed away on October 14, 2006. Puerto Rican–Greek American **Tony Orlando** won a huge following in the 1970s with such numbers as "Knock Three Times," the top song of 1971, and "Tie a Yellow Ribbon 'Round the Ole Oak Tree," which Billboard proclaimed a top song of 1973. Incidentally, both singers were honored with stars on the Hollywood Walk of Fame, Freddy Fender in 1999 and Tony Orlando in 1990.

Other gifted Latin musicians who played an important role in shaping the Latin sound before the 1980s (and in some cases after, as well) include Cuban American *congero* (conga player) **Ramon "Mongo" Santamaría**, who helped develop Latin jazz; Puerto Rican jazz flutist **Dave Valentin**; Puerto Rican jazz pianist **Hilton Ruiz**, who has a distinctive Afro-Cuban sound (he died in New Orleans on May 19, 2006); Cuban American jazz and classical saxophonist, clarinetist, and composer **Paquito D'Rivera**, a three-time Grammy winner and a recipient in 2005 both of a National Medal of Arts and a National Endowment for the Arts Jazz Masters Fellowship; Latin jazz bassist **Andy González** and his brother, trumpeter and percussionist **Jerry González**; Puerto Rican Latin jazz and salsa pianist and bandleader **Eddie Palmieri**, an eight-time Grammy winner; Cuban-born singer, percussionist, and bandleader **Frank "Machito" Grillo**, who embodied Latin jazz; 1940s bandleader **Pupi Campo**; **José Curbelo**; **Miguelito Valdéz**; **Marcelino Guerra**; **Frank Marti**; and many, many more.

Who are the Latino music stars of the 1980s, 1990s, and the first decade of the twenty-first century?

Many of the Latino performers who rose to fame in the 1960s, including **Joan Baez**, **Linda Ronstadt**, and **Celia Cruz**, are as popular now as ever.

The 1980s and 1990s also saw new generations of talented Latino singers, who continue to captivate Americans with their sound. One of the greatest is Cuban American **Gloria Estefan**, who warned America in one of her songs that "the rhythm is gonna get you"—and it has. By blending the Latin beat with rhythm and blues and pop, and by singing in both English and Spanish, Gloria Estefan and the **Miami Sound Machine** single-handedly ushered Latin music into the mainstream in a big way, first crossing over to an English-speaking audience with her "Dr. Beat" (1984) and "Conga" (1986), both international hit singles. Estefan's popularity is so tremendous that when she nearly severed her spinal cord in an accident in 1990, while traveling with her band, husband and manager **Emilio Estefan Jr.,** and son **Nayib** in their tour bus, the people of Miami held a candlelight vigil for her all night long on *Calle Ocho,* Eighth Street, in the heart of Little Havana.

Gloria Estefan made a miraculous recovery, and to celebrate, she launched an international comeback tour, performing before cheering crowds at sold-out concerts all over the world, and released an album entitled *Into the Light* (1991). A single from the album, "Coming Out of the Dark," which her accident inspired, climbed to the top of the charts. *Into the Light* was followed by numerous albums in the 1990s, including *Mi tierra* (1993), the singer's first Spanish-language album in almost a decade, for which she was honored with a Grammy for Best Tropical Album; *Abriendo puertas* (1995), which earned her another Grammy; *Destiny* (1996), a highlight of which is "Reach," the official theme song of the 1996 Summer Olympics; and *Gloria!* (1998). The new millennium brought another Spanish-language album, this one entitled *Alma caribeña,* a fusion of Cuban, Puerto Rican, Dominican, and Panamanian sounds. In 2002 Gloria delighted Olympians and the world once again by performing at the closing ceremony of the XIX Olympic Winter Games in Salt Lake City. A year later, she released *Unwrapped*, an English-language recording, and in 2006, *The Essential Gloria Estefan*. In the course of her career, she has sold more than seventy million albums and has received five Grammys, the Ellis Island Medal of Honor, the American Music Award for Lifetime Achievement, a star on the Hollywood Walk of Fame, and numerous other distinctions.

Her lyrics may often be in English, but Gloria Estefan's soul is pure Latin, and this combination has inspired many Latino musicians. Among them is fellow Cuban American **Jon Secada**, who, under the guidance of producer Emilio Estefan Jr., went from being a backup vocalist for Gloria Estefan in 1989 to an international pop superstar in 1992, after the release of his multiplatinum album *Jon Secada*. *Otro día más sin verte*, the Spanish-language version of *Jon Secada*, was the number one Latin album of 1992 and captured a Grammy for the artist, for Best Latin Pop Album. The year 1994 saw the release of Secada's second album, *Heart, Soul, & a Voice*, which went platinum; 1995, the release of his *Amor*, which brought him a second Grammy, this time for Best Latin Pop Performance; and 2005, the release of *Same Dream*. Other highlights of his career include taking the stage with opera star **Luciano Pavarotti**, performing for **Pope John Paul II**, playing in *Grease* on Broadway, and writing and producing a tribute to the victims of the September 11 terrorist attacks.

Another singer who has benefited from the genius of producer Emilio Estefan Jr. is Cuban American **Albita Rodríguez**, known simply as Albita, whom *Newsweek* magazine ranked among its "100 personalities for the XXI Century." In 1993 Albita, who by then already enjoyed a thriving singing career, defected from Cuba: Permitted to travel to Mexico, she and her band crossed the U.S.-Mexico border at El Paso and requested asylum. Soon after settling in Miami, Albita, called the Latin **k.d. lang** because of her androgynous look, was packing the house at Centro Vasco, the legendary Cuban restaurant in Little Havana, and big-name stars like **Madonna**, **Liza Minnelli**, and **Rosie O'Donnell** were flocking to see her perform. For about a decade now, she has been delighting American listeners with old numbers from prerevolutionary Cuba as well as new songs with rock and jazz elements, which can be heard on her numerous albums, among them *No se parece a nada* (1995), *Dicen qué . . .* (1996), *Una mujer como yo* (1997), *Son* (2000), *Hecho a mano* (2002), and *Albita llegó* (2004). In 1997 Albita sang the Cuban classic *"Guantanamera"* at **President Clinton**'s inaugural ball.

Pop superstar **Mariah Carey**, who has Afro-Venezuelan and Irish roots, achieved stardom with the release of her debut album, *Mariah Carey*, in 1990. The album hit number one on the U.S. Billboard 200 chart and earned the singer Grammys for Best Pop Female Vocalist and Best New Artist. In the decade after her 1990 debut, she amassed fifteen number one hits and created a multi-million-selling album every year or so. Lukewarm reviews of the motion picture *Glitter* (2001), in which Carey starred, and its tie-in soundtrack album, coupled with the singer's emotional break-down in 2001, attributed to a frenetic promotional schedule, led Virgin Records in 2002 to pay Mariah Carey $28 million to end her recording contract. With her voice, songwriting talent, and the backing of millions of fans, it was not long before Carey bounced back: in 2005 her ninth studio album, *The Emancipation of Mimi*, was the year's best-selling album in the United States and earned the singer three Grammys and rave reviews. In 2007 she received a star on the Hollywood Walk of Fame.

Pop artist/actor **Ricky Martin**, who was born in San Juan, Puerto Rico, in 1971, first took the music world by storm while performing as Little Ricky with the Puerto Rican group **Menudo** beginning in 1984 before sell-out crowds in the United States and Latin America. After touring with Menudo for five years, Martin left the group in 1989 to pursue a solo music (and acting) career, signing with Sony in 1990. In the 1990s, he put out such albums as *Ricky Martin* (1991); *Vuelve* (1998); and *Ricky Martin* (1999), which includes the singer's number one hit "Livin' la Vida Loca"; and by mid-1999 he had sold over thirteen million solo albums. Since 2000, he has released five more albums—*Sound Loaded* (2000), *La historia* (2001), *Almas del silencio* (2003), *Life* (2005), and *MTV Unplugged* (2006)—and has received many honors for his achievements, including his humanitarian efforts, through his Ricky Martin Foundation, to relieve the suffering of exploited children worldwide.

Another Puerto Rican pop star is **Marc Anthony**, who was born Marco Antonio Muñiz in New York City, has a passion for salsa, and has appeared in several motion pictures, among them **Martin Scorsese**'s *Bringing Out the Dead* (1999). In 1992 **Tito Puente** invited Anthony to perform as the opening act for his 100th Album Celebration Party at Madison Square Garden. Then came a trio of Spanish-language albums: *Otra Nota* (1993), with hit songs like "*El último beso*"; *Todo a su tiempo* (1995); and *Contra la corriente* (1997), which won the performer a Grammy for Best

Tropical Performance. In 1999 Marc Anthony made his English-language debut, releasing his triple-platinum, crossover LP, *Marc Anthony*. A hit from the album, "I Need to Know," earned the singer a Grammy for Song of the Year in 2000. Since then he has recorded a handful of albums, including *Libre* (2001), *Mended* (2002), *Amar sin mentiras* (2004), *Valió la pena* (2004), and *El cantante: Soundtrack* (2006).

Puerto Rican pop star **Carlos Ponce** also emerged in the 1990s. He began his career on the small screen, starring in commercials for Latin American audiences, hosting and producing the weekly program *Control*, which Univisión broadcasted, and starring as Renato in the television drama *Sentimientos ajenos*—a hit in Mexico and the United States. In 1997 Ponce signed with the recording label EMI Latin, and the following year, he released his debut album, *Carlos Ponce*, produced by Emilio Estefan Jr., and featuring the hits "*Decir adiós*" and "*Rezo*." Latin pop fans could not get enough, and the singer released *Todo lo que soy* (2000), followed by *Ponce* (2002). Carlos Ponce has never forgotten his love of acting. Since taking the pop music world by storm, he has appeared in myriad roles on the small and big screens, even starring as himself in the motion picture *Chasing Papi* (2003).

Multitalented superstar **Jennifer Lopez**—who was born in the Bronx, is of Puerto Rican parentage, and is known to her fans as J. Lo and La Lopez—has found fame as an actress on the small and silver screens *and* as a singer. In 1999 she delighted fans by releasing her debut album, *On the 6*, with its unique sound that she calls Latin Soul. In 2001 she put out *J. Lo*, which opened at the top of the Billboard 200, as did her *J to Tha L-O!: The Remixes* (2002), the world's best-selling remix album of all time. Then along came *This Is Me . . . Then* (2002), *Rebirth* (2005), and *Como ama una mujer* (2006), the singer's first completely Spanish album. In 2007 Jennifer Lopez topped *People en Español*'s "100 Most Influential Hispanics" list.

The year 1999 was also pivotal for multiplatinum pop singer **Christina Aguilera**. Having caught the music world's attention with her rendition of "Reflection" for the soundtrack of the 1998 Disney animated movie *Mulan*, she catapulted to fame with her first hit single, "Genie in a Bottle," from her 1999 album, *Christina Aguilera*. In 2000 the singer released two more albums, *Just Be Free* and *Mi reflejo*, and won the Grammy for Best New Artist. In 2001 she won a Latin Grammy for Best Female Pop Vocal Album for *Mi reflejo* and was nominated for two Grammys, one for her duet with Ricky Martin, "Nobody Wants to Be Lonely," and the other for her remake (with other singers) of **Patti La-Belle**'s "Lady Marmalade" for the soundtrack to the film *Moulin Rouge*. In 2002 she released her second studio album, *Stripped*, and began toying with her persona, rendering it more provocative, causing rumors to fly that she was bisexual. The year 2006 brought the release of her third studio album, *Back to Basics*, which debuted in the number one spot on the Billboard chart and hit number one in thirteen countries in all.

Latin pop/rock singer and songwriter **Shakira**, who is Colombian and Lebanese and was born Shakira Isabel Mebarak Ripoll in Barranquilla, Colombia, in 1977, caught the attention of the Latin music scene with the release in 1995 of her album *Pies descalzos*, which had several hit singles. In 1998 she began to work closely with Gloria Estefan and Emilio Estefan Jr., who produced her highly successful album *¿Dónde están los ladrones?* This partnership gave rise to Shakira's multiplatinum English-language crossover album, *Laundry Service* (2001), which established her as a Latin music superstar in mainstream America. Shakira has been especially prolific since 2002, releasing five albums: *Laundry Service (Washed and Dried)* (2002), *Grandes exitos* (2002), *Live & Off the Record* (2004), *Fijación oral, Vol. 1* (2006), and *Oral Fixation, Vol. 2* (2006). She is the recipient of three Grammys and thirteen Latin Grammys, seven of which she was awarded in 2006.

Other Latino singers and music groups who enjoy quite a following include Puerto Rican pop star **Chayanne**, who was one of *People* magazine's "Fifty Most Beautiful People" for 1993 and has recorded nine Spanish-language albums; the hard-hitting Puerto Rican pop quintet the **Barrio Boyzz**, who got together in 1991, perform everything from soul to R & B and hip-hop, and have two platinum Spanish-language albums and a number of hits on the Latin charts; the Mexican American folk/rock/Tejano band **Los Lobos**, which began as Los Lobos del Este de Los Angeles in 1973, has since released over twenty albums and captured a handful of Grammys, including one for "Mariachi Suite" on the soundtrack album to the film *Desperado*, and is still going strong; Mexican American **Flaco Jiménez**, the leading exponent of authentic South Texas conjunto and a winner of several Grammys, who, along with **Freddy Fender** and others, belonged to the Tejano supergroup the **Texas Tornados** in the 1990s and who has jammed with musicians of all kinds, from the **Rolling Stones** to **Bob Dylan** and **Linda Ronstadt**, in addition to recording his own music for the Texas *norteño* crowd; and Grammy winner **"Little Joe" Hernandez**, who helped pioneer Tejano music and who, in a career spanning over four decades, has cut over forty albums, including *Timeless* (1986), which spent over a year on Billboard's Latin chart. Others are Puerto Rican jazz trumpeter and bandleader **Charlie Sepulveda**; Puerto Rican jazz trumpeter **Humberto Ramirez**; and dance-pop and freestyle music artist **Judy Torres**, who remains one of the most celebrated freestyle performers of all time.

Is Plácido Domingo the only Latino opera star?

Plácido Domingo, who was born in Madrid to parents who were zarzuela performers, was raised in Mexico, and resides in New York City, is certainly the Latino superstar of opera. Known as the "king of opera," he sings in every major opera house in the world; has sung 119 roles, more than any other tenor in opera history; has produced over one hundred recordings, ninety-seven of which are full-length operas; has captured nine Grammys; and has made over fifty videos and three theatrically released films. Other Latinos have also earned a place in the pantheon of great opera singers, among them Puerto Rican baritone **Justino Diaz**, who debuted at the New York Metropolitan Opera as Monterone in Verdi's *Rigoletto* in 1963 and performed in major opera houses around the world until he retired in 2003. Puerto Rican tenor **César Hernández** and mezzo-soprano **Dulce Reyes** have also made their mark in the world of opera.

What about classical musicians?

World-famous Chilean pianist **Claudio Arrau**, lauded for his interpretations of Beethoven's piano music, resided in New York City from 1941 until his death in 1991. Among the most noteworthy Latino classical musicians on the stage today are Chilean-born flutist **Viviana Guzmán**; Chilean-born cellist **Andrés Díaz**; and pianist **Santiago Rodriguez**, the first Cuban American classical musician to achieve prominence. Incidentally, Santiago Rodriguez, who began studying piano at age four, was sent, with a younger brother, to the United States by his parents after **Castro** seized control of Cuba. A New Orleans orphanage under the care of Catholic Charities took the brothers in, and the nuns kept up Santiago's music lessons—thanks to a note with such a request and money that his mother had concealed on the boys. Two years after arriving in the United States, ten-year-old Santiago Rodriguez made his concert debut with the New Orleans Philharmonic.

Among the world-class conductors is Uruguayan American **Gisèle Ben-Dor**. Highlights of her illustrious career include the posts of music director (1991–2000) and conductor emerita (2000–) of the Pro Arte Chamber Orchestra of Boston, music director (1994–2006) and conductor laureate (2006–) of the Santa Barbara Symphony Orchestra, associate conductor of the New York Philharmonic, and guest conductor with major orchestras and opera houses. Gisèle Ben-Dor is known not only for her sheer genius as a conductor, but for her efforts in promoting works by Latin American composers, who have not gotten the attention they deserve.

ON THE STAGE AND THE SILVER SCREEN

Who were the first Latino actors, and what roles did they play?

Ever since Mexican American heartthrobs **Ramón Novarro** and **Gilbert Roland** seduced moviegoers with their artful expressions and dashing good looks in the 1920s and 1930s; Mexican American actresses **Dolores Del Río** and **Lupe Vélez** captivated audiences in both silent films and talkies; and Cuban American **César Romero** played both villain and Latin lover from the 1930s to the 1960s, Latino actors have been romancing the silver screen.

In fact, early Hollywood pictures capitalized on the myth of the Latin lover—the notion that Latinos are more sensual, sultry, and sexy than Anglos. Of course, Hollywood also exploited other myths—that of the dirty, devious, lazy, or stupid Mexican, in countless cowboy movies, and of the shifty Latin with the thick Spanish accent, who finds himself in such "exotic" places as Argentina, Uruguay, and the South Pacific. While Latinos were often cast in these roles (which **Ricardo Montalbán** once summed up as the "laggard, lover, or bandit"), they also went to non-Latino actors, whose hair was dyed shoe-polish black and whose pencil-thin mustaches were made to look particularly suspect. (Take a look at **Paul Newman** as a Mexican renegade in the 1964 film *The Outrage*.)

Although such overt typecasting has gone the way of the silent screen, Hollywood continues to cast Latinos in stereotypical roles. Early in her career, Cuban American actress **Elizabeth Peña**, who played an abused wife in the 1987 motion picture *La Bamba* and has acted in about two dozen other large-screen films, told the *Los Angeles Times*, "I'm usually offered the roles of the prostitute, the mother with seventeen children, or the screaming wife getting beaten up." Tired of such typecasting, Peña turned down **Robert Redford**'s invitation to play a Mexican in the 1988 feature film *The Milagro Beanfield War*.

Latinos have faced much discrimination on the stage as well. Until the innovative theatrical director and producer **Joseph Papp** invited minorities to act in productions of his New York Shakespeare Festival in Central Park and his classical plays at the Public Theater, very few audiences had ever seen a Latino play a serious dramatic part, let alone one as monumental as Hamlet. Papp nurtured such brilliant Latino actors as **Raúl Julia** and **Martin Sheen**.

Why do Latinos hate Tonto?

In *The Lone Ranger*—which first aired on the radio on January 30, 1933, and then was adapted as a television series, a comic book series, a comic strip, and novels—the hero is a white man, a masked Texas Ranger, who imparts his wisdom to his Native American sidekick, Tonto, who is portrayed as a dimwit with only a partial command of English, in the way of Charlie Chan. Tonto's lack of brainpower is underscored by his very name, which is Spanish for "dopey" or "slow-witted." (So that audiences would not be offended, in Spanish-speaking countries, the character Tonto was renamed Toro, which means "bull" in Spanish.) To add insult to injury, this Apache or Potawatomi Indian—his tribe is unspecified on the television show, but his name suggests a mixed Native American and Mexican heritage—calls his boss Kemo Sabe, which some speculate is a corruption of the Spanish *quien mas sabe*, literally "he who knows best." The duo of the Lone Ranger and Tonto emblematizes the prejudice and insensitivity that Latino groups have been laboring to abolish for decades, both in Hollywood and in mainstream society.

Who are some other famous Latino actors and directors?

José Ferrer, who was born in San Juan, Puerto Rico, in 1909, was a highly revered stage and screen star. He began his career, which spanned nearly half a century, on the stage, landing his first starring role on Broadway in 1940, when he played the title role in the farce *Charley's Aunt*. The role of Iago in the legendary 1943 Broadway production of *Othello* followed, and later a part in the 1946 Broadway production of *Cyrano de Bergerac*, for which he won the first of five Tony awards of his career. In 1950 he became the first Latino to win an Oscar—for Best Actor for his performance as the romantic, long-nosed poet in the 1950 film version of *Cyrano de Bergerac*. In the coming years, Ferrer would win Tonys for directing stage productions; would direct films and appear in a slew of them, from **John Huston**'s *Moulin Rouge* (1952) to **Woody Allen**'s *A Midsummer Night's Sex Comedy* (1982); and would appear on the small screen, including in the television series *Columbo*.

Legendary actor, writer, and director **Anthony Quinn**, who was born in Chihuahua, Mexico, on April 15, 1915, and was raised in East Los Angeles, enjoyed a long and distinguished stage and screen career. In the early days, **Cecil B. De Mille** (whose daughter Quinn married) cast the actor as a bad guy or Indian, but later Quinn landed memorable roles in films such as *Viva Zapata!* (1952), *La Strada* (1954), *Lust for Life* (1956), *Lawrence of Arabia* (1962), and *Zorba the Greek* (1964). After six decades of acting, he was still delighting audiences in the 1990s with his performances in such films as *Only the Lonely* (1991) and *Last Action Hero* (1993). In all, the actor starred in one hundred feature films, winning Oscars for his performances in *Viva Zapata!* and *Lust for Life*. Anthony Quinn died on June 3, 2001. Before a public funeral service for the eminent actor, Mexican American actor **Edward James Olmos** spoke of Quinn's contributions: "His real gift was helping people who had no voice. His gift was creativity and giving . . ."

Since the early 1940s, Mexican American **Ricardo Montalbán**, who is probably best known for his starring role as the suave Mr. Roarke in the 1978–84 television series *Fantasy Island* and for his portrayal of the evil Khan in the film *Star Trek: The Wrath of Khan* (1982), has acted in scores of television shows and films, most recently as the voice of Head of Council in the computer-animated film *The Ant Bully* (2006). He is also credited with being among the first Latinos to land nonethnic roles in national TV commercials. Remember his "Corinthian leather" lines in the 1970s commercial for the Cordoba, Chrysler's luxury coupe? As it turns out, typecasting is what got the actor that first job with Chrysler. The company hired him because they needed a person with Spanish roots to enhance the "exotic" image of their luxury car, the Cordoba. Montalbán proved so talented that he served as a Chrysler spokesman for two decades, shedding the Latin image along the way.

Famed theatrical director **José Quintero**, who was born in Panama in 1924 and came to the United States to study medicine but began a love affair with theater instead, founded, with others, Circle in the Square theatre in Greenwich Village in the 1950s. It would emerge as off-Broadway's most important theater, igniting the off-Broadway movement, before it moved to Broadway in 1972. At Circle in the Square, Quintero staged more than a dozen of **Eugene O'Neill**'s plays, including the original Broadway production of *Long Day's Journey Into Night*, which opened in 1956 and garnered a Tony Award and the *Variety* award for the director. Quintero was the premier interpreter of O'Neill and contributed immensely to the writer's legacy. But he would, in the course of his career, direct over seventy stage productions by a wide variety of writers, among them **Noel Coward**, **Thornton Wilder**, **Truman Capote**, and **Tennessee Williams**. The world of theater mourned José Quintero's passing in 1999.

Dynamic stage actress **Chita Rivera**, who is Puerto Rican and Scottish (mostly), has been a shining star on Broadway for about half a century, that is, ever since being cast in 1957 in the role of Anita in the Broadway premiere of *West Side Story*. In 1984 she was honored with a Tony Award for Best Actress for her performance in *The Rink*, and in 1993 she garnered another Tony for her acting in the Broadway hit *Kiss of the Spider Woman*. In 2002 she became the first Latina to collect the prestigious Kennedy Center Honors award, in recognition of her contributions to American culture. From late 2005 to early 2006, a seventy-two-year-old Chita Rivera performed on Broadway before packed houses in her autobiographical show, *Chita Rivera: The Dancer's Life*. Calling the show a "singing scrapbook" and a "must-have ticket for aficionados of the American musical," a *New York Times* reviewer wrote of its star on December 12, 2005, "She still has the voice, the attitude and—oh yes—the legs to magnetize all eyes in an audience."

Puerto Rican actress **Rita Moreno** made history as the first female performer and the second individual in history to receive all four of the most coveted awards in American entertainment. She won the Oscar for Best Supporting Actress in 1961 for her role as Anita in the screen version of the Broadway musical *West Side Story*, the Grammy in 1972 for her performance on the soundtrack album of the PBS children's show *The Electric Company*, the Tony in 1975 for her role as Googie Gomez in *The Ritz*, and the Emmy in 1977 for *The Muppet Show* and again in 1978 for an episode of *The Rockford Files*. (She has also been honored with a Presidential Medal of Freedom, in 2004; a star on the Hollywood Walk of Fame; and more.) Rita Moreno has been dazzling audiences since making her Broadway debut, at age thirteen, in *Skydrift*, starring **Eli Wallach**. In 2006 she was on the big screen in the romance *Play It By Ear*.

Puerto Rican actress and director **Miriam Colón** has done much on behalf of Latino actors. Among her greatest contributions is the creation, in Manhattan in 1967, of the world-renowned Puerto Rican Traveling Theatre, a bilingual theater located on West Forty-seventh Street, in the heart of Broadway. The Puerto Rican Traveling Theatre stages plays by Latinos and the classics; offers free performances in various venues around New York City and in New Jersey during the summer; provides an after-school arts education program for New York City's low- to moderate-income minority students; and has a Playwrights Unit, featuring writers' workshops, staged readings, and staged workshop productions. After moving to New York in 1954, Miriam Colón worked on stage, appearing in numerous off-Broadway and Broadway productions; on the small screen, making 250 guest appearances, primarily as a Mexican woman in Westerns, from 1954 to 1974; and on the big screen, appearing in such films as *One-Eyed Jacks* (1961) and *The Appaloosa* (1966) (opposite **Marlon Brando** in both), **John Sayles**'s *Lone Star* (1996), *All the Pretty Horses* (2000), and the *Goal!* trilogy (2005–07). In 1993, she was honored with the OBIE Award for Lifetime Achievement in the Theater.

Bolivian American **Raquel Welch**, who was born Raquel Tejada, was America's premier sex symbol in the pre-feminist 1960s and 1970s, when she starred in numerous feature films and television shows that capitalized on her physical features, not her acting ability. She was finally lauded for her acting talent in the early 1980s, when she appeared in the Broadway musical *Woman of the Year*. Raquel Welch has appeared more recently in *Tortilla Soup* (2001), *Legally Blonde* (2001), and *Forget About It* (2006).

The 1970s saw the rise of talented comedian and actor **Freddie Prinze**, who was born Frederick Karl Pruetzel in New York City in 1954 and called himself "Hungarican" because he was half–Puerto Rican and half-Hungarian. (Some say that his father was actually German, not Hungarian.) Freddie Prinze is best remembered for his costarring role as Chico, a Mexican American, in one of the first TV sitcoms with a Latino bent, NBC's smash hit *Chico and the Man*, which premiered in 1974. Tragically, Prinze ended his life three years later. Mexican American comedian and actor **Richard "Cheech" Marin**, who, with **Tommy Chong**, was awarded a Grammy for the comedy album *Cheech & Chong's Wedding Album*, also cowrote and starred in a handful of highly successful Cheech and Chong movies in the late 1970s and early 1980s. **Edward James Olmos**, whose tough-cop role as Lieutenant Martin Castillo in the popular 1980s television series *Miami Vice* made him an overnight success, is one of Tinseltown's busiest actors and directors. On the big screen, Olmos has starred in such films as *Stand and Deliver* (1988), *My Family, Mi Familia* (1995), and *Selena* (1997), about slain Mexican American Tejano music star **Selena Quintanilla Pérez**. (*My Family, Mi Familia* and *Selena* were written and directed by **Gregory Nava**, a Mexican American, who also directed the 1983 feature film *El Norte*).

Puerto Rican–Basque actor **Hector Elizondo**, who was born in New York in 1936, got his start off-Broadway and first achieved success when he won an OBIE Award for his role as God, in the guise of a Puerto Rican steam-room attendant, in the off-Broadway comedy *Steambath* in 1971. He has appeared in dozens and dozens of films and television movies and shows over the years, and is perhaps best known for his performances in *Pretty Woman* (1990) and *Runaway Bride* (1999) and for his starring role in *Tortilla Soup* (2001). **Raúl Julia**, another highly talented Puerto Rican actor, is remembered not only for his marvelous stage performances on Broadway and off, including as a leading actor with the New York Shakespeare Festival (**Joseph Papp** helped jump-start his career), but also for his spectacular acting in such films as *Eyes of Laura Mars* (1978), *Kiss of the Spider Woman* (1985), *Tango Bar* (1988), *Presumed Innocent* (1990), *The Addams Family* (1991), and *Addams Family Values* (1993). Millions mourned the actor's untimely death on October 24, 1994. At a memorial tribute held in his honor at the Joseph Papp Public Theater in Manhattan's East Village, **Meryl Streep** said of the actor, "He emanated exuberant joy."

Jimmy Smits, who is of Surinamese Dutch and Puerto Rican ancestry, rose to fame with his performances over many seasons in the popular TV series *L.A. Law* (1986–1994) and *NYPD Blue* (1993–2005). In 1990 he was awarded an Emmy for Outstanding Supporting Actor in a Drama Series for the former, and in 1995 he won a Golden Globe for Best Actor in a Television Series (Drama) for the latter. Later he starred in the final two seasons of the television serial drama *The West Wing* (1999–2006). On the big screen, Smits has acted in such films as *My Family, Mi Familia* (1995) and *Price of Glory* (2000). Academy-Award winner **Benicio Del Toro**, who was born in San German, Puerto Rico, in 1967, got his start as a guest star on the TV series *Miami Vice*, in an episode that first aired in 1987. He can be seen on the big screen in over thirty films, including *The Usual Suspects* (1995), *Snatch* (2001), *The Pledge* (2001), and *21 Grams* (2003). His many awards include an Oscar for Best Supporting Actor in 2001 for his performance in Steven Soderbergh's *Traffic*. Puerto Rican actor **Esai Morales** first made a splash in Hollywood as **Ritchie Valens**'s half brother in the motion picture *La Bamba* (1987) and later appeared on the big screen in such films as *My Family, Mi Familia* (1995) and *Fast Food Nation* (2006). For eight seasons, he played Lieutenant Tony Rodriguez in the TV police drama *NYPD Blue* (1993–2005), a role that brought him much attention. Puerto Rican entertainer **Ricky Martin** has been lauded for his talent as an actor as well as a musician. Highlights of his acting career include a role on the television soap *General Hospital* in the years 1994–95 and a role on Broadway, as the romantic lead in *Les Miserables* in 1996.

Puerto Rican actress, singer, and comedian **Liz Torres**, who started out doing comedy and singing in New York City's nightclubs with **Bette Midler** and was later the opening act for **Liza Minnelli**, **Tony Bennett**, **Helen Reddy**, and other stars, has acted and made guest appearances in numerous television series, perhaps most notably *All in the Family* in 1976 and 1977, *Murphy Brown* in 1992, *Ally McBeal* in 1998, and *ER* in 2003. She has also appeared in several feature films, including *A Million to Juan* (1994). African, Cuban, and Puerto Rican actress and singer **Irene Cara**, best known for her singing of movie themes, skyrocketed to fame with her performance of the song "Fame" (which she cowrote) in the 1980 blockbuster film with the same name. She went on to dazzle listeners with the song "Flashdance . . .What a Feeling," which she cowrote for the 1983 film *Flashdance* and which earned her an Oscar in 1983 for Best Original Song and a Grammy in 1984 for Best Pop Vocal Performance. Since "Fame," she has recorded seventeen motion picture theme songs. In 2004 the American Film Institute included "Fame" and "Flashdance . . . What a Feeling" in its list of top motion picture theme songs, "AFI's 100 Years . . . 100 Songs: America's Greatest Movie Music."

Two Puerto Rican actresses who catapulted to fame in the early 1990s are **Rosie Pérez** and **Jennifer Lopez**. Rosie Pérez has appeared on the small screen, including in episodes of the situation comedy *Frasier* in 1995 and 2004 and in the TV film *Lackawanna Blues* (2005), and she has starred in such motion pictures as *Do the Right Thing* (1989), *White Men Can't Jump* (1992), *It Could Happen to You* (1994), and *Riding in Cars with Boys* (2001). She was nominated for an Academy Award for Best Supporting Actress in 1994 for her performance in the 1993 film *Fearless*. Jennifer Lopez, nicknamed J. Lo and La Lopez, is a much-sought-after, multitalented superstar whose career got into gear when she played one of the acclaimed Fly Girls on the 1990–94 TV comedy series *In Living Color*. She achieved fame with her starring role as singer Selena Quintanilla Pérez in the 1997 motion picture *Selena* and her superb acting in *Out of Sight* (1998). Audiences saw her on the big screen again in 2002 in the motion picture *Enough*, and since then she has starred in a number of films, among them Gregory Nava's *Bordertown* (2006).

Ofelia González was honored with six awards for best actress for performances in theater, film, and television before coming to America from Cuba in 1971. (In Cuba she was cast in what is perhaps Cuban director **Tomás Gutiérrez Alea**'s most famous film, *Memorias de Subdesarrollo* [Memories of Underdevelopment, 1968].) A year after her arrival in the United States, she joined Repertorio Español, New York City's preeminent Spanish-language theater company, which was founded in 1968 by producer **Gilberto Zaldivar** and artistic director **René Buch** to showcase the best of Spanish, Latin American, and Latino theater. She remains a member to this day. Another Cuban-born actor is **Andy García**, who has earned enthusiastic applause for his performances in such films as *The Untouchables* (1987), *The Godfather: Part III* (1990), *Steal Big Steal Little* (1995), *Desperate Measures* (1998), *Ocean's Eleven* (2001), *The Man from Elysian Fields* (2001),

Modigliani (2004), and *The Lost City* (2005), which he directed and coproduced.

One of Hollywood's most prolific actors is **Martin Sheen**, whose father emigrated from Spain to America by way of Cuba, whose mother fled Ireland during the Irish War of Independence (1919–1921), and who was born **Ramón Gerardo Antonio Estévez**. Highlights of his career, which was launched on the stage in 1959, include lead roles on the big screen in **Francis Ford Coppola**'s 1979 film *Apocalypse Now* and in *Gandhi* (1982), and on the small screen in NBC's hit political drama *The West Wing* (1999–2006). Martin Sheen should also be credited for spawning a whole new generation of Latino actors—his own sons, **Charlie Sheen** and **Emilio Estevez**, both top box-office draws. **Charlie Sheen** has appeared in dozens of feature films, including *Platoon* (1986), *Wall Street* (1987), and *Being John Malkovich* (1999), and in the TV sitcoms *Spin City* (1996–2002), for which he earned a Golden Globe in 2002, and *Two and a Half Men* (2003–present). **Emilio Estevez** has captivated audiences in such films as *St. Elmo's Fire* (1985), *The Breakfast Club* (1985), *The Mighty Ducks* (1992), *D2: The Mighty Ducks* (1994), *D3: The Mighty Ducks* (1996), and *Sand* (2001). The year 2006 saw the release of *Bobby*, a Golden Globe Award–nominated film that he wrote and directed.

Another Cuban American actor to take the world by storm is **Cameron Diaz**, who was born in 1972; began her career as a fashion model; then, without ever having taken an acting lesson, landed the female lead in the motion picture *The Mask* (1994), also starring **Jim Carrey**. She later captured roles in such films as *My Best Friend's Wedding* (1997), *There's Something About Mary* (1998), *Being John Malkovich* (1999), *Shrek* (the voice of Princess Fiona, 2001), *Vanilla Sky* (2001), *Shrek 2* (2004), *In Her Shoes* (2005), and *The Holiday* (2006).

Colombian-born actor, comedian, writer, and producer **John Leguizamo**, who is of Colombian and Puerto Rican descent, earned an Obie Award and an Outer Critics Circle Award in 1991 for his one-man off-Broadway comedy *Mambo Mouth*, in which he plays seven different Latino characters. His second one-man show, *Spic-O-Rama*, in which he poked fun at Latino stereotypes and which he staged in 1993, netted him a Drama Desk Award. Leguizamo's performances in the 1993 motion pictures *Super Mario Brothers* and *Carlito's Way* made him a household name. Since then, he has appeared in numerous films; produced or coproduced nearly a dozen others; acted on the small screen, including in the television drama *ER*; appeared on Broadway in another of his comedies, *Sexaholix*; written a fascinating and funny autobiography, *Pimps, Hos, Playa Hatas, and All the Rest of My Hollywood Friends: My Life* (2006); and much more.

Since the mid-1970s, Mexican American **Lupe Ontiveros** has played in dozens of television programs, including in the award-winning television series *Desperate Housewives* (as Juanita Solis, Gabrielle's intrusive mother-in-law), and in such groundbreaking films as *El Norte* (1983), *My Family, Mi Familia* (1995), and *Selena* (1997). **Julie Carmen** has garnered resounding applause for her acting in such motion pictures as *The Milagro Beanfield War* (1988), *Fright Night Part 2* (1988), *The Penitent* (1988), **Michael Mann**'s Emmy-nominated *Drug Wars: The Cocaine Cartel* (1992), and *King of the Jungle* (2000).

Mexican American heartthrob **Mario Lopez** first garnered attention in 1989, when he appeared on the small screen as A. C. Slater, an athletic student, in the television teen sitcom *Saved by the Bell*. After his five-year run on *Saved by the Bell*, Lopez hosted Animal Planet's highly popular show *Pet Star*, cohosted *ESPN Hollywood*, and much more. In 2006 he took the dance floor as the celebrity contestant opposite professional dancer **Karina Smirnoff** in the third season of ABC's *Dancing with the Stars*, making it all the way to the final round of competition. Another Latino heartthrob is **Benjamin Bratt**, who is half-Peruvian. He became a household name in 1995, his first of five seasons as New York City homicide detective Reynaldo Curtis in the television police and legal drama *Law & Order*. Bratt has also starred in a slate of Hollywood films, most notably *Traffic* (2000), *The Next Best Thing* (2000), *Miss Congeniality* (2000), and *Catwoman* (2004).

Honduran American **America Ferrara**, who was born in Los Angeles in 1984, is the latest Latina actress to travel the road to stardom. She is the ugly duckling lead of the wildly popular ABC melodrama/comedy *Ugly Betty*, which premiered in 2006 and was adapted from the highly successful Colombian *telenovela* (soap opera) entitled *Yo soy Betty la fea*. Ferrara made her motion picture debut in the indie *Real Women Have Curves* (2002), costarring Lupe Ontiveros, then landed a role in a 2002 episode of *Touched by an Angel*, the films *The Sisterhood of the Traveling Pants* (2005) and *Lords of Dogtown* (2005), and the 2005 off-Broadway production *Dog Sees God: Confessions of a Teenage Blockhead*. In 2005 she was the recipient of a Movieline Breakthrough Award.

Among the hundreds of other Latinos and Latinas who have

made inroads in Hollywood, or are just now taking Tinseltown by storm, are **Jessica Alba, Jay Hernandez, Laura Elena Harring, Jacqueline Obradors, Clifton Collins Jr., Elpidia Carrillo, Eva Mendes, Roselyn Sanchez, Talisa Soto, Michael DeLorenzo, Tony Plana** (of *Ugly Betty* fame), **Freddy Rodríguez, Wilmer Valderrama, Rosa Blasi, Judy Reyes, Jamie-Lynn Sigler, Christina Vidal, Lisa Vidal, Lauren Vélez, Loraine Vélez, Alexis Bledel, Zoë Saldana, Aimee Garcia**, and **Michael Peña**.

Who are the Latino dancers?

The scores of Latino dancers include Cuban American **Fernando Bujones**, one of the finest classical dancers of the twentieth century and one the *New York Times* proclaimed in 1988 "the greatest American male dancer of his generation." Bujones made his professional dancing debut in 1970 with the Eglevsky Ballet in New York, joined American Ballet Theatre in New York City in 1972, and in 1974 captured the prestigious gold medal at the Seventh International Ballet Competition in Varna, Bulgaria—the Olympics of dance—the first American dancer to win the coveted award. Until he retired as a dancer in 1995, Bujones took the stage as a guest artist with over sixty companies, danced with many of the twentieth century's greatest ballerinas, and performed for **President Reagan** at the White House in 1985. After he retired from the stage, Bujones devoted himself to directing ballet companies, choreographing, and teaching. His untimely death at age fifty, in 2005, came as an enormous and unexpected blow to the ballet world. At the time, he was artistic director of Orlando Ballet.

Among other Latinos in the world of ballet are Cuban-born **Lourdes Lopez**, who retired as a principal dancer with the New York City Ballet in 1997; Puerto Rican–Navajo Indian **Jock Soto**, who retired as a principal dancer with the New York City Ballet in 2005; **Beatriz Rodriguez**, a former principal with the Joffrey Ballet of Chicago; Argentinean-born **Paloma Herrera**, a principal dancer with the American Ballet Theatre since 1995; Cuban-born **Jose Manuel Carreño**, a principal dancer with the American Ballet Theatre, who joined the company in 1995; Cuban-born **Xiomara Reyes**, a soloist with the American Ballet Theatre since 2001; Colombian-born **Flavio Salazar**, a member of the American Ballet Theatre's corps de ballet since 1993; Uruguayan-born

Maria Riccetto, a member of the American Ballet Theatre's corps de ballet since 1999; and many, many more.

All of these dancers follow in the footsteps of a great master: **José Limón** (1908–72), who emigrated from Mexico to America in 1915, went to New York in 1928 to become a painter, and there emerged instead as one of the world's greatest modern dancers and choreographers. In 1946 Limón formed the José Limon Dance Company and set about choreographing prodigiously and imparting his genius to the next generation of dancers. In 1996 the New York Public Library for the Performing Arts staged a major retrospective exhibition about the dancer and choreographer, *The Dance Heroes of José Limón*. Dancers and ballerinas on the stage today also inherited the mantle from Chilean-born **Lupe Serrano**, who in 1953 became the first Latino named a principal dancer at the American Ballet Theatre. Before retiring in 1971, she was elevated to prima ballerina and danced over fifty roles.

It must be mentioned that since its founding in 1970 by artistic director **Tina Ramirez**, the Ballet Hispanico School—which offers a unique curriculum in classical ballet, modern dance, and traditional Spanish dance—has been a nurturer of Latino talent. Some of its alumni go on to dance in the Ballet Hispanico Company, which performs works by leading Latino choreographers.

Who are the Latino comedians?

Award-winning stand-up comedian **George Lopez**, a Mexican American who grew up in California's San Fernando Valley, has a huge following, especially among Latinos, who appreciate his humorous insights about Latino life. After years on the comedy stand-up circuit, in 2002 Lopez cocreated, wrote, produced, and starred in the hit ABC sitcom *The George Lopez Show*, which remains on the air. Over the years, Lopez has released four albums of recorded stand-up comedy routines, including *Alien Nation* (1996), *Right Now Right Now* (2001), and *Team Leader* (2004). In 2007 *People en Español* selected George Lopez for its "100 Most Influential Hispanics" issue.

Mexican American stand-up comedian **Paul Rodriguez** is known for tackling ethnic stereotypes head-on. Born in Mexico and raised in East Los Angeles, he sharpened his comedic skills as a doorman at the Comedy Store, L.A.'s legendary comedy club, and got his big break doing warm-up on **Norman Lear**'s single-season television sitcom *Gloria* (1982–83). Lear liked what he heard and developed a sitcom for Rodriguez, *a.k.a. Pablo* (1984). After a few more comedy series and feature films, the comedian finally made it to the big time with his talk show *El Show de Paul Rodriguez*, which ran for four seasons. In 1994 fans saw him on the big screen in *A Million to Juan*, which he cowrote and directed; and more recently, in *Tortilla Soup* (2001) and *The World's Fastest Indian* (2005). Throughout his career, Rodriguez has showcased his humor on cable television, including in *Paul Rodriguez: Behind Bars* in 1991.

Who are some well-known Latino television hosts and news commentators?

Puerto Rican journalist and talk show host **Geraldo Rivera** is one of the most recognized faces in the media. He got his start as a reporter for WABC-TV's *Eyewitness News* in New York City in 1970 and later served as a chief reporter on *20/20*. In 1987 Rivera launched his own nationally syndicated daytime talk show, *Geraldo* (in 1996 the name was changed to *The Geraldo Rivera Show*), which ran until 1998. In 1994 he began hosting *Rivera Live*, a nighttime program on CNBC that dealt with issues in the news. Rivera left the show just a few months after the September 11, 2001, terrorist attacks to become a war correspondent for the Fox News Channel. After some controversy over his battlefield reporting, in 2003 he launched *At Large with Geraldo Rivera*, which ended in late 2005, when he began his latest syndicated show, *Geraldo at Large*. In recent times, he has also made frequent appearances on the Fox News Channel news shows *Hannity & Colmes* and *The O'Reilly Factor*. Geraldo Rivera is the recipient of many Emmy Awards, among numerous other honors.

Emmy Award–winning journalist **Jackie Nespral**, a Cuban American, earned the distinction of being the first Latino to anchor a network news program when NBC selected her in 1991 to coanchor its *Weekend Today* show. After three years of shuttling back and forth between Miami and New York, Nespral signed on as a news anchor for WTVJ-TV, the NBC affiliate in South Florida. Another Latina to reach the upper echelons of broadcast journalism is **Elizabeth Vargas**, who is of Puerto Rican and Irish American parentage. Among her numerous posts, she has served as a substitute cohost and anchor of NBC's *Today* show (1993–96), a correspondent for *Dateline NBC* (1993–96), a news anchor for

ABC's *Good Morning America* (1996–97), a correspondent and coanchor for ABC's *20/20* (1997–2004 and 2004, respectively), and a host of ABC's *20/20 Downtown* (1999–2002). In the first five months of 2006, she coanchored, with **Bob Woodruff**, ABC's evenings news broadcast, *World News Tonight*—delivering the news solo after her coanchor was seriously injured while reporting from Iraq on January 29, 2006. Currently, she coanchors ABC's *20/20*.

In the 1990s, Mexican-born **Giselle Fernandez** covered international news stories and major events for CBS and NBC, substituting for Dan Rather on the *CBS Evening News*; contributing to CBS's *Sunday Morning*, *Face the Nation*, and *48 Hours*; anchoring NBC's weekend edition of the *Today* show and the Sunday edition of *NBC Nightly News*, and much more. For her outstanding efforts, she was honored with five Emmys. From 1996 to 1998, she cohosted NBC's entertainment news program *Access Hollywood*, and in 2001 she returned to KTLA in Los Angeles, where she was once a coanchor and reporter, to coanchor the *KTLA Morning News*. Currently, she is president of her own production company and copresident of F Squared Productions, where she is engaged in developing film and television projects. Other award-winning Latino correspondents or anchors of national news programs are ABC news correspondent **Jim Avila**, who often anchors *World News Saturday*, **Arnold Diaz** of ABC's *20/20*, **Soledad O'Brien**, coanchor of CNN's *American Morning*, **Rick Sanchez** of CNN, and **John Quiñones** of ABC News.

Cuban American **Cristina Saralegui** is a household name among over one hundred million Spanish speakers in the United States and worldwide, who tune in to her Spanish-language television program, *El Show de Cristina*, and her radio show, *Cristina Opina*, and read her monthly magazine, *Cristina: La Revista*. In 1991 *El Show de Cristina*, which first aired in 1989, became the first Spanish-language talk show to capture an Emmy. *El Show de Cristina* has remained the *número uno* talk show on Spanish-language television, with nearly four thousand shows in the can, and it has received eleven Emmys (as of 2006). Among her many other honors, in 2005, *Time* magazine selected Cristina as one of America's twenty-five most influential Hispanics, and that very year, she became the first Latina to be inducted into the *Broadcasting & Cable* Hall of Fame, joining such icons as **Walter Cronkite**, **Johnny Carson**, and **Barbara Walters**. She is also the first Spanish-language television personality to receive a star on the Hollywood Walk of Fame. Over the years Cristina has made guest appearances on a number of television shows, including the popular family comedy *The George Lopez Show*.

Cuban-born television host and model **Daisy Fuentes** launched her television career in 1986, at age nineteen, as a news reporter and evening news anchor for the New York station WXTV. Before long, MTV discovered her and invited her to host its weekly syndicated Spanish-language video program *MTV Internacional*. During her six years with MTV, she also played on the ABC daytime drama *Loving*. In 1994 and 1995, Fuentes hosted her own talk show as a member of CNBC's *Talk All-Stars*. From 1998 to 2000, she cohosted, with **John Fugelsang**, the ABC television program *America's Funniest Home Videos*. In the course of her career, Daisy Fuentes has also appeared on the cover of such magazines as *Vanidades*, *Cosmopolitan*, and *Latina*, and has been a spokesmodel for American Express, Revlon, Pantene, and other companies.

Cuban American **Bob Vila** established the genre of home improvement television with the premiere of *This Old House* on PBS in 1979. He hosted the popular show until 1989, when he began hosting the nationally syndicated program *Bob Vila's Home Again*, renamed *Bob Vila* in 2005. Through his television programs, his many books on home design and historic homes, and his Web site, Bob Vila has taught audiences over the years everything from installing copper gutters to designing a wheelchair-accessible kitchen.

WRITERS AND ARTISTS

Who's writing the books?

Latino writers did not catch the attention of mainstream America until rather recently. It all started when Colombian writer **Gabriel García Márquez** stunned readers worldwide with his *One Hundred Years of Solitude* (1970), written in a surrealistic style known as "magical realism." This style had been established years before in Latin America by my father, **Lino Novas Calvo**, author of *El negrero*, a novel about the African slave trade in the Americas, among other works.

Once acquainted with the Latin spirit, mainstream American readers wanted more. It did not take them long to find the Latino writers in their midst, such as **Carlos Castaneda**, the Peruvian-born anthropologist who has penned nine books based on his training in Native American shamanism, involving hallucinatory states of consciousness he claims to have experienced with a Yaqui sorcerer named Don Juan Matus. These include *The Teachings of Don Juan: A Yaqui Way of Knowledge* (1968), *A Separate Reality: Further Conversations with Don Juan* (1971), and *Journey to Ixtlan: The Lessons of Don Juan* (1972). Castaneda, who captivated American readers (especially the antiestablishment) in the 1960s and 1970s, vanished into thin air in the 1980s (few know what he looks like), but his books are still selling well (by 1996 he had sold eight million copies in seventeen countries).

The publication of Cuban American **Oscar Hijuelos**'s Pulitzer Prize–winning second novel, *The Mambo Kings Play Songs of Love*, in 1989—and its transformation into the Hollywood motion picture *The Mambo Kings* in 1992—ushered in an era of widespread recognition for Latino writers, which has been gaining momentum ever since. Many works by Latinos nowadays crowd the shelves in libraries and bookshops, large and small, across America.

Among the Latina novelists, short story writers, and poets (and their most celebrated works) are **Chantel Acevedo**, *Love and Ghost Letters* (2005); **Kathleen Alcalá**, *Spirits of the Ordinary: A Tale of Casas Grandes* (1998), *The Flower in the Skull* (1999), and *Treasures in Heaven* (2000); **Isabel Allende**, *The House of the Spirits* (1982), which was made into a 1993 motion picture and has been translated into over two dozen languages, *Paula* (1995), *Aphrodite: A Memoir of the Senses* (1998), *Daughter of Fortune* (1999), *Zorro* (2005), and *Inés of My Soul* (2006); **Julia Alvarez**, *How the García Girls Lost Their Accents* (1991), *In the Time of the Butterflies* (1994), *¡Yo!* (1997), *In the Name of Salomé* (2000), and *Saving the World* (2006); **Marie Arana**, *American Chica: Two Worlds, One Childhood* (2002) and *Cellophane* (2006); **Elena Castedo**, *Paradise* (1990); **Ana Castillo**, *The Mixquiahuala Letters* (1986), *Loverboys: Stories* (1996), and *I Ask the Impossible: Poems* (2001); **Sandra Cisneros**, *The House on Mango Street* (1984), *Woman Hollering Creek and Other Stories* (1991), and *Caramelo* (2002); **Margarita Engle**, *Skywriting* (1995); **Rosario Ferré**, *The House on the Lagoon* (1995) and *Flight of the Swan* (2001); **Montserrat Fontes**, *Dreams of the Centaur* (1996); **Cristina Garcia**, *Dreaming in Cuban* (1993), which the *New York Times* selected as one of the best novels of that year, *The Agüero Sisters* (1998), and *Monkey Hunting* (2004); **Demetria Martinez**, *Mother Tongue* (1994) and *Confessions of a Berlitz-Tape*

Chicana (2005); **Ana Menéndez**, *In Cuba I Was a German Shepherd* (2001) and *Loving Che* (2003); **Himilce Novas**, *Mangos, Bananas and Coconuts: A Cuban Love Story* (1996) and *Princess Papaya* (2004); **Judith Ortiz Cofer**, *The Line of the Sun* (1989), *The Latin Deli* (1995), *Reaching for the Mainland & Selected New Poems* (1995), and *The Meaning of Consuelo* (2004); and **Helena María Viramontes**, *The Moths and Other Stories* (1985) and *Under the Feet of Jesus* (1995).

Among the Latino novelists, short story writers, and poets, and their most celebrated works (in alphabetical order) are **Oscar Zeta Acosta**, author of *The Autobiography of a Brown Buffalo* (1972) and *The Revolt of the Cockroach People* (1989); **Aldo Alvarez**, *Interesting Monsters* (2001); **Rudolfo Anaya**, *Bless Me, Ultima* (1972), *Tortuga* (1979), and *Albuquerque* (1995); **H. G. Carrillo**, *Loosing My Espanish* (2004); **Carlos Castaneda**, *Journey to Ixtlan: The Lessons of Don Juan* (1972); **Daniel Chacón**, *Chicano Chicanery: Short Stories* (2000); **Junot Díaz**, *Drown* (1996); **Ernesto Galarza**, *Barrio Boy* (1971); **Guy Garcia**, *Skin Deep* (1988) and *Obsidian Sky* (1994); **Oscar Hijuelos**, *The Mambo Kings Play Songs of Love* (1989), *The Fourteen Sisters of Emilio Montez O'Brien* (1993), *Mr. Ives' Christmas* (1995), *Empress of the Splendid Season* (1999), and *A Simple Habana Melody* (2002); **Tato Laviera**, *AmeRícan* (1985); **Jaime Manrique**, *Latin Moon in Manhattan* (1992), *Twilight at the Equator* (1997), and *Our Lives Are the Rivers* (2006); **Alejandro Morales**, *The Brick People* (1988) and *The Rag Doll Plagues* (1991); **Miguel Piñero**, *Short Eyes* (1975); **Ernesto Quiñonez**, *Bodega Dreams* (2000); **John Rechy**, *City of Night* (1963), *Numbers* (1967), *The Coming of the Night* (1999), and *The Life and Adventures of Lyle Clemens* (2003); **Edward Rivera**, *Family Installments: Memories of Growing Up Hispanic* (1982); **Tomás Rivera**, *And the Earth Did Not Devour Him* (1971); **Pedro Juan Soto**, *Spiks* (1973); **Virgil Suárez**, *Going Under* (1996); **Piri Thomas**, *Down These Mean Streets* (1967) and *Seven Long Times* (1974); **Sergio Troncoso**, *The Last Tortilla & Other Stories* (1999) and *The Nature of Truth* (2003); **Ed Vega**, *Mendoza's Dreams* (1987); **José Antonio Villarreal**, *Pocho* (1970) and *The Fifth Horseman* (1974); and **Victor Villaseñor**, *Rain of Gold* (1991) and *Crazy Loco Love: A Memoir* (2006).

THIRTY-THREE IMPORTANT BOOKS WRITTEN BY LATINOS

1. John Rechy, *City of Night* (1963)

2. Piri Thomas, *Down These Mean Streets* (1967)

3. José Antonio Villarreal, *Pocho* (1970)

4. Tomás Rivera, *And the Earth Did Not Devour Him* (1971)

5. Rudolfo Anaya, *Bless Me, Ultima* (1972)

6. Carlos Castaneda, *Journey to Ixtlan: The Lessons of Don Juan* (1972)

7. Oscar Zeta Acosta, *The Autobiography of a Brown Buffalo* (1972)

8. Nicholasa Mohr, *Nilda* (1973)

9. Pedro Juan Soto, *Spiks* (1973)

10. Miguel Piñero, *Short Eyes* (1975)

11. Alfredo Mirandé and Evangelina Enríquez, *La Chicana: The Mexican-American Woman* (1979)

12. Gloria Anzaldúa and Cherríe Moraga, eds., *This Bridge Called My Back: Writings by Radical Women of Color* (1981)

13. Edward Rivera, *Family Installments: Memories of Growing Up Hispanic* (1982)

14. Cherríe Moraga, *Loving in the War Years* (1983)

15. Sandra Cisneros, *The House on Mango Street* (1984)

16. Helena María Viramontes, *The Moths and Other Stories* (1985)

17. Isabel Allende, *The House of the Spirits* (1982)

18. Ana Castillo, *The Mixquiahuala Letters* (1986)

19. Oscar Hijuelos, *The Mambo Kings Play Songs of Love* (1989)

20. Judith Ortiz Cofer, *Silent Dancing: A Partial Remembrance of a Puerto Rican Childhood* (1990)

21. Julia Alvarez, *How the García Girls Lost Their Accents* (1991)

22. Sandra Cisneros, *Woman Hollering Creek and Other Stories* (1991)

23. Victor Villaseñor, *Rain of Gold* (1991)

24. Richard Rodriguez, *Days of Obligation: An Argument with My Mexican Father* (1992)

25. Cristina Garcia, *Dreaming in Cuban* (1993)

26. Esmeralda Santiago, *When I Was Puerto Rican* (1993)

27. Demetria Martinez, *Mother Tongue* (1994)

28. Montserrat Fontes, *Dreams of the Centaur* (1996)

29. Himilce Novas, *Mangos, Bananas and Coconuts: A Cuban Love Story* (1996)

30. Sandra Cisneros, *Caramelo* (2002)

31. Marie Arana, *American Chica: Two Worlds, One Childhood* (2002)

32. Ana Menéndez, *Loving Che* (2003)

33. Richard Rodriguez, *Brown: The Last Discovery of America* (2003)

Who's painting the pictures?

While Latino artists have yet to achieve the visibility they deserve, as the *New York Times* observed in 2006, they have, nonetheless, over the decades engaged fervently in the creation of art and, in the process, have enriched art's millennia-old dialogue with their unique sensibilities and perspectives, much to the delight of the global art establishment, art critics, and art appreciators.

One of the greatest Latino artists is Venezuelan-born sculptor **Marisol** (Marisol Escobar), who attained enormous notoriety in the 1960s and 1970s. While she was influenced by pop artists **Andy Warhol** and **Roy Lichtenstein**, and others, her style was unique. In her early work, she created small figurines from bronze, terra-cotta, and wood, but in 1961 she began to integrate drawing, painting, and objets trouvés into large-scale assemblages, which, at their core, are three-dimensional portraits of public figures, family members, and friends, some rather satirical. Marisol's works are on exhibit at the National Gallery of Art, the Metropolitan Museum of Art, the Museum of Modern Art in New York City, the Museum of Contemporary Art in Chicago, and elsewhere. She has served as an inspiration to the new crop of Latino artists practicing their craft in America today.

Cuban-born artist **Ana Mendieta** (1948–85)—who was sent by her parents into exile in the United States in 1961, soon after **Castro** seized control of Cuba—was at once a sculptor, earth artist, conceptual artist, performance artist, photographer, filmmaker, and feminist and managed in her rather short life to make quite a significant artistic contribution. The immateriality of 1970s conceptual art resonated with her, and a good deal of her art involved outdoor performances and site-specific sculptures constructed of elemental things—such as fire, water, earth—and meant to disappear. Oftentimes, only the artist and a photographer witnessed the works, and so much of what remains of her art takes the form of mere slides, negatives, photographs, and short films. Mendieta's work influenced generations of artists who, following in her footsteps, continue to explore gender and identity themes. In 1985, at age thirty-six, she fell to her death from her Greenwich Village apartment in New York City. Her husband, sculptor **Carl Andre**, was thrice indicted on a murder charge in her death, but he was acquitted, despite what prosecutors perceived as a trail of damning evidence that he pushed her out the window. Since her death, several retrospective exhibitions of her art have been mounted, including at the New Museum of Contemporary Art in New York in 1987 and at the Whitney Museum of American Art in 2004.

Another Latino artist whose career was cut short by tragedy was **Jean-Michel Basquiat** (1960–88). Of Haitian and Puerto Rican parentage, Basquiat was born in New York City and started out as a graffiti artist. In 1980 he began exhibiting his canvases, depicting skeletal figures and faces, automobiles, buildings, police, and other urban images, alongside other artists, including **Keith Haring**. By 1982 he had aligned himself with the artistic movement neo-expressionism, which was a reaction to the minimalist and conceptual art of the 1970s and returned recognizable objects, such as the human form, to the canvas. In 1983 Basquiat began what would be a close friendship with Andy Warhol, with whom he created a number of collaborative works, and in 1985, having achieved international success, he made the cover of the *New York Times Magazine*. Sadly, he succumbed to a heroin overdose in his studio loft in 1988, which some have attributed to the depression the artist experienced after the death of Andy Warhol in 1987.

Other Latino artists whose works hang at leading American galleries and museums are internationally renowned Mexican American sculptor **Luis Jiménez**, who created, until he died in a freak accident in his studio in 2006, larger-than-life works—from bronze, fiberglass, and plastic—of cowboys, dancers, and workers; Mexican American **Rupert García**, who played a prominent role in the Chicano art movement of the late 1960s and early 1970s, and in the civil rights movement and the Vietnam War protests, and who first garnered widespread attention with his political posters delving into the themes of politics, race, and the Vietnam War; Mexican American narrative artist **Carmen Lomas Garza**, who paints everyday Mexican American life, drawing on her childhood memories of South Texas, and who has authored three children's books; and Mexican American **Charlie Carrillo**, who is considered the leading contemporary New Mexican *santero*, or maker of religious artifacts (which are nowadays collected as art).

Others are Brooklyn-born **Juan Sánchez**, through whose mixed-media paintings and installations the theme of Puerto Rican independence runs; Puerto Rican artist **Pepón Osorio**, whose large-scale multimedia installations explore Latino culture; **Arturo Cuenca**—considered one of Cuba's most prominent young artists before he emigrated to the United States in 1989—who creates painting, sculptures, and installations using photographic and cinematic techniques; **German Pérez**, a Dominican American artist whose canvases vibrate with primary colors and the flavor of the Caribbean; Argentinean American sculptor **Susana Jaime-Mena**, whose works combine painting and sculpture and have been exhibited extensively; **Jorge Tacla**, a Chilean-born New York artist who creates—on cloth, jute, paper, and canvas—paintings of real and imaginary trips, deserts, New York culture, and classical architecture, often incorporating graphic elements; and Peruvian-born **Kukuli Velarde**, the recipient of the Anonymous Is a Woman Award in 2000 and a PEW Fellowship in 2003, who creates clay sculptures and mixed-media installations that reflect Peru's indigenous culture and its "violent encounter" with foreign cultures, and the cultural hybridization that resulted.

A PASSION FOR FASHION

Who are some Latino fashion designers?

One of the world's top fashion designers is **Oscar de la Renta**, who was born in the Dominican Republic. In his youth he went to Spain to study painting but was drawn to design and began sketching for prominent Spanish fashion houses, which eventuated in an apprenticeship with Cristóbal Balenciaga, Spain's most prestigious couturier. De la Renta made his way to New York in 1963 to design the couture collection for Elizabeth Arden. Two years later, he launched his signature ready-to-wear label and went on to create a billion-dollar international clothing business, headquartered in New York. It nowadays runs the gamut from haute couture to ready-to-wear and from ties to fragrances. In the years 1993–2002, he designed the haute couture collection for the classic house of Pierre Balmain, becoming the first American designer to design for a French couturier. Throughout the years, Oscar de la Renta has contributed to the wardrobes of first ladies **Nancy Reagan**, **Hillary Clinton**, and **Laura Bush**. His designs are as coveted in the new millennium as in the old: in 2002 he set a Bergdorf Goodman record with his $2.5 million in sales at a trunk show for his fall collection. Among his numerous honors, Oscar de la Renta was inducted into the Coty Hall of Fame in 1973, was awarded the Gold Medal of Bellas Artes from the king of Spain in 1990, and received the Council of Fashion Designers of America (CFDA) Lifetime Achievement Award in 1990 and the CFDA Womenswear Designer of the Year Award in 2000.

Cuban-born **Adolfo Sardina** (known to the world simply as Adolfo) immigrated to the United States in 1948, worked as an apprentice millinery designer at Bergdorf Goodman in Manhattan, and opened his own New York salon in 1962, early on designing hats for some of the most prominent women in society, including **Betsy Bloomingdale**, **Gloria Vanderbilt**, **Babe Paley**, and **Lady Bird Johnson**. In the 1980s, he was the favorite designer of First Lady **Nancy Reagan**. In 1993 Adolfo closed his Fifth Avenue salon and retired from designing to focus his efforts on licensing ventures. Over the years, he has licensed his name for furs, handbags, fragrances, shoes, men's clothing, and more.

Isabel Toledo, who was born in Cuba in 1961 and came to the United States at age five, first took the fashion scene by storm in the mid-1980s. Designated one of the "100 Designers that Count Around the World" by *Women's Wear Daily*, she has won applause for her remarkable designs that combine fabrics and strong shapes to create an air of elegant whimsy as well as novel architectural style. Her designs are for sale at exclusive stores, such as Bergdorf Goodman and Barneys in New York. On some of her designs, Isabel Toledo has collaborated with her husband, Cuban American fashion illustrator/artist **Ruben Toledo**, whose fashion drawings, watercolors, and pen-and-ink portraits fill the pages of the volume *Ruben Toledo: Fashionation* (2006). Together, the two run Toledo Studio. Their collaborative relationship was chronicled in an exhibition entitled Toledo/Toledo: A Marriage of Art and Fashion, which ran at the Fashion Institute of Technology in New York City. A companion book to the exhibition was published in 1999. In 2005 Isabel Toledo and Ruben Toledo received the Cooper-Hewitt National Design Award for Fashion Design. In 2006 Anne Klein, a division of Jones Apparel Group, Inc., chose Isabel Toledo as its new creative director of the Anne Klein Designer Collection.

Venezuelan-born fashion designer **Carolina Herrera** relocated her family to New York in 1980 and established her own design firm, Carolina Herrera, Ltd., divisions of which include a signature fashion collection, bridal collection, accessories collection, color cosmetics, and fragrances. Herrera has built a tremendous following. In her later years, **Jacqueline Kennedy Onassis** considered her one of her favorite designers. Carolina Herrera is the recipient of many fragrance awards and the 2004 CFDA Women's Designer of the Year Award. Another designer with roots in South America is Chilean-born **Maria Cornejo**, who enjoys an international reputation as a designer of women's wear. Upon graduating from Ravensbourne College of Design in London in 1984, she started the Richmond Cornejo line with designer **John Richmond**. It did well, and in 1987 Cornejo launched her own line. After working as a design consultant and then designing for Tehen in Paris, she settled in New York in

1996, where, a year later, she launched her Zero line, which has been described as minimal, architectural, modern, and feminine all at the same time. In 2006 Maria Cornejo was presented with the Cooper-Hewitt National Design Award for fashion design.

Noteworthy Latino design talents who arrived on the fashion scene in the 1990s include Mexican American **David Rodriguez**, who launched his first collection in 1997 and in 1999 received the Moët & Chandon Designer Debut Award; Mexican American **Marisol Deluna**, a women's clothing and textile designer and the founder of Deluna By Design, Inc., who, since 1997, has designed a line of handbags, scarves, and ties under her own label, Marisol Deluna New York; Cuban American **Narciso Rodriguez**, who began his career in 1985 as a design assistant at Anne Klein and then at Calvin Klein, launched his own label in 1998, and took the fashion world by storm with the bridal dress he designed for **Carolyn Bessette**, for her wedding to **John F. Kennedy Jr.**; Puerto Rican shoe designer **Edmundo Castillo**, nowadays the head designer for Sergio Rossi shoes, who designed footwear for Donna Karan and then, in 1999, began designing his own line of women's shoes, and in 2001 received the CFDA's Perry Ellis Award for Accessories; and Dominican-born **Lourdes Atencio Libman**, who is based in Miami and who is a favorite designer of the first lady of the Dominican Republic and numerous celebrities.

Who is Cesar Pelli?

A designer, too—but of buildings. In 1991 the American Institute of Architects (AIA) named **Cesar Pelli** one of the nation's ten most influential living architects. Pelli, who was born in Argentina in 1926 and immigrated to the United States in 1952, was the first Latino to earn such a distinction. Among his many other distinctions, in 1995 he was awarded the AIA Gold Medal for his architectural contributions. Some of the buildings he has designed are the United States Embassy in Tokyo (1972); the Pacific Design Center in Los Angeles (1972); the World Financial Center and Winter Garden at Battery Park in New York City (1981–87); Canary Wharf tower in London (1986); the Aronoff Center for the Arts in Cincinnati (1991); the Petronas Towers in Kuala Lumpur, Malaysia, the world's tallest buildings (1998); the Goldman Sachs Tower, in Jersey City, New Jersey (2004); the Cira Centre in Philadelphia (2005); and the National Museum of Contemporary Art in Osaka, Japan (2005).

Incidentally, the World Financial Center's Winter Garden, a grand, 45,000-square-foot space, sustained severe damage to its east side during the September 11, 2001, terrorist attack on the World Trade Center. The restoration of the Winter Garden included replacing two thousand glass panes, which comprise about 70 percent of the ceiling; the marble flooring; and half of the grand staircase. In addition, the North Bridge, the spacious pedestrian bridge that connected the World Trade Center to the World Financial Center, was demolished in the attack. It was replaced with glass windows.

ON THE CUTTING EDGE OF SCIENCE AND TECHNOLOGY

Who are the great Latino scientists?

Puerto Rican **Antonia Coello Novello**, a specialist in pediatric nephrology, held one of the highest posts in the National Institutes of Health before **President George Bush** (senior) appointed her the nation's first woman and first Latino U.S. surgeon general in 1990. During her tenure as surgeon general from 1990 to 1993, Antonia Novello did much to draw attention to the health issues of the country's constituencies that have historically been neglected—namely, women, children, and minorities. From 1993 to 1996, Novello served as the United Nations Children's Fund (UNICEF) special representative for health and nutrition, and in 1996 she was appointed visiting professor of health policy and management at the Johns Hopkins School of Hygiene and Public Health. In 1999 she became commissioner of health for the State of New York, a post she holds to this day.

Luis W. Alvarez (1911–88) was one of the world's leading scientists in the field of elementary particle physics. During World War II, Alvarez took part in the Manhattan Project, which developed and constructed the world's first nuclear weapons and detonated three, two of them over Japan. During this period, he also worked on the development of radar as it relates to aviation, designing a system that facilitates the safe landing of aircraft in poor visibility conditions. Among his many distinctions, in 1968 Alvarez was honored with the Nobel Prize in Physics for developing a liquid hydrogen bubble chamber that allowed scientists to observe more subnuclear particles than ever before. Called the "wild idea man," he holds over forty patents and was inducted into the National Inventors Hall of Fame in 1978. In 1980 Luis Alvarez, his son **Walter Alvarez**, a respected field geologist, and two chemists proposed the asteroid-impact theory to explain the high levels of iridium in the sedimentary layers at the Cretaceous-Tertiary boundary all over the world. Since iridium is extremely rare in the earth's crust but plentiful in meteorites, the Alvarez team deduced that an asteroid must have hit the earth at the time of the Cretaceous-Tertiary boundary, the consequence of which was a mass extinction of species, including the dinosaurs.

Mexican American physicist **Alberto Baez**, the father of singer **Joan Baez**, moved forward the field of X-ray imaging optics. While a graduate student at Stanford in 1948, he developed, with Stanford professor **Paul Kirkpatrick**, the first X-ray microscope, the Kirkpatrick-Baez X-ray microscope. The imaging technique they generated is still in use, particularly in medicine and in astronomy, to take pictures of the galaxies. Another leading Latino physicist is Guatemalan American **Victor Pérez-Mendez** (1923–2005), a specialist in particle and nuclear physics, medical physics, and radiation detection, who worked in various divisions of the University of California from 1955 to 1995. Among his many contributions, he was part of a small team of scientists at Lawrence Berkeley National Laboratory who developed, in the 1990s, an electronic method of x-raying teeth that delivers a much lower dosage of X-ray radiation to patients compared to conventional methods. He holds several patents, including one for an apparatus and method for improving particle detector spatial resolution.

In 1980 leading primatologist **Richard Wrangham** sent samples of a leaf that he discovered chimpanzees in Tanzania chewing—despite its unpleasant taste—to Mexican American biochemist **Eloy Rodriguez**. When analyzing the leaf, Dr. Rodriguez uncovered compounds that hinder the growth of particular disease-causing parasites. With that discovery, he pioneered a whole new field—zoopharmacognosy, the study of how animals medicate themselves by carefully selecting and ingesting, or otherwise utilizing, plants, insects, and soils, to prevent or treat disease. This field has enormous significance because these plants may potentially be used to treat humans. Eloy Rodriguez, who in his youth picked cotton as a migrant farmworker, is a professor at Cornell and one of few Latinos to hold an endowed chair in science at an American university.

The first Latino to travel into the cosmos was Costa Rican American **Franklin R. Chang-Diaz**, a physical scientist who was selected by NASA in 1980 and took part in seven NASA space flights before retiring in 2005. The first Latina in space was Mexican American **Ellen Ochoa**, who was selected by NASA in 1990 and is a veteran of four NASA space flights, the last of which was the thirteenth space shuttle mission to visit the International Space Station in April 2002. She currently directs NASA's Astronaut Office and Aircraft Operations. The other Latino members of the NASA astronaut corps are Mexican American **Sidney M. Gutiérrez**, a veteran of two space flights, who retired from NASA in 1994 and joined Sandia National Laboratories; Argentinean-born **Fernando "Frank" Caldeiro**, class of 1994; Peruvian-born **Carlos I. Noriega**, class of 1995; **Christopher "Gus" Loria**, class of 1996; **John D. Olivas** and **George D. Zamka**, class of 1998; and Mexican-born **José M. Hernández** and **Joseph M. Acaba**, class of 2004.

Latinos are also hard at work at NASA in other capacities besides space flight. **Adriana Ocampo**, a planetary geologist who was born in Colombia and raised in Argentina, has been a research scientist at NASA's Jet Propulsion Laboratory since 1973. She worked on NASA's *Viking* mission to explore Mars and was also a science coordinator for the *Galileo* mission to Jupiter. In addition to working on planetary missions, Adriana Ocampo began studying the Chicxulub impact crater in 1988, which scientists believe was formed when an asteroid the size of a small city slammed into the earth sixty-five million years ago, causing the extinction of the dinosaurs—just as Luis Alvarez and Walter Alvarez had proposed in 1980. Ocampo was the first to realize that a ring of sinkholes discovered near the present-day village of Chicxulub on the Yucatán Peninsula was associated with the impact crater. As chief scientist at NASA from 1993 to 1996, **France Anne Córdova** worked on various satellite projects, including the Hubble Space Telescope. In 1996 she was awarded NASA's highest honor, the Distinguished Service Medal. That same year she was appointed a professor of physics and vice chancellor for research at the University of California, Santa Barbara, a post she held until 2002, when she was named chancellor of the University of California, Riverside.

TAKE ME OUT TO THE BALL GAME . . . BOXING RING . . . TENNIS COURT

Is soccer número uno *among Latinos?*

Of all professional sports, baseball is the all-time Latino favorite. But soccer runs a close second. Latin Americans who immigrated to America after World War II brought with them their love of soccer, or *fútbol,* and the sport grew in popularity in Latino neighborhoods across the country. Nowadays many Latinos, young and not so young, play in weekend soccer leagues, organized games in their neighborhoods, and the occasional *cascarita* (pickup game). Newer immigrants especially love to watch international matches on television and cheer for the old country and their favorite players.

Thanks to Latinos (and newer immigrants from Europe), soccer began to catch on in mainstream America around the mid-1990s. And thanks also to Latinos, the U.S. soccer team has garnered more respect abroad since 1994, the year five Latinos, **Marcelo Balboa**, **Fernando Clavijo**, **Hugo Perez**, **Tab Ramos**, and **Claudio Reyna**, helped steer the U.S. team to the second round in World Cup play, a feat that stunned the international soccer world. Nowadays there are many Latino players in Major League Soccer, the U.S. professional soccer league.

Who are the Latino baseball legends, and who are the great players of today?

Latinos' love of baseball dates all the way back to pre-Columbian times, when the native Taino and Siboney peoples of the Caribbean played a similar game with a wooden stick and a ball, a game the Spanish colonizers and Africans adopted. The game of baseball as we know it today developed in North America in the eighteenth century and is undoubtedly based on cricket and rounders, two English games. Baseball achieved popularity in the United States by the mid-nineteenth century, around the time that the first organized team, the Knickerbocker Baseball Club, was formed in New York.

One of the earliest Latino achievers in baseball—and one of the sport's greatest players—is Hall of Famer **Vernon "Lefty" Gómez**, a left-hander of Mexican descent, who pitched in the major leagues for fourteen years (1930–43). As a New York Yankees pitcher in the 1930s, he helped lead the Yanks to seven pennants and five World Series championships. Gómez's World Series record of six wins without a loss still stands. Another of his records that has gone unchallenged for decades is his record five starts and three wins (1933, 1935, 1937) in All-Star game competition. Gómez twice won the pitching version of the Triple Crown, in 1934 and 1937, leading the American League in wins, ERA, and strikeouts. In 1972 Vernon "Lefty" Gómez became the second Latino player inducted into the National Baseball Hall of Fame.

Perhaps the greatest Latino baseball legend is **Roberto Walker Clemente**. Born on August 18, 1934, in Carolina, Puerto Rico, Clemente joined the Pittsburgh Pirates in 1955 and spent his entire eighteen-year major league career with the team. He is considered one of baseball's finest outfielders and won National League batting titles in 1961, 1964, 1965, and 1967. Among his other distinctions, Clemente played in every All-Star game from 1960 to 1972, earned National League MVP honors in 1966, led the Pirates to world championships in 1960 and 1971, and batted .414 in the 1971 World Series. Roberto Clemente was as great a humanitarian as he was a baseball player. After a catastrophic earthquake shook Managua, Nicaragua, in December 1972, Clemente loaded up a cargo plane with supplies and set off to aid in the relief effort. Shortly after takeoff, the plane crashed, killing all on board. In homage to the great player, the Baseball Writers Association of America waived the five-year wait for induction for the second and last time in history and elected Roberto Clemente to the National Baseball Hall of Fame in 1973.

Baseball great **Orlando Cepeda** was unanimously voted National League Rookie of the Year in 1958, his first season with the San Francisco Giants, after hitting .312 with twenty-five home runs. Wearing the St. Louis Cardinals' uniform in 1967, he became the first player selected the National League's MVP by a unanimous vote since **Carl Hubbell** in 1936. During his seventeen-year career in the major leagues, Cepeda was a National League All-Star seven times. In 1999 he was inducted into the National Baseball Hall of Fame. Another baseball great is **Juan Marichal**, "the Dominican Dandy," who was born in the Dominican Republic. He pitched the San Francisco Giants to 191 victories in the 1960s, more than any other National League pitcher. Over sixteen seasons, he won 243 games and lost a mere 142. In

1983 Marichal became the first Dominican inducted into the National Baseball Hall of Fame.

Other Latinos who excelled in professional baseball in the 1960s, 1970s, and 1980s include Cuban American outfielder **Tony Oliva**, who won the American League batting title three times while with Minnesota from 1962 to 1976. **Lou Piniella** had a stellar decade-long career with the Yankees before retiring from play in 1984. In 1990, as Cincinnati Reds manager, Piniella steered the team to a World Series victory. After his last year with the Reds, in 1992, he first managed the Seattle Mariners (1993–2002), molding the team into one with play-off potential and capturing the American League Manager of the Year Award in 1995 and 2001, and then the Tampa Bay Devil Rays (2003–05). In October 2006, Piniella signed on to manage the Chicago Cubs. Cuban American infielder **Tony Pérez**, who played mostly with the Cincinnati Reds from 1964 to 1986, was a National League All-Star seven times. His 1,652 career RBIs are the most in major league history by a player with Latin American roots. Perez was inducted into the National Baseball Hall of Fame in 2000.

Panamanian-born **Rod Carew**, who immigrated to the United States in the early 1960s, played for the Minnesota Twins from 1967 to 1978 and for the California Angels from 1979 to 1985. He received the American League Rookie of the Year Award, was an All-Star in every season but his last, was the American League's MVP in 1977, accrued seven batting titles, and was elected to the National Baseball Hall of Fame in 1991. As a rookie pitcher in 1981, Mexican American pitcher **Fernando Valenzuela** helped the Los Angeles Dodgers capture their first World Series since 1965. "Fernandomania" hit Los Angeles and the nation. For his efforts that season, Valenzuela was awarded the Cy Young Award, the first rookie to receive pitching's highest honor. He was selected for the All-Star team from 1981 to 1986, and in 1986 the Dodgers issued him a $5.5 million contract, making him the highest-paid Latino in baseball at the time. Valenzuela remained with the Dodgers until the 1991 season and retired from baseball in 1997.

Other Latino baseball greats who made their mark in the 1980s and 1990s include **Keith Hernandez**, who won eleven consecutive Gold Glove awards and had a lifetime batting average of .296 in a career that lasted from 1974 to 1990; **Bobby Bonilla**, who was voted a member of the National League All-Star team six times during his sixteen seasons, which began in 1986, set the record for career home runs by a switch hitter, and helped the Florida Marlins capture the 1997 World Series; Cuban-born **José Canseco** of the Oakland Athletics, who was Rookie of the Year in 1986, became the first player to hit forty homers and steal forty bases in a single season, in 1988, and finished his career in May 2002 with 462 home runs, 1,407 RBIs, and 200 stolen bases; and **Edgar Martinez**, who made his major league debut in 1987 with the Seattle Mariners and remained with the team until retiring in 2004, and who some consider the greatest designated hitter in the annals of baseball.

By the mid-1990s, the Latino presence in the big leagues was extraordinary. In 1996, 17 percent of the players on major league rosters were Latino or Latin American. And the number of Latinos sporting major league baseball uniforms rose over the next decade: in 2005, Latinos and Latin Americans comprised 25 percent of major league rosters. The Latino presence on the baseball diamond will invariably continue to grow, as evidenced by the fact that in 2005 almost 50 percent of minor leaguers were Latino or Latin American. The majority of Latinos in baseball today are foreign born and have roots (in descending order) in the Dominican Republic, Puerto Rico, Venezuela, Cuba, Mexico, Panama, Nicaragua, Colombia, and Honduras.

While there are far too many to mention in these pages (see latinobaseball.com for a detailed account of Latinos in major league baseball), some of the top Latino players who debuted in the majors during the 1990s and the early years of the new millennium are Panamanian-born pitcher **Mariano "Mo" Rivera**, who began his career with the Yankees in 1995 and still plays for them, has helped the Yanks to four World Series titles (1996, 1998, 1999, and 2000), and as the all-time major league postseason leader in saves and ERA, has been called the greatest postseason relief pitcher in baseball history; Puerto Rican outfielder **Bernie Williams**, who debuted with the Yankees in 1991 and has played for them ever since, facilitated the Yankees' World Series victories in 1996, 1998, 1999, and 2000; was the ALCS MVP in 1996; became the first player to capture a batting title, a Gold Glove Award, and the World Series championship in a single season (1998); was an All-Star from 1997 to 2001; and won the Gold Glove Award four times (1997–2000); and Puerto Rican **Juan González**, who debuted with the Texas Rangers in 1989; won the American League's MVP Award in 1996; and played with

Detroit in 2000, Cleveland in 2001, and back with the Rangers in 2002, which marked the beginning of the end of his major league baseball career, due to injuries.

Others are Dominican pitcher **Pedro Martinez**, called the Strikeout King, who has played for the New York Mets since 2005, is one of the greatest pitchers of all time, has won three Cy Young Awards, and became a two-hundred-game winner in 2006; Dominican **Manny Ramirez**, who made his debut in the majors in 1993 with the Cleveland Indians, hit 165 RBIs in the 1999 season as he pursued **Hack Wilson**'s record, set in 1930, of 191 RBIs in a single season, has been an All-Star ten times (1995 and 1998–2006), and has played for the Boston Red Sox since 2001; and Dominican **Sammy Sosa**, who made major league history when, in 1998, he (and **Mark McGwire**) broke **Roger Maris**'s 1961 record of sixty-one home runs in a single season, in 1999 became the first baseball player ever to hit sixty homers in two seasons, and in 2000 became one of only three players in the annals of baseball (**Babe Ruth** and Mark McGwire are the others) to hit fifty home runs in three different seasons. Unfortunately, throughout his career, which ended in 2006, Sosa was embroiled in quite a bit of controversy.

One of the best all-around major league players is **Vladimir Guerrero**, who was born in the Dominican Republic in 1976, made his debut with the Montreal Expos in 1996, and now wears the uniform of the Los Angeles Angels of Anaheim. Dominican American **Alex Rodriguez**, who was born in Manhattan in 1975, played shortstop first with the Seattle Mariners (1994–2000), then the Texas Rangers (2001–03), before signing with the Yankees in 2004 as a third baseman. Four times he has led the American League in home runs, he's frequently been called the best all-around baseball player of the present day, and he signed the richest deal (as of 2006) in the history of sport: a ten-year, $252,000,000 contract. Another Dominican American player is **Albert Pujols**, who was born in the Dominican Republic, immigrated to the United States with his family in the early 1990s, debuted with the St. Louis Cardinals in 2001, and has often been cited as one of the game's best offensive players. In 2006 he became the first major league player to hit thirty home runs in each of his first six seasons and the first since **Ted Williams** to hit one hundred RBIs in his first six seasons. That same year, he received his first Gold Glove Award. Puerto Rican **Carlos Beltrán** played for the Kansas City Royals (1998–2004) and the Houston Astros

(2004), and has been with the New York Mets since 2005. He was the American League's Rookie of the Year in 1998, and in 2006 he won the National League Gold Glove and Silver Slugger awards. One of the most promising players in all of baseball is **José Reyes**, who was born in the Dominican Republic and debuted with the New York Mets in 2003. Many in the baseball world have called him the best shortstop in the game. In 2006, after a stellar season, he received the National League Silver Slugger Award for shortstops.

Who are the Latino stars on the tennis court?

Tennis is another sport in which Latinos have excelled, but not before breaking down the ethnic barriers on the court. Mexican American **Ricardo Alonso "Pancho" González**, who never took formal tennis lessons, was the first Latino to gain fame in the sport. He caught the attention of tennis fans in 1948, when he defeated **Eric Sturgess** in the U.S. National Championships at Forest Hills. Gonzáles clinched the same title again in 1949, the year he turned pro. Open tennis (professional tennis) was brand new then, and some tournaments, such as Wimbledon, were against it and did not allow pros to mix with amateurs. As a result, González was barred from playing in the world's premier tennis tournament while he was in his prime. Many believe that had he been allowed to compete regularly at Wimbledon, he would have captured many titles.

He did manage to compete once. In 1969, a year after open tennis came to Wimbledon, a forty-one-year-old González amazed the tennis world by defeating **Charles Pasarell** in a 112-game match lasting five hours and twelve minutes, what was then the tournament's longest match in history. While he may have been barred from Wimbledon, González, with his power serve and formidable court play, was still one of the world's greatest tennis players, as the cover of the June 16, 1958, issue of *Sports Illustrated* proclaimed him. In 1968 Pancho González was inducted into the International Tennis Hall of Fame. When he died on July 3, 1995, all of tennis mourned the passing of a hero.

Another tennis hero is Ecuadoran American **Francisco Olegario "Pancho" Segura**, whose legs were deformed by premature birth and diseases he suffered in childhood. Despite the odds, Segura excelled in tennis, turning pro in 1947. From 1950 to 1952, he won the U.S. Pro Championships, defeating Pancho González in the finals in 1951 and 1952. Open tennis arrived too late for Pancho Segura; he played in only one open tournament, the men's doubles of the first open Wimbledon. From the late 1960s to the mid-1970s, Segura coached **Jimmy Connors**, helping him clinch his first Wimbledon title in 1974. In 1984 Pancho Segura was inducted into the International Tennis Hall of Fame.

Among the top Latina tennis players is Salvadoran American **Rosemary Casals**, a distant relative of the cello virtuoso **Pablo Casals**, who won over ninety tournaments in a career that began in 1966. She and **Billie Jean King** dominated women's doubles in the late 1960s and early 1970s, capturing five Wimbledon women's doubles titles (1967–68, 1970–71, and 1973), the U.S. Championships doubles title in 1967, and the U.S. Open doubles title in 1971 and 1974, among others. Casals was instrumental in ridding tennis of sexism and gender inequality, which would enable women's tennis to flourish as a popular sport in the 1980s, 1990s, and beyond. In 1996 Rosemary Casals was inducted into the International Tennis Hall of Fame.

Among the beneficiaries of women tennis players' efforts in the 1970s to bring gender equality to professional tennis were such Latina players as Puerto Rican **Gigi Fernández**, one of the world's premier doubles players. She captured seventeen Grand Slam women's doubles titles, including the U.S. Open in 1990, the French Open in 1991, and the French Open, Wimbledon, and the U.S. Open in 1992, before retiring from the professional tennis circuit in 1997, the year she was named coach of the women's tennis team at the University of South Florida. Another is Dominican American **Mary Joe Fernández** (of no relation to Gigi), who made her first appearance at Wimbledon in 1986, at the tender age of fourteen, and won seven career singles titles and nineteen career doubles titles before retiring from the tour in 2000. At both the 1992 and 1996 Summer Olympics, she and partner Gigi Fernández captured a gold medal in women's doubles.

Who are some Latinos in the world of golf?

Mention the name **Lee Trevino**, one of the most venerated players in the history of golf, and sports fans smile. That's because the Mexican American player loves to crack jokes and chatter on the green, and because he has a heart of gold, rarely leaving a tournament he has won without donating a large portion of the prize to charity. Despite his good humor, Lee Trevino has never forgotten his rough early days. Born on December 1, 1939, in Dallas, Trevino rose from abject poverty to stun the golfing world at the U.S. Open in 1968, where he defeated **Jack Nicklaus**. In spite of his talent, when he played in the Masters, he was made to change his spikes outside the doors of country clubs, which looked down upon the minority player. Lee Trevino has won many titles and trophies in his illustrious career and continues to bring much excitement to the Senior PGA Tour.

Back in the days when Lee Trevino turned pro, virtually the only other Latino on the green was **Juan "Chi Chi" Rodríguez**, who was born on October 23, 1935, in Río Piedras, Puerto Rico. In 1963 Rodríguez captured his first PGA title at the Denver Open, but his career really peaked after he joined the Senior Tour in 1985. By 1993 he had won so many tournaments that he belonged to the $5 million club for overall earnings, whose members include golf legends Lee Trevino, Jack Nicklaus, and others. He continues to amaze the crowds at Senior tournaments, though in recent years he has played in a limited number of events. Over the course of his career, Rodríguez has also contributed to many philanthropies. In 1979 he founded the Chi Chi Rodríguez Youth Foundation, in Clearwater, Florida, which provides at-risk children with tutoring, vocational training, and a little bit of golf. He also underwrites college tuition for many high school graduates each year, and much more.

Mexican American **Nancy López** would later follow in the footsteps of Lee Trevino and Chi Chi Rodríguez and master a sport dominated by Anglo Americans—as well as break new ground for women athletes. López has shattered many records in her illustrious career. In 1978 she won a record five consecutive LPGA events and was named LPGA Rookie of the Year and Player of the Year, the only golfer to enjoy both distinctions in a single year. Thanks to her spectacular performance, attendance tripled for the LPGA Tour, and along with the fans came the media and corporate sponsorship, which women's golf so desperately needed. In 1989 López was inducted into the PGA / World Golf Hall of Fame. With forty-eight tournament and three majors victories, López made 2002 her last full-time season on the LPGA Tour. A great humanitarian, Nancy López is committed to many causes on behalf of children.

TWENTY-EIGHT GREAT LATINO ATHLETES

1. Bobby Bonilla (baseball)

This outfielder and slugger made the National League All-Star Team half a dozen times during his sixteen seasons, which began in 1986; set the record for career home runs by a switch hitter; and helped the Florida Marlins win the 1997 World Series.

2. José Canseco (baseball)

Canseco was Rookie of the Year in 1986 and the American League's Most Valuable Player in 1988, the year he became the first player to hit forty homers and steal forty bases in a single season. He retired in 2002 with 462 career home runs, 1,407 RBIs, and two hundred stolen bases.

3. Rosemary Casals (tennis)

Rosie Casals won over ninety tournaments, including five Wimbledon doubles titles, in the 1960s and 1970s, with Billie Jean King. She was inducted into the International Tennis Hall of Fame in 1996.

4. Orlando Cepeda (baseball)

Selected National League Rookie of the Year by a unanimous vote in 1958, in 1967 Orlando Cepeda became the first player to be unanimously voted the National League's MVP since Carl Hubbell in 1936. During his seventeen years in the majors, Cepeda was a seven-time National League All-Star. In 1999 he was inducted into the National Baseball Hall of Fame.

5. Roberto Clemente (baseball)

A sports legend and a humanitarian, Clemente played for the Pittsburgh Pirates from 1955 to 1972 and earned twelve Gold Glove awards. In 1973 he became the second Latino inducted into the National Baseball Hall of Fame.

6. Angel Cordero Jr. (horse racing)

This top jockey broke a record by winning the Kentucky Derby for the third time in 1985. In 1988 he became the first Puerto

7. Oscar De La Hoya (boxing)

Rican to be inducted into the National Thoroughbred Racing Hall of Fame.

Oscar De La Hoya won the only gold medal in boxing for America at the 1992 Summer Olympics and captured the world welterweight boxing championship in 1996 by defeating Mexican great Julio César Chávez. By May 2006, he had won thirty-eight professional bouts, with thirty knockouts, and had lost only four.

8. Donna De Varona (swimming)

Donna De Varona became the first Latino to win a gold medal in swimming when she captured gold in two events at the 1964 Summer Olympics in Tokyo.

9. Trent Dimas (gymnastics)

Dimas captured a gold medal at the 1992 Summer Olympics in Barcelona.

10. Mary Joe Fernández (tennis)

Competing in her first Wimbledon tournament in 1986, at the age of fourteen, she went on to win a gold medal in doubles with Gigi Fernández at the 1992 and the 1996 Summer Olympics.

11. Gigi Fernández (tennis)

The winner of numerous Grand Slam doubles titles, including the U.S. Open in 1990, the French Open in 1991, and the French Open, Wimbledon, and the U.S. Open in 1992, she took the gold in doubles at the 1992 and 1996 Summer Olympics.

12. Lisa Fernández (softball)

Lisa Fernández pitched the U.S. women's softball team to gold medals at the 1996 Summer Olympics in Atlanta, the 2000 Summer Olympics in Sydney, and the 2004 Summer Olympics in Athens.

13. Tom Flores (football)

Tom Flores made history by quarterbacking the Kansas City Chiefs to Super Bowl I in 1967. He achieved victory at the Super Bowl in the 1980s, first as head coach of the Oakland Raiders, in 1981, and then as head coach of the Los Angeles Raiders, in 1984.

14. Vernon Gomez (baseball)

As a New York Yankees pitcher in the 1930s, Gomez helped guide the Yanks to seven pennants and five World Series championships. His World Series record of six victories without a loss has gone unchallenged, as has his record five starts and three wins in All-Star game competition. Gomez twice won the pitching version of the Triple Crown, leading the American League in wins, ERA, and strikeouts. In 1972 he became the first Latino inducted into the National Baseball Hall of Fame.

15. Pancho González (tennis)

This legend of the court was victorious at the U.S. National Championships and the U.S. Clay Court Championships in 1948 and 1949. In 1969, at age forty-one, he stunned the tennis world by defeating Charles Pasarell in a 112-game match at Wimbledon. González was inducted into the International Tennis Hall of Fame in 1968.

16. Nancy López (golf)

After winning a record five consecutive LPGA events, Nancy López was named LPGA Rookie of the Year and the Player of the Year in 1978. She was inducted into the PGA/World Golf Hall of Fame in 1989. During the course of her illustrious career, she opened the door for Latinas and all women in golf.

17. Juan Marichal (baseball)

In the 1960s, Juan Marichal pitched the San Francisco Giants to 191 victories, more than any other National League pitcher. He won 243 games and lost just 142 during his sixteen years in the majors. In 1983 Marichal became the first Dominican inducted into the National Baseball Hall of Fame.

18. Pedro Pablo Morales (swimming)

Morales won a gold medal and two silver medals at the 1984 Summer Olympics in Los Angeles and garnered two more gold at the 1992 Summer Olympics in Barcelona.

19. Anthony Muñoz (football)

Drafted by the Cincinnati Bengals in 1980, Muñoz was elected to eleven consecutive Pro Bowls and was named All-Pro eleven consecutive times between 1981 and 1991. He played in two Super Bowls and was selected NFL Offensive Lineman of the Year in 1981, 1987, and 1988. In 1998 he became the first Latino inducted into the Pro Football Hall of Fame.

20. Derek Parra (speedskating)

Parra became the first Mexican American to win a Winter Olympics medal when he captured the silver in the 5,000-meter speedskate event at the 2002 Winter Games in Salt Lake City. Nine days later, he broke the world record in the 1,500-meter speedskate event and won Olympic gold.

21. Lou Piniella (baseball)

Rookie of the Year in 1969, Piniella helped the Yankees win the 1977 World Series by batting .333 in the series. After retiring in 1984, he managed first the Yankees, then the Cincinnati Reds, guiding the Reds to a World Series victory in 1990, and has been the Seattle Mariners' manager since 1993. Under Piniella's guidance, the Mariners made it to the American League Championship series in 2000 and 2001, losing to the Yanks both times.

22. Chi Chi Rodríguez (golf)

One of the first Latino pro golfers, Rodríguez's real success began in 1985, when he joined the Senior Tour. By 1993 he was victorious in so many tournaments that he belonged to the $5 million club for overall earnings. He continues to astound the crowds at Senior tournaments.

23. John Ruiz (boxing)

Ruiz turned pro in 1992 and defeated Evander Holyfield in 2001 to become the first Latino World Boxing Association heavyweight champion of the world. In the ensuing years, Ruiz lost and then regained the title several times, before losing it again at the end of 2005, to Nikolai Valuev. As of 2006, he was setting his sights on recapturing the heavyweight belt.

24. Alberto Salazar (running)	This distance runner crossed the finish line first at the New York Marathon in 1981, 1982, and 1983, and at the Boston Marathon in 1982. He also qualified for the U.S. Olympic team in 1980 and 1984.
25. Pancho Segura (tennis)	This tennis legend won the U.S. Pro Championships singles from 1950 to 1952 and the doubles in 1954 and 1956. He coached Jimmy Connors to his first Wimbledon title in 1974 and was inducted into the International Tennis Hall of Fame in 1984.
26. Sammy Sosa (baseball)	Sosa made major league history in 1998, when he shattered Roger Maris's record, set back in 1961, of sixty-one home runs in a single season. In 1999 Sosa became the first baseball player ever to hit sixty homers in two seasons, and in 2000 he became one of only three players in baseball history to hit fifty homers in three different seasons. His career, which ended in 2006, saw a fair share of controversy.
27. Lee Trevino (golf)	In 1971 this legendary golfer won the U.S. Open, the British Open, and the Canadian Open, a feat for which he was given many honors. He continues to enliven the green and exhilarate fans on the Senior Tour.
28. Fernando Valenzuela (baseball)	In 1981 Valenzuela became the first rookie to win the Cy Young Award. He played on the All-Star team from 1981 to 1986, and in 1986 the Dodgers signed him to a $5.5 million contract, making him the highest-paid Latino in baseball at the time.

Who are the Latino football players?

Football, a great American sport, has traditionally enjoyed only a small Latino fan base and attracted a meager number of Latino players, largely because football does not have much popularity in Latin American countries or among Latinos in the United States. In recent years, the NFL has made a conscious effort to change all that, seeking to tap into Latinos' ever-expanding purchasing power and sports talent. As part of this effort, the NFL now celebrates Hispanic Heritage Month by highlighting Latinos' contributions to professional football and offering in-stadium entertainment geared to Latinos. In 2005 the NFL launched a Spanish-language media blitz to promote football among Latinos, which included spots on Telemundo and ESPN Deportes, and in 2006 the league unveiled a newly revamped Spanish-language Web site, www.NFLatino.com, which contains the latest NFL and team news, Latino player diaries, information for football neophytes, and more. The NFL's efforts are beginning to pay off: While there were only seven Latinos, mostly kickers, in the NFL in 1989, and only twenty in 1999, according to NFLatino.com, the NFL boasted twenty-three Latinos in 2006, a growing pool of Latino NFL draft prospects, and more Latino fans.

The first Latino to play professional football was Cuban-born **Ignacio "Lou" Molinet**, who was a halfback for the Frankford Yellowjackets in the 1927 season, a fact that only resurfaced in the year 2000, when Molinet's granddaughter donated his NFL contract to the Pro Football Hall of Fame. The second was **Jesse Rodriguez**, who was a punter and fullback for the Buffalo Bisons in 1929. From 1929 until the NFL-AFL merger in 1970, only thirty Latinos played in the NFL (though more may come to light in the way of Ignacio Molinet). Among these is Mexican-born **Tom Fears**, a receiver with the Los Angeles Rams from 1948 through 1956, who led the NFL in receptions in each of his first three seasons with the Rams and was the first Latino to receive All-League honors (1949), to be elected to the Pro Football Hall of Fame (1970), and to become a head coach. (He coached the New Orleans Saints from 1967 to 1970.) Another is Minnesota Vikings quarterback **Joe Kapp**, a Mexican American, who steered the Vikings to their first divisional title and play-off game in 1968 and, in 1970, led the team to Super Bowl IV against the Kansas City Chiefs. In 1970 Kapp retired from football.

Another superb Latino player in the NFL in the 1960s, who was also the NFL's first Latino quarterback, was **Tom Flores**, the son of Mexican American farmworkers, who guided the Kansas City Chiefs to Super Bowl I in 1967, where they went down in defeat to Green Bay. Flores would later enjoy two Super Bowl victories, first as head coach of the Oakland Raiders, in 1981, and then as head coach of the Los Angeles Raiders, in 1984. He has had a profound impact on the world of football; in fact, his autobiography, *Fire in the Iceman*, is considered a classic.

Tom Flores was instrumental in the football career of Mexican American **Jim Plunkett**. The Heisman Trophy winner in 1970, Plunkett was the first Latino ever selected first overall in the NFL draft, when the then Boston Patriots chose him in 1971. He was an instant success, earning the title of NFL Rookie of the Year for his quarterbacking skills. With the superior coaching of Tom Flores, Plunkett led the Oakland Raiders to a 27–10 victory over Philadelphia in Super Bowl XV in 1980 and was named Most Valuable Player for his effort. He repeated his stellar performance in 1983, helping the Raiders defeat the Washington Redskins 38–9 in Super Bowl XVIII. In 1988 a shoulder condition forced Plunkett to retire from football. Another Latino to enter the ranks of professional football players in 1971 was **Lyle Alzado**. The former All-Pro lineman, who started with the Denver Broncos before joining the Cleveland Browns and then the Los Angeles Raiders, enjoyed scores of victories, including a Super Bowl win in 1984, with the Raiders. Alzado tragically succumbed to brain cancer in 1992, at the age of forty-two.

Another Latino player who exhilarated the fans in the 1980s was offensive lineman **Anthony Muñoz**, who was drafted as a first-round pick by the Cincinnati Bengals in 1980 and was designated a starter that very year. Muñoz was elected to eleven consecutive Pro Bowls and was named All-Pro eleven times in a row between 1981 and 1991. He took the field in two Super Bowls and was selected NFL Offensive Lineman of the Year in 1981, 1987, and 1988. In 1998 Anthony Muñoz was inducted into the Pro Football Hall of Fame. The 1980s also saw the rise of a whole dynasty of Latino pro kickers when five members of the **Zendejas** family made it into in the NFL. The most famous is probably **Tony Zendejas**, who spent most of his career (1985–95) kicking for the Oilers and the Rams. His brother **Marty** and cousins **Luis**, **Max**, and **Joaquin** also retired from successful careers in the sport.

Latinos who have contributed much to the sport of football since the 1990s include Mexican-Irish American **Jeff Garcia**, currently a Philadelphia Eagles quarterback, who was the starting quarterback for the San Francisco 49ers from 1999 to 2003, threw for a career-high and team-record 4,278 yards in 2000, and led the 49ers to the playoffs in the 2001 and 2002 seasons; and Detroit

Lions punter **Leo Araguz**, who joined the NFL in 1996 as an Oakland Raider, set an NFL record for punts in a game, with sixteen against the Chargers in 1998, and as of 2006 was a Baltimore Ravens veteran punter. The twenty-two other Latinos who played in the NFL in the 2006 season are **Tony Romo**, **Roberto Ortiz**, **Martín Gramática**, **Luis Berlanga**, **Joselio Hanson**, **Greg Camarillo**, **Antonio Garay**, **Ken Amato**, **Tony González**, **Richard Angulo**, **Adam Archuleta**, **Jason Babin**, **Rolando Cantu**, **J. P. Losman**, **Luis Castillo**, **Jorge Córdova**, **Ronnie Cruz**, **Donnie Edwards**, **Jeff Garcia**, **Marco Rivera**, **Roberto Garza**, and **Frank Davis**.

Who are some Latinos in other sports?

Boxing boasts a good number of Latino greats. Puerto Rican **Carlos Ortiz** is a boxing legend. He defeated **Joe Brown** to win the world lightweight title in 1962 and held on to it, for the most part, until 1968. Ortiz was inducted into the International Boxing Hall of Fame in 1991. Another legendary fighter is Puerto Rican **Wilfredo Benitez**, who was born in New York in 1958 and is known to his fans as El Radar. At age seventeen, Benitez became the youngest fighter to win a world title in the annals of professional boxing. Before leaving the sport, he reigned in three separate divisions and achieved an impressive 53-8-1 record with thirty-one knockouts. In 1996, at thirty-seven, Benitez became the youngest fighter to be inducted into the International Boxing Hall of Fame.

Nowadays Mexican American boxer **Oscar De La Hoya** and **John "the Quiet Man" Ruiz** are role models for young Latinos all across America who dream of fame in the ring. Oscar De La Hoya posted an amateur career record of 223 wins and just 5 losses, won gold at the 1992 Summer Olympics in Barcelona, and later that year made his professional debut. He totally dominated the welterweight division until he went down in defeat to **Felix Trinidad** on September 18, 1999, a fight that broke pay-per-view box office records. As of May 2006, he had won thirty-eight professional bouts, with thirty knockouts, and lost only four. He is the only boxer in the sport's history to capture world titles in six weight classes. Oscar De La Hoya is as talented a Latin pop singer as he is a boxer. In 2000 he released his debut album, *Oscar De La Hoya*, which hovered at the top of Billboard's Latin Dance charts for several weeks. A single from this Latin Pop album, *"Ven a mi,"* was nominated for a Grammy.

John "the Quiet Man" Ruiz, who turned pro in 1992, defeated **Evander Holyfield** in March 2001 to become the first Latino World Boxing Association (WBA) heavyweight champion. That same year, the magazine *Hispanic Business* ranked Ruiz among the one hundred most influential Hispanics. Ruiz lost the WBA heavyweight title to **Roy Jones Jr.** in March 2003 but regained it in December 2003, after defeating **Hasim Rahman** by unanimous decision. On April 30, 2005, Ruiz lost the heavyweight belt a second time, to **James "Lights-Out" Toney**, and hung up his gloves, but he emerged from retirement days later, when it was reported that Toney had tested positive for anabolic steroids. Ruiz was given back his title, but he lost it at the end of 2005, to **Nikolai Valuev**, "the Russian Giant," and as of 2006 was seeking to regain it.

The 1992 Summer Olympics in Barcelona, Spain, proved fertile ground for other Latino athletes. Cuban American **Pedro Pablo Morales** captured two gold medals in swimming (to add to the one gold medal and two silver medals he won at the 1984 Summer Olympics); **Dara Torres** also got a gold in swimming (she competed in four Summer Olympics in all, winning ten medals, four of them gold); **Mary Joe Fernández** and **Gigi Fernández** captured a gold medal in women's doubles tennis in 1992 (they grabbed Olympic gold again in Atlanta in 1996); and **Trent Dimas** clinched a gold medal in gymnastics. It was a proud moment when Americans with roots in Spanish-speaking Latin America won gold right in the heart of Spain.

At the 1996 Atlanta Summer Olympics, the 2000 Sydney Summer Olympics, and the 2004 Athens Summer Olympics, Puerto Rican–Cuban American **Lisa Fernández**, one of the biggest names in the sport of softball, pitched the U.S. women's Olympic softball team to gold medals. In 1996 **Rebecca Lobo** became the first Latina to capture an Olympic gold medal in basketball. One of the original players of the WNBA, she played professional basketball from 1997 to 2003, spending most of her pro career with the New York Liberty. At the 2000 Sydney Summer Games and the 2004 Athens Summer Games, **Steven Lopez** captured Olympic gold in tae kwon do. And at the 2002 Winter Games in Salt Lake City, **Derek Parra** became the first Mexican American to win a Winter Olympics medal when he won the silver in the 5,000-meter speedskate event. He went on, nine days later in Salt Lake, to break the world record in the 1,500-meter speed-skate event and win the gold medal.

In other sports, Cuban American distance runner **Alberto Salazar** won the New York Marathon in 1980, 1982, and 1983, and the Boston Marathon in 1982, and qualified for the U.S. Olympic team in 1980 and 1984. Puerto Rican jockey **Angel Cordero Jr.** broke a record by winning the Kentucky Derby for a third time in 1985. By the time his career, spanning three decades, ended in 1992, after a riding accident, Cordero had racked up 7,057 wins in 38,646 starts and had won the Preakness Stakes twice (1980 and 1984) and the Belmont Stakes once (1976), making him the first and only Puerto Rican jockey to prevail in all three legs of the Triple Crown of thoroughbred racing (not in the same year). In 1988 he earned the distinction of being the first Puerto Rican inducted into the National Thoroughbred Racing Hall of Fame. Mexican American figure skating champion **Rudy Galindo** won the men's title at the U.S. National Figure Skating Championships in 1996 after the judges awarded him a 6.0, the first perfect score in a national competition since 1988. That year he became the first Latino to medal in the World Figure Skating Championships when he captured the bronze. Galindo is not only the first Mexican American to achieve prominence in his sport, he is also the first openly gay American figure skating champion.

What *is* lucha libre?

Lucha libre, meaning "free fight," is a form of professional wrestling popular in Mexico (and in many Latin American countries) in which the wrestler, or *luchador*, wearing a mask, executes rapid sequences of holds and moves. In some matches, the *luchadores* attempt to unmask each other, and in others the loser must shave his head. *Lucha libre* has the villain-hero dichotomy and many of the same rules as American pro wrestling, but the similarities end there. *Lucha libre* actually got its start in the United States in the 1930s: It was the brainchild of an American promoter, who took the idea south, to Mexico, where it caught on because masks were a key feature of pre-Columbian native ceremonies. Nowadays, *lucha libre* has devotees on both sides of the U.S.-Mexico border. In the United States, Mexican Americans and non-Latinos have embraced this sport and cultural phenomenon. There are non-Latino rock bands whose members wear *lucha* masks, *lucha* Web sites, and even a bizarre Los Angeles–based *lucha* touring show, called Lucha Va Voom, complete with *lucha* performers, strippers, and caped midgets.

Long a subject for the Mexican silver screen, Hollywood finally took notice of *lucha libre*'s crossover to the American mainstream culture, and its avid following among American hipsters, in 2006, which saw the release of the motion picture *Nacho Libre* (2006). This comedy spoof is based loosely on the story of *luchador* Fray Tormenta (Brother Storm), aka **Rev. Sergio Gutiérrez Benítez**, a real-life Mexican Catholic priest who enjoyed a twenty-three-year career behind the *lucha* mask, competing to support the orphanage he directed.

What's on the Internet?

With the maturing of the Internet, the number of Web sites dedicated to Latinas/os has increased exponentially. Here are a few sites that serve as a great starting point for exploring Latino topics in cyberspace.

batanga.com
This bilingual Web site offers free Internet radio, with stations playing Latin jazz, salsa, merengue, *cumbia*, mariachi, hip-hop, tango, and more.

hispanicbusiness.com
This is the official Web site of *Hispanic Business*, the magazine for Latino professionals and entrepreneurs.

hispaniconline.com
This is the official Web site of *Hispanic*, the magazine for those who want to stay current on issues important to Latinos.

labloga.blogspot.com
This blog, run by Daniel A. Olivas and other Chicano/a writers, provides insightful commentary on Chicano/a literature and much more.

lamusica.com
This bilingual Latin music and entertainment site contains music reviews, concert information, artist interviews, videos, contests, original content, and more.

latina.com
This site—the official Web site of *Latina* magazine—is packed with information on entertainment, fashion, health and fitness, beauty, cuisine, and more.

latinola.com
This site contains up-to-date listings of entertainment and cultural and educational events of interest to Latinos in Los Angeles, feature stories about issues impacting Latinos everywhere, a list of employment opportunities and career advice for Latinos in Los Angeles and beyond, and more.

latinolink.com
"A meeting place for the Latino community," this bilingual Web site features ads related to real estate, personals, swap, community, jobs, services, vehicles, pets, and miscellany and also has Latino-oriented chat forums covering a variety of topics.

latinoweeklyreview.com
The is the official Web site of the *Latino Weekly Review*, a free bicultural and bilingual publication covering the arts, entertainment, culture, and politics from a Latino perspective. While *LTW* is distributed in Los Angeles, its thought-provoking contents transcend geographical boundaries.

mundolatino.org
The Mundo Latino Web site provides country-specific links to Web sites related to newspapers, radio, television, finance, arts, travel, family, work, and more. Just click on Argentina, Chile, Colombia, the United States, Mexico, or other nations to get started.

pocho.com
This Web site, filled with "satire, news *y* chat for the Spanglish generation," provides the Latino inside scoop on what's happening on the political and cultural front.

quepasa.com
This bilingual cybercommunity devoted to Latinos features the latest news in entertainment, sports, fashion, health, immigration, and Latin America, as well as a chatroom, forums, videos, radio, ringtones, and more.

somosprimos.com
This is the free monthly e-magazine of the Society of Hispanic Historical and Ancestral Research, a nonprofit organization devoted to unearthing the Latino past by aiding Latinos in researching their family history and by providing a treasure trove of information on the vast contributions that Latinos have made to the development of the United States.

supernovas.org
This is the official Himilce Novas home page.

vivirlatino.com
This Web site provides the latest news and information on U.S. and world politics, entertainment, the media, celebrities, culture, and much more, as well as links to cutting-edge Latino-related blogs.

xispas.com
This Web site is devoted to Chicano art, literature, culture, and politics.

Selected Readings

GENERAL WORKS

Abalos, David T. *Latinos in the United States: The Sacred and the Political.* Notre Dame, IN: University of Notre Dame Press, 1986.

Acosta-Belén, Edna, and Barbara R. Sjostrom, eds. *The Hispanic Experience in the United States: Contemporary Issues and Perspectives.* New York: Praeger, 1988.

Alarcón, Norma, and Sylvia Kossnar. *Bibliography of Hispanic Women Writers.* Bloomington, IN: Chicano-Riqueño Studies, 1980.

Augenbraum, Harold, and Ilan Stavans, eds. *Growing Up Latino: Memoirs and Stories.* New York: Houghton Mifflin, 1993.

Bodnar, John. *The Transplanted: A History of Immigrants in Urban America.* Bloomington: Indiana University Press, 1985.

Bohon, Stephanie. *Latinos in Ethnic Enclaves: Immigrant Workers and the Competition for Jobs.* New York: Garland, 2001.

Borjas, George J. *Friends or Strangers: The Impact of Immigrants on the U.S. Economy.* New York: Basic Books, 1990.

Cafferty, Pastora San Juan, Barry R. Chiswick, Andrew M. Greeley, and Teresa A. Sullivan. *The Dilemma of American Immigration: Beyond the Golden Door.* New Brunswick, NJ: Transaction Books, 1983.

Cantó, Leandro. *Todos fuimos a Miami.* Caracas: SEDECO, 1986.

Chavez, Linda. *Out of the Barrio: Toward a New Politics of Hispanic Assimilation.* New York: Basic Books, 1991.

Christensen, Thomas, and Carol Christensen, eds. *The Discovery of America & Other Myths: A New World Reader.* San Francisco: Chronicle, 1992.

Cockcraft, James D. *The Hispanic Struggle for Social Justice: The Hispanic Experience in the Americas.* New York: Franklin Watts, 1994.

Collier, Simon, Thomas E. Skidmore, and Harold Blakemore, eds. *The Cambridge Encyclopedia of Latin America and the Caribbean.* New York: Cambridge University Press, 1992.

Contreras, Carlos Alberto, and James W. Wilkie, eds. *Statistical Abstract of Latin America.* Los Angeles: UCLA Latin American Center Publications, 1991.

Crawford, James. *Bilingual Education: History, Politics, Theory, and Practice.* Trenton, NJ: Crane, 1989.

Dávila, Arlene. *Barrio Dreams: Puerto Ricans, Latinos, and the Neoliberal City.* Berkeley: University of California Press, 2004.

————. *Latinos, Inc.: The Marketing and Making of a People.* Berkeley: University of California, 2001.

DeFreitas, Gregory. *Inequality at Work: Hispanics in the U.S. Labor Force.* New York: Oxford University Press, 1991.

DeSipio, Louis. *Counting on the Latino Vote: Latinos as a New Electorate.* Charlottesville: University of Virginia Press, 1996.

Dinnerstein, Leonard, and David M. Reimers. *Ethnic Americans: A History of Immigration.* New York: Harper & Row, 1988.

Fernández-Shaw, Carlos M. *Presencia española en los Estados Unidos.* New York: Facts on File, 1992.

Foner, Nancy, ed. *New Immigrants in New York.* New York: Colombia University Press, 1987.

Ford Foundation. *Los hispanos: Problemas y oportunidades.* New York: Ford Foundation, 1984.

Fox, Geoffrey. *Hispanic Nation: Culture, Politics, and the Constructing of Identity.* Secaucus, NJ: Carol, 1996.

Gann, Lewis H., and Peter J. Duignan. *The Hispanics in the United States: A History.* Boulder, CO: Westview, 1986.

Garcia, F. Chris, ed. *Pursuing Power: Latinos and the Political System.* Notre Dame, IN: University of Notre Dame Press, 1997.

Garza, Hedda. *Latinas: Hispanic Women in the United States.* Albuquerque: University of New Mexico Press, 2001.

Glazer, Nathan, ed. *Clamor at the Gates: The New American Immigration.* San Francisco: ICS Press, 1985.

González, Carolina, and Seth Kugel. *Nueva York: The Complete Guide to Latino Life in the Five Boroughs.* New York: St. Martin's, 2006.

González, Ray, ed. *After Aztlan: Latino Poets of the Nineties.* Boston: David R. Godine, 1992.

González-Wippler, Migene. *The Santería Experience.* Englewood Cliffs, NJ: Prentice-Hall, 1982.

González Echevarría, Roberto, and Enrique Pupo-Walker, eds. *The Cambridge History of Latin American Literature.* Cambridge: Cambridge University Press, 1996.

Hadley-Garcia, George. *Hispanic Hollywood: The Latins in Motion Pictures.* New York: Carol, 1990.

Hague, Eleanor. *Latin American Music: Past and Present.* Detroit: B. Etheridge, 1982.

Handlin, Oscar. *A Pictorial History of Immigration.* New York: Crown, 1972.

Haslip-Viera, Gabriel, and Sherrie L. Baver, eds. *Latinos in New York: Communities in Transition.* Notre Dame, IN: University of Notre Dame Press, 1996.

Henderson, James D., and Linda Roddy Henderson. *Ten Notable Women of Latin America.* Chicago: Nelson-Hall, 1978.

Hernández-Chávez, Eduardo. "Language Maintenance, Bilingual Education, and Philosophies of Bilingualism in the United States," in James E. Alatis, ed., *International Dimensions of Bilingual Education.* Washington DC: Georgetown University Press, 1978.

Higham, John. *Strangers in the Land: Patterns of American Nativism, 1860–1925.* New Brunswick, NJ: Rutgers University Press, 1988.

Kanellos, Nicolás. *The Hispanic Almanac: From Columbus to Corporate America.* Detroit: Visible Ink, 1994.

Kanellos, Nicolás, with Cristelia Pérez. *Chronology of Hispanic-American History: From Pre-Columbian Times to the Present.* New York: Gale Research, 1995.

Lachaga, José María de. *El pueblo hispano en USA: Minorías étnicas y la Iglesia Católica.* Bilbao: Desclée de Brouwer, 1982.

Lamm, Richard D., and Gary Imhoff. *The Immigration Time Bomb: The Fragmenting of America.* New York: Truman Talley, 1985.

Lockhart, James, and Stuart B. Schwartz. *Early Latin America: A History of Colonial Spanish America and Brazil.* Cambridge: Cambridge University Press, 1983.

Longoria, Mario. *Athletes Remembered: Mexicano / Latino Professional Football Players, 1929–1970.* Tempe, AZ: Bilingual Press / Editorial Bilingüe, 1997.

Moncada, Alberto. *La americanización de los hispanos.* Barcelona: Plaza & Janes, 1986.

Monsivais, George I. *Hispanic Immigrant Identity: Political Allegiance vs. Cultural Preference.* New York: LFB Scholarly Publishing, 2004.

Moore, Joan, and Harry Pachon. *Hispanics in the United States.* Englewood Cliffs, NJ: Prentice-Hall, 1985.

Moreno Fraginals, Manuel, Frank Moya Pons, and Stanley L. Engerman, eds. *Between Slavery and Free Labor: The Spanish-Speaking Caribbean in the Nineteenth Century.* Baltimore: Johns Hopkins University Press, 1985.

Muller, Thomas, and Thomas J. Espenshade. *The Fourth Wave: California's Newest Immigrants.* Washington DC: Urban Institute Press, 1985.

Natella, Arthur A., Jr. *The Spanish in America, 1513–1974: A Chronology and Fact Book.* Dobbs Ferry, NY: Oceana, 1975.

Nevins, Joseph. *Operation Gatekeeper: The Rise of the "Illegal Alien" and the Making of the U.S.-Mexico Boundary.* New York: Routledge, 2002.

Novas, Himilce. *The Hispanic 100: A Ranking of the Latino Men and Women Who Have Most Influenced American Thought and Culture.* New York: Carol, 1995.

Novas, Himilce, and Rosemary Silva. *Latin American Cooking Across the U.S.A.* New York: Alfred. A. Knopf, 1997.

Oboler, Suzanne. *Ethnic Labels, Latino Lives: Identity and the Politics of (Re)Presentation in the United States.* Minneapolis: University of Minnesota Press, 1995.

Olmos, Edward James, Lea Ybarra, and Manuel Monterrey. *Americanos: Latino Life in the United States / La Vida Latina en los Estados Unidos.* Boston: Little, Brown, 1999.

Ortiz, Elizabeth Lambert. *The Book of Latin American Cooking.* New York: Alfred A. Knopf, 1979.

O'Shaughnessy, Hugh. *Latin Americans.* London: BBC Books, 1988.

Pachon, Harry, and Louis DeSipio. *New Americans By Choice: Political Perspectives of Latino Immigrants.* Boulder, CO: Westview, 1994.

Perpetusa-Seva, Immaculada, and Lourde Torres, eds. *Tortilleras: Hispanic and U.S. Latina Lesbian Expression.* Philadelphia: Temple University Press, 2003.

Poey, Delia, and Virgil Suarez, eds. *Iguana Dreams: New Latino Fiction.* New York: Harper Perennial, 1992.

Porter, Rosalie Pedalino. *Forked Tongue: The Politics of Bilingual Education.* New York: Basic Books, 1990.

Ramos, Jorge. *The Latino Wave: How Hispanics Are Transforming Politics in America.* New York: HarperCollins, 2005. First published as *The Latino Wave: How Hispanics Will Elect the Next American President,* 2004, by Rayo.

Ratliff, William E. *Castroism and Communism in Latin America, 1959–1976: The Varieties of Marxist-Leninist Experience.* Washington

DC: American Enterprise Institute for Public Policy Research, 1976.

Reimers, David M. *Still the Golden Door: The Third World Comes to America*. New York: Columbia University Press, 1992.

Richard, Alfred Charles, Jr. *The Hispanic Image on the Silver Screen: An Interpretive Filmography from Silents into Sound, 1898–1935*. New York: Greenwood, 1992.

Roberts, John Storm. *The Latin Tinge: The Impact of Latin American Music on the United States*. New York: Oxford University Press, 1979.

Rochin, Refugio I., ed. *Immigration and Ethnic Communities: A Focus on Latinos*. East Lansing, MI: Julian Samora Research Institute, 1996.

Rodríguez, Juana María. *Queer Latinidad: Identity Practices, Discursive Spaces*. New York: New York University Press, 2003.

Rodriguez, Richard. *Brown: The Last Discovery of America*. New York: Viking, 2002.

Romero, Mary, Pierrette Hondagneu-Sotelo, and Vilma Ortiz, eds. *Challenging Fronteras: Structuring Latina and Latino Lives in the U.S.* New York: Routledge, 1997.

Sandoval, Moises. *On the Move: A History of the Hispanic Church in the United States*. Maryknoll, NY: Orbis, 1990.

Santoli, Al. *New Americans: An Oral History.* New York: Viking, 1988.

Shorris, Earl. *Latinos: A Biography of the People*. New York: W. W. Norton, 1992.

Simon, Julian Lincoln. *The Economic Consequences of Immigration*. Cambridge: B. Blackwell, 1989.

Smith, Peter H. *Talons of the Eagle: Dynamics of U.S.-Latin American Relations*. New York: Oxford University Press, 1996.

Sotomayor, Marta, ed. *Empowering Hispanic Families: A Critical Issue for the '90s*. Milwaukee: Family Service America, 1991.

Suárez-Orozco, Marcelo M. and Mariela M. Páez. *Latinos: Remaking America*. Berkeley: University of California Press, 2002.

Sutton, Constance R., and Elsa M. Chaney, eds. *Caribbean Life in New York City: Sociocultural Dimensions*. New York: Center for Migration Studies of New York, 1987.

Valdés, M. Isabel, and Marta H. Seoane. *Hispanic Market Handbook*. Detroit: Gale Research, 1995.

Vigil, Maurilio E. *Hispanics in American Politics: The Search for Political Power.* Lanham, MD: University Press of America, 1987.

Villarreal, Roberto E., and Norma G. Hernandez, eds. *Latinos and Political Coalitions: Political Empowerment for the 1990s*. New York: Greenwood, 1991.

Weyr, Thomas. *Hispanic U.S.A.: Breaking the Melting Pot*. New York: Harper & Row, 1988.

Williamson, Edwin. *The Penguin History of Latin America*. London: Penguin, 1992.

Zucker, Norman L., and Naomi Flink Zucker. *The Guarded Gate: The Reality of American Refugee Policy*. San Diego: Harcourt, Brace, Jovanovich, 1987.

THE SPANISH CONQUEST

Bernáldez, Andrés. *Historia de los reyes católicos D. Fernando y Da. Isabel*. Granada: Imprenta y librería de José María Zamora, 1856. English translation: *Select Documents Illustrating the Four Voyages of Columbus*, vol. 1. London: Hakluyt Society, 1930.

Cabeza de Vaca, A. N. *Naufragios y comentarios*. Madrid: Taurus, 1969. English translation: *Adventures in the Unknown Interior of America*. New York: Collier, 1961.

Casas, Bartolomé de las. *Opúsculos, cartas y memoriales*, vol. 110. Madrid: Biblioteca de Autores Españoles, 1958. English translation: *The Devastation of the Indies: A Brief Account*. New York: Seabury, 1974.

Colón, C. *Raccolta colombiana, I*, vols 1 and 2. Rome, 1892–94. English translation: *Journals and Other Documents on the Life and Voyages of Christopher Columbus*. New York: Heritage, 1963.

Díaz del Castillo, Bernal. *Historia verdadera de la conquista de la Nueva España*. 2 vols. Mexico: Porrúa, 1955. English translation: *The True History of the Conquest of New Spain*. 5 vols. London: Hakluyt Society, 1908–16.

Durán, Diego. *Historia de las Indias de Nueva España e islas de tierra firme*. 2 vols. Mexico: Porrua, 1967. English translation: *Book of the Gods and Rites and the Ancient Calendar*. Norman: University of Oklahoma Press, 1971.

Godoy, Diego. "Relación a H. Cortés." In *Historiadores primitivos de Indias*, vol. 1. Madrid: Biblioteca de Autores Españoles, 1877.

Hassig, Ross. *Mexico and the Spanish Conquest*. 2nd ed. Norman: University of Oklahoma Press, 2006.

Lockhart, James. *Spanish Peru, 1532–1560*. Madison: University of Wisconsin Press, 1968.

Todorov, Tzvetan. *The Conquest of America: The Question of the Other*. New York: Harper & Row, 1984.

MEXICAN AMERICANS

Acuña, Rodolfo F. *Anything But Mexican: Chicanos in Contemporary Los Angeles*. London: Verso, 1996.

————. *Occupied America: A History of Chicanos*. New York: Harper & Row, 1988.

Andreas, Peter. *Border Games: Policing the U.S.-Mexico Divide*. Ithaca: Cornell University Press, 2000.

Bayless, Rick, with Deann Groen Bayless. *Authentic Mexican: Regional Cooking from the Heart of Mexico*. New York: William Morrow, 1987.

Binder, Wolfgang, ed. *Partial Autobiographies: Interviews with Twenty Chicano Poets*. Erlangen, Germany: Palm & Enke, 1985.

Blea, Irene I. *La Chicana and the Intersection of Race, Class, and Gender*. New York: Praeger, 1992.

Bruce-Novoa, Juan. *RetroSpace: Collected Essays on Chicano Literature: Theory and History*. Houston: Arte Público, 1990.

Calderón, Héctor, and José David Saldívar, eds. *Criticism in the Borderlands: Studies in Chicano Literature, Culture, and Ideology*. Durham, NC: Duke University Press, 1991.

Coe, Michael D. *Mexico: From the Olmecs to the Aztecs*. New York: Thames and Hudson, 1994.

Commission on Civil Rights. *The Excluded Student: Educational Practices Affecting Mexican Americans in the Southwest*. Washington DC: Government Printing Office, 1972.

De Anda, Roberto M., ed. *Chicanas and Chicanos in Contemporary Society*. Boston: Allyn and Bacon, 1996.

Elizondo, Virgilio P. *The Future is Mestizo: Life Where Cultures Meet*. Oak Park, IL: Meyer-Stone, 1988.

Galarza, Ernesto. *Barrio Boy*. Notre Dame, IN: University of Notre Dame Press, 1971.

García, Juan Ramon. *Operation Wetback: The Mass Deportation of Mexican Undocumented Workers in 1954*. Westport, CT: Greenwood, 1980.

García, Mario T. *Memories of Chicano History: The Life and Narrative of Bert Corona*. Berkeley: University of California Press, 1994.

Glazer, Mark. *A Dictionary of Mexican American Proverbs*. New York: Greenwood, 1987.

González, Gilbert G., and Raul A. Fernández. *A Century of Chicano History: Empire, Nations, and Migration*. New York: Routledge, 2003.

Graham, Joe S., ed. *Hecho en Tejas: Texas-Mexican Folk Arts and Crafts*. Denton: University of North Texas Press, 1991.

Herrera-Sobek, María. *The Bracero Experience: Elitelore Versus Folklore*. Los Angeles: UCLA Latin American Center Publications, 1979.

Iglesias Prieto, Norma. *Medios de communicación en la frontera norte*.

Mexico: Fundación Manuel Buendia; Programa Cultural de las Fronteras, 1990.

Jussawalla, Feroza, and Reed Way Dasenbrock, eds. *Interviews with Writers of the Post-Colonial World*. Jackson: University Press of Mississippi, 1992.

Kanellos, Nicolás. *Understanding the Chicano Experience Through Literature*. Houston: University of Texas Press, 1981.

Langley, Lester D. *MexAmerica: Two Countries, One Future*. New York: Crown, 1988.

Lattin, Vernon E., ed. *Contemporary Chicano Fiction: A Critical Survey*. Binghamton, NY: Bilingual Press / Editorial Bilingüe, 1986.

León, Luis D. *La Llorona's Children: Religion, Life, and Death in the U.S.-Mexican Borderlands*. Berkeley: University of California Press, 2004.

Limón, José Eduardo. *Mexican Ballads, Chicano Poems: History and Influence in Mexican-American Social Poetry*. Berkeley: University of California Press, 1992.

Long, Haniel. *The Marvelous Adventure of Cabeza de Vaca*. Clearlake, CA: Dawn Horse, 1992.

López de Gómara, Francisco. *Historia de la conquista de México*. Mexico City: Editorial Pedro Robredo, 1943. English translation: *Cortés: The Life of the Conqueror by His Secretary*. Berkeley: University of California Press, 1964.

Maciel, David R., and Isidro D. Ortiz, eds. *Chicanas/Chicanos at the Crossroads: Social, Economic, and Political Change*. Tucson: University of Arizona Press, 1996.

Martínez, Oscar J. *Mexican-Origin People in the United States: A Topical History*. Tucson: University of Arizona Press, 2001.

Martinez, Ruben. *Crossing Over: A Mexican Family on the Migrant Trail*. New York: Metropolitan Books, 2001.

Mayberry, Jodine. *Mexicans*. New York: Franklin Watts, 1990.

McWilliams, Carey. *North from Mexico: The Spanish-Speaking People of the United States*. New York: Greenwood, 1990.

Meier, Matt S., and Feliciano Ribera. *Mexican Americans / American Mexicans: From Conquistadors to Chicanos*. New York: Hill and Wang, 1993.

Miller, Tom. *On the Border: Portraits of America's Southwestern Frontier*. Tucson: University of Arizona Press, 1981.

Montejano, David, ed. *Chicano Politics and Society in the Late Twentieth Century*. Austin: University of Texas Press, 1999.

Moquin, Wayne, with Charles Van Doren, eds. *A Documentary History of the Mexican Americans*. New York: Praeger, 1971.

Noriega, Chon A. *Shot in America: Television, the State, and the Rise of Chicano Cinema*. Minneapolis: University of Minnesota Press, 2000.

Paz, Octavio. *The Labyrinth of Solitude.* New York: Grove, 1985.

Peñuelas, Marcelino C. *Cultura hispánica en los Estados Unidos: Los chicanos.* Madrid: Ediciones Cultura Hispánica del Centro Ibero-américano de Cooperación, 1978.

Pérez, Emma. *The Decolonial Imaginary: Writing Chicanas Into History.* Bloomington: Indiana University Press, 1999.

Pettit, Arthur G. *Images of the Mexican-American in Fiction and Film.* College Station: Texas A&M University Press, 1980.

Pierri, Ettore. *Chicanos, el poder mestizo.* Mexico City: Mexicanos Unidos, 1979.

Rodriguez, Richard. *Hunger of Memory: The Education of Richard Rodriguez.* New York: Bantam, 1983.

Samora, Julian, and Patricia Vandel Simon. *A History of the Mexican-American People.* Notre Dame, IN: University of Notre Dame Press, 1977.

Sánchez, George J. *Becoming Mexican American: Ethnicity, Culture and Identity in Chicano Los Angeles, 1900–1945.* New York: Oxford University Press, 1993.

Sewell, Dorita. *Knowing People: A Mexican-American Community's Concept of a Person.* New York: AMS, 1989.

Skerry, Peter. *Mexican Americans: The Ambivalent Minority.* New York: Macmillan, 1993.

Smith, Robert Courtney. *Mexican New York: Transnational Lives of New Immigrants.* Berkeley: University of California Press, 2006.

Tafolla, Carmen. *To Split a Human: Mitos, Machos y la Mujer Chicana.* San Antonio: Mexican American Cultural Center, 1985.

Tatum, Charles M., ed. *New Chicana/Chicano Writing.* Tucson: University of Arizona Press, 1992.

Time-Life Books, eds. *Mexico.* Alexandria, VA: Time-Life Books, 1986.

Trujillo, Carla, ed. *Chicana Lesbians: The Girls Our Mothers Warned Us About.* Berkeley, CA: Third Woman, 1991.

Tywoniak, Frances Esquibel, and Mario T. García. *Migrant Daughter: Coming of Age as a Mexican American Woman.* Berkeley: University of California Press, 2000.

Weigle, Marta, ed. *Two Guadalupes: Hispanic Legends and Magic Tales from Northern New Mexico.* Santa Fe: Ancient City, 1987.

Weigle, Marta, and Peter White. *The Lore of New Mexico.* Albuquerque: University of New Mexico Press, 1988.

West, John O., ed. *Mexican-American Folklore: Legends, Songs, Festivals, Proverbs, Crafts, Tales of Saints, of Revolutionaries, and More.* Little Rock, AR: August House, 1988.

PUERTO RICANS

Aliotta, Jerome J. *The Puerto Ricans*. New York: Chelsea House, 1991.

Bothwell Gonzalez, Reece B. *La ciudadanía en Puerto Rico*. Rio Piedras: Editorial Universitaria, Universidad de Puerto Rico, 1980.

Carr, Raymond. *Puerto Rico: A Colonial Experiment*. New York: New York University Press, 1984.

Carrión, Arturo Morales, ed. *Puerto Rico: A Political and Cultural History*. New York: W. W. Norton, 1984.

Coll y Toste, Cayetano. *Puertorriqueños ilustres*. Rio Piedras, PR: Editorial Cultural, 1971.

Cruz, Wilfredo. *Puerto Rican Chicago*. Charleston, SC: Arcadia, 2004.

Dietz, James L. *Economic History of Puerto Rico: Institutional Change and Capitalist Development*. Princeton, NJ: Princeton University Press, 1986.

Fitzpatrick, Joseph P. *Puerto Rican Americans: The Meaning of Migration to the Mainland*. Englewood Cliffs, NJ: Prentice-Hall, 1987.

Flores, Juan. *Divided Borders: Essays on Puerto Rican Identity*. Houston: Arte Público, 1991.

Haslip-Viera, Gabriel, Angelo Falcón, and Félix Matos-Rodríguez, eds. *Boricuas in Gotham: Puerto Ricans in the Making of Modern New York City*. Princeton, NJ: Markus Wiener, 2004.

Hauberg, Clifford A. *Puerto Rico and the Puerto Ricans*. New York: Twayne, 1975.

Hauptly, Denis J. *Puerto Rico: An Unfinished Story*. New York: Atheneum, 1991.

Larsen, Ronald J. *The Puerto Ricans in America*. Minneapolis: Lerner, 1989.

López, Adalberto, and James F. Petras, eds. *Puerto Rico and the Puerto Ricans: Studies in History and Society*. Cambridge, MA: Schenkman, 1974.

Matos-Rodríguez, Félix V., and Pedro Juan Hernández. *Pioneros: Puerto Ricans in New York City 1896–1948*. Charleston, SC: Arcadia, 2001.

Melendez, Edwin, and Edgardo Melendez, eds. *Colonial Dilemma: Critical Perspectives on Contemporary Puerto Rico*. Boston: South End, 1993.

Mohr, Eugene V. *The Nuyorican Experience: Literature of the Puerto Rican Minority*. Westport, CT: Greenwood, 1982.

Negrón-Muntaner, Frances, ed. *None of the Above: Puerto Ricans in the Global Era*. New York: Palgrave Macmillan, 2006.

Perez y Mena, Andres Isidoro. *Speaking with the Dead: Development of Afro-Latin Religion Among Puerto Ricans in the United States—A Study into the Interpenetration of Civilizations in the New World*. New York: AMS Press, 1991.

Samoiloff, Louise Cripps. *A Portrait of Puerto Rico.* New York: Cornwall, 1984.

Sánchez Korrol, Virginia. *From Colonia to Community: The History of Puerto Ricans in New York City, 1917–1948.* Berkeley: University of California Press, 1994.

Turner, Faythe. *Puerto Rican Writers at Home in the USA: An Anthology.* Seattle: Open Hand Publishing, 1991.

Whalen, Carmen Teresa. *El Viaje: Puerto Ricans of Philadelphia.* Charleston, SC: Arcadia, 2006.

—————. *From Puerto Rico to Philadelphia: Puerto Rican Workers and Postwar Economies.* Philadelphia: Temple University Press, 2001.

CUBAN AMERICANS

Blight, James G. *The Shattered Crystal Ball: Fear and Learning in the Cuban Missile Crisis.* Savage, MD: Rowman & Littlefield, 1990.

Bonachea, Ramón L., and Marta San Martin. *The Cuban Insurrection, 1952–1959.* New Brunswick, NJ: Transaction, 1974.

Bosch, Lynette M. F. *Cuban-American Art in Miami: Exile, Identity and the Neo-Baroque.* Burlington, VT: Lund Humphries, 2004.

Boswell, Thomas D., and James R. Curtis. *The Cuban-American Experience: Culture, Images, and Perspectives.* Totowa, NJ: Rowman & Allanheld, 1984.

Cortes, Carlos E., ed. *The Cuban Experience in the United States.* New York: Arno, 1980.

Cruz, Celia. *Celia: Mi vida. Una autobiografía.* With Ana Cristina Reymundo. New York: HarperCollins, 2004.

Del Aguila, Juan M. *Cuba: Dilemmas of a Revolution.* Boulder, CO: Westview, 1994.

Del Mar, Marcia. *A Cuban Story.* Winston-Salem, NC: John F. Blair, 1979.

Duncan, Walter Raymond. *The Soviet Union and Cuba: Interests and Influence.* New York: Praeger, 1985.

Fernández, Alfredo A. *Adrift: The Cuban Raft People.* Houston: Arte Público, 2000.

Garcia, Maria Cristina. *Havana USA: Cuban Exiles and Cuban Americans in South Florida, 1959–1994.* Berkeley: University of California Press, 1996.

Geyer, Georgie Anne. *Guerrilla Prince: The Untold Story of Fidel Castro.* Boston: Little, Brown, 1991.

Grillo, Evelio. *Black Cuban, Black American: A Memoir.* Houston: Arte Público, 2000.

Grupo Areíto. *Contra viento y marea: Jóvenes cubanos hablan desde su exilio en Estados Unidos.* Havana: Casa de las Americas, 1978.

Kiple, Kenneth F. *Blacks in Colonial Cuba, 1774–1899.* Gainesville: University Presses of Florida, 1976.

Levine, Robert M., and Moisés Asís. *Cuban Miami.* Piscataway, NJ: Rutgers University Press, 2000.

Llanes, José. *Cuban Americans: Masters of Survival.* Cambridge, MA: ABT, 1982.

Medina, Pablo. *Exiled Memories: A Cuban Childhood.* Austin: University of Texas Press, 1990.

Mesa-Lago, Carmelo. *The Economy of Socialist Cuba: A Two-Decade Appraisal.* Albuquerque: University of New Mexico Press, 1981.

Murphy, Joseph M. *Santería: An African Religion in America.* New York: Original Publications, 1989.

Ojito, Mirta. *Finding Mañana: A Memoir of a Cuban Exodus.* New York: Penguin, 2005.

Olson, James S., and Judith E. Olson. *Cuban Americans: From Trauma to Triumph.* New York: Twayne, 1995.

Padilla, Heberto. *Self-Portrait of the Other: A Memoir.* New York: Farrar, Straus & Giroux, 1990.

Pérez, Louis A., Jr. *Cuba: Between Reform and Revolution.* New York: Oxford University Press, 1988.

Pérez Firmat, Gustavo. *Life on the Hyphen: The Cuban-American Way.* Austin: University of Texas Press, 1994.

Rieff, David. *The Exile: Cuba in the Heart of Miami.* New York: Simon & Schuster, 1993.

Rogg, Eleanor. *The Assimilation of Cuban Exiles: The Role of the Community and Class.* New York: Aberdeen, 1974.

Scott, Rebecca J. *Slave Emancipation in Cuba: The Transition to Free Labor, 1860–1899.* Princeton, NJ: Princeton University Press, 1985.

Suchlicki, Jaime. *Cuba: From Columbus to Castro.* Washington, DC: Pergamon-Brassey's, 1986.

Suarez, Virgil. *Spared Angola: Memories from a Cuban-American Childhood.* Albuquerque: Arte Público, 1997.

Timerman, Jacobo. *Cuba: A Journey.* New York: Alfred A. Knopf, 1990.

DOMINICAN AMERICANS

Aparicio, Ana. *Dominican-Americans and the Politics of Empowerment.* Gainesville: University Press of Florida, 2006.

Atkins, G. Pope, and Larman C. Wilson. *The Dominican Republic and the United States: From Imperialism to Transnationalism.* Athens: The University of Georgia Press, 1998.

Bailey, Benjamin H. *Language, Race, and Negotiation of Identity: A Study of Dominican Americans.* New York: LFB Scholarly Publishing, 2002.

Betances, Emelio. *State and Society in the Dominican Republic*. Boulder, CO: Westview, 1995.

Bogen, Elizabeth. *Caribbean Immigrants in New York City: A Demographic Summary*. New York: Department of City Planning / Office of Immigrant Affairs and Population Analysis Division, 1988.

Brown, Isabel Zakrzewski. *Culture and Customs of the Dominican Republic*. Westport, CT: Greenwood, 1999.

Cambeira, Alan. *Quisqueya la Bella: The Dominican Republic in Historical and Cultural Perspective*. Armonk, NY: M. E. Sharpe. 1997.

Grasmuck, Sherri, and Patricia R. Pessar. *Between Two Islands: Dominican International Migration*. Berkeley: University of California Press, 1991.

Gray, Dulce María. *High Literacy and Ethnic Identity: Dominican American Schooling in Transition*. Lanham, MD: Rowman & Littlefield Publishers, 2001.

Haggerty, Richard A., ed. *Dominican Republic and Haiti: Country Studies*. Washington DC: Federal Research Division, Library of Congress, 1991.

Hall, Michael R. *Sugar and Power in the Dominican Republic: Eisenhower, Kennedy, and the Trujillos*. Westport, CT: Greenwood, 2000.

Hendricks, Glenn. *The Dominican Diaspora: From the Dominican Republic to New York City—Villagers in Transition*. New York: Teachers College Press, 1974.

Klein, Alan M. *Sugarball: The American Game, the Dominican Dream*. New Haven, CT: Yale University Press, 1991.

Pessar, Patricia R. *A Visa for a Dream: Dominicans in the United States*. Boston: Allyn & Bacon, 1995.

Rodman, Selden. *Quisqueya: A History of the Dominican Republic*. Seattle: University of Washington Press, 1964.

Slater, Jerome. *Intervention and Negotiation: The United States and the Dominican Revolution*. New York: Harper & Row, 1970.

AMERICANS OF CENTRAL AND SOUTH AMERICAN DESCENT

Anderson, Thomas P. *Politics in Central America: Guatemala, El Salvador, Honduras, and Nicaragua*. New York: Praeger, 1982.

Arana, Marie. *American Chica: Two Worlds, One Childhood*. New York: Dial Press, 2001.

Barry, Tom. *Roots of Rebellion: Land and Hunger in Central America*. Boston: South End, 1987.

Biesanz, Richard, Karen Zubris Biesanz, and Mavis Hiltunen Biesanz. *The Costa Ricans*. Englewood Cliffs, NJ: Prentice-Hall, 1982.

Black, George. *The Good Neighbor: How the United States Wrote the History of Central America and the Caribbean*. New York: Pantheon, 1988.

Buckley, Kevin. *Panama: The Whole Story*. New York: Simon & Schuster, 1991.

Buckley, Tom. *Violent Neighbors: El Salvador, Central America, and the United States*. New York: Times Books, 1984.

Child, Jack, ed. *Conflict in Central America: Approaches to Peace and Security*. London: C. Hurst, 1986.

Cordova, Carlos B. *The Salvadoran Americans*. Westport, CT: Greenwood, 2005.

Crawley, Eduardo. *Nicaragua in Perspective*. New York: St. Martin's, 1984.

Didion, Joan. *Salvador*. New York: Simon & Schuster, 1983.

Faugsted, George E., Jr. *Chilenos in the California Gold Rush*. San Francisco: R & E Research Associates, 1973.

García, María Cristina. *Seeking Refuge: Central American Migration to Mexico, the United States, and Canada*. Berkeley: University of California Press, 2006.

Gleijeses, Piero. *Shattered Hope: The Guatemalan Revolution and the United States, 1944–1954*. Princeton: Princeton University Press, 1991.

Hamilton, Nora, Jeffry A. Frieden, Linda Fuller, and Manuel Pastor, Jr., eds. *Crisis in Central America: Regional Dynamics and U.S. Policy in the 1980s*. Boulder, CO: Westview, 1988.

Immerman, Richard H. *The CIA in Guatemala: The Foreign Policy of Intervention*. Austin: University of Texas Press, 1982.

Kohpahl, Gabriele. *Voices of Guatemalan Women in Los Angeles: Understanding Their Immigration*. New York: Garland, 1998.

Krauss, Clifford. *Inside Central America: Its People, Politics, and History*. New York: Summit, 1991.

López, Carlos U. *Chilenos in California: A Study of the 1850, 1852 and 1860 Censuses*. San Francisco: R & E Research Associates, 1973.

Mahler, Sarah J. *Salvadorans in Suburbia: Symbiosis and Conflict*. Boston: Allyn & Bacon, 1995.

Manz, Beatriz. *Paradise in Ashes: A Guatemalan Journey of Courage, Terror, and Hope*. Berkeley: University of California Press, 2004.

McNeil, Frank. *War and Peace in Central America: Reality and Illusion*. New York: Scribner's, 1988.

Menjívar, Cecilia. *Fragmented Ties: Salvadoran Immigrant Networks in America*. Berkeley: University of California Press, 2000.

Monaghan, Jay. *Chile, Peru, and the California Gold Rush of 1849*. Berkeley: University of California Press, 1973.

Painter, James. *Guatemala: False Hope, False Freedom: The Rich, the Poor and the Christian Democrats.* London: Catholic Institute for International Relations, 1987.

Simon, Jean-Marie. *Guatemala: Eternal Spring, Eternal Tyranny.* New York: W. W. Norton, 1987.

Williams, Robert G. *Export Agriculture and the Crisis in Central America.* Chapel Hill: University of North Carolina Press, 1986.

Woodward, Ralph Lee. *Central America: A Nation Divided.* New York: Oxford University Press, 1985.

Index

Index

Nahuatl language, 30, 54, 55
Napoléon Bonaparte, 66
Napoléon III, 123, 138
Napolitano, Grace, 294
Narváez, Pánfilo de, 57, 61
National Council of La Raza (NCLR), 287
National Farm Workers Association (NFWA), 51, 108
National Puerto Rican Coalition, Inc. (NPRC), 287
Nava, Gregory, 260, 333
Negro/negrito, 133
Nelson, Hugh, 172
Nespral, Jackie, 340
New Deal, 90, 119
Newfoundland, 20
New Granada, 271
New Jersey:
  Argentinean Americans in, 279
  Chilean Americans in, 281
  Colombian Americans in, 275
  Costa Rican Americans in, 271
  Cuban Americans in, 12, 194, 212
  Dominican Americans in, 14, 15, 232
  Ecuadoran Americans in, 277
  Honduran Americans in, 269
  Latino population in, 6
  Nicaraguan Americans in, 269
  Peruvian Americans in, 278
  Puerto Ricans in, 11
New Mexico, 56–58, 60, 66–69, 73, 89, 91
New York:
  Argentinean Americans in, 279
  Chilean Americans in, 281
  Colombian Americans in, 274, 275
  Costa Rican Americans in, 271
  Cuban Americans in, 12, 194, 212
  Dominican Americans in, 14, 232
  Ecuadoran Americans in, 277
  Guatemalan Americans in, 261
  Honduran Americans in, 269
  Nicaraguan Americans in, 269
  Panamanian Americans in, 270
  Peruvian Americans in, 278
  Puerto Ricans in, 11, 12
  Salvadoran Americans in, 252
New York City:
  Dominican Americans in, 14–15, 232, 234
  Puerto Ricans in, 12, 155–58, 159, 163–64

Nicaragua, xiii, 2, 23, 138, 243, 255, 261–68
Nicaraguan Adjustment and Central American Relief Act (NACARA) of 1997, 204, 251–52, 260, 268, 293
Nicaraguan Americans, 17, 204, 214, 240, 250, 268–69
Niza, Marcos, 57–58
No Child Left Behind law, 313
Noriega, Carlos I., 354
North Carolina, Latino population in, 9–10
North Dakota, Latino population in, 6
Northwest Passage, 59
Novarro, Ramón, 161–62, 328
Novas, Himilce, 344, 346
Novas Calvo, Lino, 342
Novello, Antonia Coello, xii, 307–8, 352
Nunes, Devin, 290
Núñez de Balboa, Vasco, 40

O'Brien, Soledad, 341
Ocampo, Adriana, 354
Ochoa, Ellen, 354
Ojeda Ríos, Filiberto, 150
Olé, 41
Oliva, Tony, 357
Olivas, John D., 354
Olmecs, 25–27, 118
Olmos, Edward James, 227, 330, 333
Oñate, Juan de, 59–60
100 Hispanic Women, Inc., 287–88
Ontiveros, Lupe, 337
Operation Gatekeeper, 102
Operation Power Back, 228
Operation Rescue, 246
Operation Wetback, 95–96, 302
Operation Zapata, 190
Oregon Trail, 76
O'Reilly, Alejandro, 135
Organization of American States (OAS), 226, 228
Orinoco River, 38, 271
Orlando, Tony, 321
Orozco, José Clemente, 118–19
Ortega Saavedra, Daniel, 266–68
Ortiz, Carlos, 370
Ortiz, Solomon, 294
Ortiz de Dominguez, Doña Josefa, 115
Osorio, Pepón, 33, 348
Ostend Manifesto, 173
O'Sullivan, John, 67